THE CARL HOVLAND MEMORIAL LECTURES

THE RESOLUTION OF CONFLICT

CONSTRUCTIVE AND DESTRUCTIVE PROCESSES

Morton Deutsch

New Haven and London: Yale University Press

Library of Congress catalog card number: 73–80080
International standard book numbers: 0–300–01683–2 cloth
0–300–02186–0 paper
Designed by Sally Sullivan
and set in Times Roman type.
Printed in the United States of America by
Vail-Ballou Press, Inc., Binghamton, N.Y.

13   12   11   10   9

The Carl Hovland Memorial Lectures

CARL IVER HOVLAND was one of those rare people whom any university with pride in the quality of its faculty hopes to attract and retain. He came to Yale as a graduate student and as soon as he received his Ph.D. in 1936 was appointed to the faculty in psychology. He rose rapidly through the ranks to become professor in 1945 and Sterling professor in 1947. This early arrival at a position of eminence in Yale was matched by a rapid rise in knowledge of and respect for his work in the scientific community outside his own institution.

In addition to serving as chairman of his academic department, as its director of graduate studies, and as one of its most stimulating seminar leaders, Carl had a sequence of prolific research careers and perhaps was reaching the peak of his productivity just before his untimely death in 1961. His work in human learning first demonstrated his very great competence in experimental work. Although he had several other secondary interests, such as that in personnel selection, it was probably his work with films intended to educate and to change attitudes among World War II soldiers that, back at Yale, led to his major developments in experimental work in attitude change. It was in this area that he perhaps influenced more students and colleagues than in any other, but almost simultaneously he was moving into research in thinking and problem-solving, continuing to show a high order of theoretical and experimental brilliance.

It was out of respect not only for his scientific accomplishments but for his gentle yet effective relationships with people, that his students, friends, and colleagues across the nation established the Hovland Memorial Lecture Series. As these lectures become books they will periodically remind us of the remarkable man to whom they are dedicated.

Contents

Preface

Throughout my career in social psychology, I have been concerned with the interrelations among experimental research, theory, and social policy. I started my graduate study not long after Hiroshima and Nagasaki, and my work in social psychology has been shadowed by the atomic cloud ever since. The efforts reported in this book reflect my continuing interest in contributing to the understanding of how to prevent destructive conflict and initiate cooperation. Much of the book presents, in a generalized form, theoretical analysis and research bearing upon these issues; however, I have not hesitated to express my views on current social preoccupations whenever I felt that those views were likely to have benefited from the serious thought that I have given to the issues in conflict resolution.

The stimulus for this book was the Carl Hovland Memorial Lectures which I gave at Yale University several years ago. The lectures contained a summary of my theoretical and empirical work on the topic of conflict resolution. At that time, I was requested to expand my lectures into a book, and this collection of my own theoretical essays and of research papers by both my students and myself is a response to that request. My objective is to present my own thought and work in this area rather than to survey the literature; no systematic attempt is made to describe the important work being done by other scholars in the field.

This book assembles for the first time within one volume research that has, in many cases, been described in previous publications. The earlier published versions are acknowledged in footnotes, with full citations being given in the bibliography. For permission to use material that first appeared in the *Journal of Abnormal and Social Psychology,* the *American Psychologist,* and the *Journal of Personality and Social Psychology,* I wish to thank the American Psychological Association;

for material from the *Journal of Experimental Social Psychology*, I wish to thank the Academic Press, Inc.; for material from the *Journal of Conflict Resolution*, I wish to thank Sage Publications, Inc.; and for material from *Human Relations*, I wish to thank Planum Publishing Co., Ltd. Portions from "Strategies of Inducing Cooperation: An Experimental Study," by M. Deutsch, Y. Epstein, D. Canavan, and P. Gumpert, are reprinted from *The Journal of Conflict Resolution* Volume 11 (1967), pp. 345–60; portions from "Trust and Suspicion," by M. Deutsch, are reprinted from *The Journal of Conflict Resolution* Volume 2 (1958), pp. 256–79; "Studies of Interpersonal Bargaining," by M. Deutsch and R. M. Krauss, are reprinted from *The Journal of Conflict Resolution* Volume 6 (1962), pp. 42–76; the excerpt of " 'Locking-in' Effects During a Game of Chicken," by M. Deutsch and R. J. Lewicki is reprinted from *The Journal of Conflict Resolution* Volume 14 (1970), pp. 376–78; all are reprinted by permission of the Publisher, Sage Publications, Inc.

Most of the theoretical essays were written especially for this volume and are published here for the first time. They deal with a wide range of subject matter even though their common concern is to contribute to the understanding of the conditions which lead to the constructive resolution of conflict. In discussing particular topics I have felt free to digress from the main theme of this volume in order to come to grips with the issue being considered.

A word about my relations with Carl Hovland. I knew him personally through our mutual connection to the psychological research unit, which he was instrumental in initiating, at the Bell Telephone Laboratories. In addition to being a first-rate scientist with an unusually broad range of interests and knowledge, he was a rare human being with a warm sensitivity for the needs of other people. He knew that science had to have a heart as well as a mind if it were to meet human needs. I am proud to have had his encouragement and support for my work.

I also wish to acknowledge my considerable debt to the many students and colleagues who have contributed to the research reported here. This research includes doctoral dissertations by Bert Brown, Peter Gumpert, Madeline Heilman, Harvey A. Hornstein, Robert M. Krauss, James Loomis, and Leonard Solomon. It also includes studies in which I have collaborated with Barbara Bunker, Donnah Canavan, Mary Chase, King Collins, Yakov Epstein, Katherine Garner, Peter

Gumpert, Robert M. Krauss, Julie Hover, Sharon Kaplan, Roy Lewicki, and Jeffrey Rubin.

I must further acknowledge my indebtedness to the National Science Foundation, the Office of Naval Research, and the Bell Telephone Laboratories for supporting the research presented herein. The opinions, findings, conclusions, and recommendations in this book are my own, however, and do not necessarily reflect the views of any organization.

In conclusion, I would like to thank those who helped me produce this book. Jane Isay of the Yale University Press provided the necessary prodding and encouragement to keep me working on it. Professor Robert Abelson of Yale University was an unusually astute reader whose insightful comments were very valuable in making revisions. Among the many who assisted with the secretarial and bibliographical chores were Dorothy Thorne, Laura Zwilich, and Marilyn Seiler.

M. D.

New York City
January 1973

PART ONE: THEORETICAL ESSAYS

1. Introduction

Some time ago, in the garden of a friend's house, my five-year-old son and his chum were struggling over possession of a water hose. Each wanted to use it first to water the flowers. Each was tugging at it in an effort to get it away from the other, and both were crying. Each was very frustrated, and neither was able to use the hose to sprinkle the flowers as he had desired. After reaching a deadlock in their tug-of-war, they began to punch one another and call each other names. The escalation of the conflict to physical violence led to the intervention of a powerful third party (an adult), who suggested a game to determine who would use the hose first. The boys, somewhat frightened by the violence of the struggle, were relieved to agree to the suggestion. They quickly became absorbed in trying to find a small object I had hidden and obediently followed the rule that the winner would have a first turn of two minutes with the hose. Soon they tired of the water hose and began to pick blackberries, which they threw provocatively at a ten year old who responded to their ineffectual sallies with amused tolerance.

Even a simple episode like this suggests many questions pertinent to conflicts of all sorts: intrapersonal, interpersonal, intragroup, intergroup, and international. Thus one might inquire about the participants in the conflict—how their individual characteristics (strength, cognitive resources, personality, emotional state, etc.) and their prior relationship with one another affected the development and course of the dispute. One might expect, for instance, that if the disputants in the above example had been men rather than boys the resort to physical violence would have been less likely. May we assume that this would have been because violence is more painful and dangerous among men than among boys, and hence the social and personal restraints against adults punching one another are likely to be stronger?

3

Or could it be that violence was less likely because of the greater intellectual resourcefulness of adults? Also, it seems reasonable to assume that girls would have been less likely to punch one another than boys. If these assumptions are correct, how is it possible to socialize or otherwise indoctrinate people so that certain methods of waging conflict are so alien that they become "unthinkable"?

Or one might ask about the issue in the conflict, its motivational significance and its phrasing. Was there anything about the possession or nonpossession of that water hose that might have been of particular emotional significance to the quarrelers? A Freudian might stress the phallic symbolism and the intensity of the rivalrous and anxious feelings that a boy of five years is likely to have about the possession of a big and powerful water sprinkler. Moreover, the issue might have been phrased so that its magnitude was large or small, so that the legitimate claim of both or of only one was recognized. Thus, the issue could have been defined as all or none: the hose either became one boy's exclusive possession and under his sole control, or its use was alternated. Questions might also be raised about the broader social environment within which the conflict occurred. For example, was conflict more likely because neither child had clear territorial rights (both were visitors in an unfamiliar locale)? Did the known presence of an interested and significant audience (parents) affect the course of conflict in particular ways? More generally, what modes of intervention by a third party are likely to be most effective in resolving a conflict of a given type? What characteristics of the third party, including his relationship to the parties in conflict, determine how acceptable his intervention will be? The two five year olds probably would not have been much influenced by a cease-and-desist order from a four year old. Yet, it is not unknown for a physically powerless third party to help prevent the conflict of more powerful parties from escalating into violent forms. What characteristics of third parties aid in resolving conflict, and what characteristics promote deadlock and interminable conflict?

An Outline of Variables Affecting the Course of Conflict

There are many other questions that can be raised about this episode of conflict. Whether the conflict under scrutiny is between union and management, between nations, between a husband and wife, or between children, it is useful to know something about:

1. *The characteristics of the parties in conflict (their values and motivations; their aspirations and objectives; their physical, intellectual, and social resources for waging or resolving conflict; their beliefs about conflict, including their conceptions of strategy and tactics; and so forth).* For groups as well as for kids in conflict, it is helpful to know what the respective parties will consider a reward or gain and what they will consider a punishment or loss. For individuals as well as for nations, knowledge of the weapons and tools available to them and of their skill in employing those resources to wage or resolve conflict is clearly relevant to predicting and understanding the course of conflict. Similarly, it is pertinent to know whether a given conflict is between equals (two boys) or unequals (an adult and a child), between parts of a whole (New York and New Jersey) or between a part and the whole (Mississippi and the United States), or between wholes (the United States and the Soviet Union).

2. *Their prior relationship to one another (their attitudes, beliefs, and expectations about one another, including each one's belief about the other's view of him, and particularly the degree of polarization that has occurred on such evaluations as "good-bad", "trustworthy-untrustworthy").* A specific controversy, whether between Egypt and Israel, between union and management, or between husband and wife, will be colored and affected by the prior relations and preexisting attitudes between the parties. A husband or wife who has lost confidence in the benevolence of the other's intentions is as unlikely as Egypt and Israel or an embittered union and management to come to an agreement necessitating mutual trust to be effective.

3. *The nature of the issue giving rise to the conflict (its scope, rigidity, motivational significance, formulation, periodicity, etc.).* The issue or issues in conflict between nations, groups, or individuals may be diffuse and generalized, as in ideological conflict, or specific and limited, as in the conflict over possession of a certain property; the issue may be important or trivial to the parties involved; it may permit compromise or require the submission of one side to the other.

4. *The social environment within which the conflict occurs (the facilities and restraints, the encouragements and deterrents it provides with regard to the different strategies and tactics of waging or resolving conflict, including the nature of the social norms and institutional*

forms for regulating conflict). Individuals as well as groups and nations may find themselves in social environments in which there is little tradition of cooperative conflict resolution and in which few institutions, norms, facilities, or resources have been developed to foster
peaceful resolution of disputes. Of course, it is true that the present
environment of nations is more impoverished in such traditions and
institutions than the environments of most individuals or groups.

5. *The interested audiences to the conflict (their relationships to
the parties in conflict and to one another, their interests in the conflict
and its outcomes, their characteristics).* Many conflicts take place in a
public spotlight, and the course of conflict may be greatly influenced
by the participants' conceptions of their audience and how it will
react—as well as by the actual behavior of interested third parties.
Thus, one of the proclaimed goals of the United States in the Vietnam
conflict was to discourage "wars of liberation" everywhere. The conflict in the Middle East is exacerbated by the arms race, which is nur-
tured and supported by third parties. Similarly, a conflict between individuals or groups can be either egged on or curbed by the desire to
maintain or gain face with third parties and by the promises or threats
of others.

6. *The strategy and tactics employed by the parties in the conflict
(in assessing and / or changing one another's utilities, disutilities, and
subjective probabilities; and in influencing the other's conceptions of
one's own utilities and disutilities through tactics that vary along such
dimensions as legitimacy-illegitimacy, the relative use of positive and
negative incentives such as promises and rewards or threats and punishments, freedom of choice-coercion, the openness and veracity of
communication and sharing of information, the degree of credibility,
the degree of commitment, the types of motives appealed to, and so
on).* Much has been written about these topics by students of bargaining (e.g., Schelling 1960; Boulding 1962; Stevens 1963; Walton and
McKersie 1965). It is evident that the processes of bargaining, influence, and communication occur between nations as well as between
people. Knowledge about such processes as coercion, persuasion,
blackmail, ingratiation, and seduction is equally important for those
who would advise parents as for those who would advise kings.

7. *The consequences of the conflict to each of the participants and
to other interested parties (the gains or losses relating to the immediate issue in conflict, the precedents established, the internal changes in*

the participants resulting from having engaged in conflict, the long-term effects on the relationship between the parties involved, the reputation that each party develops in the eyes of the various interested audiences). The actions taken during the course of conflict and the consequences of conflict rarely leave the participants unchanged.

The dynamics of interpersonal, intergroup, and international conflict seem to have similar characteristics and appear to rest on such common underlying processes as "the self-fulfilling prophecy," biased perception and judgment, and "unwitting commitment." For example, it seems likely that for groups as well as individuals the self-fulfilling prophecy operates to produce hostility on the part of a disputant when hostile action toward him is initiated, based on the expectation of the other's hostility. Similarly, groups as well as individuals are likely to view their own actions toward another as more legitimate and well-intended than the actions of the other.

This outline of some of the variables entailed in conflict involving different types of units—individuals, groups, organizations, and nations—is not meant to imply that the mechanisms or capabilities of acquiring information, making decisions, and acting are necessarily similar in the different types of units. One should not commit the "group mind" fallacy. Yet one should not ignore the fact that nations as well as individuals have the capacity to act even though each unit cannot do the same kinds of things: a nation can declare war, a man cannot; a man can make love, a nation cannot.

It is beyond the scope of this volume to attempt to make explicit the conceptual framework that underlies the assumption that it is fruitful to view interpersonal, intergroup, and international conflict in the same terms, but it is well to recognize that my approach at all levels herein is *social-psychological*. Several key notions in a social-psychological approach are:

1. Each participant in a social interaction responds to the other in terms of his perceptions and cognitions of the other; these may or may not correspond to the other's actualities.

2. Each participant in a social interaction, being cognizant of the other's capacity for awareness, is influenced by his own expectations concerning the other's actions as well as by his perceptions of the other's conduct. These expectations may or may not be accurate; the ability to take the role of the other and to predict the other's behavior is not notable in either interpersonal or international crises.

3. Social interaction is not only initiated by motives but also generates new motives and alters old ones. It is not only determined but also determining. In the process of rationalizing and justifying actions that have been taken and effects that have been produced, new values and motives emerge. Moreover, social interaction exposes one to models and exemplars which may be identified with and imitated. Thus, a child's personality is shaped largely by the interactions he has with his parents and peers and by the people with whom he identifies. Similarly, a nation's institutions may be considerably influenced by its interrelations with other nations and by the existing models of functioning that other nations provide.

4. Social interaction takes place in a social environment—in a family, a group, a community, a nation, a civilization—that has developed techniques, symbols, categories, rules, and values that are relevant to human interactions. Hence, to understand the events that occur in social interactions one must comprehend the interplay of these events with the broader social context in which they occur.

5. Even though each participant in a social interaction, whether an individual or a group, is a complex unit composed of many interacting subsystems, it can act in a unified way toward some aspect of its environment. Decision making within the individual as within the nation can entail a struggle among different interests and values for control over action. Internal structure and internal process, while less observable in individuals than in groups, are characteristic of all social units.

THE FUNCTIONS OF CONFLICT

The legitimacy of employing similar concepts to discuss conflict between different types of units is stressed in order to justify the approach to the question that is taken in this volume. The main thrust here concerns the conditions that determine whether a conflict will be resolved with constructive or destructive consequences. The approach is to examine different levels of conflict to see whether or not there are some central notions that can throw light on varied situations of conflict and, then, to investigate these notions in laboratory experiments.

The central question underlying this investigation assumes that conflict is potentially of personal and social value. Conflict has many positive functions (Simmel 1955; Coser 1956). It prevents stagnation, it stimulates interest and curiosity, it is the medium through which problems can be aired and solutions arrived at, it is the root of personal and social change. Conflict is often part of the process of testing and assessing oneself and, as such, may be highly enjoyable as one experiences the pleasure of the full and active use of one's capacities. In addition, conflict demarcates groups from one another and thus helps establish group and personal identities; external conflict often fosters internal cohesiveness. Moreover, as Coser (1956, pp. 154–55) has indicated:

> In loosely-structured groups and open societies, conflict, which aims at a resolution of tension between antagonists, is likely to have stabilizing and integrative functions for the relationship. By permitting immediate and direct expression of rival claims, such social systems are able to readjust their structures by eliminating the sources of dissatisfaction. The multiple conflicts which they experience may serve to eliminate the causes for dissociation and to re-establish unity. These systems avail themselves, through the toleration and institutionalization of conflict, of an important stabilizing mechanism.
>
> In addition, conflict within a group frequently helps to revitalize existent norms; or it contributes to the emergence of new norms. In this sense, social conflict is a mechanism for adjustment of norms adequate to new conditions. A flexible society benefits from conflict because such behavior, by helping to create and modify norms, assures its continuance under changed conditions. Such a mechanism for readjustment of norms is hardly available to rigid systems: by suppressing conflict, the latter smother a useful warning signal, thereby maximizing the danger of catastrophic breakdown.
>
> Internal conflict can also serve as a means for ascertaining the relative strength of antagonistic interests within the structure, and in this way constitute a mechanism for the maintenance or continual readjustment of the balance of power. Since the outbreak of a conflict indicates a rejection of a previous accommodation between parties, once the respective power of the contenders has been ascertained through conflict, a new equilibrium can be established and the relationship can proceed on this new basis.

I stress the positive functions of conflict, and I have by no means provided an exhaustive listing, because many discussions of conflict cast it in the role of the villain, as though conflict per se were the cause of psychopathology, social disorder, war. A superficial reading of psychoanalytic theory with its emphasis on the "pleasure principle," field theory with its stress on tension reduction, and dissonance theory with its preoccupation with dissonance reduction would seem to suggest that the psychological utopia would be a conflict-free existence. Yet it is apparent that most people seek out conflict in competitive sports and games, by going to the theater or reading a novel, by attending to the news, in the teasing interplay of intimate encounters, and in their intellectual work. Fortunately, no one has to face the prospect of a conflict-free existence. Conflict can neither be eliminated nor even suppressed for long.

SOME DEFINITIONS

At this point it would be well to define some of the key terms used in this text. A *conflict* exists whenever *incompatible* activities occur. The incompatible actions may originate in one person, group, or nation; such conflicts are called *intra*personal, *intra*group, or *intra*national. Or they may reflect incompatible actions of two or more persons, groups, or nations; such conflicts are called *inter*personal, *inter*group, or *inter*national. An action that is incompatible with another action prevents, obstructs, interferes, injures, or in some way makes the latter less likely or less effective.

The terms *competition* and *conflict* are often used synonymously or interchangeably. This reflects a basic confusion. Although competition produces conflict, not all instances of conflict reflect competition. Competition implies an opposition in the goals of the interdependent parties such that the probability of goal attainment for one decreases as the probability for the other increases. In conflict that is derived from competition, the incompatible actions reflect incompatible goals. However, conflict may occur even when there is no perceived or actual incompatibility of goals. Thus if a husband and wife are in conflict about how to treat their son's mosquito bites, it is not because they have mutually exclusive goals; here, their goals are concordant. This distinction between conflict and competition is not made merely to split hairs. It is important and basic to a theme that underlies the work discussed in this book. Namely, conflict can occur in a cooperative or a competitive context, and the processes of conflict resolution that are likely to be displayed will be strongly influenced by the context within which the conflict occurs.

This text is concerned with psychological or perceived conflict—i.e., with conflicts that exist psychologically for the parties involved. It does not assume that perceptions are always veridical or that actual incompatibilities are always perceived.

The possibility that the nature of a relationship may be misperceived indicates that whether or not conflict occurs may be determined by a misunderstanding of or misinformation about the objective state of affairs. Thus the presence or absence of conflict is never rigidly determined by the objective state of affairs. Apart from the possibility of misperception, psychological factors enter into the determination of conflict in yet another crucial way. Conflict is also determined by what is valued by the conflicting parties. Even the classical example of pure conflict—two starving men on a lifeboat with only enough food for the survival of one—loses its impact if one or both of the men have social or religious values that can become more dominant psychologically than the hunger need or the desire for survival.

The point of these remarks is that neither the occurrence nor the outcome of conflict is completely and rigidly determined by objective circumstances. This means that the fate of the participants in a situation of conflict is not inevitably determined by the external circumstances in which they find themselves. Whether conflict takes a productive or a destructive course is thus open to influence even under the most unfavorable objective conditions. Similarly, even under the most favorable objective circumstances, psychological factors can cause a conflict to take a destructive course. The importance of "real" conflict cannot be denied; nevertheless, the psychological process of perceiving and evaluating are also "real," and they are involved in turning objective conditions into experienced conflict.

A TYPOLOGY OF CONFLICTS

Although many different typologies of conflict have been developed (see, for example, Boulding 1962; Rapoport 1960; and various articles in the first issue of the *Journal of Conflict Resolution,* 1957), in table 1.1 still another one is presented. In it, conflicts are distinguished in terms of the relationship between the objective state of affairs and the state of affairs as perceived by the conflicting parties. Six such types of conflict are characterized below.

Veridical conflict. This type of conflict exists objectively and is perceived accurately. It is not contingent upon some easily altered feature of the environment. Thus if a wife wants to use the spare room in the house as a studio for painting and her husband wishes to use it as a study, they have a "true conflict." This is especially true if their time schedules are such that she can only paint and he can only study at the same time and if the spare room cannot be subdivided to permit both activities simultaneously. Veridical conflicts are difficult to resolve amicably unless there is either sufficient cooperativeness between the two parties for them to work collaboratively to solve

TABLE 1.1. A Typology of Conflicts

Type	Objective Conflict Between A & B	Experienced [1] Conflict Between A & B	Type of Misperception [1]		
			Contingency of Conflict	Issues in Conflict	Parties in Conflict
I. Veridical Conflict	Yes	Yes	No	No	No
II. Contingent Conflict	Yes	Yes	Yes	No	No
III. Displaced Conflict	Yes	Yes	No	Yes	No
IV. Misattributed Conflict	Yes	No	No	No	Yes
V. Latent Conflict	Yes	No			
VI. False Conflict	No	Yes	Yes or	Yes or	Yes

[1] The state of affairs as experienced and perceived by one of the parties to the conflict. The other party may, of course, experience and perceive it differently. Thus A may be displacing the conflict, and for B the conflict may be a latent one.

their mutual problem of establishing priorities or they can agree upon an impartial, jointly accepted, institutional mechanism for resolving the conflict (e.g., binding arbitration, flipping a coin).

Contingent conflict. Here the existence of the conflict is dependent upon readily rearranged circumstances, but this is not recognized by the conflicting parties. Thus the veridical conflict of the preceding paragraph would be classified as a contingent conflict if there were an attic or garage or some other space that could be easily converted into a study or studio. The contingent conflict would disappear if the available alternative resources for satisfying the "conflicting" needs were recognized. Contingent conflicts are difficult to resolve only when the perspectives of the conflicting parties are narrow and rigid as a result of either insufficient cognitive and problem-solving resources or excessive emotional tension. In addition, of course, if the issues at stake in the contingent conflict have escalated so that accepting an equivalent substitute entails a loss of "face," the conflict has lost its contingency.

Displaced conflict. Here, the parties in conflict are, so to speak, arguing about the wrong thing. A husband and wife, for example, may quarrel over household bills (Am I getting enough for what I give her? Does he really give me enough?) as a displacement of an unexpressed conflict over sexual relations. The conflict being experienced is the *manifest* conflict, the one that is not being directly expressed is the *underlying* conflict. The manifest conflict will usually express the underlying conflict in a symbolic or idiomatic form; the indirect form is a "safer" way of talking about conflicts that may seem too volatile and dangerous to deal with directly. Or the manifest conflict may simply reflect the general irritability and tension in the relations between the conflicting parties that results from an unresolved, underlying conflict—the unresolved tension leading each side to be unduly sensitive to slights, to be argumentative, and the like.

Manifest conflicts take such diverse forms as the conflict of an obsessional patient over whether or not she should check to see if she really turned off the stove; the argument of two brothers over which TV program is to be tuned in; the controversy between a school board and a teachers' union over the transfer of a teacher; or an international dispute involving alleged violations of a territory by alien aircraft. Each of these manifest conflicts may be symptomatic of an underlying conflict. The obsessional patient may want to trust herself but be afraid that she has impulses that would be destructive if unchecked; the two brothers may be fighting to obtain what each considers to be his fair share of the family rewards; and so on. Often manifest conflict can only be resolved temporarily—unless the underlying conflict is dealt with or unless the manifest conflict can be separated from the underlying conflict and treated in isolation. On the other hand, sometimes the resolution of an underlying conflict is expedited by dealing with it initially in its safer, displaced forms, which often seem more approachable because they are less cosmic in their implications than the underlying conflict.

Misattributed conflict. In this type, the conflict is between the wrong parties and, as a consequence, usually over the wrong issues. Such misattribution may be unwitting, as when one blames a child for something she was instructed to do by her parents, or the misattribution may be fostered by those who would gain from it. "Divide and conquer" is a well-known strategy for weakening a group by inducing internal conflict to obscure the conflict between the group and its conqueror. Similarly, when there is a shortage of good jobs, antagonism rather than cooperation between white and black workers may reflect a faulty attribution: the source of one's difficulties being attributed to competition from the other racial group rather than to the industrial system or to the government. Such faulty attribution may be indirectly fostered through ideologies that attribute economic problems to the defects of individuals and groups rather than to the functioning of the economic system. One of the inevitable concerns of groups interested in producing social change is to reduce misattribution and the resulting false or divisive conflicts so that effective cooperation can take place between low-power groups. Effective cooperation will, presumably, enhance their mutual power to bring about change.

Latent conflict. This is, in effect, a conflict that should be occurring but is not. One may not be consciously experiencing a conflict the way he should be because it has been repressed, displaced, or misattributed or because it does not yet exist psychologically. If a woman thinks it is natural for men to have superior economic and legal rights, she is unlikely to contest male chauvinists, but, even if she rejects the doctrine of male superiority, she may not be a partisan of women's rights until she is conscious of discrimination against women. Thus one of the objectives of those interested in social betterment is to turn latent conflict into conscious conflict. "Consciousness-raising" occurs in the simultaneous enhancement of awareness of one's identity (as a woman, as a black, as a worker) and increase in the saliency of conflict with others who denigrate his identity.

False conflict. This is the occurrence of conflict when there is no objective basis for it. Such conflict always implies misperception or misunderstanding. Given the notorious inaccuracy in perception by individuals, groups, and nations, it is not unlikely that such conflicts are pervasive. A conflict may, of course, start out as a false one but elicit new motives and attitudes that turn it into a true conflict. Such a transformation is more likely to occur in a competitive-suspicious atmosphere than in a cooperative-trusting one.

The six types of conflict, described above, are not mutually exclusive. The existence of a displaced or misattributed conflict implies that there is also an unrecognized or latent one. Moreover, in any given situation of conflict, the interaction between the conflicting parties may transform the conflict from one type to another. In addition, an actual conflict may be complex, involving several issues and several parties. There may be a veridical conflict on one issue, a displaced conflict on another, and elements of misattribution in relation to several of the issues in conflict.

A conflict, whatever its reality, is usually about one or another of several types of issues. The five basic types of issues are described below.

Control over resources. Such resources as space, money, property, power, prestige, food, and so forth may be viewed as nonsharable, and if two or more parties seek exclusive possession or use of a resource or a given part of it, conflict is apt to occur between them. Conflicts of this kind are difficult to resolve constructively when there is a rigid fixation on the particular resource at issue and little possibility of finding a satisfactory substitute for it.

Preferences and nuisances. Many conflicts arise because the activities or tastes of one person or group impinge upon another's preferences, sensitivities, or sensibilities. A bride-to-be loves her cats and wants to keep them; her future husband dislikes cats and does not want them. A neighbor plays the piano incessantly and badly; the walls are paper thin. The issue is not the abstract right of the other to his preferences and activities but whether he can exercise his right if by so doing he creates a nuisance or disturbance for you. Such conflict is usually readily handled by avoidance and segregation so that the opposed sensibilities or preferences do not come into play in the same space or time. Sometimes, however, the opposed sensibilities become enmeshed in a deeper struggle of relative power or relative love (Does he love me enough to put up with my cats?), and this symbolic struggle is difficult to resolve as long as the underlying issue is not clear.

Values. Many conflicts concern what "should be." One person may prefer a system of government that emphasizes social justice, another

that emphasizes individual liberty. Value conflicts can be over relatively isolated issues (Should chemical sprays be used against the
gypsy moth?) or take the larger form of religious or ideological conflicts in which systems of values are put in opposition to one another.
It is not the differences in values per se that lead to conflict but rather
the claim that one value should dominate or be applied generally,
even by those who hold different values. Value conflict is most likely
to occur when opposing values become implicated in legal or political
action, e.g., when the state legislature has to decide whether to support a bill banning abortion or when the village council has to vote
upon whether to permit chemical spraying of the trees under its juris-
diction. A value perspective that claims no intrinsic superiority and
does not seek to force its moral views upon nonbelievers is least likely
to be involved in value conflict.

Beliefs. Many conflicts are over what "is": over facts, information,
knowledge, or beliefs about reality. The conflicts may be about something as open and direct as the perceptions of two people looking at
the same thing. The notorious conflicting testimony of eyewitnesses to
an accident is an illustration. Or, the conflict may be more subtle, as
in the difference of basic assumptions about how things relate to one
another. One economist may believe that the best way to predict
trends in the national economy is to watch variables X, Y, and Z; another may think A, B, and C are better indicators. The work of Asch
and his collaborators (1956) studying perceptual conflict, and the research of Hammond and his colleagues (1965) investigating conflicts
over cognitive assumptions have demonstrated that such conflicts can
be emotionally upsetting when the opponent or his views cannot be
dismissed as being incompetent or mischievous. Opposition to one's
securely held fundamental beliefs is a challenge to one's grasp on reality. If you cannot have confidence in what you perceive and believe,
your ability to act rationally is undermined.

Not all discrepancies in belief lead to conflict. A wife may believe
that suntanning is good for the skin, and her husband may think the
opposite, but no conflict will result unless they must act jointly in an
area relevant to their beliefs, unless one or both of them decide that
his or her belief should dominate and be accepted by the other, or unless their beliefs are so fundamental to their views of reality and so
based on social consensus that challenges to them must be negated.

The nature of the relationship between the parties. Two people may conflict because of opposing views and desires in their relationship. Both may want to be dominant, or both may desire to be dominated; one may want more "togetherness" than the other; and so on. Sometimes a conflict over the relationship is too difficult to face directly and, as a consequence, it remains latent or is displaced or misattributed.

DESTRUCTIVE AND CONSTRUCTIVE CONFLICTS

Another useful distinction among conflicts, which differs from those made in the typology presented above, is that between *destructive* and *constructive* conflicts.

At the extremes, these terms are easy to define. Thus a conflict clearly has destructive consequences if its participants are dissatisfied with the outcomes and feel they have lost as a result of the conflict. Similarly, a conflict has productive consequences if the participants all are satisfied with their outcomes and feel that they have gained as a result of the conflict. Also, in most instances, a conflict in which the outcomes are satisfying to all the participants will be more constructive than one that is satisfying to some and dissatisfying to others.

It is, of course, easier to identify and measure satisfactions-dissatisfactions and gains-losses in simple laboratory conflict situations than it is in the complex conflicts of groups in everyday life. Yet even in these complex situations, it is not impossible to compare conflicts in terms of their outcomes. In some instances, union-management negotiations may lead to a prolonged strike with considerable loss and ill will resulting to both parties; in other instances, such negotiations may lead to a mutually satisfying agreement from which both sides obtain something they want. In some cases, a quarrel between a husband and wife will clear up unexpressed misunderstandings and lead to greater intimacy; in others, it may produce only bitterness and estrangement.

THE QUERY

We may now return to the basic question to which this work is addressed: how to prevent conflict from being destructive. The point is *not* how to eliminate or prevent conflict but rather how to make it productive. We shall not deal with situations of "pure" conflict in which one side inevitably loses what the other gains. The interest here is in conflict where there is a mixture of cooperative and competitive interests, where a variety of outcomes is possible: mutual loss, gain for one and loss for the other, and mutual gain. Thus, the thesis of this book can be restated as an investigation of the conditions under which the participants will evolve a cooperative or a competitive relationship in a situation which permits either.

It should be stressed that the elimination of pure conflict is not very restricting. As has been indicated above, conflict is determined by what is valued by the conflicting parties and by what beliefs and perceptions those parties hold. But values, beliefs, and perceptions are not always unalterable. In addition, there are few circumstances, particularly if the situation is repetitive or if the participants are involved in many different relationships together, that are so rigidly structured as to cause one's gains to come inevitably from the other's losses. It is, of course, true that the participants may nearsightedly define an occasion that permits mutual gain as a situation of pure conflict and respond to one another in a purely competitive manner.

There is an important advantage to be gained from the reformulation of the original query into a statement concerning the conditions under which a cooperative or competitive relationship will evolve among participants who have a mixture of cooperative and competitive interests in regard to one another. It permits the application of considerable previous theoretical and research work to the characterization of two major processes of interrelationships in dealing with conflict: a cooperative process and a competitive one. It may be assumed that the development of one or the other type of relationship will be manifest not only in the outcomes of conflict but also in the processes of dealing with it.

In the next chapter, we shall characterize the major differences between cooperative and competitive processes as they have been revealed in theoretical and experimental work. In subsequent chapters in Part One, we shall examine conflict at different levels—intrapersonal, interpersonal, and intergroup—to see if it is possible to arrive at some broad generalizations concerning the conditions that give rise to one rather than the other process of conflict resolution. In Part Two, some experimental investigations, conducted in the author's laboratory and which bear upon these generalizations, will be described.

In Part Three are described the typical characteristics of destructive and constructive conflicts and the factors that determine which mode of conflict resolution will be dominant. In this part, the regulation of conflict and the role of third parties in this process are also discussed. Finally, some of the special issues relating to conflict between the weak and the strong are considered.

2. Cooperative and Competitive Processes

A Theoretical Analysis of Cooperation and Competition

Kurt Lewin, with whom I studied as a graduate student, had a favorite question: "What is the essence of the phenomena?" This question was of central importance in the formulation of my doctoral dissertation on the effects of cooperation and competition (Deutsch 1948). It seemed that implicit in the then sparse scholarly literature on the subject, as well as in everyday usage, had been the notion that the crux of the differences between cooperation and competition lies in the nature of the way the goals of the participants in each of the situations are linked. In a cooperative situation the goals are so linked that everybody "sinks or swims" together, while in the competitive situation if one swims, the other must sink.

With this idea in mind, I have defined a cooperative situation as one in which the goals of the participants are so linked that any participant can attain his goal if, and only if, the others with whom he is linked can attain their goals. The term *promotive interdependence* has been used to characterize all goal linkages in which there is a positive correlation between the attainments of the linked participants. The degree of promotive interdependence refers to the amount of positive correlation; it can vary in value from 0 to $+1$.

Similarly, in a competitive situation the goals for the participants are *contriently interdependent*. Contrient interdependence is the condition in which participants are so linked together that there is a negative correlation between their goal attainments. The degree of contrient interdependence refers to the amount of negative correlation; it can vary in value from 0 to -1. In the limiting case of pure competition, a participant can attain his goal if, and only if, the others with whom he is linked cannot attain their goals.

The theoretical discussion here will cover only pure situations of cooperation and competition that are symmetrical and are perceived consonantly. Figure 2.1 illustrates a case of symmetrical promotive interdependence; consonant perception implies that the relationship is perceived by both parties (P_1 and P_2) to be promotively interdependent. Figure 2.1 also illustrates symmetrical contrient interdependence and the case of noninterdependence between the goals of P_1 and P_2.

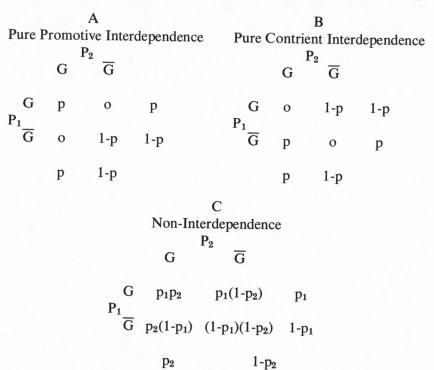

A
Pure Promotive Interdependence

B
Pure Contrient Interdependence

C
Non-Interdependence

Figure 2.1. Three basic types of goal relations between the probabilities of goal attainment of two people, P_1 and P_2. G = goal attainment; $\overline{G}$ = lack of goal attainment; p, p_1, and p_2 refer to probabilities.

It may be noted that few real-life situations correspond to pure cooperative or competitive situations as defined herein. Most situations of everyday life involve a complex set of goals and subgoals. Consequently, it is possible for individuals to be promotively interdependent with respect to one goal and contriently interdependent in relation to another. The members of a basketball team may be cooperatively interrelated with respect to winning the game but competitive with respect to being the "star" of the team. Also, people may be promotively interdependent with respect to subgoals and contriently interdependent with respect to main goals, or vice versa. Firms manufacturing the same product may be cooperative with regard to expanding the total market but competitive with regard to the share of it that each obtains. Moreover, there are certain situations in which people may compete about the terms of their cooperation, as in bargaining. Indeed, extrapolation from the "pure" situation is often nearly unnecessary to understand the more complex one: when the occasions for cooperation and competition are not rigidly segregated, it is likely that the relative strengths of the cooperative and competitive linkages between the parties (as determined by the importance of the goals that are linked together and the degree of their linkage or interdependence) will determine the direction of the resulting process.

THE EFFECTS OF COOPERATION AND COMPETITION

In a cooperative situation when a participant behaves in such a way as to increase his chances of goal attainment, he increases the chances that the others, with whom he is promotively linked, will also attain their goals. In contrast, in a competitive situation when a participant behaves in such a way as to increase his own chances of goal attainment, he decreases the chances of the others. In order to understand the differing consequences of cooperative and competitive situations, it would be well to examine their effects upon such central social-psychological processes as "substitutability" (the willingness to allow someone else's actions to be substitutable for one's own), "cathexis" (the development of positive or negative attitudes), and "inducibility" (the readiness to be influenced positively by another).

Substitutability. If P_1 has moved toward his goal as a consequence of P_2's actions, P_2's actions are substitutable for similarly intended actions by P_1, and repetition would be perceived as superfluous. Hence, in a cooperative situation, one would expect that there would be little need for the cooperators to duplicate one another's activities. On the other hand, if P_1's chances of attaining his goal are reduced while P_2's chances are enhanced because of P_2's successful actions, one would expect no substitutability. Hence, in a competitive situation, P_1 would instead attempt to cover the same ground as P_2 by attempting to imitate or outdo him.

Positive cathexis. If P_1 has moved toward his goal as a consequence of P_2's effective actions, in a cooperative situation it seems likely that P_1 will cathect positively P_2's actions and may generalize the cathexis to P_2 so that he (P_1) will want to cooperate with P_2 in other situations. On the other hand, if P_1's chance of reaching his goal has been reduced as a consequence of P_2's able, competitive behavior, it seems likely that P_1 will negatively cathect P_2 and his behavior and will not want to compete with P_2 in the future. A negative attitude toward an effective opponent such as P_2, however, would be inconsistent with an attempt to imitate or outdo P_2's behavior; hence, P_1 will be in self-conflict in the competitive social situation when doing badly.

Inducibility. If P_2's successful cooperative actions move P_1 toward his goals, it may be expected that P_1 will facilitate P_2's actions. Thus in a cooperative relationship, one would expect people to be mutually helpful and responsive to one another's requests. If P_2's actions move P_1 away from his goals, one would expect P_1 to be obstructive and resistant to P_2's efforts. Competitors are more likely to attempt to hinder than aid one another.

Note that in the description of the effects described above, the situations have all concerned what happens when P_2's actions affect P_1's chances of goal attainment positively or negatively. Until now, I have made the simplifying assumption that P_2's actions are successful or effective actions; hence, in a cooperative situation P_2's actions would help P_1, but those same actions would harm P_1 if it were a competitive situation. However, P_2's behavior may be bungling or relatively ineffective (less effective than that of another potential cooperator or competitor who serves as a base of comparison). Instead of helping P_1, with whom he is cooperatively linked, P_2 might actually reduce his chances of goal attainment; or instead of harming P_1, with whom he is competitively linked, P_2 might enhance his chances. If this were the case, the predictions for the cooperative and competitive situations would be reversed. In the cooperative situation, there would be no substitutability: P_1 would hinder rather than facilitate P_2's actions, he would dislike rather than like, he would reject rather than be satisfied with P_2's actions. And in the competitive situation, P_1 would facilitate and like P_2's bungling actions but feel no need to imitate or outdo them.

Elsewhere (Deutsch 1949a, 1962), some of the further consequences of the differences between a cooperative and a competitive social process have been detailed. Here, some of the main results of this theoretical analysis are summarized. In brief, a cooperative process, by permitting more substitutability, encourages more division of labor and role specialization; this permits more economic use of personnel and resources which, in turn, leads to greater task productivity. The development of more favorable attitudes toward one another in the cooperative situation fosters more mutual trust and openness of communication as well as provides a more stable basis for continuing cooperation despite the waxing and waning of particular goals. It also encourages a perception of similarity of attitudes. Since participants in the cooperative situation are more easily influenced than those in the competitive situation, the former are usually more attentive to one another. This lessens communication difficulties and encourages the use of techniques of persuasion rather than of coercion when there are differences of viewpoint.

The cooperative process, however, contains within it some typical "pathologies": the division of labor and role specialization tend to create vested interests in the specialized functions, so that the specialists become more oriented to the fulfillment of their own functions than to the fulfillment of the overall requirements of the cooperative undertaking; the development of friendly personal relations encourages favoritism or nepotism, which may be an impediment to the fulfillment of task-requirements, a source of internal conflict, and a basis for the erosion of universalistic rules that may conflict with the ties of a personal relationship; and the susceptibility to social influence in the cooperative situation may lead to overconformity as well as to the inhibition of disagreement and differences which, in turn, may retard innovation and improvements in the process of cooperation.

By now, there has been a good deal of experimental research bearing upon my theoretical analysis of the processes of cooperation and competition. Most of the research has investigated *intra*group cooperation and competition. In the next section, a summary of a study on this topic by this writer is presented. In the following section, an investigation by Sherif and his associates that deals with *inter*group cooperation and competition is summarized. Although Sherif's work was not guided by the theoretical analysis presented above, his data are clearly relevant to it, and the results of his study of *inter*group cooperation and competition parallel remarkably well the results of my research on *intra*group cooperation and competition.

A STUDY OF INTRAGROUP COOPERATION AND COMPETITION

In the spring semester of 1948, I conducted an experiment with M.I.T. undergraduates who were enrolled in sections of an introductory psychology course that I was teaching. I subdivided the sections into ten groups, each composed of five students, and met with each group for three hours once a week for six weeks. Each group followed the same routine at its meetings. First, the members were given the task of solving together a rather tricky intellectual puzzle as rapidly as they could. (For example: There must have been a dearth of eligible young ladies in Kinsleydale, for each of five men there has married the widowed mother of one of the others. Jenkin's stepson, Tomkins, is the stepfather of Perkins. Jenkin's mother is a friend of Mrs. Watkins, whose husband's mother is a cousin of Mrs. Perkins. What is the name of the stepson of Simkins? [Answer: Watkins.]) During the next fifty minutes they were constituted as a "board of human relations advisors" and were asked to formulate, after group discussion, a written response to a letter asking their advice about a personal or social problem. They discussed such problems as how to respond to an incident involving prejudice in a barber shop and what to recommend to a returning soldier who felt guilty about being unfaithful to his wife while overseas. During the remainder of the period, I led the group in a discussion of psychological concepts and principles relating to such topics as learning, perception, cognition, and motivation.

After the first week of such meetings, the groups were divided into equated pairs based upon their group performances in the first meeting. One group in each equated pair was then assigned at random to a competitive grading system and the other group to a cooperative grading system. Half of the groups were told that their discussions of the human relations problem would be graded competitively: each individual's contribution to the group's discussion and group product would be compared with the contributions of each of the other group members, and the best contributor would get an *A*, the next best a *B*, and so on. The other half of the groups were told that they would be graded cooperatively: every person in the group would get the same grade, the grade being determined by how well the group's discussion and product compared with those of four other similar groups; all the members in the best group would get *A*'s, those in the next best group

would get *B*'s, and so on. The students accepted the grading procedures in both types of groups without question or protest. Since
grades were quite important at M.I.T., the students were highly motivated to achieve a high grade in both conditions.

All groups were observed systematically by three research assistants
who categorized and rated such different aspects of the discussions as
their friendliness, orderliness, and quality. They also noted who spoke
to whom and how much attentiveness and mutual understanding there
was during the discussions. In addition, the students filled out questionnaires after each discussion in which they rated various aspects of
the discussion, their own reactions during it, and their attitudes toward other group members.

The results of the experiment showed striking differences between
the cooperative and competitive groups. As compared with the competitively graded groups, the cooperative ones showed the following
characteristics:

1. More effective intermember communication. More ideas were
verbalized, and members were more attentive to one another and
more acceptant of and influenced by one another's ideas. They had
fewer difficulties in communicating with or understanding others.

2. More friendliness, more helpfulness, and less obstructiveness
was expressed in the discussion. Members were also more satisfied
with the group and its solutions and more favorably impressed by the
contributions of the other group members. In addition, members of
the cooperative groups rated themselves higher in desire to win the respect of their colleagues and in obligation to the other members.

3. More coordination of effort, more division of labor, more orientation to task achievement, more orderliness in discussion, and higher
productivity were manifested in the cooperative groups.

4. More feeling of agreement and similarity in ideas and more confidence in one's own ideas and in the value that other members
attached to those ideas were obtained in the cooperative groups.

The above findings, which are described more fully in my article,
"An Experimental Study of the Effects of Cooperation and Competition Upon Group Process" (Deutsch 1949b), have been supported by
the studies of many other investigators (Back 1951; Berkowitz 1957;
Gerard 1953; Gottheil 1955; Grossack 1954; Levy 1953; Margolin
1954; Mintz 1951; Mizuhara 1952; Mizuhara and Tamai 1952;
Raven and Eachus 1963; Thomas 1957; Workie 1967). All these stud-

ies except Workie's, however, were confined to comparisons of competitive and cooperative relations among individuals. Workie studied *inter*group as well as *intra*group cooperation and competition. His research indicates that whether the units being looked at are groups or individuals, the same basic findings are obtained. The total productivity of a system of interdependent groups is smaller when the reward structure orients the groups toward intergroup competition rather than cooperation. Not surprisingly, more intergroup goal-blocking and deceptiveness occur between groups that are in competition with one another than between groups that are cooperatively interdependent.

A STUDY OF INTERGROUP COOPERATION AND COMPETITION

The most detailed investigations of intergroup cooperation and competition to date have been conducted by Muzafer Sherif and by Blake and Mouton (Sherif *et al.* 1961; Sherif 1966; Blake and Mouton 1961a, b and 1962 a, b). These studies are notable for their ingenious use of natural rather than laboratory settings. Sherif and his associates conducted their now classic "Robbers Cave" study at a specially arranged campsite in which the campers (boys of eleven and twelve) interacted in activities that appeared natural to them; they were not aware of the fact that their behavior was under observation.

The experiment proceeded in three stages. The first stage was designed to produce groups with distinct internal structures and group norms, so that they could be confronted with intergroup problems. This stage of group formation lasted about a week. It was initiated by having each of two groups of campers come to camp in a separate bus and then live in a separate cabin. The boys in each cabin engaged in a variety of cooperative activities: camping out, cooking, improving swimming places, transporting canoes over rough terrain to the water, and so on. Each group developed an organization and specific customs, and each manifested the signs of "we-feeling" and the joint accomplishments that mark a cohesive group. In the second stage of the experiment, tension and conflict were produced between the two groups by introducing conditions conducive to competition between them. A series of situations was created in which one group could achieve its goal only at the expense of the other group—e.g., through a tournament of competitive events with desirable prizes only for the winning group. As a result, members of each group developed hostile attitudes and highly unfavorable stereotypes toward the other group and its members. Conflict was manifested in derogatory name calling and invectives ("stinkers," "sneaks," and "cheats"), flare-ups of physical conflict, and raids on each other's cabins. At the same time, there was an increase in ingroup solidarity and cooperativeness and a significant change in the status relations within groups, such that those who were particularly effective in intergroup competition rose in status. Clearly, intragroup cooperation and harmony does not inevitably lead to intergroup harmony.

In the third stage, different approaches to reducing intergroup conflict were evaluated: contact between groups in activities highly pleasant to each group but not involving interdependence between them (going to the movies, eating in the same dining room, shooting off fireworks on July 4); and, in contrast, the introduction of superordinate goals, which had a compelling appeal for each group but which neither group could achieve without the cooperation of the other. Such other techniques as "disseminating favorable information about the other group" and "summit conferences between leaders of the two groups" were rejected on a priori grounds as ineffective. Intergroup contacts without the existence of superordinate goals were ineffective in reducing conflict; in fact, such intergroup contacts often degenerated into conflict. But joint efforts toward accomplishing superordinate goals (such as repairing the water supply system of the camp after the experimenters covertly arranged to have it break down, raising the funds necessary to go to a highly desired movie, moving a camp truck that had "broken down") gradually and cumulatively changed the relations between the two groups from a pattern of hostile to one of friendly interaction.

Sherif's findings have been supported by the work of other investigators, particularly Blake and Mouton (1961a, b), who have been especially interested in the effects of win-lose conflicts on the negotiations between groups. They have studied intergroup conflict in human relations training laboratories among ad hoc, temporary groups as well as between union and management in industry. In findings similar to Sherif's, they report that intergroup competition has characteristic effects on ingroup relations (an increased ingroup cohesion, a shift to a conflict-oriented leadership, more personal identification by members with their group), on perception of the outgroup (an increase in negative stereotyping and in perception of dissimilarity), and on negotiations between the groups to resolve their differences. Between highly competitive groups, negotiations are characterized by: a tendency to overvalue the recommendations of one's own group and to disparage those of the other group; mutual misunderstandings of positions, such that common values are overlooked and differences emphasized; a tendency to prize victory more than agreement, so that a negotiator who compromises is seen as a traitor while one who is unyielding is seen as a hero; a tendency to discredit a neutral third party if he makes a recommendation that is not clearly favorable to one's own group; frequent deadlocking rather than arrival at a mutually satisfying agreement.

Clearly, there is a marked parallel in the results of the research on both cooperation and competition within groups and between groups. The research findings, as well as the theoretical analysis, indicate that the differences between the processes involved in cooperation and competition (comparing them in their pure or extreme forms) can be summarized as follows:

1. *Communication*

a) A cooperative process is characterized by open and honest communication of relevant information between the participants. Each is interested in informing, and being informed by, the other.

b) A competitive process is characterized by either lack of communication or misleading communication. It also gives rise to espionage or other techniques of obtaining information about the other that the other is unwilling to communicate. In addition to obtaining such information, each party is interested in providing discouraging or misleading information to the other.

2. *Perception*

a) A cooperative process tends to increase sensitivity to similarities and common interests while minimizing the salience of differences. It stimulates a convergence and conformity of beliefs and values.

b) A competitive process tends to increase sensitivity to differences and threats while minimizing the awareness of similarities. It stimulates the sense of complete oppositeness: "You are bad; I am good." It seems likely that competition produces a stronger bias toward misperceiving the other's neutral or conciliatory actions as malevolently motivated than the bias induced by cooperation to see the other's actions as benevolently intended.

3. *Attitudes toward one another*

a) A cooperative process leads to a trusting, friendly attitude, and it increases the willingness to respond helpfully to the other's needs and requests.

b) A competitive process leads to a suspicious, hostile attitude, and it increases the readiness to exploit the other's needs and respond negatively to the other's requests.

4. *Task orientation*

a) A cooperative process enables the participants to approach the mutually acknowledged problem in a way that utilizes their special talents and enables them to substitute for one another in their joint work, so that duplication of effort is reduced. The enhancement of mutual power and resources becomes an objective. It leads to the defining of conflicting interests as a mutual problem to be solved by collaborative effort. It facilitates the recognition of the legitimacy of each other's interests and of the necessity of searching for a solution that is responsive to the needs of all. It tends to limit rather than expand the scope of conflicting interests. Attempts to influence the other tend to be limited to processes of persuasion.

b) A competitive process stimulates the view that the solution of a conflict can only be one that is imposed by one side on the other. The enhancement of one's own power and the minimization of the legitimacy of the other side's interests in the situation become objectives. It fosters the expansion of the scope of the issues in conflict so that the conflict becomes a matter of general principle and is no longer confined to a particular issue at a given time and place. The escalation of the conflict increases its motivational significance to the participants and intensifies their emotional involvement in it; these factors, in turn, may make a limited defeat less acceptable or more humiliating than mutual disaster might be. Duplication of effort, so that the competitors become mirror-images of one another, is more likely than division of effort. Coercive processes tend to be employed in the attempt to influence the other.

This sketch of some aspects of competitive and cooperative processes suggests that each process tends to be self-confirming, so that the experience of cooperation will induce a benign spiral of increasing co-operation, while competition will induce a vicious spiral of intensifying competition. This is true to some extent, but there are restraints that usually operate to limit the spiraling of both processes. Not the least of these restraints arises from the fact that a person or group is usually involved in many situations and relationships simultaneously, and his other involvements and relationships usually prevent or contain what might be termed an obsessive intensification of any particular relationship.

A PARADOX?

I have now characterized the central social-psychological manifestation of the cooperative and competitive approaches to the resolution of conflicting interests. I have also suggested that it may be fruitful to think of the mutually destructive consequences of conflict as resulting from a competitive process of conflict resolution and the mutually constructive consequences as emerging from the cooperative process. One may ask again then: in a situation of conflict, what conditions determine which process will dominate? Here, we must face an apparent contradiction in this presentation so far. Earlier it was indicated that conflict has positive individual and social functions, and yet now we see that a competitive process of conflict resolution is likely to be destructive.

There are several points to be made. First, conflict is not confined to competitive processes; controversy over the means to achieve a mutually desired objective is a common part of cooperation. Conflict of this sort is not competitive so long as each cooperator is motivated to select the best means to achieve the mutual objective rather than the method that he advocated initially. There is no reason to think of this kind of conflict as being destructive. Second, competition is not inevitably destructive to both sides. Often one side is more powerful, more determined, or more resourceful than the other, and it may be able to impose its initially preferred solution to the conflict. It is, of course, possible that the defeat of an individual, group, or nation in a conflict may be constructive for others besides the immediate victor, and occasionally it is so even for the defeated party. Competition also provides a useful social mechanism for selecting those who are more rather than less able to perform the activities involved in the competition. (The greater skill in performance may, of course, reflect differences in training and resources as well as differences in endowment or motivation.) Third, competitive conflict, with its resulting losses to one or both of the parties involved, may be a necessary precondition to motivate the parties to engage in a cooperative process. An affluent, complacent authority or majority may be unresponsive to a dissatisfied subordinate minority until the threats and losses of a competitive conflict motivate it to seek a cooperative solution. Finally, it seems reasonable to speculate that much of the pleasure of competition arises when it occurs in a cooperative encounter; then there is a cooperative interest in having a mutually enjoyable competition rather than a primary interest in defeating the other.

We may turn back now to a consideration of the conditions that give rise to one rather than another process of conflict resolution. In an attempt to arrive at some broad generalizations, I shall examine conflict at the intrapersonal and intergroup levels in the next several chapters.

3. Intrapsychic Conflict

Inner conflict is an experience no one can avoid. It occurs in relation to such temptations as eating a piece of Nesselrode pie rather than staying on one's low calorie diet as well as in such major decisions as whether to resist or submit to an unjust authority. It is experienced as one attempts to juggle the conflicting responsibilities of various social roles: father, husband, teacher, scholar, citizen, and so forth.

The pervasive character of intrapsychic conflict is indicated by the distinguished roster of psychological theorists who have concerned themselves with it. A partial listing would include Freud, Pavlov, Lewin, Miller, Hull, Guthrie, Brown, Heider, Festinger, the role theorists, and the decision theorists. I shall not attempt to summarize the works of these theorists individually, but rather I will draw freely on their contributions to see what insights can be gathered from the different groups of theorists—especially the learning, consistency, role, and psychoanalytic theorists—about the conditions that determine whether an intrapersonal conflict will be easy or difficult to resolve. In this presentation the differences among the theorists who fall under a given heading will not be detailed, nor will the theories or experimental findings be presented as such; rather I shall focus on the relevant conclusions that can be drawn in relation to the theme of this volume.

Learning Theorists

In their approach to conflict, learning theorists stress the view (Brown 1957, p. 36) "that the important determinants of behavior in conflict-producing situations are indistinguishable from those in ordinary unambivalent situations and that no sharp dividing line can be drawn between the two kinds of behavior." The basic conflict paradigm, which is presented in figure 3.1, involves a stimulus complex (S) capable of arousing two tendencies (T_1 and T_2) to perform antagonistic responses (R_1 and R_2).

A distinction is made between the *tendency to approach* something one likes or wants and the *tendency to avoid* something one dislikes or fears. As Lewin (1931) and Miller (1944) have pointed out, there are three fundamental conflict situations: an *approach-approach* conflict, in which the individual is torn between two desires; an *avoidance-avoidance* conflict, in which the individual is caught between two fears; and an *approach-avoidance* conflict in which the individual fears to approach something he desires.

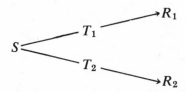

Figure 3.1. The basic stimulus-response conflict paradigm.

While it is assumed that both the approach and the avoidance tendencies decrease in strength the farther the person is from the goal (toward or away from which the tendencies are directed), it is also usually assumed that the strength of the avoidance tendency falls off more rapidly. From these assumptions, one can predict that a pure approach-approach conflict would be easy to resolve since movement toward one, rather than the other, of the competing desirable goals would increase the strength of the approach tendency toward it at the same time as it would weaken the approach tendency toward the other goal by making it farther away.

However, many conflicts that seem to be simple approach-approach conflicts on closer inspection turn out to be double approach-avoidance conflicts—wherein gaining one alternative also means losing the other one, and the alternatives are not mutually substitutable. Approach-avoidance and avoidance-avoidance conflicts are thornier than approach-approach ones. In both of these, because of the rapidly increasing strength of the avoidance tendency as you get closer to the aversive object (i.e., the closer you come to resolving the conflict by moving toward the desired goal in the approach-avoidance conflict or away from one of the feared or disliked regions in the avoidance-

avoidance conflict), the stronger will be the tendency pushing you in the direction that leads back into the center of conflict. In the avoidance-avoidance conflict, however, there will be a tendency to "escape from the field" and thus avoid both negative regions unless the conflict is so structured that this is not possible. A girl who must either marry an unpleasant suitor or become an impoverished spinster, if she remains in her village, may leave the village if she can do so.

The strength of each response tendency, approach or avoidant, is conceived to be determined not only by the person's closeness to his desired or feared object but also by such other factors as the response tendency's "habit strength," the strength of the "drive" associated with it, and the "stimulus intensity" or "incentive value of the stimulus." The various learning theorists differ among themselves as to how "response strength" is related to such other concepts as "habit strength" and "drive" and as to how these other concepts relate to one another and to events that can be observed and measured. Few of them would disagree, however, that performance of a given response in a given situation can be influenced by such factors as the amount, kind, immediacy, and distribution of rewards associated with prior performances; the kind and intensity of the subject's motivation; the amount of work connected with making the response; the distinctiveness of the stimulus situation from other situations to which competing or interfering responses have been learned; and the similarity of the stimulus situation to other situations in which similar or facilitating responses have been learned.

As the strength of each competing response tendency increases, it seems evident that conflict will be more intense and more difficult to resolve. Thus, a conflict will be more difficult to resolve if each conflicting behavior tendency has an intense motivation underlying it, has a strong habit strength as a result of the prior history of reward associated with it, and has strongly activating stimuli connected with it. One can also assume that the more equal the competing tendencies are in strength, the greater will be the difficulty in resolving the conflict.

So far, I have described the learning theory approach to conflict by using the imagery of movement in physical space. Although this approach was originally conceived in such terms, it has been elaborated (Miller 1948; Brown 1957) to apply to all dimensions of qualitative stimulus similarity. Dollard and Miller (1950, p. 354) thus state: "Therefore, we would expect gradients of approach and avoidance, respectively, to exist in any situation that involves regular sequences of cues that become progressively more similar to those present at the goal or point of punishment." In other words, if a person learns to make an approach or avoidance response to a certain cue, this response will tend to generalize to other, similar cues, with more generalization occurring to stimuli that are more similar.

Attaching the same label (communism) to different stimuli (Russia, China, Yugoslavia, Rumania, Cuba) increases the amount of generalization of a given response tendency (disapproval); attaching different labels to similar cues (Stalinism, Titoism, Castroism, Maoism, Leninism) decreases the amount of generalization and thus makes subsequent discrimination easier to learn. It is apparent that the nature of the labels that are applied to stimuli, and also to responses, can either promote internal conflict or reduce its likelihood. For example, if a student burns his draft card, his response to his own behavior will involve less self-conflict if he labels the behavior a courageous protest against war than if he labels it an illegal act and thus puts it in the same category as vandalism.

The learning theorists discuss the resolution of conflict essentially in terms of two basic notions: response displacement and reinforcement. They assume that if a response tendency, such as making a direct sexual approach to a woman, is blocked by an opposing response tendency arising from the fear of disapproval or rejection, there will be a shift away from the original response until a response such as "hinting" occurs, which will not be blocked or inhibited by the fear. The displaced response of hinting may become the dominant initial approach tendency if it is reinforced by the successful reduction of the fear of rejection or by the gratification of the sexual drive activating this response. In effect, past experiences involving the successful reduction of fear or anxiety may become a principal factor in determining which response will be made in a situation of conflict. As Atkinson (1964) has pointed out, there are differences in the tendency of individuals to be "achievement oriented" or "failure oriented," and, undoubtedly, such differences may make this "reduction of fear" a more potent reinforcer for some and "positive gratification" more potent for others.

Although the learning theorists have suggested that conflict per se may evoke drives other than those underlying the competing response tendencies, they have not paid much attention to the processes instigated by conflict. This has been the main concern of the consistency theorists, among whom Heider, Festinger, Osgood, McGuire, Abelson, and Rosenberg are especially outstanding.

CONSISTENCY THEORISTS

A central theme of the consistency theorists is that it is psychologically noxious to have inner conflict (imbalance, dissonance, incongruence, or inconsistency) among one's beliefs or between one's values. These theorists posit that people will seek to reduce or eliminate inconsistency if it occurs and to prevent it if it threatens to arise. An interesting implication of this view is that people will not only attempt to act in a way that is consistent with their beliefs, but also, conversely, they will attempt to make their beliefs consistent with their actions. Thus experimental research (Brock and Buss 1962, 1964; Davis and Jones 1960; Glass 1964) indicates that we may come to dislike those we harm or may tend to minimize the harm we have done to people we cannot dislike.

The tendency to make beliefs consistent with actions is significant for understanding why people sometimes find themselves involved and committed, albeit unwittingly, to doing things that they did not start out to do and did not initially intend. To rationalize the unanticipated costs of an activity that a person has engaged in, he may come to view the activity as important, thus making further additional costs easier for him to justify. Thus from the perspective offered by the consistency theories, the war in Vietnam became important to the United States because of the costs incurred there. Once it became important, it was easier to justify additional expenditures of men and resources. Before the 1960s, few responsible government officials would have felt that Vietnam was sufficiently important to justify the costs that have since occurred as a result of our involvement in this far-off, tragic land.

The consistency theorists, and particularly the dissonance theorists, thus suggest the proposition that in the course of conflict, a person who has chosen a course of action and feels responsible for it will become even more committed to it if he experiences unexpected difficulty, pain, or loss as a consequence of his choice. The notion that by inflicting hurt or loss on an opponent one will weaken his commitment to the conflict is, according to this proposition, not well grounded.

Another proposition suggested by the consistency theorists is that the pressure for psychological consistency will tend to produce cognitive distortions and an oversimplified black-white view of the entities in conflict. Such distortions will foster either a benign or a vicious spiral that will make the interactions mutually benevolent or mutually destructive. As I have stated elsewhere (Deutsch 1962):

> If an individual feels afraid, he tends to perceive his world as frightening; if he feels weak and vulnerable, he is apt to see it as exploitative and powerful; if he is torn by self-doubt and self-conflict, he will tend to see the external world in such a way as to justify his feelings and beliefs but also as to justify his behavior. If an individual is a heavy smoker, he is apt to perceive cigarette smoking as less injurious to health than a nonsmoker; if he drives a car and injures a pedestrian, he is likely to blame the pedestrian; if he invests in something (e.g., a munitions industry), he will attempt to justify and protect his investment. Moreover, there is much evidence that an individual tends to perceive the different parts of his world as consistent with one another. Thus, if somebody disagrees with you, you are likely to expect him to agree with someone who disagrees with you.

Although the pressure for self-consistency is a natural process that occurs in all people, in its extreme forms it manifests itself in an intolerance for ambiguity, an oversimplified black-white view of the world, and an inclination toward rigid, dogmatic positions. Rokeach (1960) has investigated some of the factors that contribute to the development of the "closed mind." He indicates that dogmatism tends to increase with anxiety or the experience of fundamental threat from the environment. This finding, with regard to intrapsychic processes, parallels conclusions that have been drawn for intragroup processes: group cohesion increases and the tolerance of deviance within the group decreases as external threat increases.

ROLE THEORISTS

Conflict has generally been considered by role theorists to be one of the primary motivations for deviant behavior (behavior that violates the social norms defining legitimate goals or legitimate means for attaining goals within a community). Deviant behavior may also reflect inadequate or inappropriate socialization. That is, the deviant individual may never have been adequately trained to guide his conduct by the relevant social norms, or he may have been trained to abide by social norms that run counter to the dominant norms in his community. Inadequate socialization is illustrated by the case of a feebleminded person who has never been able to acquire the behavioral skills necessary to become a self-reliant adult; inappropriate socialization is illustrated by the child in a slum area who has internalized values relating to "immediate" gratification and physical aggressiveness that are counter to the dominant norms in the school he attends.

Although an individual may be both adequately and appropriately socialized, he may nevertheless find himself confronted with conflicting expectations or expectations that exceed his ability, and, as a consequence, he may experience inner conflict and exhibit deviant behavior. Viewing deviance as a failure to conform to norms governing goals or means, Merton (1957) has provided a classification in terms of the following types: *innovation, ritualism, retreatism,* and *rebellion.*

Innovation, which is characterized by an acceptance of the prescribed goals and the rejection of prescribed means, may involve either the covert use of forbidden methods or the attempt to introduce and obtain public acceptance of new methods as a substitute for the old ones. The businessman who cheats his customers in order to make a higher profit, the looter who steals a television set from a store in order to be able to watch television at home, the student who copies the work of another student in order to get a passing mark are all pursuing culturally accepted goals by forbidden means. The inventor and the political reformer who seek to introduce new methods are also innovators, but, unlike the antisocial innovator, they act overtly and seek public acceptance for their innovations.

Ritualism is manifested by a conformity to approved means but a failure to strive for the culturally accepted goals. A bureaucrat who adheres to the letter of the law and, in so doing, defeats its purposes provides an illustration.

Retreatism is indicated by a rejection of both the approved goals and means without any attempt to change them. It is expressed in a withdrawal from direct involvement in the community. Illustrations of this type of deviance are found among hippies, hoboes, alcoholics, drug addicts, and psychotics.

Rebellion is indicated by a rejection of culturally accepted goals and means and an active attempt to substitute new ones. Examples are to be found in the various radical political and religious movements.

In addition to the four types of deviance described above, some sociologists have cited "overconformity" or "hypernormality" as a fifth type of deviance. This type is characterized by a more rigid adherence to convention and a more zealous pursuit of accepted goals than is generally expected or approved.

The unique insights offered by the role theorists in their discussions of conflict follow from their recognition that internal conflict, and the resulting deviance, is often a reflection of external conflict or of a malintegration of the social system. These insights give rise to such propositions as:

1. *The occurrence of different types of internal conflict will be influenced by the individual's positions and roles within the social structures of which he is a part.* A foreman, because of his conflicting obligations to his work group and to management, may experience more inner conflicts than members of either of the two groups to which he has responsibilities. A black physician may be faced with dilemmas that a white physician would not encouter as a result of the conflicting rights and obligations of "a physician" and "a black" in American society.

2. *The opportunities and techniques for dealing with inner conflict are differentially available at different positions within a social system.* Thus the power to restructure one's environment so as to reduce externally induced inner conflict is not equally available to the poor and to the wealthy. The opportunities to learn and to engage in different forms of criminal behavior—embezzlement and mugging, for example—differ as a function of one's social environment. The costs of adopting differing techniques of dealing with conflict vary as a function of social position; open defiance of a social norm is likely to be more costly for those in highly paid than in lowly paid positions.

3. *Internal conflict that is a reflection of environmental inconsistencies, or malintegration, is best handled by altering the social environment.* As Merton (1957) has pointed out, one method of resolving externally caused conflict is to make the conflicting demands observable to each of the demanding parties, so that the focus of the problem is shifted from the self to the conflicting parties. The problem is

turned into one in which *they* have to resolve *their* conflicting demands. Another method of reducing externally generated role conflict entails seeking the social support of others who are subjected to the same or similar sets of conflicting demands. Organizing people occupying similar status into occupational, professional, and political associations serves to develop a normative system which anticipates and thereby mitigates the conflicting demands made upon those in a given status. Such associations minimize the need to improvise individual adjustments to role conflict, and they provide social support to the individual as he resists entrapment in the dilemmas of conflicting demands.

However, not all externally generated conflicts can be resolved by environmental restructuring. Such restructuring may be impossible to accomplish or, if accomplishable, it may not be sufficient because the conflicting norms may be *internalized*. In violating a social norm, not only does a person risk the costs of social sanctions, but he also may risk a lowering of self-esteem and the development of a sense of guilt, such as are expressed in the feeling of being "less of a man" or of being "a heel" for not living up to a conflicting expectation. The psychopathologists, and particularly the psychoanalysts, have been concerned with the intrapsychic processes arising from inner conflict. What follows is a discussion of some of their ideas about the factors contributing to the pathological or healthy solution of internal conflict.

PSYCHOANALYTIC THEORISTS

The psychoanalytic literature dealing with psychopathology (e.g., Fenichel 1945) suggests that conflicts between fear or guilt and important drives become pathological only if these drives are cut off from the remainder of the personality. As a result of being cut off, they are denied periodic gratification, and, in addition, they remain unchanged as the rest of the personality matures. The warding-off of the drive means that it no longer has direct access either to consciousness or to the perceptual-motor apparatus of the ego necessary to achieve gratification. Such warding-off occurs to prevent the ego from being overwhelmed by anxiety. The anxiety is thought to arise either from the intensity of the stimulation associated with the drive or from an expected internal censure. The stronger the ego and the less intense the anxiety, the greater the ability to cope with anxiety without resorting to techniques that ward off or dissociate a danger-evoking drive. When the warded-off drive is deprived of its opportunity for direct discharge, it uses any opportunity for indirect discharge, displacing its energy to any other impulse that is associatively connected with it. Such a substitute impulse, thus, is a derivative both of the drive and of the defense mechanisms that are employed to ward it off, since it arises as an attempt to obtain some indirect gratification by evading or circumventing the warding-off process. Most neurotic symptoms are considered to be such derivates.

Anxiety. The term *anxiety* is used in many different ways, but it is commonly distinguished from fear on the basis that fear comes from without while anxiety comes from within. As Sartre (1945, p. 29) has written, "A situation provokes anguish to the extent that I distrust myself and my own reactions in the situation. The artillery preparation which precedes the attack can provoke fear in the soldier who undergoes bombardment but anguish is born in him when he tries to foresee the conduct with which he will face the bombardment, when he asks himself if he is going to be able to 'hold up'." Fear, then, is an expectation of external danger or misfortune, while anxiety is an expectation that one would not be able to control his fears, or, more generally, it is an expectation of damage to one's conception of one's self.

Psychic conflict elicits anxiety when a defeat of one or another of the competing intrapsychic tendencies would lead to a damaging change to one's self-concept. For example, consider the conflict of a deeply religious and amorous man whose wife is sexually rejecting and whose religion strictly forbids extramarital intercourse. If he adheres to his religious conception of himself and fails to live up to his conception of himself as a sexually desirable male, his view of himself as a man may be impaired. On the other hand, if he conforms to his view of himself as a sexually potent male by involving himself in extramarital affairs, his conception of himself as a person of moral character may be damaged.

A win-lose intrapsychic conflict of this sort, where victory for one conflicting tendency implies defeat for another, not only leads to anxiety because of the anticipated damage to one's self-conception, but it may also lead to all the usual manifestations of the competitive process of conflict resolution as one intrapsychic tendency tries to defeat the other: mutual suspicion, mutual derogation, accentuation of incompatibility, expansion of the scope of conflict, etc. In addition, the process of intrapsychic communication may be hampered and distorted. Making the conflict unconscious is one form of such distortion of communication.

Unconscious Conflict

The notion of unconscious conflict contains within it the paradox of self-deception, whereby the deceiver and the deceived may be the same person. However, this paradox disappears if one does not assume that the self is a discrete, self-contained, and highly unified entity. While the conception of a tightly unified self is prevalent in modern, complex societies, it is by no means universal. As Beattie (1969, p. 23) has pointed out, in many small-scale societies "when mental processes have to be described, the description is in terms of the interaction of parts of the self as separate agents, which can converse with one another as man to man. . . ." Similarly, Simon and Weiner (1966) point out that in Ancient Greece there was no notion of a unified or single self: a person had a manifold identity which reflected the events he participated in, actively or passively. Thus there is no necessity to conceive of the self as a monolithic entity rather than as an organization with many parts or subsystems. Although the subsystems may be able to communicate with one another, they do not necessarily have the power to inspect each other. Either side to a conflicted self may attempt to deny the existence of the other side, misrepresent the other side, deny its own existence, or misrepresent itself. Thus some women will pretend to experience no sexual pleasure during the sexual act in order to prove to themselves that they are only doing it as a sacrifice for the man's pleasure.

It is not surprising that the dialogue of nonrecognition, concealment, distortion, and misrepresentation between conflicting aspects of the self may resemble the dialogue between people in an intense struggle. The internal dialogue is, as George Herbert Mead pointed out many years ago, often an internalization of the experienced relationship between oneself and a significant other. The tactics of self and other deception are both neatly catalogued in the so-called mechanisms of defense: denial, projection, repression, displacement, reaction-formation, undoing, isolation, regression, etc. By the reaction-formation of frigidity, a woman can conceal her sexual obsession from herself or from her sexual partner; by isolation a person can make a hostile feeling seem insignificant and accidental to himself or to another; by repression one can conceal from oneself or from another the nature of one's intentions; by projection one can shift attention from one's own fault to the faults of another and gain praise for one's moral vigilance; by regression one can obtain an excuse for one's faults in terms of one's helplessness; and so on. If the tactics of misleading communications are similar in intrapsychic and interpersonal conflict, it seems likely that a study of such tactics would provide useful insights into intrapsychic dynamics. In fact, the term *mechanism of defense* may be too confining. Are we not dealing with mechanisms or tactics of conflict that include both aggressive and defensive forms of deception?

The connection between self-deception (unconsciousness) and the pathology of psychic conflict resides in the likelihood that the distortions may prevent the discovery that the original conflict is no longer present—and that the expected loss of self-esteem for certain kinds of actions or thoughts will not occur. Self-deception may also hinder the development of a cooperative conflict resolution that would permit gratification for both of the once-opposed tendencies. For example, a woman who denies her sexual interest in men in order to prove her respectability to herself may be unable to affirm her interest again, even when it is respectable to do so, because she has been committed to her denial (to express herself would be to negate her original denial). A major psychological investment may have been made in the denial, and she may have even developed a way of life to support her denial.

Thus self-deception is elicited by anxiety, a threat to a central conception of oneself. But it seems reasonable to suppose that individual vulnerability to such threat varies and, further, that anxiety does not inevitably kindle an unbridled, no-holds-barred, competitive process of conflict resolution. The psychoanalysts have used the term *ego strength* to refer to both the individual's invulnerability to threats to his self-esteem and his ability to cope with conflict-induced anxiety without resorting to an inner tooth-and-nail struggle. A strong ego enables the individual to cope with external difficulties and serves to regulate and integrate diverse internal processes into a coordinated, cooperative system.

What are the characteristics of a strong ego? Erik Erikson (1964), in his paper "Human Strength and the Cycle of Generations," has given us a useful list: hope, will, purpose, competence, fidelity, love, care, and wisdom. Many other theorists have made attempts to characterize the related concept of mental health (see Jahoda 1958). However, neither Erikson nor others have yet specified in any detail the conditions under which these virtues develop. Perhaps the safest quick generalization is that ego strength develops from experiences of a moderately high degree of success in coping with a moderately difficult and demanding environment. In other words, an individual needs the experience of coping successfully with external conflict, but he also needs the experience of coping successfully with failure. To have such experiences, the developing individual needs a social environment that is responsive to, but not enslaved by, his needs, that can trust his capabilities and place realistic demands upon them, and that provides a basis for identification with effective models for coping with difficulties and conflict. I stress the importance of the opportunity to learn effective techniques of conflict resolution through the observation of how conflict is actually resolved in one's social environment. Possibly styles of conflict resolution can be cultivated systematically through special techniques of training. If so, it may well be that many of the pathological consequences of conflict could be prevented through carefully planned educational efforts.

More is known about the conditions that breed ego weakness than about those that lead to ego strength. Such conditions include: a social environment that lacks the virtues Erikson has described; massive exposure to failure and derogation; overprotection and lack of exposure to conflict and difficulty; loss of status; a prolonged experience of internal conflict; a prolonged experience of powerlessness and helplessness; isolation and lack of contact with social reality; fatigue, intoxication, and illness. Ego weakness, for any of these reasons, is likely to make the individual more vulnerable to threats to his self-esteem and is likely to stimulate a competitive process of conflict resolution, self-deception, and the conditions that perpetuate the conflict.

SUMMARY

This chapter may be summarized in terms of some propositions about conflict that are inherent in the works of the theorists who have been concerned with intrapersonal conflict. Although many of these propositions have substantial empirical support from research on intrapsychic conflict, they are not presented here as well-established "laws" of conflict but rather as ideas that merit investigation at levels other than the intrapsychic.

PROPOSITION 1. *Conflict instigated by fears or aversions in the conflicting parties is more difficult to resolve cooperatively than conflict instigated by desires.*

Conflicts that are initially perceived in terms of deciding "who suffers" are more difficult to resolve than those that are perceived in terms of deciding "who gains."

PROPOSITION 2. *The less intense a conflict is, the easier it is to resolve cooperatively.*

The intensity of a conflict will be greater the stronger the motives involved in the conflict and the stronger and more rigid the habitual tendency to fulfill the motives by the particular course of action that has led to the conflict. The strength of the motive of any party involved in the conflict will be greater the higher the value attached to the goals involved in the conflict, the higher the level of aspiration of the party, and the more central and salient the needs that will be satisfied by attaining the desired goal (or by avoiding the feared goal). The strength of the response tendencies involved in the conflict will be affected not only by the intensity of the motivations underlying it but also by the prior history of reward associated with it and by the strength and relevance of the external stimuli activating it. The rigidity of the response tendency will be determined by the perceived availability of alternative response tendencies, which can function as satisfactory substitutes for the initially dominant tendency.

PROPOSITION 3. As important corollaries to the above proposition, one can state that (a) *conflict that threatens the self-esteem of the parties involved is more difficult to resolve cooperatively than conflict that does not;* (b) *conflict over large issues of principle is less likely to be resolved cooperatively than conflict over specific issues relating to the application of a principle.*

PROPOSITION 4. *Conflict between parties who mutually perceive themselves to be equal in power and legitimacy is more difficult to resolve cooperatively than conflict in which there is a mutual recognition of differential power and legitimacy.*

PROPOSITION 5. *Unacknowledged or unconscious conflict is more difficult to resolve than conflict that is recognized by the parties involved. Also, conflict between parties who do not recognize the existence and legitimacy of one another is more difficult to resolve than conflict in which there is such recognition.*

PROPOSITION 6. *Conflict that is resolved by a more powerful tendency suppressing or repressing a weaker one, without the extinction of the weaker tendency's underlying motives, leads to the return of the repressed tendency in disguised form whenever the vigilance or defenses of the more powerful tendency are lowered.*

PROPOSITION 7. *As the costs of engaging in a course of action during conflict increase, there are two opposing effects: the degree of commitment to the conflict increases, and the degree of opposition to it also increases. When the present and anticipated future costs are small in relation to the stake involved in the conflict (the recoverable past costs and the future gain expected from the conflict), the readiness to increase one's commitments by incurring additional costs will increase at a faster rate than the degree of opposition; as the present and anticipated costs become equal to or surpass the stake in the conflict, the degree of opposition will increase at a faster rate than the degree of commitment.*

This proposition suggests that inflicting small to moderate costs on an opponent during a conflict will generally increase his determination unless he interprets his costs as indicating that he will be exposed to such sizable future costs that winning anything from the conflict, or even being able to continue it, seems unlikely.

PROPOSITION 8. *There are pathogenic processes inherent in competitive conflict—such as perceptual distortion, self-deception, unwitting involvement—that tend to magnify and perpetuate conflict.*

4. Group Formation

In the preceding chapter, we looked at the individual from the inside. From this perspective, he is seen to be composed of interdependent subunits that interact with one another in a manner resembling that of members in a tightly knit group.[1] Just as from the outside the individual can be considered a unit and from the inside he can be viewed as a system of interdependent subunits, so, too, is the group a unit from the exterior and a system of cooperatively interdependent members from the interior. In this chapter, we shall be concerned primarily with the formation of groups or, in other words, with the conditions that determine whether or not cooperation will be initiated among the potential members of a group. First we shall treat the question: What is a group? Then we shall discuss group formation; finally, the relationship between group membership and personal identity will be considered.

What Is a Group?

An examination of the different usages of the term *group* suggests that each combines a greater or lesser number of the following distinguishing criteria: a group consists of two or more persons who (1) have one

1. To be sure, the individual as a "group" has many special features. I mention only a few: its members cannot survive outside the group and, thus, cannot join other groups; the pressures toward internal consistency are relatively strong; its members are specialized with the consequences that there are highly developed centralized subunits for coordinating and integrating the activities of the specialized components; contact with the outside (in perception or in action) is not directly available to all members but is highly specialized and is controlled by the centralized subunits; the organizational structure, the systems of internal communication, and the relative power of different subsystems is largely determined by biological inheritance.

or more characteristics in common; (2) perceive themselves as forming a distinguishable entity; (3) are aware of the positive interdependence of some of their goals or interests; (4) interact with one another; and (5) pursue their promotively interdependent goals together. In addition, writers concerned with persisting social units indicate that groups endure over a period of time and as a result develop (6) a set of norms that regulate and guide member interaction; and (7) a set of roles, each of which has specific activities, obligations, and rights associated with it.

The term *group* is commonly used to signify at least the first three of the criteria listed above. Several different degrees of "groupness" are often distinguished: "quasi-groups," which have only the first three characteristics listed; "functioning groups," which have the first five attributes; and "organized groups," which have all the criteria listed. This multifaceted usage of the term *group* is consonant with the intuitive notion that minimally a group is an entity consisting of people who are aware of being psychologically bound together by mutually linked interests. Thus a group is to be distinguished from an aggregate, class, category, or type, which consists of people who are classified together because of some common characteristic. "Group" implies a psychological or perceived bond, not merely an objective linkage, between the members' interests or goals. Moreover, the psychological linkage has some cohesive feature to it—i.e., members of a group see that in some respects they sink or swim together. This latter statement is not meant to deny that divisive and disruptive tendencies may exist within a group; rather, it is meant to indicate that, by definition, a group does not exist if its cohesive bonds are not strong enough to contain its disunifying influences.

Our discussion of the concept *group* implies that not all aggregates of people who have something in common or whose interests are positively interrelated will act together in pursuit of their common interests. We shall consider below some of the conditions that affect whether or not a category of people will become an interacting organized group. Surely, it makes a difference whether a collection of people are a group or not; in addition, it makes a difference what characteristics they have as a group. How cohesive are they? How many members are there? What kind of structure or organization do they have? As members of an organized group, individuals are part of a cooperative system, and their behavior toward others in the group and toward those not part of the system is affected by their membership in that system and by the particular characteristics of the system.

In chapter 2, some of the features of cooperative relations were delineated; individuals who are part of an organized group are more likely to manifest such features than individuals who do not form one. Thus members of such a group are more prone to attend to and understand one another; communication among them is more effective and more frequent; they are more ready to be influenced by one another, to respond helpfully to others, and to facilitate each other's actions; their attitudes toward one another are more often friendly and trusting; they are more apt to develop similar beliefs, values, and customs and to expect other members to conform to them; they are more inclined to organize themselves so as to pool their specialized skills and responses in a coordinated effort to achieve their interrelated objectives; when conflicts occur, they are more prone to view them as mutual problems to be solved by collaborative effort and are less likely to use coercive techniques to influence one another or to expand the scope of the issues in conflict.

To illustrate the difference between an organized group and an aggregate of people with similar interests, consider tenants in a New York apartment house who are, as individuals, discontent with many aspects of their housing. If they recognize that the discontent is shared and if they interact with the objective of changing conditions in their housing, the tenants will in the process transform themselves into a functioning group. If they cooperate effectively, their relations to one another will change. Instead of remaining strangers who interact rarely and cautiously, they will develop many of the "symptoms" of cooperation outlined in the preceding paragraph.

GROUP FORMATION

In light of the great variety of groups, it is unlikely that there is a single answer to the question of how a collection of individuals comes to be a cooperative system. As Cartwright and Zander (1968, p. 54) point out, a group may be established deliberately by one or more people to accomplish some objective, it may be formed spontaneously by those who become members, or it may be created because other people treat a collection of individuals as a group. Despite the many different ways in which a group can originate, it seems possible to identify several minimal conditions that must be met before a collection of individuals will turn into a cooperative system.

First, the individuals must be aware of one another's existence. Second, they must have some motives (interests, goals, or values) whose fulfillment they prefer to seek through cooperative interaction with the others—i.e., they must choose to cooperate with the others. Third, cooperative interaction must be initiated and reciprocated in such a way that the interaction serves to confirm for each of the potential group members his expectation of a mutually desired cooperative relationship. Finally, the individuals must become aware of themselves as a distinguishable entity. Factors affecting the realization of each of these basic conditions are discussed below.

Becoming Known to One Another

There has been little systematic study of the many factors, direct or indirect, that influence the likelihood that any collection of individuals will come to know of each other's existence. Propinquity has been the factor most thoroughly investigated, and the overwhelming evidence suggests that propinquity plays a very important role in establishing social relationships (Lundberg and Beasley 1948; Hollingshead 1949; Festinger, Schachter, and Back 1950; Deutsch and Collins 1951). Other ecological factors, such as the availability of communication and transportation facilities, have an influence similar to that of propinquity (Zipf 1949). Propinquity and other physical factors influencing ease of contact may themselves be determined indirectly by demographic variables—i.e., by the tendency of people of similar economic, religious, racial, or occupational backgrounds to live, work, and/or play in close proximity to one another (Form 1951). The existence of various institutionalized settings such as schools, factories, churches, hospitals, shopping centers, recreational centers, bars, and meeting halls will also affect the likelihood that people will get to know one another. In addition, of course, such personal factors as age, health, sex, social position, and personality will influence the individual's ability and willingness to get to know others and to become known. The aged, the disabled, and the poor often are limited in their physical mobility, and thus if they are widely scattered, it will be rather difficult for them to have sufficient contact with kindred people to develop a basis for group formation and effective group action.

Choosing to Cooperate

The choice to cooperate or not is in many respects similar to any other choice. Hence, such general theories of choice as level-of-aspiration theory (Lewin et al. 1944) or utility theory (Edwards 1954) are applicable. A basic assumption in such theories is that an individual will choose, from a set of perceived alternatives, the positively valued alternative that has the highest "effective attractiveness." As applied to the choice of cooperating or not, this statement means that an individual will want to cooperate when he sees that this is the best or only way to achieve a goal (or goals) that he is motivated to attain.

It is obvious that many goals are social in nature and intrinsically require the collaboration of others for their attainment—e.g., to belong to a given group, to achieve racial and sexual equality, to have an intimate relationship, to play a game of tennis, to participate in an interesting conversation, to sell or buy anything, to obtain someone's approval or support. Other goals, though not intrinsically social, may nevertheless be impossible to attain without collaboration of others— e.g., to have a lobster dinner in Chicago, to travel from the United States to Europe, to live in a better house than one could construct oneself. Of course, there are many types of nonsocial goals that can be attained through either individual or collaborative effort—e.g., to build a canoe, to solve a problem, to repaint the living room. There are, moreover, certain types of goals relating to self-expression or self-activity from which it would be intrinsically impossible to gain personal satisfaction through the activities of others alone—e.g., to *make* a painting or to *eat* a lobster. For other types of goals, the activities of others may be entirely self-sufficient—e.g., to see that a blind man crosses a street safely, to have a nursery school organized so that one's children may have an opportunity to engage in supervised activities with other children.

Whether or not one's goals require or permit cooperation for their attainment will obviously be an important determinant of the choice to cooperate or not. If one's goals permit but do not require cooperation, the choice to cooperate will be determined by the effective attractiveness of cooperation as compared to other perceived alternatives. The effective attraction of an alternative is a function of two sets of factors: those that influence its desirability or undesirability and those that influence the subjective probability that it will lead to the desired result.

The desirability of cooperation is determined by the gains, pleasures, and values one hopes to realize through it; its undesirability by the costs, pains, and disvalues one expects. Clearly, a choice to cooperate is unlikely if it is anticipated that the "negatives" will outweigh the "positives"—unless, of course, cooperation is chosen as the lesser of evils. In addition to the nature of one's objectives, several other major types of determinants influence the desirability of cooperation. Personality dispositions affect both one's general inclination to be cooperative and one's preferences regarding with whom one would like to cooperate (see Terhune 1970 a, b for a review). It is also evident, as Mead (1937) has demonstrated in her classical study of *Cooperation and Competition Among Primitive Peoples,* that societal values may be more or less oriented toward cooperation. In addition to the more enduring general influences of personality dispositions and cultural values, the desirability of cooperation is influenced by a host of such specific external factors as the social and personality characteristics of other group members, the reputation of the group, and one's anticipated activities and status within the group.

No matter how desirable the various aspects of cooperation may seem, cooperation is not likely to be undertaken unless there is some hope that what one wants from it will be attained. This is especially the case when unsuccessful cooperation is seen to be costly. There are many determinants of an individual's estimate of his chances of success in a given situation. These include his prior experiences in similar situations, his perceptions of the judgments of others, and his personality. Thus if he has had a prior history of success or if his friends assure him that he will be successful, and if he is inclined to be optimistic, he is likely to be quite confident. There are, of course, considerable differences among individuals in terms of how much confidence of success each requires before he will initiate cooperation. Nevertheless, if one cannot *trust* that the other potential group members will have the motivation and ability to cooperate effectively, one is not likely to enter a cooperative process. Because of the centrality of trust to the initiation of cooperation, a separate chapter (chapter 7) will be concerned with this topic. Trust is, however, only one of the three key problems of *mutuality* that must be resolved if cooperative interaction is to be successfully initiated and reciprocated. The others are *coordination* and *bargaining*. Each of these problems is discussed below in terms of the question it poses for the potential cooperators.

Problems of Mutuality in the Initiation of Cooperation

No individual, by his choice alone, can successfully initiate cooperation. Cooperation is a mutual endeavor, and for cooperative interaction to occur, the choice to cooperate must be reciprocated. Contrast this with a choice involving inanimate objects. If I choose to have yogurt rather than pastry for dessert, the yogurt does not have to choose me for my choice to be successfully consummated. Arising out of the requirement that cooperation be mutual and reciprocated are the three problems mentioned above: trust, coordination, and bargaining.

Trust. The problem of trust raises the question of whether or not the potential cooperators can trust one another sufficiently to take the risks involved in initiating cooperation. Suppose, for example, that I wish to sell an antique clock and you wish to buy one. There is a possibility that what I am offering you is not a genuine antique but only an imitation; analogously, you may attempt to pay me with a bogus credit card or forged check. For me to sell the clock to you, I must trust that your credit card or check is valid, and for you to buy it, you must trust that I have not misrepresented the clock.

Figure 4.1 illustrates the problem of trust in an abstract form. P_1 has to choose between *C* and *D* and has to announce his choice before he knows what P_2 has chosen. The situation is the same for P_2. Clearly, unless he can trust that the other will choose *C* rather than *D*, each is forced to choose *D*. If both choose *D* then both will lose, despite the fact that both can gain by cooperating and choosing *C*. Each may, however, feel that the other might be tempted to gain

		P_2	
		C	D
P_1	C	$+1, +1$	$-2, +2$
	D	$+2, -2$	$-1, -1$

Figure 4.1. The trust problem. This and the following matrices should be read as follows: P_1 chooses between rows C and D, P_2 between columns C and D. P_1's payoffs are the first numbers in the cell; P_2's are the second numbers. For illustrative purposes, consider that the payoffs are in money and that each person would prefer to gain rather than lose, as well as gain $+2$ rather than $+1$, or lose -1 rather than -2.

more by choosing *D*. Or, even if the other can be trusted, it may be difficult to resist the temptation oneself.

Matrices, like the one illustrated in figure 4.1, have been employed in many studies to investigate the conditions affecting "trust" and "trustworthiness." (See chapter 8 for reports of such research done by my associates and myself.) It is well to recognize that a relationship of mutual trust is not always based upon knowledge of the other's personal trustworthiness. Trust may be rooted in factors that are external to the particular relationship, such as confidence that existing social institutions will discourage untrustworthy behavior, confidence in third parties who can vouch for the other, or a general confidence in the trustworthiness of people who are viewed as similar to oneself.

Particularistic trust, which is based upon personal knowledge of the other, is characteristic of small, traditionalistic communities. *Universalistic trust,* which depends upon the social rather than the personal characteristics of the other, seems to be a necessary ingredient in the development and functioning of complex modern societies.

Generalized trust as a norm among individuals in a given society appears to be essential for the operation of large-scale organizations, which must rely heavily on interpersonal relationships among strangers. In the modern, organizational society, one must trust that an unknown mailman will bring your letters conscientiously rather than throw them away, that an unknown worker in a pharmacy will fill your prescription correctly, that a bank clerk will not make incorrect entries into your account, that your physician will have obtained his degree through competence rather than through political influence, and so on. When generalized trust is impaired, one can expect a corresponding increase in suspiciousness, irresponsibility, and untrustworthiness. Public opinion data reported by the Survey Research Center of the University of Michigan in November 1971 indicate that from 1966 to 1971, paralleling the increased involvement of the United States in the Vietnam war, there was a sharp decline, particularly among the youth, in the generalized trust toward the government and other major social institutions. Symptomatic of this decline were more social disorder and disruption, greater apprehensiveness, and an increased sense of lack of participation in a meaningful community.

The level of generalized trust existing in a community determines whether or not the different individual resources existing within it can be shared or combined for mutual benefit. The existence of trust is itself a resource of cooperation, and without it the benefits that can be derived from organized cooperative activity are drastically curtailed. The development of revolving credit and mutual loan associations within a community are likely to be inhibited with a low level of trust. Without such institutions, however, economic activity and growth will be cumbersome and, as a consequence, deterred. Similarly, the development and effective functioning of all community institutions and organizations—schools, cultural centers, and community organizations—will be strangled by excessive red tape, meetings, and disruptions if there is little trust. A university, for example, cannot function effectively if faculty, students, and administrators are all suspicious of one another. If each has to monitor the other constantly because of insufficient trust, none will have time to perform its own functions adequately, and its failure to do so will confirm the other's suspicions.

There is a variety of evidence to suggest that levels of trust are usually higher in communities of higher socioeconomic status than in those of lower, and higher among the advantaged groups than among the disadvantaged groups within a community. It is not surprising that blacks and the poor are less trusting than whites and the well-off: they have less reason to be so. However, insofar as the low level of trust is not only characteristic of the relations with the outgroup but also of the relations within the group, it serves to perpetuate and enhance the weakness of the disadvantaged group. If the level of trust within a disadvantaged group is low, the group cannot develop a strong community with effective institutions that would enhance its collective power and enable its members to cooperate effectively to overcome their disadvantages. Of course, an exploitative group that seeks to maintain its advantages will often utilize any tactics necessary to deter the development of group cohesion among the exploited.

Bargaining. The question of mutuality posed by the bargaining problem is whether the potential cooperators can resolve differences in preferences with regard to the terms of their cooperation. The buyer-seller transaction provides an illustration of such problems. The buyer and seller have concordant interests in that they both desire that a sale take place. However, they also have conflicting interests in that the seller would prefer a sale at a high price and the buyer at a low one. If the seller's minimum acceptable sale price is lower than the buyer's maximum acceptable purchase price, a mutually acceptable agreement is possible. Whether or not the buyer and the seller reach an agreement will be determined by how successfully they bargain together.

Bargaining is not only characteristic of economic transactions but is a feature of all social relationships. Husbands and wives who want to spend an evening out together but have dissimilar preferences on where to go will bargain to determine the nature of their cooperation; similarly, parents and children who have dissimilar views about "bedtime" will often engage in elaborate negotiations in the process of working out an agreement. Students and faculty who may have different preferences regarding the timing of various academic events nevertheless will need to come to an agreement to prevent an academic impasse.

Figure 4.2 presents the bargaining problem in abstract form. It is evident that each side is better off if they can agree.

$$P_2$$

	x	y
A	0, 0	+2, +4
B	+4, +2	0, 0

P_1 is at the left of rows A and B.

Figure 4.2. The bargaining problem.

P_1 would, however, prefer *Bx* while P_2 would prefer *Ay*. What determines whether or not P_1 and P_2 will be able to come to a mutually acceptable agreement in such situations? What are the effects of different methods of attempting to influence the other to yield? These and other related questions are the focus of inquiry in a series of studies reported in chapters 9, 10, and 11. Because of the pervasiveness of threats and promises in bargaining, a theoretical discussion of these modes of social influence is presented in chapter 6.

Coordination. Even if potential cooperators trust one another and agree completely on how to cooperate, they still confront the problem of coordination. For example, suppose a man and woman meet briefly, by chance, at a cocktail party in New York. They immediately are taken with each other and would very much like to meet again. Unfortunately, they forget to exchange last names, addresses, and phone numbers before leaving the party. They want to get together, but how, when, and where can they meet? They face the problem of coordination. Suppose each of them decides to meet the other by going to some hangout for "singles" for the next several nights. Where should each go and at what time to maximize their chance of meeting?

An abstract version of the couple's problem is presented in figure 4.3. In this version, P_1 and P_2 both want to converge on the same choice, but they do not know what the other is going to choose. In such a situation, P_1's best course of action depends on the action he expects P_2 to take, which depends in turn on P_2's expectation of P_1's action. Each must try to guess what the other thinks he will guess, and so on. What permits the convergence of expectations rather than an endless spiral of "second-guessing"? (See Schelling 1960 for an insightful discussion.)

		A	B	C
			P_2	
		A	B	C
	A	+4, +4	0, 0	0, 0
P_1	B	0, 0	+4, +4	0, 0
	C	0, 0	0, 0	+4, +4

Figure 4.3. The coordination problem.

Communication is an obvious way of solving the coordination problem—e.g., P_1 says to P_2: "You choose column A and I'll choose row A." However, there are many situations in which communication is impossible or too costly, and in these cases coordination has to be accomplished tacitly rather than explicitly. Moreover, even when communication is feasible, there is often some necessity for selecting what one communicates from that limited range of possibilities that are likely to be mutually acceptable. Thus Schelling (1960, p. 70) has pointed out:

> Most bargaining situations ultimately involve some range of possibility outcomes within which each party would rather make a concession than fail to reach agreement at all. . . . The final outcome must be a point from which neither expects the other to retreat; yet the main ingredient of this expectation is what one thinks the other expects the first to expect, and so on. . . . These infinitely reflexive

expectations must somehow converge on a single point, at which each expects the other not to expect to be expected to retreat.

The problem of coordination encompasses more than the convergence of expectations in situations of tacit communication. Even explicit communication may be misunderstood; the speaker and the listener may not interpret what is said in the same ways. Misunderstandings, of course, are very likely when the speaker and listener are from rather different cultural backgrounds and are not fully aware of their differences. The stock conversation of returning tourists consists of amusing or embarrassing anecdotes based upon misunderstandings of this sort. Even within a given society, unrecognized cultural differences may give the same act or word a different significance to blacks and whites, to men and women, to members of different ethnic groups, to people of different class backgrounds, to scientists and nonscientists.

Thus, for example, only in recent years has there developed some awareness that lower-class black children, when they enter school, often speak a form of English that is different from standard American. Before this was recognized, many teachers assumed that the speech of these students was simply an inferior, impoverished version of standard, middle-class American speech. This faulty view buttressed educators' low expectations regarding the intellectual potential of black children and contributed to a vicious cycle in which the black children became increasingly alienated from their schools.

Although husbands and wives may speak the same form of English, it is not uncommon for a couple to misunderstand one another because their styles of emotional communication differ enormously. There may be differences in what is attended to: the husband may consider *what* is said (the words) to be more important, the wife may attend more to *how* it is said (the tone of voice, the circumstances). There may be differences in amplitude and frequency of emotional expressiveness, the husband expressing his emotions in low key, infrequently, and the wife expressing hers at high intensity, frequently. Each may judge the other's expressiveness in terms of his or her own norms, the husband judging his wife as very emotional, the wife viewing her husband as unemotional. Lack of recognition, lack of understanding, or intolerance of such stylistic differences in communication can create misunderstandings, resentment, and hurt feelings that may impair cooperation.

The Perception of the Group as a Distinguishable Entity

In the previous sections, I have considered how potential cooperators get to know one another, some of the determinants of the choice to co-operate, and the problems of mutuality arising from the fact that cooperation can not be consummated unless it is reciprocated. This discussion has assumed that a group is a voluntary cooperative system and, hence, that the development of cooperation and group formation are clearly related topics. However, a group is more than an assemblage of cooperating people. It is composed of members who are aware of themselves as an entity: a group is conscious of itself. In addition, it is evident that membership in many groups (such as family, racial, and ethnic groups) is by inheritance and not choice. In such instances, the development of a positive group consciousness may be the precondition for the development of cooperation, rather than vice versa. Also, the development of cooperation and the growth of group consciousness may each foster the other. Thus it is apparent that the onset of group consciousness may precede, follow, or be concurrent with the development of cooperative relations within the group.

In addition to the experience of successful cooperation, several factors seem to play key roles in the development of group consciousness. They include (1) *the treatment by others.* If others treat members of the group in a similar way and identify them as one group for varous purposes, group consciousness will be promoted; (2) *an abrupt discontinuity between the characteristics of members and nonmembers of the group.* Thus if members are rather similar in such matters as beliefs, values, appearances, proximity, past experience, language, customs, and style but sharply different in these respects from the remainder of the people in their surroundings, group consciousness will be heightened; (3) *the use of symbols to represent the group.* The existence of a name, insignia, uniforms, differentiated and labeled statuses within the group, and group ceremonials all intensify group awareness; (4) *differences in rates, types, and styles of interaction between members and nonmembers.* The more members interact with one another about topics and in a manner that differs from the way they interact with nonmembers, the more intense will be their group awareness; and (5) *a history of cooperating together.* The existence of an historical time perspective, with a sense of continuity of relatedness, and an awareness of shared memories of past events contributes to a heightened consciousness of a group identity. A time perspective that extends from the past to the future is central to a stable group identity.

The operation of these factors in raising group consciousness can be illustrated by a hypothetical example. Suppose that in a large lecture class I wished to create two groups: *the shorties* (those 5'6" and under) and *the longies* (those over 5'6" in height). To do this, I would treat the groups differently: require them to enter and exit the classroom by different doors, give them different assignments and tests, assign different teaching assistants to work with them, allow them to visit me in my office only at clearly different hours, and encourage others to treat them differently. If this were not sufficient, I could assign them to sit in clearly separated areas of the classroom so that the two groups would be quite distinct visually. In addition, I could refer to the groups by different names and give them distinctive collective tasks to perform that would encourage interaction within each group but interfere with interaction between "longies" and "shorties." I would do this over a period of time, creating distinctive histories and memories for the two groups as well as expectations that the future would be continuous with the present. Such behavior on my part would create two groups whose members were highly conscious of their group membership.

Typically, one would expect that the more conscious an individual is of his membership in a group in a given situation, the more likely is his behavior to be affected by his group membership. Moreover, as an individual's group consciousness increases, the probability that his behavior will be affected by the group in more situations also increases. Although the enhancement of group consciousness often raises cohesiveness, the member may become more negative toward the group as its salience increases when his attitude toward it is negative. Such a situation may occur when a person belongs to a group he dislikes but cannot leave because of external restraints.

GROUP MEMBERSHIP AND PERSONAL IDENTITY

George Herbert Mead, in his classic work *Mind, Self, and Society* (1934), pointed out that the individual's self as well as his capacity for reflective thought develop in the course of social interaction with the members of his family and other groups in the community to which he belongs. By taking the role of others and responding to his own actions as they would, the individual learns to anticipate the social effects of his actions. In addition, he learns that he and others are expected to behave toward one another in specified ways as a function of his and their particular personal and social attributes—such as age, sex, social class, race, religion, ethnic background, and nationality.

Thus a black child learns to behave differently toward black than toward white children, and he learns to expect whites to behave differently toward him than they do toward whites. Similarly, children learn that certain activities are "feminine" and others are "masculine" and that disapproval is risked by engaging in behavior that is considered appropriate for the opposite sex but not for one's own. However, each child's experience is in some respects unique, and thus the conceptions among a group of what it is to be a member of that group will not be identical. Moreover, the meaning of any particular subidentity, such as "black," is influenced by the total configuration of social identities of which it is an element. Thus the conception of "black," like that of "Jew," is affected by the linking of the two attributes in the configuration "black Jew." Adding other elements to the configuration, such as "rich," "young," "woman," and "Brazilian," further alters and defines the meaning of the initially specified subidentity "black."

Although the meaning of any personal subidentity is influenced by the total configuration of subidentities, it would be a mistake to assume that all elements are equally influential in determining an individual's thoughts, feelings, and behavior. It is evident that situational factors help determine which subidentity will be elicited most strongly at a given time: different subidentities are likely to be most salient and most influential in different social situations. The subidentity of "white" is more likely to be elicited in the presence of blacks than in the presence of other whites—unless the other whites are discussing blacks or interracial relations. A New Yorker and a Texan are more likely to feel a common identity as Americans in China than in the United States. Thus a subidentity is made salient in a situation by contrast with the presence of members of other different or antithetical groups that are used to mark off the boundaries of one's own group (Herman 1970). It is also made salient by the presence of threats, danger, discrimination, or other potential harm to oneself because of membership in a given group. If derogatory comments or discriminatory actions are liable to be directed at you or other members of your group at any time from almost anybody, then you will be continuously aware of your membership in this group. A subidentity is also made salient by the prospect of reward or other potential gain resulting from membership in a particular group. More generally, the more eliciting stimuli that are present in a situation—whether those stimuli be negative or positive in implication—the more salient will be the identity in that situation.

It is apparent that subidentities differ in their readiness to be evoked. Some subidentities are more pervasive than others and are readily aroused in many different types of situations. My subidentity as a member of my family group enters into many more situations than my subidentity as a member of the Accabonac Tennis Club. It connects with more people and with more of my other subidentities, and thus it is a more pervasive influence on my thoughts, feelings, and behavior.

Subidentities also differ in how central or important they are to the individual's self-esteem; the more central a subidentity is, the more likely it is to be evoked, and the more influential it will be when evoked. One measure of the centrality of a subidentity is one's readiness to resist its derogation or elimination. Thus I am more willing to give up being a squash player than a tennis player, and I would abandon either of these rather than quit my profession. Similarly, I am more ready to resist derogation of my ethnic group than my age group.

The importance of a subidentity to one's self-esteem is determined by the strength of the different types of bonds binding one to it. Several different types of bonds can be distinguished (McCall 1970): ascribed bonds, bonds of commitment, bonds due to investment, bonds of attachment, and instrumental bonds. The first three types of bonds (ascription, commitment, and investment) are in large measure "restraining bonds"; they restrain one from leaving a group even if he desires to do so. The latter two (attachment and instrumental) are "attracting bonds," which pull the individual toward the group.

The strongest restraining bonds are those arising out of certain *ascribed* statuses—such as family, sex, racial, ethnic, and national group membership, all of which one acquires by birth rather than by choice. Such statuses can rarely be changed. It is the combination of their unalterability and their social significance that gives these ascribed statuses their personal importance. One's handedness, left or right, may be as difficult to alter as one's race, but it is by no means as socially significant. Membership in a family, racial, sexual, ethnic, or national group affects one's thoughts and actions in many situations; these effects are pervasive. In addition, by common definition, membership in such groups typically excludes membership in other groups of a similar type. That is, if you are black, you are not also white; if you are male, you are not also female; if you are Jewish, you are not also Christian. Thus being a member is thought to be more or less distinctive, and since membership is linked to experiences from early on in one's life, it is not unusual for one to get emotionally attached to such groups, with the result that these memberships play an important positive role in determining one's sense of identity.

Bonds of *commitment* may also tie one to a group and to the identity connected with it. The commitment may be to other members of the group or to interested outsiders. Thus a girl who is engaged but no longer interested in marrying may be reluctant to break the engagement because of her commitment to her fiancé or because of the expected disappointment of her parents and friends. Similarly, one's *investments* in a given identity—the amount of time, energy, life's chances, money, and emotion previously expended in establishing and maintaining the identity—will generally serve to bind one to continue it even when one might not otherwise choose to do so. Nevertheless, it should be noted that people do break up long-standing marriages or change well-established careers if they expect that continued investments will be costly and not worthwhile. This is particularly likely if they are aware of a more rewarding alternative for their future investments. The restraining bonds of commitment and investment are, however, usually easier to break than those of ascription.

Bonds of *attachment* attract one to a group; such bonds develop when significant personal needs—for security, acceptance, and meaning—have been fulfilled in the group, and the group is thought to be largely irreplaceable or nonsubstitutable as a source of fulfillment for these needs. A group is likely to be viewed as irreplaceable when no readily available alternatives are perceived (as in the case of the small child in relation to the nuclear family), when the feasibility of leaving the group to go to another one is small (as is the case of the citizens of most nations), or when, as a result of an extended history of participation in the group, the group has taken on a unique significance (as is the case of family and ethnic groups).

Bonds of attachment provide a diffuse, nonspecific form of attraction to a group and to the idea of expressing one's identity by membership in the group. In contrast, *instrumental* bonds arise from the success of the group in providing dependable rewards for fulfilling one's specific roles or functions within the group and for being identified as a member of the group. Instrumental bonds are linked to the specific success of the group in providing specific satisfactions. However, the more success the group has in doing this, and the wider the range of satisfactions it provides, the more likely it is that diffuse bonds of attachment will also develop.

It is evident that an individual who is getting ample instrumental satisfactions from his group and is deeply attached to it will not find himself in conflict, because his investments and ascription will restrain him from abandoning his identification with the group. To the contrary, the more the individual is attracted to a group, the more willing he will be to make investments in it, to make personal commitments to it, and to bind himself irrevocably to it. Conversely, the less he is attracted to a group, the less willing he will be to bind himself so tightly that it would be difficult to leave it if he should choose to do so.

Suppose that one is emotionally attached to one's subidentity as a Jew, woman, or black—and irrevocably bound to it by bonds of ascription, commitment, and investment—but that it places one at a distinct instrumental disadvantage in obtaining many kinds of opportunities and rewards. How one copes with this situation will be largely determined by whether one views the disadvantages to be just or unjust. If those who are disadvantaged by their group identity accept their disadvantages as being warranted, they are unlikely to challenge and conflict with those who are profiting from their relatively advantaged positions. The sense of being treated unjustly because of one's membership in a group to which one is strongly attached and bound is the energizer for much intergroup conflict. The sense of injustice is felt particularly intensely in interracial, interethnic, and intersex conflicts because of the centrality of these group identities to the individual's self esteem. When women or blacks or Jews are devalued as a group, those who are identified and identify with the groups also are personally devalued.

It is evident that those groups who gain from the disadvantaging of other groups are usually the more powerful ones. They are more likely to set the terms of their relationship with other groups and, through their control of the state and other social institutions, to establish the legal and other reigning definitions of "justice." Thus in addition to their gains from exploitative actions, they commonly have the reassurance of the official definition of justice and the support of such major social institutions as the church, the press, and the schools to deaden their sensitivities to the injustices inherent in their relations with the disadvantaged group. The disadvantaged may, of course, be taken in by the official definitions and the indoctrination emanating from social institutions and, as a result, lose their sensitivity to their situation of injustice. Even when they are not brainwashed into accepting their inferior positions as just, a sense of hopelessness about the possibility of change may keep the disadvantaged quiescent. As I have pointed out elsewhere (Deutsch 1972), the process of activating the sense of injustice so that it is a stimulant to intergroup conflict and social change entails falsifying and delegitimizing the officially sanctioned ideologies and myths that "justify" the injustices; exposing the disadvantaged to new ideologies, new models, and new reference groups that justify and give life to the possibilities of change in their status; stimulating hope by successful efforts to improve their situation; and reducing their fear by increasing their relative bargaining strength.

It would be a mistake to assume that the only form of intergroup conflict is that between exploiting and exploited groups. In the next chapter, intergroup conflict is considered more broadly. However, it is well to recognize that deep passions are aroused whenever the value and merit of an individual's personal identity are challenged, and this is quite likely to happen when a group that he is closely identified with is involved in a conflict with another group over such central values as justice and superiority-inferiority.

5. Intergroup Conflict

This chapter, which is concerned with intergroup conflict, is divided into three sections. The first discusses some of the external conditions conducive to conflict. The second deals with several internal properties of groups as they are related to intergroup conflict. In the third section, class conflict and race conflict are considered as examples in an attempt to uncover some general propositions about the resolution of conflict.

EXTERNAL CONDITIONS CONDUCIVE TO INTERGROUP CONFLICT

Contact

It takes two to tangle. Conflicting, as well as harmonious, interaction requires a partner. Thus one of the factors contributing to the development of discord between groups is the opportunity to interact. People or groups that have little or no contact with one another are unlikely to have either conflicting or harmonious relations.

In our discussion of group formation in the preceding chapter, we considered some of the factors that influence the chances that two or more people will become known to one another. Such "pair attributes" as proximity, communication facilities, interdependence, and similarity and such "individual attributes" as physical and social position, the amount of resources available to overcome distance, and various personality characteristics affect the likelihood that contact will occur. Pairs of groups that are physically close to one another, are functionally interdependent, share common facilities, are easily able to communicate with one another, and are similar are more likely to find themselves in contact than are pairs lacking these characteristics. A group has more "contact potential" if it is centrally located, powerful, large, expansive, and has a high need for interaction with other groups because of its lack of self-sufficiency.

Paradoxically, if contact leads to the development of a cooperative relationship, this will as a consequence promote more frequent interaction, which will in turn increase the chances of conflict. In other words, cooperative relations provide a greater opportunity for the occurrence of conflict than the absence of interaction. Conflicts do occur frequently in the course of cooperative interrelations, but such conflicts are often less problematic and hence less dramatic than the conflicts arising in a noncooperative context. The cooperative surroundings often enable the conflict to be resolved productively rather than destructively (Deutsch 1969), because the attitudes of the conflicting parties and the pressures and resources of the cooperative system facilitate a cooperative rather than a competitive process of conflict resolution.

Contact and interaction provide an opportunity for intergroup conflict. But what other factors help determine whether the relations between groups become conflicting or not? Williams (1947), in a survey of research on intergroup relations, has indicated that the necessary conditions for conflict include "visibility" and "competition" in addition to contact. He quotes Young (1932. p. 586) to this effect: "Group antagonisms seem to be inevitable when two peoples in contact with each other may be distinguished by differentiating characteristics, either inborn or cultural, and are actual or potential competitors. Only by eliminating the outward evidences of distinction such as color, dress, or language, or by removing the competitive factor, may racial antagonisms be destroyed."

Visibility

The distinction between "ingroup" and "outgroup" is obviously a necessary condition for intergroup relations; the outgroup must be visible and in some way distinguishable from the ingroup. But it would be a mistake to stress physical differences as the primary determinants of the differentiation between ingroup and outgroup members. If one considers the many different circumstances in which intergroup conflict occurs—such as between a sales and an engineering department within a factory, between psychologists and physicians about the practice of psychotherapy, between different religious groups—it is evident that intergroup conflict can occur even in the absence of distinguishing physical characteristics between the members of the different groups. Differentiation is often made on the basis of social and psychological criteria such as the nature and degree of interdependence within each group as compared to those between the groups, the types of activities each engages in, the beliefs and values that each espouses, the people or groups with whom each interacts, the treatment each receives from other people or groups, the nature of the past experiences and cultural heritage of each, and the types of locales and settings in which each engages in its activities. Distinctions between groups that arise on one basis may be maintained on another basis. Thus skin color may come to distinguish groups that were initially differentiated in terms of their positions in the master-slave relationship because of the association between skin color and social caste.

There is considerable evidence to suggest that the categorization of people into groups on the basis of any distinguishing characteristic commonly has the result that, perceptually, the differences between each category tend to be enhanced (Tajfel 1969). Thus if people are categorized into groups of "black" and "white" on the basis of skin color, the differences between "black" and "white" will be perceptually accentuated or exaggerated, while the differences among "white" and among "black" will be deemphasized. This phenomenon is often more generalized. If a person has the view that certain features (e.g., skin color, social class, conduct, intelligence, and attitudes) are highly correlated, and if he categorizes people into groups according to one of the characteristics such as skin color, then he is likely to accentuate the differences *between* the groups on the other attributes that he believes to be associated with skin color.

Is the existence of a recognized difference between two categories of people enough, by itself, to lead the people in each category to think of themselves in terms of ingroup and outgroup? Research (Chase 1971; Deutsch, Thomas, and Garner, in manuscript) indicates that the mere recognition of a difference between two categories of people is not a sufficient condition for the formation of distinctive beliefs and attitudes toward the different categories, unless the difference is utilized by a prestigious authority to classify the people into distinctive groups. Experiments by Rabbie and Horwitz (1969), Rabbie and Soutendijk (1967), and Tajfel (1970) have shown that classification of people into two groups by a respected experimenter who makes distinctions between them leads to a significant ingroup-outgroup differentiation. Clearly, the type of difference among a collection of people and its significance to the people involved are important in determining whether an aggregate of individuals will be polarized into an ingroup and an outgroup.

Although the existence of differences does not necessarily lead to ingroup-outgroup formation, one may wonder whether clearly recognized differences between people who think of themselves as groups will increase the likelihood of intergroup conflict. There is a considerable body of theoretical writing that suggests that similarity leads to favorable attitudes while dissimilarity leads to unfavorable attitudes. (See Rokeach 1960; Byrne 1969; Tajfel 1970.) Such theorizing implies that visible differences between groups enhance group conflict. There is a good deal of research support for this proposition. Yet it seems too simplistic to accept the view that similarity is always positive and dissimilarity always negative in result.

It seems more reasonable to assume that the attributes of another group may be viewed as potentially beneficial, neutral, or harmful to one's own group and that similarity and dissimilarity are not invariably associated with benefit and harm, respectively. A complementary dissimilarity (male and female) could be positive while an oppositional similarity (both seeking possession of the same thing) could be negative. An experiment by Stembridge and Deutsch (1972) documents this. Dissimilarity of beliefs and values is often oppositional because it precludes effective cooperation; it also challenges the objectivity and, hence, the validity of one's own beliefs and values. On the other hand, dissimilarity between groups in the types of skills and resources that they possess is often positive because it makes cooperation between them valuable.

Competition

If not contact or the awareness of intergroup differences, what, then, are the characteristics of relations between groups that are both necessary and sufficient to produce a sense of opposition? Almost all scholars include the real conflicts of interest that arise from the competition for such scarce resources as wealth, power, prestige, and territory. Others also stress the opposition that arises from ideological and cultural differences, differences in beliefs and values about what is universally true and right. Still others would indicate that it is not the "real" conflict of interest or "real" ideological differences that create opposition but rather the "perception" of such conflict.

Perception may be incorrect: no real opposition exists, but there is nevertheless the perception that it does. Sometimes misperception can be benevolent rather than malevolent: real opposition is not recognized as such. Attention to the possibilities of misperception and misunderstanding as contributors to intergroup conflict suggests a variety of other "real" factors, in addition to real conflict of interest and real ideological difference, which may be pertinent to consider. These are the factors that influence perception and communication—such factors as the properties of the communication system between the interacting groups. One wants to know, for example, what distorting characteristics are introduced in the communication of messages as a result of the encoding, transmission, and decoding processes. Some perceptual and communication systems seem to be conflict-enhancing and some conflict-dampening.

Social Change

A further general source of intergroup conflict that has been singled out by many scholars is social change. As Mack and Snyder (1957, pp. 225–26) have suggested:

> Social change affects conflict in a number of ways. Changes are constantly shifting the bases of potentially antagonistic interests and the relative power positions of individuals and groups. As the value potentiality of the social environment shifts, new demands, new frustrations, and new incompatibilities arise. Population growth, invention, urbanization, mobility—indeed all the changes which result in and are resultants of greater social complexity—affect the sources of conflict, the nature and number of parties to conflict, the instrumentalities of conflict, modes of settlement, and so on.

Moreover, it is evident that social change often brings with it conflict between age groups—the "generation gap." Many people acquire their basic value orientations and cognitive schemes for viewing the world from the educational experiences and social conditions to which they were exposed in their youth. In a rapidly changing world, these may undergo profound alterations within a generation. The education and other formative experiences of parent and child in modern societies, in contrast to traditional ones, may have little in common and may, indeed, have incompatible implications. Youths are apt to be better educated than their parents. They are more likely to challenge some of the assumptions that were unquestioned by their parents—in such fundamental areas as sexual behavior, the relation of men and women, economic achievement and aspirations, patriotism, and race relations. The challenges from youth arising from social change and the responses to them by those in authority can rejuvenate a social order or produce tragedies such as those that have occurred at the Kent State and Jackson State massacres.

Internal Properties of Groups and Intergroup Conflict

Groups differ in countless ways. Among the many different internal characteristics that distinguish groups from one another, three have been mentioned most frequently in the literature on intergroup relations. They are cohesiveness, structure, and power. Each is discussed below.

Group Cohesiveness

In everyday usage, "cohesiveness" refers to the tendency to stick together; its usage in social psychology is much the same. It refers to the strength and types of linkages that bind the members of a group together. Since group cohesiveness is central to the existence of groups, it is natural that its determinants and also its consequences have been studied extensively (for summaries see Hare 1962; Collins and Guetzkow 1964; McGrath and Altman 1966; Cartwright and Zander 1968). Research findings, in general, indicate that cohesiveness (as measured by interpersonal congeniality, the desire to remain a member of the group, positive attitudes toward the group's functioning, or similar measures) is associated with greater communication between group members, greater readiness of group members to be influenced by the group, more consensus among members on attitudes and beliefs that relate to group functioning, more sense of responsibility toward each other among group members, and so forth. Also, task effectiveness is generally positively correlated with cohesiveness if high accomplishment of the task is valued by the group (some groups restrict performance to achieve their objectives) and if the task is such that its performance is likely to be enhanced by increased group effort. It should be noted that the causal arrow is bidirectional: group cohesiveness not only increases intragroup communication and group success, but group success and intragroup communication increase group cohesiveness.

The connection between ingroup cohesion and outgroup relations has been a topic of considerable interest to social scientists since Sumner, in his *Folkways* of 1906, asserted that "the relationship of comradeship and peace in the we-group and that of hostility and war towards other-groups are correlative to each other. . . . Loyalty to the group, sacrifice for it, hatred and contempt for outsiders, brotherhood within, warlikeness without—all grow together, common products of the same situation." Sumner coined the term *ethnocentrism* to characterize the syndrome of pride in one's own group combined with a sense of its superiority over other groups and an antipathy toward outgroups. Some writers (e.g., Rosenblatt 1964) indicate that nationalism and ethnocentrism overlap in that each stresses the association between ingroup loyalty and antipathy toward outgroups.

Rosenblatt (1964), Campbell (1965), and LeVine and Campbell (1972) have prepared extensive summaries of the social science literature dealing with ethnocentrism. In the comments that follow, I am heavily indebted to their summaries, even though my analysis of the issues involved departs from theirs. Most social scientists would agree that Sumner was correct in noting the pervasive association between ingroup solidarity and outgroup hostility; some, however, contend that the association, while pervasive, is far from universal. Furthermore, there are disagreements about the conclusions to be drawn from this association. Some assert that the causal arrow points from ingroup cohesion to outgroup hostility, others say the arrow points in the opposite direction, while still others stress the bidirectionality or even circularity of the causal process involved.

Ingroup cohesion as the cause of outgroup hostility. One point of view emphasizes that outgroup hostility is a consequence of the processes involved in maintaining or increasing ingroup cohesion. There are many different versions of this viewpoint. One prominent version centers around the concept of *displacement:* ingroup cohesion is fostered or preserved by displacing internal conflict and internal frustration onto other groups, thus reducing internal dissension. Group leaders may deliberately foster antipathy to another group as a ploy to maintain or increase ingroup loyalty to their leadership. Also, antipathy may be employed to discredit internal opposition by identifying the opponents with the hated outgroup. The reader will have no difficulty supplying illustrations of these methods if he brings to mind relations between the United States and the Communist nations during the Cold War or current relations between Israel and the Arab countries.

As the psychoanalytic origin of the term suggests, displacement may reflect unconscious rather than deliberate processes. In its extreme and most pessimistic form, as articulated by Freud in his *Civilization and Its Discontents* (1930), the displacement theory posits that outgroup hostility is an inevitable consequence of the restraints and inhibitions inherent in civilized group life. Group cohesion and survival require obedience to authority, restraint on covetousness, willingness to delay immediate gratification for future gains, and inhibition of aggressiveness toward the perceived sources of the frustration. However, due to the protracted helplessness of the human infant and the strong mutual dependence of adult group members, it is dangerous to act upon or even harbor conscious ill feelings toward one's own group or its leaders; doing so might lead to rejection and ostracism or to the disruption of the group upon whom one is dependent. Projection of one's repressed urges (such as rebelliousness toward authority, unrestrained sexuality, covetousness, aggressiveness) onto an outgroup and, simultaneously, attack of the outgroup dissociate the group member from his feelings of alienation toward his own group and enable vicarious satisfaction of some of his repressed urges. According to this view, outgroup hostility is necessary to preserve ingroup cohesion and also to maintain the inner equilibrium of the inevitably frustrated participant in organized group life.

More recent and less fatalistic versions of what LeVine and Campbell term the *frustration-aggression-displacement* theory offer several new emphases. Thus while group life may be acknowledged to be frustrating, groups differ in how much frustration they impose upon their members, and different segments, positions, and individuals within a group can vary in how much frustration they experience. A group that is experiencing considerable deprivation and difficulty has more need for outgroup hostility; similarly, members of a group who are frustrated, marginal, or under considerable pressure are more likely to be ethnocentric and nationalistic. Moreover, groups, subgroups, and individuals differ in how they manage frustration. In many instances, frustration is not likely to lead to aggressiveness; hence the need for its repression and displacement onto outgroups becomes less compelling. Finally, there is an increasing awareness that displacement of repressed hostility onto an outgroup is not a simple, automatic process. For such a displacement onto a particular outgroup to occur in a unified manner, there must be a socially institutionalized mechanism for identifying an appropriate target and for channeling the displaced hostility in a socially coordinated fashion. In effect, outgroup hostility as a displacement mechanism becomes less likely when it is difficult to achieve internal consensus about the appropriateness and safety of engaging in particular expressions of hostility toward specified outgroups.

Although the frustration-aggression-displacement theory is the most widely discussed explanation for the assumed causal sequence that posits that outgroup hostility is an effect of the processes involved in attempting to achieve ingroup unity, there are other possible explanations for such a causal sequence. Thus one might suppose that ingroup loyalty would be enhanced if members conceive their group to be unique and superior to the other groups available and relevant for purposes of comparison. However, a sense of superiority implies a derogation of other groups, and to the extent that the derogated outgroup does not acquiesce in the judgment of its inferiority, one may also expect hostility toward the outgroup. Another ingroup process that might result in outgroup hostility could be described as follows: intragroup communication leads to familiarity, a sense of similarity, and convergence in beliefs and values among group members. This, in turn, leads to a preference for and a discrimination in favor of ingroup members; the necessity to maintain and justify the ingroup favoritism produces the sense of one's own superiority and a derogation of the outgroup.

Intergroup conflict as the cause of ingroup cohesiveness. Many social science theorists reject the view that intergroup conflict is an inevitable product of the intragroup process. Instead, they postulate (see Campbell 1965) that real conflicts of group interests cause intergroup conflict and pose a real threat which is correctly perceived. The perception of threat from an outgroup, whether the threat is real or not, is hypothesized to have a number of consequences: it causes hostility toward the outgroup; it increases ingroup solidarity; it magnifies ingroup virtues and exaggerates outgroup vices; it increases the tightness of group boundaries; and it increases the punishment and rejection of deviants. A further hypothesis suggests that when external threat is reduced or nonexistent, a group will become less unified, member loyalty will diminish, and the group will tend to break up into smaller units.

There is much evidence from history and from the research laboratory (Deutsch 1949; Blake and Mouton 1962; Fiedler 1967) illustrating the views that intergroup competition enhances ingroup cohesiveness and ethnocentrism and that the diminution of external threat reduces group unity. Thus conflict with the colonial powers allowed many emerging African nations to overcome tribal rivalries and achieve a temporary unity; with the withdrawal of the colonial powers, retribalization has occurred in several of these new nations. The retribalization has often led to considerable internal conflict and a loss in national cohesion (Mazrui 1969).

Although war often leads to an upsurge of nationalism and patriotism, it frequently also has divisive effects. Consider the internal dissension in the United States associated with the war in Vietnam and recall the internal effects of Russia's involvement in World War I. In fact, many writers on revolution suggest that war may lead to conditions that are particularly condusive to revolutions (Laqueur 1968). The conditions under which real conflict between groups has divisive rather than cohesive effects are not yet definitively established. However, it seems likely that external conflict will be internally disruptive rather than unifying when its costs are clearly perceived to outweigh its potential gains, when the costs are viewed as being borne unjustly and disproportionately by only certain segments of the group, when important segments of the ingroup have strong ties with the conflicting outgroup, when the conflict persists over an extended period of time, or when the conflict violates traditional beliefs and values of the ingroup.

Ingroup cohesion and outgroup hostility as factors influencing one another. It seems evident that intergroup conflict can promote ingroup cohesion and, also, that the need to increase ingroup cohesion can stimulate ethnocentrism and outgroup hostility; the causal arrow is bidirectional. After all, the knowledge is widespread that external threat can increase ingroup loyalty. So it is not surprising that group leaders often resort to the tactic of attempting to increase the sense of external danger as a means of inhibiting internal dissension. However, not every outgroup can be "used" in this manner. One can state as a general principle that the more unresolved opposition in values and interests there has been between an ingroup and an outgroup in the recent past, the more useful will the outgroup be as a target. In other words, the tactic of whipping up hostility to an outgroup is most likely to work when there is an existing active predisposition to perceive the outgroup in terms of well-established hostile or fearful stereotypes. Intergroup conflict and differences give rise to outgroup stereotypes, and these, in turn, can be used to promote or activate intergroup conflict.

Group Structure

Group structure refers to the ways in which the parts or elements of a group are interrelated. Since there are many different types of relations connecting the parts of a group, it would be more apt to use the term *structures* rather than *structure*. One could characterize the relations among the parts in terms of their physical proximity, the amount and types of communication that take place among them, the domain and scope of the power and authority each has over the other, their affective relations, their similarities in value orientation, their interconnectedness in relation to work, the flow of people between subgroups, their relative access to such advantages as prestige, education, and well-being.

For each of the ways in which the parts of a group may be interrelated, one could ask how variations in that type of relation within a group are likely to affect or be affected by the character of the group's relations with other groups. Unfortunately, such questions have rarely been asked; as a consequence, there is little systematic information available with which to answer them. There has, however, been some suggestion that such structural characteristics as type of leadership and the degree of structural disequilibrium within the group might be relevant to intergroup relations. These characteristics are considered below.

Leadership. There are two widely held propositions about the relationship between ingroup leadership and intergroup relations. The first is that authoritarian leadership tends to produce internal frustration and hostility which is likely to be displaced onto outgroups. The second is that stress, whether it be the internal stress of ingroup frustration or the external stress of intergroup conflict, creates a demand for authoritarian, highly structured leadership (see Korten 1962).

The first proposition implicitly rests on the frustration-aggression-displacement theory of ethnocentrism, which we have discussed in the section on group cohesion. Embedded in it is the assumption that authoritarian forms of leadership are intrinsically more frustrating than democratic forms. The most direct evidence in support of this assumption comes from a series of research studies comparing democratic and authoritarian leadership; these were stimulated by the pioneering investigation of Lewin, Lippitt, and White (1939). The studies (see Likert 1961 for a summary of many studies of leadership), in general, support the views that group members are less frustrated and more productive when they can participate in making the decisions that affect them and that leaders who exercise a participative rather than authoritarian leadership are more commonly liked by the group members.

Fiedler (1964), on the other hand, has shown that the effectiveness of different types of leaders is very closely related to the situation confronting the group. His findings indicate that controlling, authoritarian leaders tend to be more effective than democratic leaders in situations where the group and task conditions are either very favorable or very unfavorable. In the former, the leader-member relations are positive, the task is clear and well structured, the leader has well-defined authority and power; in unfavorable situations, the leader-member relations are not good, the task is unclear, the leader's role is ill-defined. In the favorable situation, the leader can assume that the group will go along with his decisions willingly because what is required is self-evident, and little difference of opinion among the members is expected: discussion would be ritualistic and a waste of time. In the unfavorable situation, the leader can assume that the distrust and lack of clarity among the group members is so great that no consensus is likely and that the group would get bogged down in bickering and strife, to the detriment of the possibilities of effective action, if it were involved in the decision-making process.

Fiedler's results would suggest that democratic leadership is less frustrating than authoritarian leadership only when the conditions are neither extremely favorable nor extremely unfavorable to obtaining a group consensus on the course of action to take. In the former instance, democratic leadership is not necessary, and in the latter, presumably, it would not work. Thus the aforementioned proposition about the effects of authoritarian leadership should perhaps be modified to read that leadership that is inappropriate to the group's situation is likely to induce frustration: under extreme conditions authoritarian leadership is more likely to be effective than democratic leadership; under most other conditions, the reverse is likely to be true. It also seems probable that the particular characteristics of given situations will tend to induce leadership that is situationally appropriate. This last statement implies that leadership change or political instability is likely until a congruence between type of leadership and type of situation has been achieved.

The Feierabends (1966) have constructed for many nations indices measuring the coerciveness of the political regime, the degree of frustration of the "wants" of the population, the degree of political stability, the extent of external aggression, and the like. Their data indicate a significant association between the coerciveness of the political regime and the amount of socioeconomic frustration within the country. Thus sixteen out of twenty-two countries that are considered to have a high rate of satisfaction of the wants of their people have permissive regimes; none of the seventeen countries with a low rate of satisfaction has this type of government. Further, of the sixteen nations that have permissive regimes and a satisfied populace, fifteen are considered to be highly stable; on the other hand, less than half of the countries that have both a socioeconomically satisfied population and a coercive regime exhibit a high degree of political stability.

Although it is impossible to state causal directions from such data as the Feierabends have presented, one may speculate that when the leadership is not as permissive as it should be, given the internal conditions within the group, there will be attempts to change the leadership. A parallel process seems to occur under conditions of high frustration of the wants of the population: a highly coercive regime induces more political stability than a moderately coercive regime. It should be noted, however, that the political equilibrium reached even by highly coercive regimes with frustrated populations is considerably less stable than that reached by permissive leaders dealing with satisfied populations. None of the former is rated as highly stable, but more than 90 percent of the latter are so considered. Thus political equilibrium for a satisfied population is associated with a permissive leadership; relative political equilibrium for a highly frustrated population is correlated with a highly coercive regime. Hence it seems reasonable to conclude that group tranquility is not simply a function of either the extent of internal frustration or the type of group leadership, permissive or coercive. Rather, internal stability results from the appropriate match between the two.

Their results for external aggression (which omit the data for the major powers) lead the Feierabends to suggest that the country that is sufficiently frustrated to be politically unstable has the strongest possibility of also being externally aggressive. While the satisfied country has the greatest probability of being both internally stable and externally nonaggressive, external aggression is more closely related to political instability than it is to internal frustration. Other investigators (e.g., Rummel 1969) have not found evidence of a significant relationship between domestic and external conflict such as obtained in the Feierabend study. This may be due to the fact, as Wilkenfeld (1969) has suggested, that the relationship between internal and external conflict may differ for different types of nations. Lumping all nations together for statistical analysis may obscure these underlying differences. However, even more importantly, most analyses of the relations between internal and external conflict make the obviously false assumption that the nature of a group's external environment can be disregarded. Consider Israel, a nation with much external conflict but one whose populace is relatively satisfied and whose government is relatively stable and permissive. Is it not apparent that attempts to characterize the relationship between a group's internal properties and its external conflict are bound to be incomplete and distorted unless its external environment is meaningfully delineated?

Structural disequilibrium. There is often a correspondence among the positions that an individual (or subgroup) holds in the different structures of a group. An individual who holds a central position in one structure (e.g., the communication structure) is likely to hold a central position in other structures (power, friendship, and prestige). The research of Galtung (1964) in Norway indicates that this is the case for Norwegian society: people who are more central on social variables (income, education, occupation, residence, age, and sex) are also more central in the communication and power structures. To explain the tendency for the different statuses of an individual to be congruent with one another, Benoit-Smullyan (1944), Lasswell and Kaplan (1950), Homans (1961), and many others (see Berger, Zelditch, and Anderson 1966) have advanced the *status-equilibration* hypothesis. This hypothesis asserts that when the ranks or positions of a person or group in different status structures are dissimilar, a state of disequilibrium exists, and forces arise to induce the changes necessary to make the statuses similar. In an experiment, Burnstein and Zajonc (1965 a, b) manipulated, at different times, the individual's status within the group and his task performance. Their results demonstrated that when an individual's performance rank improved, the group increased the importance of his position within the group; similarly, when the importance of his position within the group was increased, his performance improved.

However, status equilibrium is not always achieved. Research with air crews by Adams (1953) demonstrated that lack of congruence on such status dimensions as age, military rank, education, reputed ability, popularity, combat time, and position importance was related to poor morale, less friendliness, and lack of mutual confidence. Exline and Ziller (1959), working with experimentally created groups, found that groups constructed so as to have incongruent status hierarchies manifested more interpersonal conflict and less productivity than congruent groups.

Galtung (1964, pp. 95–119) has outlined a *structural theory of aggression* which is based on the hypothesis that "aggression is more likely to arise in social positions in rank-disequilibrium. In a system of individuals it may take the form of crime, in a system of groups the form of revolutions, and in a system of nations the form of war." He points out that the extreme forms of aggression are unlikely unless other methods of equilibration have been tried and failed and unless, in addition, the culture predisposes to violence. From Galtung's hypothesis, such interesting corollaries follow as: aggression is less likely from those who are the underdogs in all respects than from those who are the underdogs in some characteristics but not in others; social change that improves an underdog's position in some respects (education) but not in others (political influence, affluence) is likely to increase the amount of aggression; the smaller the number of dimensions on which social units are ranked and the smaller the number of social units being ranked, the more disruptive is any rank-disequilibrium to the system of units.

If one assumes that progress toward social equality of the races is uneven and that such progress initially increases the structural disequilibrium, one will predict more open interracial conflict in the United States than in South Africa, and more in the North than in the South. Similarly, analysis of many revolutionary situations suggests (Davies 1962) that they often occur when there is an improvement of the underdog's position in some respect (e.g., education) and a worsening in other respects (availability of suitable employment, etc.). Himmelstrand (1969), in a discussion of the relation between tribal conflict and rank-disequilibrium in the positions of the various tribes in Nigeria, indicates that the strains induced by the disequilibrium were conducive to the development of the intertribal conflict that led to their civil war. However, he suggests that other rank-equilibrating responses than intergroup aggression were possible, but he does not define the conditions that led to strife rather than to other types of equilibrating actions.

The hypothesis that aggression may arise from structural disequilibrium is intriguing. However, as Hernes (1969) points out, it needs to be more precisely specified before it can be adequately tested. This is true not only with regard to the meaning and measurement of its key concepts but also with regard to the conditions under which aggression (rather than other actions) will occur as a response to rank-disequilibrium. Rank-disequilibrium is, obviously, neither a necessary nor a sufficient condition for the occurrence of aggression. It is probably more fruitful to conceive of structural disequilibrium as providing a motivation to produce an upward change in one's disequilibrated statuses rather than as producing a motivation to aggress. Aggression may result as a reaction to the resistance of others to a change in one's status, but it is unlikely without the experience of resistance and the resulting frustrations. But even resistance and frustration do not necessarily lead to aggression, except under rather specific conditions. Some of these have been touched upon in our prior discussion of the frustration-aggression-displacement theory of outgroup hostility.

Pyramidal-segmentary and cross-cutting structure. In most societies, people are members of more than one group. They are likely to be members of a kinship group, a political association, a recreation group, and many others. LeVine and Campbell (1972) point out that social anthropologists have characterized two basic types of social structures, the pyramidal-segmentary and the cross-cutting. In the *pyramidal-segmentary* type, each smaller unit that an individual belongs to is included as a segment of each larger group that he is a member of. Thus in some folk societies, an individual may live in a small family group, in a small farming community, which is part of a larger kinship group, which, in turn, is a segment of a larger ethnic group, which is one component of a larger society. In the *cross-cutting* type, as the name implies, the groups to which a member belongs cut across rather than nest in one another. His residence group is not necessarily included in his kinship group, and his work group may be composed of people from many different ethnic groups. These two types, of course, rarely exist in their pure forms. Most social structures tend to be mixtures, with one or the other predominating.

There is considerable evidence from the anthropological literature (see LeVine and Campbell for a summary and references) that the pyramidal-segmentary structure is more conducive to destructive intergroup strife within a society than the cross-cutting type. The reason for this is easy to see. If, for example, in a society which has a pyramidal-segmentary structure, a conflict arises between two ethnic groups in the society (e.g., about which group's language shall be paramount in the total society), then the individual's membership in all the groups that are nested within his ethnic group (his neighborhood, his recreation group, his kinship group, etc.) will strengthen his loyalty to his ethnic group's position. But this will happen on both sides, making it more difficult to resolve the differences between the two groups. On the other hand, in a cross-cutting social structure, members of the conflicting ethnic groups are likely to be members of common work groups, common neighborhood groups, and so on. Their common memberships will make it difficult to polarize individual attitudes about the ethnic conflict. Doing so would place the individual in the dilemma of choosing between loyalty to his ethnic group and loyalty to his other groups that cut across ethnic lines. Thus cross-cutting memberships and loyalties tend to function as a moderating influence in resolving any particular intergroup conflict within a society.

Thoden van Velsen and van Wettering (1960), in a study of a sample of fifty folk societies, provide some relevant evidence. They found that intrasocietal violence was considerably higher in patrilocal as compared to matrilocal societies. Since matrilocal societies involve a change of residence for the male, so that he moves from the community in which he was born to a different community, it is reasonable to suppose that the difference in internal violence may be due to the possibility that the change of residence encourages the growth of cross-cutting loyalties which, in turn, dampen the development of destructive conflict. More generally, it seems reasonable to hypothesize that population mobility, whether it be residential or social, would lead to the development of cross-cutting ties and would serve to prevent the polarization of intergroup conflict into a struggle between groups that feel they have no mutual interests.

Yet it would seem logical to assume that mobility would increase rank-disequilibrium and that, according to Galtung's hypothesis of structural aggression, this would give rise to social conflict. The contradictory predictions may both be correct, each for a different stage of the total process. Thus before there has been an erosion of the primary segmental loyalties (which are characteristic in the pyramidal-segmental type of social structure) and before the growth of cross-cutting loyalties, residential and social mobility might enhance social conflict. However, after mobility has led to the development of cross-cutting loyalties, the scope of intergroup conflict might be narrowed. Cross-cutting memberships might also be expected to individualize the social elements in the society and thus to increase their numbers, since fewer individuals might be expected to have parallel memberships in cross-cutting groups. As a consequence of the individualization and proliferation of the social units, rank-disequilibrium might be expected to have only minor consequences for intergroup relations. Nevertheless, insofar as rank-disequilibrium is individually frustrating, the frustration-aggression-displacement theory would predict that interpersonal tension and conflict would be enhanced.

Power

As Dahl (1968) has pointed out, there is little consensus about this widely employed concept other than that it is a useful one in the analysis of behavior. I shall not attempt to summarize the many different conceptions of "power" but will, instead, offer some notions of my own which have been stimulated by the writings of many others (e.g., Lasswell and Kaplan 1950; Cartwright 1959).

An actor (a term used here to refer to either a group or an individual) has power in a given situation (*situational power*) to the degree that he can satisfy the purposes (goals, desires, or wants) that he is attempting to fulfill in that situation. Power is a relational concept; it does not reside in the individual but rather in the relationship of the person to his environment. Thus, the power of an actor in a given situation is determined by the characteristics of the situation as well as by his own characteristics. It follows that an actor has more power to satisfy his desires when his environment is "facilitative" rather than "resistive" to his goal achievement; that is, he has more power to overcome another when the other's resistance is weak. Also, he has more power when his wants are readily satisfied as, for example, when his aspirations are low or when, in Hindu or Zen fashion, he can exercise control over his own desires.

Many theorists who have been concerned with power have focused on it as an attribute solely of the actor. This neglects its relational aspects and implicitly assumes that it remains constant across situations, an assumption which is clearly false. However, it would be equally incorrect to assume that power is determined only by situational characteristics. It is obvious that the resources of the actor play an important role in determining his power in a given situation. Such resources as wealth, physical strength, weapons, health, intelligence, knowledge, organizational skill, respect, and affection are ingredients of power in many situations, and they may be possessed, to a greater or a lesser degree, fairly constantly by a given actor. Thus it is possible to compare individuals, groups, or nations with one another in terms of their possession of the ingredients of power, even though their relative rankings on situational power may vary from situation to situation. Moreover, doing so is more useful than might be anticipated from a situational perspective, because there is a tendency for rank-equilibrium with regard to access to different capabilities and resources and also across different situations. As Lasswell and Kaplan (1950, p. 57) have stated: "The rich tend also to be the healthy, respected, informed, and so on, and the poor to be the sickly, despised, and ignorant." Thus there is some meaning to the abstract statement that "A is more powerful than B," even though the statement is not qualified in terms of specific contexts.

There are three distinct meanings of *power* submerged in the statement "A is more powerful than B": *environmental power,* or "A is usually more able to favorably influence his overall environment and/or to overcome its resistance than is B"; *relationship power,* or "A is usually more able to influence B favorably and/or to overcome B's resistance than B is able to do with A"; and *personal power,* or "A is usually more able to satisfy his desires than is B." Although these different forms of power are usually positively correlated, this is not inevitably so.

Let us look at one of the possibilities. B has so little environmental power that he has little expectation of satisfying large wants, and thus he wants little. A, on the other hand, has high aspirations because of his high environmental power. As a result of A's high aspirations and B's low aspirations, A is more vulnerable to B's threats of noncooperation or antagonistic behavior than B is to A's. Thus despite A's superior environmental power, he may be in an inferior bargaining position to that of B. Experienced bargainers know that the best way to get a merchant in a Turkish market to lower his price is to appear to have no interest in what he is offering to sell. And Karl Marx knew that workers could increase their power if they recognized that they had nothing to lose but their chains. More generally, by being devoid of wants and beyond "costs," one can place himself in a powerful position to influence anyone who wants anything from him. A depressed child who does not want to eat or an apathetic adult who does not care whether he lives or dies, by emptying himself of desire, makes those who care about his well-being feel helpless and very responsive to any possibility of arousing the depressed person's interest. Unfortunately, in establishing the credibility of his apathy and depression, the depressed person may lose touch with the wants that initially gave rise to this bargaining tactic.

The preceding discussion suggests that in a relationship between A and B, A does not necessarily have more influence over B when B is in a situation of low environmental power. It is also true that it is not always favorable to A's environmental and personal power for him to be in a dominating rather than an equal relationship with B. In some instances, A may be even better off if he increases B's power in the relationship rather than his own. Thus a faculty that shares some of its resources and decision-making powers with students may find that the students are more responsible and cooperative in efforts to improve the educational quality of the university than they would be if these powers were not shared.

In many discussions, the concept of power is linked only to the ability to overcome resistance; in such discussions (e.g., Lasswell and Kaplan 1950, p. 98), "the exercise of power is simply the exercise of a high degree of coerciveness." This seems too narrow a view. It overlooks the possibility that power can be facilitative as well as coercive, that it can liberate as well as restrain, that it can be "for" as well as "against." The emphasis on the coercive aspects of power possibly arises from the attempt to distinguish "power" from "influence": power is defined by Lasswell and Kaplan as, in essence, being coercive influence. I suggest that it would be more appropriate to conceive of power as *deliberate* or *purposive* influence. Without intending to do so, one may influence another's values, beliefs, or behaviors. One may even be powerless to prevent another from being influenced by oneself —as is the case with many parents who do not want their children to imitate their bad habits. Power is purposive influence; it may be coercive but it need not be. Coercion is only one of several forms of power.

It is useful to distinguish six types of power to influence another (see French and Raven 1959; Cartwright and Zander 1968): *coercive power,* which uses negative incentives, such as threats to physical well-being, wealth, reputation, or social status, to influence the other; *reward or exchange power,* which employs positive incentives, such as promises of gain in well-being, wealth, and the like, in exchange for what is desired from the other; *ecological power,* which entails sufficient control over the other's social or physical environment to permit one to modify it so that the modified environment induces the desired behavior or prevents the undesired behavior (e.g., erecting a fence may stop rabbits from eating one's vegetable garden); *normative power,* which is based on the obligations that the other has to accept one's influence as a result of the social norms governing the relationship; *referent power,* which uses the other's desire to identify with or be similar to some person or group in order to alter his attitudes and values; and *expert power,* which is grounded in the other's acceptance of one's superior knowledge or skill.

It is reasonable to suppose that the different types of power are likely to produce more or less alienation in those subjected to the power (Etzioni 1968). The most alienation could be expected to result from the use of coercive power and the least from the employment of expert and referent power. The tendency to alienation is also undoubtedly affected by whether the power is perceived to be employed legitimately or illegitimately. If the power user is perceived to have no right to use the type of power, if he is perceived to be using it excessively, or if he is perceived to be using it inappropriately (e.g., at the wrong time or in the wrong manner), resistance to his influence and alienation from his purposes are the probable consequences. In summary, illegitimate use of threat or reward that is inappropriate and excessive is most likely to elicit resistance and alienation. However, when the coercion or bribery is of sufficient magnitude to elicit overt compliance, inauthentic cooperation with covert resistance is the likely outcome.

The preceding discussion suggests that the use of power may entail costs and that the costs may differ for different types of power and as a function of how the power is employed. Alienation is one type of cost; it reduces the powerholder's resources for the future employment of normative, referent, expert, and possibly also reward power by making the other less trusting of and less receptive to the powerholder. Without the other's trust as an asset, power is essentially limited to the coercive and ecological types, the types that require and consume most in the way of physical and economic resources. Moreover, it must be recognized that once the other has become alienated, untrusting, and unreceptive, a considerable expenditure of time and resources may be required to reestablish more favorable attitudes. In the short run, the use of coercive and ecological power may be more effective in producing compliance from the alienated than the attempt to develop the attitudinal resources that underlie the effective employment of noncoercive power. Nevertheless, because it seems likely that the costs of maintaining effective coercive and ecological power far outweigh the costs of maintaining the noncoercive forms, it is generally a short-lived economy to employ coercion as a substitute for the effort involved in developing a trusting relationship with the other.

It is a commonly held view about groups, as well as about men, that they tend to be shortsighted and that they value coercion as the primary form of power. Thus it is not surprising that the most widely accepted proposition about power is the one articulated by Michels, the political theorist (1911, p. 207): "Every human power seeks to enlarge its prerogatives. He who has acquired power will almost always endeavor to consolidate it and to extend it. . . ."

The assumption implicit in this proposition is that power relations are intrinsically coercive and competitive; the more power A has, the less power available for B. A corollary of this is that there is always a struggle for power. The struggle may be *latent* because both sides agree on its probable outcome or agree that the resulting changes would not be worth the costs; the struggle may be *regulated* and *con-*

trolled so that it takes place under rules that limit its destructiveness, as in a boxing match; or the struggle may be *unregulated* and *overt* as in a no-holds-barred fight.

The earlier discussion of environmental power and personal power implies that power is not intrinsically competitive. While power is often gained at another's expense, in many situations it can only be enhanced cooperatively. And when the relations are cooperative, enhancement of the other's power also enhances one's own. Clearly it is possible for A's influence over B to increase at the same time as B's influence over A grows. This is what happens when two strangers, who have little influence over one another, become acquainted and fall in love. They develop great power over one another. This mutual increase in power to affect the other is a typical consequence in a cooperative relationship.

Why is it, then, that a competitive view of power is so widespread? This is probably a result of the fact that differential rankings of statuses, status hierarchies, are universal characteristics of human societies. As Barnard (1946) has suggested, status distinctions and associated distinctions of authority (the right to exercise influence in certain matters over certain statuses) are necessary for the effective functioning and survival of any group above a certain size. The competitive drive for superior rank and power, to the extent that it exists, probably derives from the existence of status hierarchies: the greater advantages usually associated with high as compared to low status provide the incentives to seek high relative power.

However, it would be unreasonable to assume there is an innately determined human tendency for everyone to want to be "top dog." Most people would rather not be President! While the striving for changes in power is usually upward rather than downward in direction, there are notable exceptions. The desire to avoid the responsibilities of high position and the fear of achieving competitive success are well-established phenomena. However, even when striving is upward, it is rarely directed to a rank beyond one's range of social comparison. Aspirations are generally determined by comparing oneself with others whose opinions or abilities are similar to one's own, rather than widely discrepant (Festinger 1954) and by comparing one's position with the other available opportunities (Thibaut and Kelley 1959). Thus it would be reasonable to assume that the power aspirations of most people are by no means unlimited.

It is well to note that the desire to increase power can be directed toward increasing the resources that underlie power (such as wealth, physical strength, organization, knowledge, skill, respect, and affection), or it can be directed toward increasing the effectiveness with which the resources of power are employed. Potential power may not get converted into effective power for two primary reasons. There may be little motivation to use the power; some potentially powerful groups and people prefer not to exercise it. Or, the conversion of power resources into effective power may be made inefficiently and unskillfully, so that much power potential is wasted. This may occur, for example, when power is used inappropriately or excessively. Thus effective power depends upon the following key elements: the control or possession of resources to generate power; the motivation to employ these resources to influence others; skill in converting the resources into usable power; and good judgment in employing this power so that its use is appropriate in type and magnitude to the situation in which it is used.

After this introduction on various aspects of power, we must turn to the question of how a group's powers are likely to affect its relationship with other groups. By definition, the possession of great power increases a group's chances of getting what it desires. Therefore, one would predict that the members of very powerful groups would be more satisfied with their groups and less personally discontent than members of low-power groups. Studies in industry (Porter and Lawler 1965) and of the people in various nations (Cantril 1965) provide strong support for this proposition. Second, one would expect more powerful groups to have a longer time perspective, to plan further into the future, and to have more freedom to initiate activities without consultation with others. Third, powerful groups are more likely to take actions that affect others and are more likely to influence the welfare of other groups than are less powerful groups.

Low-power groups face a situation that has many inherent disadvantages and potential frustrations. Their welfare is dependent upon the actions of others, they cannot plan far ahead, and there is likely to be discontent among their members. In such a situation, a low-power group has a limited number of alternative courses of action open to it. First, it may attempt to change the power relation itself by increasing its share of the resources at the base of power, by increasing its own resources and its effectiveness in using them, by finding allies, and/or by decreasing the resources or increasing the costs of the more powerful group. Or it may seek to induce the high-power group to use its power benevolently through such techniques as ingratiation, the arousal of guilt, the appeal of helplessness, or the appeal to general norms of equity or justice. Finally, it may try to withdraw from interaction and insulate itself from the high-power group by changing its objectives so that it will be less dependent on the high-power group and less noticeable to it.

It is difficult to predict which alternative will be taken by a low-power group. However, it is reasonable to assume that such a group is unlikely to attempt to change the power relations unless it is an effectively organized, cohesive group with a high level of frustrated aspiration, a significant degree of optimism about the possibilities of change, and considerable freedom from fear of the high-power group. Also, one might assume that if a low-power group considers itself helpless and powerless, it is likely to seek to ingratiate itself in a submissive relationship with the high-power group rather than attempt to change that group.

The frustrations inherent in the situation of the low-power group act as an instigator for change. The same is not true for the situation of those in high power. It is evident that those who are satisfied with their roles in, and the outcomes of, an interaction process often develop both a vested interest in preserving the existing arrangements and appropriate rationales to justify their position. For those in high power, these rationales generally take the form of attributing greater competence (more ability, knowledge, skill) and/or superior moral value (greater initiative, drive, sense of responsibility, self-control) to oneself than to those of lower status. From the point of view of those in power, lack of power and affluence is little enough punishment for people so deficient in morality, competence, and maturity that they have failed to make their own way in society. The rationales supporting the status quo are usually accompanied by corresponding sentiments that lead their possessors to react with disapproval and resistance to attempts to change the power relations and with apprehension and defensiveness to the possibility that these attempts might succeed. The apprehension is often a response to the expectation that the change will leave one in a powerless position under the control of those who are incompetent and irresponsible or at the mercy of those seeking revenge for past injuries.

If such rationales, sentiments, and expectations have been developed, those in power are likely to employ one or more defense mechanisms in dealing with the conflict-inducing dissatisfactions of the subordinated group: *avoidance,* which seeks to minimize human contact with those in low status by establishing a social distance that permits contact only under conditions of clear status differences; *denial,* which is expressed by a blindness and insensitivity to the dissatisfactions and often results in an unexpected revolt; *repression,* which pushes the dissatisfactions underground and often eventuates in guerrilla-type war; *aggression,* which may lead to masochistic sham cooperation or escalated counteraggression; *displacement* which attempts to divert the responsibility for the dissatisfactions onto other groups and, if successful, averts the conflict temporarily; *reaction-formation,* which allows expressions of concern and guilt to serve as substitutes for action to relieve the dissatisfaction of the underprivileged and which, in doing so, may temporarily confuse and mislead those who are dissatisfied; *tokenism,* which attempts to appease the frustrated group by providing it with token benefits and gains; *sublimation,* which attempts to find substitute solutions—e.g., instead of increasing the decision-making power of Harlem residents over their schools, those in power provide more facilities for the Harlem schools.

Although defensiveness is a common reaction by those with high power to the efforts of low-power groups to decrease the power differences, it is well to recognize that other reactions can and do occur. Those in high power sometimes voluntarily give up or share their power: political leaders leave office, parents often reduce their power and increase the decision-making responsibilities of their children as they grow up, some administrators and faculties willingly share their powers with students. Little is known about the conditions under which a high-power group will be willing to share its power with those in low power rather than attempt to defend and maintain the status quo. However, it seems reasonable to assume that such a group is most likely to do so when it expects that this course will increase rather than decrease its environmental and personal power. Thus if the group members believe that there will be gains in their assets or decreases in their costs due to an increased cooperativeness of the other group, they may feel that the sharing of power will be beneficial rather than harmful to them. A dean of students may, for example, feel that students will be more committed to obeying dormitory rules and regulations if they participate in formulating and enforcing them; he may consider their increased commitment an important asset which more than compensates for the inconveniences of sharing power. Of course, if those in high power expect to be humiliated or frustrated in major ways by a redistribution of power, they will resist it and seek to defend or extend their superior position.

CLASS AND RACE CONFLICT

Although it is evident from everyday life as well as from research that intergroup conflict can arise between groups of equal power, the most pervasive form of social conflict is between dominant and subordinate groups, between the "haves" and the "have-nots." Such conflict is latent in any social system, large or small, whenever there are differences in authority, power, or other forms of advantage associated with different social categories—e.g., employee-employer, black-white, students-faculty, women-men, homo-heterosexual, Catholic-Protestant, aged-young, disabled-nondisabled. We shall discuss class conflict and racial conflict to see what light such conflicts can throw upon the conditions affecting the course of conflict.

It is well to recognize that not all latent intergroup conflicts become actualized. Nor, of course, do they inevitably become competitive struggles. The members of a disadvantaged social category may not feel actively frustrated by their relative lack of hope, or they may have accepted their inferior status as natural and legitimate, not having conceived of any other possible state of affairs. Neither beasts of burden nor their masters are likely to conceive the possibility that a conflict could exist between them. In the past, conflict between slaves and masters was sometimes latent rather than active because the slave, as well as the master, could not conceive that another type of relationship between them was natural or possible. Similarly, women in many traditional societies view their subordinate relationship to men as a natural one, and the idea of challenging it is unlikely to occur to them. To be actively disturbed with one's social position requires more than unhappiness or dissatisfaction. There must also be a recognition that change is possible, and that such change would not be a violation of the natural order.

Even if there is a painful discrepancy between the aspirations of people in a particular social category and their reality, they may have little opportunity to interact with others in a similar plight, little possibility to develop consciousness of common interests and grievances, and little chance to develop into a "group." Intergroup conflict, however, requires more than an awareness of common grievances and the definition of common objectives if it is to be manifested in group actions. It requires, in addition, the resources and talents necessary to develop the organizational structures, normative controls, institutional facilities, and group procedures that permit coordinated group action. However, there is essentially a self-reinforcing cycle at work. As Karl Marx stressed, individuals form a class (or group) only insofar as they are engaged in a common struggle with another class. In other words, intergroup conflict stimulates the development and organization of each of the conflicting groups, and this, in turn, permits latent intergroup conflict to be expressed in overt struggle. It is likely that the ability of a group to engage in an intergroup struggle is a function of how well organized it is, as well as a function of its resources. And it is also likely that a struggle will aid a group to mobilize and organize its resources and will contribute to the group's development if the struggle is oriented toward objectives that are perceived to be attainable rather than hopeless.

Latent social conflicts over authority or power, thus, are likely to be actualized when the disadvantaged become acutely frustrated by their disadvantaged position, when they develop a group identity, and when they organize themselves for group action. However, not all such conflicts inevitably result in a competitive process of conflict resolution, even though it seems likely that most such conflicts will take a competitive form in their initial phases. Dominant groups, as we have pointed out in the preceding section, are rarely discontent with the power relations that exist between themselves and a subordinate group, and they often believe that an increase in the power of a disadvantaged group will result in a decrease in their own power. As a consequence, the disadvantaged group may perceive no other effective way to motivate the members of the powerful group to accept the possibility of significant social change except that of threatening harm to the powerful group's security and vital interests.

As our earlier discussion of structural disequilibrium would suggest, small gains by the disadvantaged—i.e., gains large enough to raise aspirations but too small to satisfy them—may be more provocative of active competitive conflict than a more stagnant intergroup situation that both offers and promises little. In the latter case, the conflict may remain latent until it is activated by changing circumstances that either increase aspirations or worsen current realities.

Below, we shall consider class conflict and then racial conflict, two widespread forms of the conflict between the "haves" and "have-nots," to obtain generalizable insights into the factors that influence whether the course of a conflict will be productive or destructive.

Class Conflict

One of the most fully developed theories of intergroup conflict was presented by Karl Marx in his theory of class conflict. His theory assumes that class conflict typically gives rise to a competitive process that spirals into an increasing intensity of conflict until a revolutionary change occurs in the power relations of the conflicting classes. Marx postulated that class conflict arises because there is a category of persons who possess private property (ownership of capital or the means of production), which is the basis of power, and another category of persons who have no such property or power and who must, as a consequence, hire themselves out as wage laborers to those who own capital. The inherent conflict of interest with regard to the distribution of the fruits of production gives rise to classes as individuals within one category engage in a common struggle against individuals from another category. As the struggle proceeds, "the whole society breaks up more and more into two great hostile camps, two great, directly antagonistic classes: bourgeoisie and proletariat." The classes polarize so that they become internally more homogeneous and more and more sharply distinguished from one another in wealth and power. The initial power advantage of the ruling class is used to augment its power vis-à-vis the working class, leading to a progressive impoverishment of the working class and the swelling of its ranks by the impoverishment of groups (the petite bourgeoisie, the small industrialists, the farmers) that were previously marginal between the two classes. The increasing intensity of the conflict and the resulting class homogenization leads the enlarging oppressed proletariat to unite in effective action to overthrow the ruling minority.

The Marxian theory of class conflict seems to be a perfectly reasonable description of what might have happened in several places if such conflict had followed the dynamics of a strictly competitive process of conflict resolution. But class conflict generally did not turn into such a process despite the widespread violence that occurred in industrial disputes in the United States and other countries (Roberts 1969; Taft and Ross 1969). However, industrial violence continued until the ruling groups recognized the rights of workers to organize themselves into unions and to bargain collectively. Much of the violence was initiated by employers, or by government forces acting in behalf of the interest of the employers, in an attempt to discourage workers from organizing and taking such collective actions as strikes and picketing. While employer-initiated violence was sometimes successful in intimidating workers, it was not generally a useful intimidating tactic in the hands of labor. Thus Taft and Ross (1969, p. 362) state: "There is little evidence that violence succeeded in gaining advantages for strikers. Not only does the roll call of lost strikes confirm such a view, but the use of employer agents, disguised as union members or union officials, for advocating violence within the union testifies to the advantage such practices gave the employer." Despite its ineffectiveness, large-scale, worker-initiated violence in labor disputes persisted as long as employers refused to recognize the legitimacy of labor unions and engage in collective bargaining. However, when violence occurred, it did not escalate into class war. Many factors were operating to make such a polarization unlikely. It is of interest to consider what prevented this development and, hence, reduced the possibility of a violent class struggle.

Marx's theory of the political and economic development of the capitalist society was incorrect in several major respects (Dahrendorf 1959). First, the growth of capital did not occur at labor's expense, nor did it lead to labor's absolute or relative pauperization as Marx predicted. Rather, it helped to increase the productivity of labor— which resulted in a general improvement of living standards. Thus gains by both sides lessened the intensity of conflict.

Second, the nature of economic and technological development in industrial society did not produce an increasing homogeneity within the so-called bourgeoisie and proletariat as Marx assumed. Rather, it led to an increasing heterogeneity within each class and some blurring of class distinctions in their common roles as consumers and citizens. Within the bourgeoisie there is not only the distinction between owners or shareholders and managers, there are also many different types of owners and managers. Moreover, the meaning of "capital" itself became more differentiated. There is ownership or control of: the physical means of production, different kinds of knowledge and expertise, the techniques of persuasion, the techniques of violence, and so on. Similarly, there was the development of different forms of labor, requiring different skills and training, rather than the predicted leveling of workers into an undifferentiated, unskilled uniformity. Thus differences within and similarities between classes restrained the polarization process.

Third, contrary to Marx's prediction that social mobility would be primarily downward from the bourgeoisie and petite bourgeoisie to the working class, social mobility has been upward as well as downward. The continuous expansion of industry has required the recruitment of many workers for managerial positions. The possibility of upward mobility from class to class has interfered with the development of allegiances to one's class of origin.

Fourth, for reasons that are partly economic, partly educational, partly technological, and partly resultant from the struggle by various interest groups competing for the allegiances of large audiences, the status of citizenship has been endowed with a growing array of rights, which has to some extent led to the dissociation between political power and industrial power. This has also served to reduce the polarization of conflict by enabling individuals to obtain economic gains through the political process as well as through direct confrontation. In addition, it has led to the institutionalization of patterns of conflict regulation, which serve to limit the destructiveness of conflict when it occurs.

Finally, conflict resolution within industry has been progressively institutionalized through the recognition of labor unions and the development of procedures for collective bargaining, mediation, and arbitration; thus conflict between labor and management is conducted under an increasingly wide area of norms shared by both sides in the conflict. This institutionalization not only reduces the likelihood of destructive conflict but gives the conflicting parties a common interest in maintaining the institutionalized system of rules for dealing with conflict.

This analysis of why class conflict did not develop into the intensely competitive process predicted by Marx's theory can be generalized so as to suggest some propositions that may be applicable to all forms of intergroup conflict and, possibly, to conflict at the interpersonal and international levels as well.

PROPOSITION 1. *Any attempt to introduce a change in the existing re-*
lationship between two parties is more likely to be accepted if each
expects some net gain from the change than if either side expects
that the other side will gain at its expense.

The enormous growth of capital and the rapid development of
technology would have been resisted more bitterly had they not been
accompanied by an improvement in the living standards of laborers as
well as of capitalists.

It is, of course, true that both sides in a conflict may gain because
they may form an implicit or explicit coalition against a third party,
who suffers a loss as a consequence. This is the thesis advanced by
some Marxists in underdeveloped countries to explain the relative
lack of conflict between labor and capital in the advanced industrial
nations. Namely, labor and capital in the industrialized countries are
both profiting from the exploitation of the underdeveloped nations.
Thus the basis for conflict between the exploiters and the exploited is
reduced *within* the industrialized nations, and the basis for conflict *be-*
tween the exploiting and exploited nations is enhanced. Whether or not
this view is accurate, it is apparent that agreement between labor and
management is often facilitated when the costs of the agreement
(higher prices, reduced service, and the like) can be passed on to a
powerless third party such as the consumer.

However, even when the two potentially conflicting parties do not
form a coalition to the detriment of a third party, it may be possible
for both sides to gain from a change in their existing relationship. The
gains may be economic, or there may be gains in other values such as
psychological or physical well-being, respect, affection, moral recti-
tude, knowledge, prestige, or the power to elicit authentic cooperation. The nature of the gains may be different for the initially opposed
parties. One may gain economically while the other may gain morally.

The emphasis on the possibility of mutual gain—for one's
opponent as well as for oneself—underlies the approach to intergroup
conflict of Gandhi, Martin Luther King, and many other advocates of
nonviolence. Essentially, the Gandhian system of ethics (Naess 1958)
postulates that an agreement that injures the other or is arrived at by
coercing the other is self-defeating because it negates the full realization of one's capacity to relate lovingly to the other. Such agreement

is also unstable because the other will not cooperate, authentically and reliably, in relation to an agreement he dislikes. In addition, it is conducive to future violence, since coercion begets violence by the attitudes it creates and the model it provides as a guide to future behavior.

The Gandhian approach assumes a fundamental decency in mankind, and it assumes that an individual and his opponent share this common decency. Thus it is supposed that one will only advocate just causes and that one's opponent can be persuaded by an intelligent, respectful, and persistent appeal in favor of a good cause. History has, of course, recorded many rebuffs to well-argued appeals in favor of good causes. It is evident that, at least in the short run, the appeal to the nobler motives or to conscience may not be sufficiently persuasive. This is particularly likely to be the case when the other does not include you in the community toward whom the norms governing his customary moral conduct apply.

Nevertheless, it seems likely that a change that is accomplished by gains for both sides—even if the gains involve satisfaction of the less altruistic motives—is more likely to produce authentic cooperation than a change that is coercively imposed. Moreover, it seems reasonable to suppose that the complement to the preceding proposition is valid: namely, that any attempt to introduce a change in the existing relationship is more likely to be resisted if one side expects to be disadvantaged as a result. Thus if an agreement implies a loss of "face," a humiliation, a loss of wealth, a loss of virtue, a loss of well-being, a loss of legitimacy, or a loss of power, it is likely to be achieved only if one side can successfully coerce or intimidate the other.

PROPOSITION 2. *Conflict is more likely to be resolved by a competitive process when each of the parties in conflict is internally homogeneous but distinctly different from one another in a variety of characteristics (such as class, race, religion, political affiliation, area of residence, and group memberships) than when each is internally heterogeneous and both have overlapping characteristics.*

Heterogeneity within each group is likely to be reflected in a diversity of interests and values among group members—with the consequence that the differences between the conflicting groups may be smaller than the differences within each group. The intragroup differences may individualize the separate components of the group and make it difficult to obtain their allegiance to the group goals that are involved in an intragroup conflict. The differences within each group may also increase the sense of overlapping interests with elements of the other group, if the other group is also seen to be composed of heterogeneous units. The lack of unified support for group goals and the awareness of intergroup common interests are not conducive to the development of an intergroup struggle.

Our discussion in a preceding section of cross-cutting and pyramidal-segmentary types of social structures essentially led to much the same conclusion as stated above. The cross-cutting ties that restrain destructive intergroup conflict are also encouraged by permeable group boundaries that permit social mobility from one group to another. The fact that more than two-thirds of the sons of unskilled workers (the lowest occupational category) have moved into a higher occupational status than their fathers is undoubtedly one of the factors moderating class conflict in the industrialized nations of the West (see Goldhamer 1968 for a presentation of some relevant data). On the basis of similar reasoning, one would expect that racial conflict is likely to be more destructive than class conflict because of the strong caste-like barriers that restrict social mobility from occupations or neighborhoods associated with one race to those associated with another race.

Generally, the free and continuing exchange of members between groups increases the likelihood of cooperative management of conflict between them, while the existence of impermeable boundaries between them fosters a competitive process when conflict occurs.

PROPOSITION 3. *The greater the number and the stronger the concurrent competitive links between the two groups, the less likely it is that a conflict will be resolved cooperatively; the greater the number and the stronger the concurrent cooperative bonds between the groups, the less likely it is that they will resolve their conflict by a competitive process.*

In other words, conflict is likely to be resolved cooperatively in situations where the parties involved perceive that they have less at stake in the conflict than they have in the continuing relationships between them or in the community, institutions, procedures, and facilities they share.

The growth of a superordinate community with institutions and procedures for promoting general welfare and resolving conflicts and the development of allegiances and loyalties to the superordinate community and its institutions serve to reduce the likelihood of disruptive conflict. Too much of value would be lost if a conflict destroyed worthwhile cooperative bonds or shattered an encompassing community. Thus there is little doubt that the development of an effective na-' tional political community, which commands the loyalty of its citizens, serves to inhibit destructive conflict between classes within that community. (Thus there may be merit in the Marxist view that nationalistic ideologies serve the interests of the bourgeoisie by enabling challenges to existing relations within the nation to be labeled as divisive and unpatriotic.) Likewise, conflict between different groups within a university tends to be resolved cooperatively as long as each of the groups values the university as a community and wishes to preserve the existing cooperative bonds. However, when there is widespread disenchantment and alienation and a sense of betrayal of the community's values by its authorities, there are likely to be few common bonds and allegiances to inhibit the occurrence of the destructive forms of conflict.

PROPOSITION 4. *The institutionalization and regulation of conflict decreases the likelihood that conflict will take a destructive course.*

One of the most pertinent facts about the history of industrial conflict in the industrialized nations of the West is that such conflict has become increasingly institutionalized and subject to regulation. As a consequence, industrial conflict is characterized by much less personal violence and damage to property than used to be the case. Because of the central significance of the regulation of conflict, we consider it in greater detail in chapter 13.

Interracial Conflict

The emergence of a racist ideology. Across different societies there are clear variations in the way dominant groups treat subordinate ones. A major variable explaining differences among societies in this regard seems to be the ideological residue of social revolutions. As Stinchcombe (1968) points out, egalitarianism was not as prevalent in the United States before as after the Revolutionary War. And certainly it was not as prevalent in Russia or China before their revolutions. The egalitarian ideals spread initially by the American and French revolutions made it difficult for the newly emerging dominant classes to maintain that the members of subordinate classes were innately inferior, that their origin and thus their biological constitution inherently made them unfit to have liberty and equality.

In one of the great paradoxes of history, racism as an ideology of biological superiority was a child, albeit a foster child, of egalitarianism. Although an elaborately developed system of racial exploitation was in existence in the United States and other parts of the New World by the beginning of the seventeenth century, racism as an ideology came of age only in the third or fourth decade of the nineteenth century, achieving its fullest development approximately between 1880 and 1920. As Myrdal (1944, p. 89) has written: "The fateful word *race* itself is actually not yet two hundred years old. The biological ideology had to be utilized as an intellectual explanation of, and moral apology for, slavery in a society which went out emphatically to invoke as its highest principles the ideals of the inalienable rights of all men to freedom and equality of opportunity."

The democratic, egalitarian, and libertarian ideals of the Enlightenment spread by the American and French revolutions were reconciled with slavery by restricting the definition of humanity to apply only to whites. Thus Chief Justice Taney concluded in his notorious Dred Scott decision of 1857 that Negroes were "beings of an inferior order . . . so far inferior that they had not rights which the white man was bound to respect." (van den Berghe 1967, p. 78).

With the publication in 1859 of Darwin's epochal work, *On the Origin of Species by Means of Natural Selection: or The Preservation of Favored Races in the Struggle for Life,* and the subsequent vulgarization of his ideas in the form of "social Darwinism," the basis for an intellectual rationale for racism was at hand. Such ideas as "survival of the fittest," "hereditary determinism," and "stages of evolution" were eagerly misapplied to the relations between different human social groups—classes and nations as well as social races—to justify existing exploitative social relations and to rationalize imperialist policies. The influence of evolutionary thinking was so strong that, as a critic suggested, it gave rise to a new imperialist beatitude: "Blessed are the strong, for they shall prey upon the weak" (Banton 1967, p. 48). The rich and powerful were biologically superior; they had achieved their positions as a result of natural selection. It would be against nature to interfere with the inequality and suffering of the poor and weak. Imperialism was patriotism "in a race endowed with the genius for empire," or the "manifest destiny" of those superior peoples meant to lead inferior people. Negroes were slaves as a result of their being at a lower stage of evolution, closer to the apes, than whites, who presumably were at the highest evolutionary stage. Unfortunately, much of today's racial folklore is a derivative of the pseudoscience of fifty to a hundred years ago.

Social race. The term *race* in popular usage is applied to such diverse groups as the Jews, the Germans, the Negroes, the Chinese, and the Gypsies. It is evident that such usage has little in common with the somewhat unsuccessful attempts by biologists and anthropologists to classify the human species into subspecies or races that differ in their frequencies of certain genes. Nevertheless, the folk and scientific usages share the conception that membership in racial groups derives principally from inheritance. One becomes a member by descent rather than by choice. Many social scientists, similarly, employ the term *social race* to refer to any human group that defines itself, or is defined by other groups, by rules of descent (Harris 1968). In addition, social races are usually conceived (by themselves or others) to have distinctive physical, intellectual, moral, or cultural characteristics as a result of their unique descents.

Social races are socially defined groups; they may, in fact, differ little or not at all in their biological or genetic characteristics from other groups. Similarly, rules of descent are socially defined codes that vary from society to society and from time to time. Thus in Nazi Germany people who had one or more Jewish grandparents were defined as "Jews" even though their parents and they, themselves, were members of the Catholic church. Similarly, in the United States many people with white skins are considered "black" because one or more of their ancestors were classified as "Negroes."

It is apparent that the rules of membership by descent for any particular social race may not originate in the group itself but may be foisted upon it by a more dominant group. Also, it is evident that the rules employed by the group itself to define its membership may differ from those employed by outgroups and, further, that the individual who is being categorized as a member may or may not himself be following a different set of rules than either the ingroup or the outgroup. Moreover, the rules defined by the individual, the ingroup, or the outgroup may be internally inconsistent or consistent, clear or ambiguous, complete or incomplete. It is evident that for a system of race relations to endure, there must be some correspondence among the rules of descent that are employed to define an individual's membership by the outgroup, the ingroup, and the person being classified. The system will break down if people can readily pass from one social race to another or if they can be disowned or can disown their own group. Thus continuation of a system of interacting racial groups implies that marriages will be within rather than between groups and that there will be a high level of agreement about the rules defining membership in the social races. A high level of agreement presupposes that each of the groups and their potential members are motivated to agree to the rules and that the rules can be so clearly defined that they are unambiguous in their interpretation and application.

A high level of agreement can be imposed by a dominant and powerful group which employs severe sanctions if the rules that it prefers are not followed. Thus in South Africa the dominant white minority has enforced regulations that require a person's race to be on his identity card; falsification of the identity card or failure to carry it can lead to imprisonment. As a result of being categorized together and being treated in a like manner by the dominant group, an aggregate of people may develop a group consciousness and a sense of group identity that it otherwise would not have had. This happened with Africans in the New World who, prior to their enslavement, often came from different tribal groups in Africa—groups that did not think of themselves as belonging to one people.

At first, an imposed group identity may be negative, an acceptance of the dominant's group conception or a reaction against it. At a later stage, the sense of common problems and common attempts to cope with them will often lead to a feeling of belonging to a group that is distinct from and morally superior to the dominant group. In this latter period, there may be mutual desire between the two groups to have a clear separation between them and unambiguous methods of identifying their members. The motivation of the dominant and subordinate groups will, of course, have different bases. The dominant group will want high identifiability and segregation to perpetuate its dominance. The subordinate group will want these things because it hopes that such conditions will enable it to mobilize itself more effectively or change the power relations between the groups—or because it hopes to insulate itself from the constant exposure to the indignities of its relationship with the dominant group.

Agreement on identification of ingroup and outgroup members may also originate in the separate interests of both groups. Both groups, and not merely the dominant one, may desire to maintain separate identities in order to preserve their unique traditions and cultures. However, whether such a situation is enforced by the dominant group or sought by both groups, it is inherently unstable if the dominant group utilizes the other's distinctive characteristics as a means of successfully exploiting or rationalizing its exploitation of the less powerful group. Under such circumstances, the members of the subordinate group will be motivated to change or destroy the system that exploits them or to escape from their own group if they see little possibility of overcoming their oppression. Masochistic submission to overwhelming force does, of course, occur. However, over time it tends to turn the subordinated group into sullen, lethargic, and ineffectual individuals who harbor a seething volcano of unerupted rage under their apathetic exterior. Such a group provides only marginal gains to their exploiters. As Genovese (1965) has documented, the Negro slaves worked badly, without interest or effort, and their use retarded the economic development of the slaveholding South.

Color and race. The need for relatively unambiguous methods of membership identification has two common consequences. It may lead to the definition of the two groups in terms of physical characteristics, which are easily discernable and not readily changed or falsified, and it may also lead to the creation of external conditions that permit the groups to be quickly and reliably distinguished. By the latter, I mean such devices as the physical segregation of the races; the differential access to places, institutions, and occupations; the development of a distinctive outward appearance through dress and insignia; the use of identity cards; and the development of distinctive cultural characteristics, including special dialects and patterns of speech. Such modes of group identification are often used when there is an absence of distinguishing physical characteristics or when physical characteristics are an unreliable sign of social race because of the prior occurrence of considerable miscegenation.

Skin color is, of course, a highly visible characteristic and it is one of the prime bases for distinguishing social races. However, skin color is not the only genetically determined physical trait on which people differ. A race classification based on characteristics such as head shapes, height, or eye color would give rise to different groupings than those based on skin color. The advantage of skin color as a basis of social classification is that it is more easily observed and less readily disguised than other physical characteristics.

Although in the Western world dark skin came to be a stigma of inferior status, a mark of a group that had been in the brutish and degraded position of the slave, it was not always thus. As Snowden (1970, pp. 216–17) has written: "Xenophanes, the first European to contrast the physical characteristics of Negroes and Whites, described Ethiopians and Thracians as he saw them and implied nothing as to the superiority or inferiority of either, whether physical, aesthetic, mental, or moral. . . . In short, those Greeks who first described and depicted dark or Negroid peoples did so without bias. . . ." Similarly, Davidson (1961, p. 5), in summarizing European attitudes toward Africans prior to the development of the massive African slave trade, comments: "They supposed no natural inferiority in Africans, no inherent failure to develop and mature. That was to be the great myth of later years: the central myth of European expansion that first took shape on the deck of a slaving ship."

The myth that associated dark skin with inferiority grew slowly. The first twelve slaves plucked from the western coast of Africa in 1441 by Goncalvez, a youthful Portuguese adventurer, were not considered a different order of human. Nor were the African chieftains and traders with whom the European slave merchants negotiated the purchase of slaves considered to be inferior humans by their white counterparts.

White slavery, after all, had not yet disappeared from western Europe by the time the Spanish were setting foot in the New World. In fact, Queen Isabella, Christopher Columbus's benefactress, allowed the export of white slaves only to the West Indies because of the fear that the rebelliousness of the African slaves would be transmitted to the Indian natives. However, the decimation of the Indian natives by disease, the limited supply of white slaves (mostly criminals, debtors, orphans, infidels, and prostitutes), and the ever-increasing need for manual labor to help with the very profitable sugar, tobacco, and cotton crops, soon led to a rapidly increasing importation of African slaves. By the end of the seventeenth century, *white* slavery had almost completely disappeared in the New World.

There is reason to believe that the end of white slavery was one of the ingredients necessary to solidify the distinction between the freeman and the slave. If it were difficult to distinguish a slave from a freeman, it would be hard to keep the slaves in bondage in lands with sufficient cities and distances to permit easy disappearances. As Banton (1967, pp. 117–18) has written:

Extreme subordination could not be maintained on the plantation if the slaves could easily escape. . . . But the slaves and employers could not be isolated from local life outside the plantation. Therefore the planters—who held the political power—were obliged to see that similar principles of racial subordination obtained outside. The status distinctions on the plantation (which coincided with the colour line) were generalized to the wider society where the criterion of colour did not fit so well. . . . White supremacy and solidarity became a political doctrine, sometimes overlooked in private relations but never in public matters. Part of the price of the support of the non-slaveholding White was the maintenance of the status gap between White and Black. If the equation of status with race was to be enforced, intermediate groups who fitted in neither of the major categories were troublesome anomalies whose very existence called into question the basic assumptions of the system; therefore they could not be tolerated. Free Negroes appeared dangerous so they had to be reduced to subjugation whenever possible. Children of mixed parentage could not be accepted as intermediates, but had to be assigned to the lower category.

The progress of the immigrants compared to the lack of progress of the former slaves. There can be little doubt that the character of the relations between blacks and whites in the New World has largely been determined by the fact that the Africans came involuntarily, as slaves with neither rights nor resources, arriving under conditions that typically destroyed their families, their group identities, and their self-esteem. In contrast, other low-ranking minorities such as the Italians, the Irish, the Polish, and the Jews came to the Americas voluntarily with rights and social resources, under conditions that enabled them to preserve their group identities and families and to maintain their self-respect. Their political bargaining power in relation to the dominant groups was enormously higher than that of the enslaved Africans because of the cohesiveness of their own internal communities.

As the Italians, the Irish, and the Jews rose from the impoverished low-status positions of "newly-arrived immigrants," their skin color could not be used as a reliable mark of social inferiority. As a consequence, members of these initially low-ranking groups could more readily move into the vacant positions in the rapidly expanding socio-economic frontiers of the New World than could the descendants of the African slaves. The greater opportunities available to the European immigrants kept the hopes with which they came to the New World alive. These opportunities also motivated them to persist in sustained attempts to better their social positions. In addition, it provided them with the resources and circumstances, such as money, successful experience, group pride, and education, to improve their capabilities for making progress in the socioeconomic sphere. The progress itself, in a self-reinforcing benevolent spiral, served to make further progress easier. It did so by reducing their objective "social inferiority" and thus diminishing the prejudice and discrimination against them; it also did so by increasing their motivation and capabilities to achieve further progress in the social and economic spheres.

The African slaves, on the other hand, came to the New World with no hope and few resources, and their circumstances as slaves were not conducive to the development of either the motivation or the capabilities for advancing themselves socially or economically. The abolition of slavery raised hopes, but the lack of resources of the former slaves and their descendants—in education, in experience as freemen, in community and family organization, in material possessions—gave them little possibility of overcoming the barriers of prejudice and discrimination. The few who were able to advance themselves despite the stigma of color were never sure of the permanence of their step forward, nor could their enhanced resources wipe out for themselves or for their children the stigma of social inferiority embedded in their skin color. Thus, for the former slaves and their descendants, a vicious cycle existed: their lack of progress lowered their hope and their motivation to advance themselves, and it limited their resources for overcoming the barriers that kept them in a socially inferior status. These consequences of the prejudice and discrimination against them, in turn, served to provide rationales (such as "they are lazy and incapable") for the perpetuation of the racial barriers erected by the dominant white group. Thus, because dark color serves as a mark of racial inferiority as well as of group membership, it makes the prevalent social and economic barriers imposed against low-status groups more difficult for blacks to overcome than for whites.

In addition to the extra difficulties imposed by their skin color and their legacy of social deficits inherited from their experience in slavery, blacks have not been as lucky as white immigrants. When white immigrants were arriving in large numbers, America was becoming an urbanized, industrial society that needed great pools of unskilled labor. The European immigrants were easily able to gain an economic foothold and to help their children move up the socioeconomic ladder. In contrast, the black migrants from the rural South have, since the end of World War II, found that there is little demand for the unskilled labor they possess. America's urban-industrial society requires more and more skilled labor in its technologically advanced industries but provides few opportunities for advancement for those with inadequate education and few skills.

Although skin color has been an important factor in making the progress of blacks more difficult, it would be a mistake to overemphasize its role as an independent causal factor. The Chinese and Japanese, who are also distinctively different from whites in physical appearance, have had much less difficulty than the blacks in improving their social and economic positions. They came to the United States, like the European immigrants and unlike the African slaves, out of choice and under conditions that enabled them to preserve their group cultures and self-esteem. The initial antipathy and color prejudice against these groups arose largely as a result of competition in mining and agriculture with white European immigrants. The Chinese and Japanese, under hostile and often brutal attacks, withdrew from competitive forms of labor and business and segregated themselves from the hostile white community. They entered occupations and businesses not sought by whites and made considerable progress because of the mutual support that derives from family and group cohesion. Because of their relatively small numbers, a large proportion of them have been able to move out of the "Chinatowns" unobtrusively since World War II. In doing so, the color prejudice that they have had to face has been much smaller than that facing blacks. It seems likely that color prejudice has played a more pervasive and persisting role in relation to Africans, as compared to Orientals, because of slavery and the difference in numbers of their different population groups. Elaborate rationales and a complex network of institutional arrangements necessary to the maintenance of blacks in a subordinate role were developed and embedded in the American culture and society—much more so than with regard to the various groups from the Far East. In addition, slavery stripped the Africans of their cultural, group, and family resources, and such resources have been of enormous help to the Chinese and Japanese in overcoming the color barriers to economic and social progress.

The paradox of race relations in the United States. Despite the obvious progress made in the United States since World War II in eliminating legally sanctioned segregation and discrimination, it is evident that racial conflict and polarization have increased in recent years. Many explanations have been offered for this seeming paradox. Basically, the explanations are of three types: racial progress causes or increases racial tensions; racial tensions cause or increase racial progress; and racial progress has been illusory or minimal, and the increased racial tension is a result of the lack of significant improvements. These explanations are not mutually exclusive; each undoubtedly contains an element of truth.

It seems reasonable to suppose that *racial progress will increase racial tensions* because those who favor the status quo in race relations are likely to be upset by racial change and to resist such change. The giving-up of long-held, elaborately rationalized attitudes and customs rarely comes about without defensiveness and resistance—except when careful and extensive efforts are made to help reduce the apprehensions of those who must change and to help them see the advantages that may result from the changes. It is evident that very little systematic effort has been made to reduce the prejudices and discriminatory practices of the white majority in a way that would be least likely to elicit their defensiveness and resistance. Unless such efforts are made, one may expect that tension will increase as changes occur and that, as the modifications become more extensive, it will continue to increase until it is apparent that the new policies and practices are irreversible.

Increased tension with racial progress may also be apparent in the subordinate group, which, presumably, should be happy that change is occurring. The occurrence of reform may whet the group's appetite for further change by signifying that progress is more possible than it initially thought. However, the resistance of whites may increase the subordinates' suspicions and hostility toward whites even as their aspirations are increasing. In such circumstances, the racial gains may well be perceived as the result of the pressures of the blacks against the resistance of the whites rather than as the consequence of enhanced cooperation between the racial groups. Such an interpretation is likely to lead to increased ill will between the races. The white liberals who have supported reforms will feel unappreciated and devalued; the blacks who have been optimistic about the goodwill of whites will be embittered and disillusioned.

A second explanation of the association between racial progress and racial tension is that *racial tension is necessary to achieve racial progress*. As we have indicated earlier in this and the preceding chapter, the impetus for a move toward equality is unlikely to come from the dominant group in a dominant-subordinate relationship. It is, after all, improbable that the dominant group will be dissatisfied with its superior status; hence it is not very likely to initiate attempts to alter the status quo. The subordinate group is, thus, often faced with the necessity of motivating the dominant group to want a modification of the existing state of affairs. However, by the very nature of its lower status, it is rarely in the position to persuasively offer the more powerful group increased rewards and benefits to renounce their superior position. This is, of course, less true when the subordinated group is able to form alliances with powerful elements of the dominant group or when it is able to enlist the cooperation of powerful third parties. Nevertheless, the methods most available to low-status groups are the ones that challenge or disrupt the existing exploitative relationships and that make attempts to continue such relationships unrewarding to the dominant group. These methods include: the withdrawal of cooperation from all forms of unequal relationship; the confrontation of the dominant group when it acts exploitatively; the harassment of the dominant group if it seeks to insulate itself from the discontent of the subordinate group; and the use of obstructive and destructive techniques if the dominant group is unresponsive and repressive.

There are, of course, many instances that demonstrate that the threat of increased racial tension or its actual occurrence may lead to racial progress. Thus President Roosevelt in 1941 issued an executive order establishing the federal Fair Employment Practices Commission in order to avert a threatened mass Negro convergence on Washington. College student sit-ins achieved the desegregation of lunch counters in many communities during the winter and spring of 1960. Various bills protecting civil rights were passed by Congress under the pressure of massive confrontations between demonstrators and repressive local authorities. Boycotts, street demonstrations, and other direct action techniques have compelled employers, from supermarkets to banks, to add many Negroes to their work force.

Riots have sometimes served as a "signaling device" to indicate to those in power that changes must be made or further destructiveness will occur. Moreover, as Skolnick (1969, pp. 341–42) has pointed out, ". . . one need not be fond of revolutions to observe that riots are sometimes the preface to an even more organized overthrow of existing arrangements with the substitution of new regimes. And one need not admire the consequences of the Russian revolution to appreciate those of America or France. All three began with rioting."

The reaction of the dominant group to pressures for changes from a subordinate group may lead to progress, but under certain circumstances it may also lead to reaction and repression. Little scientific knowledge exists about the conditions that determine whether progress or reaction will be the outcome. However, one may speculate that "tension" follows the general rule for motivation: namely, enhancement of tension will have facilitating effects until an optimal level is reached, and beyond this level additional increases will accelerFatingly have interfering effects. One may further speculate that the height of the optimal level is inversely related to the defensiveness of the dominant group: the higher the defensiveness, the lower the optimal level. Presumably, the defensiveness of the dominant group would be greater the more it expects to lose as a result of gains by the subordinate group. In addition, one would expect the extent of defensiveness to be inversely related to the perceived legitimacy of the methods of pressuring for a change and the perceived justifiability of the grievances instigating the pressures. The amount of tension resulting from any pressure from the subordinate group would be a function of the extent of change that that group is attempting to induce in a given period of time. The larger the amount of change or the more frequent the number of changes pressed for in a given period of time, the more tension that one can expect.

If these speculations have merit, progress in race relations would occur when the tensions due to pressures from the subordinate group are high and the defensiveness of the dominant group is low. Reaction or revolution, if the pressures are strong enough to overwhelm the dominant group, would be the outcome when the pressures and defensiveness are both high. Neither progress nor reaction (or revolution) could be expected if tensions are low. In other words, pressure from the subordinate group is necessary to alter a relationship with which it is discontent and with which the dominant group is satisfied. Yet the more discontent the subordinate is, the greater changes it presses for, and the quicker it seeks such change, the more likely these pressures are to be perceived as threatening the interests of the dominant group and the more defensive and resistive the latter is likely to become. The defensiveness and resistance is, in turn, conducive to a sense of frustration and desperation in the group seeking a change and may propel it to employ pressure tactics that are perceived to be illegitimate and that have the effect of further alienating the already defensive dominant group.

In such circumstances the development of an escalating spiral of force and counterforce is not uncommon. Unless a neutral authority can intervene to reverse the upward spiral of violence, it will continue until one side exhausts, vanquishes, or persuades the other or until the costs of the escalating hostilities become intolerable to both sides. Although the usual response to violence is the employment of counterviolence, in some rare instances the resort to violence may be persuasive of the seriousness and intensity, and also of the legitimacy, of the grievances of the subordinate group. This is most likely when the violence is seen as an act of desperation, as irrational, and as having no chance of significantly harming or intimidating the more powerful party. Under such conditions, the violence may be regarded as an urgent cry for help and may be responded to as such, rather than as a threat. (See chapter 6 for a further discussion of the effects of threat.)

Although it is useful for certain purposes to treat the dominant white group and the subordinate black group as though each were internally homogeneous, doing so is a considerable oversimplification. It is well to recognize that the extent and types of grievances and the potential for protest vary in the different segments of the black population as a function of such factors as age, sex, locale, class, and education. Thus the young black males have more protest potential and more economic grievances than older blacks of either sex. Similarly, the extent of defensiveness varies among the white population as a function of how much each segment expects to lose from black progress or from instituting the conditions necessary to achieve such progress. While it is beyond the present purposes to analyze the white American society from this perspective, the questions that must be asked to achieve such answers include: What groups believe that they would be adversely affected by a reordering of American priorities such that a greater proportion of the national, state, and municipal budgets would be spent on improving the education, employment, housing, community services, etc. that are available to the black and other disadvantaged groups? What groups believe that they would be harmed if more blacks voted and otherwise exerted political influence? What groups feel that they would lose if blacks could enter the various occupations as freely as whites? What groups think that their mortgages and the quality of their children's education will be threatened if blacks moved into their residential areas?

If such questions were asked and adequately answered, it would be evident that different segments of the white population are defensive about different issues. The members of the so-called military-industrial complex may prefer to spend money on the development of the antiballistic missile (ABM) rather than on improving the educational and employment opportunities of blacks; yet they may not oppose the elimination of discrimination in suburban housing. The lower-middle- and working-class whites who have most of their limited savings invested in their homes may fearfully resist the entrance of blacks into their neighborhoods but may not be supporters of the ABM. The point is that pressures for racial progress need not elicit the defensiveness of the entire white population (and, in fact, can draw support from major elements of the dominant group) if the pressures are aimed at specific objectives rather than formulated in terms of a basic opposition between blacks and whites.

A third explanation for the seeming paradox of the odd concurrence of racial progress and racial tension is contained in the view that racial progress has been minimal and that the *increased racial tension is a result of lack of significant changes* at a time when the expectation of improvement is high. *The Report of the National Advisory Commission on Civil Disorders* (the so-called Kerner report, 1968), in explaining the causes of recent disorders, places its primary emphasis on the lack of significant racial progress. It states: "White racism is essentially responsible for the explosive mixture which has been accumulating in our cities since the end of World War II" (p. 203).

Although the Kerner report emphasizes the role of white prejudice and discrimination in determining the conditions that have given rise to the recent racial disorders, it is clear that other factors are also at work. Public-opinion data clearly indicate a marked and continuing decrease in racially prejudiced attitudes among the white population since 1940 (see Skolnick 1969, chapter 5, and Campbell 1971 for a summary of research on racial attitudes of whites), and certainly there has been a decrease in recent years in many forms of officially supported discrimination. Moreover, recent census data (Bureau of Labor Statistics Report #394, July 1971) indicate that there has been a substantial improvement in the real income of Negro families, even though the gap between the income of whites and blacks still remains large—black families have only 61 percent of the income of white families.

Although the objective circumstances of life for urban Negroes are on the average considerably more modest than those of white urban residents, most of the dissatisfactions that black people express in interview surveys are not directly related to their economic, educational, or occupational attainments. More than their socioeconomic status, black people are dissatisfied with their housing, with the services they receive from the city—their schools, the police, the garbage collection, the parks—and with the stores and merchants in their neighborhoods (see Campbell 1971).

These dissatisfactions are the outcome of a process that was accelerated by World War II. The war produced an unprecedented increase in opportunities for workers with little or no prior industrial experience, and this, in turn, induced a flood of northward migration by southern Negroes whose means of livelihood had been undermined by the long decline of southern agriculture. The migrating Negroes were drawn to the big, established cities of heavy industry in the north central regions and on the East and West coasts. The seeking of their own kind and the patterns of segregated housing led to their concentration in the central cities. After the Korean War, the demand for less-skilled workers in manufacturing began a sharp, continuing decline, in part due to a shift in the nature of defense spending to more sophisticated, complex, space-age weaponry, and in part due to a general shift in industry toward more-skilled, white-collar employment with a relative decline in blue-collar jobs. Connected with these industrial changes was an increasing decentralization of manufacturing activity and an associated exodus of whites to the suburbs—to the disadvantage of the old industrial centers and the Negroes who were massed in them. Deterioration of public transportation facilities and the barriers to housing for Negroes increased the Negro's isolation from the growing suburbs. At the same time, the central cities entered a period of sharp decline which was accelerated by the increasing gap between the financial resources available to them and the needs of their population for such public services as schools, police protection, garbage collection and street cleaning, welfare assistance, and the like. Thus there is reason to suppose that the quality of life for blacks in urban areas has worsened as the cities have deteriorated. This impairment of the quality of everyday life has undoubtedly increased the sense of dissatisfaction among blacks, despite the improvement in their educational status and income.

What can be done? The diagnosis is clear. The legacy of centuries of slavery and decades of prejudice and discrimination have left large segments of the black population with handicaps and deficits for playing the American success game. As Coleman (1969) has pointed out, the Afro-Americans have relative deficits in freedom, economic power, political power, community cohesion, and family cohesion and in such personal resources as education, health, and self-esteem. Their comparative deficiency in these important resources means that they have an impaired ability as a group, and as individuals, to obtain their fair share of the goods and goodies of the American way of life. Even if racial prejudice and discrimination were to be suddenly wiped out, they would still be at a relative disadvantage. But, alas, the racial barriers are still high in many areas of American life and are not likely to disappear immediately. The problem is, thus, two-headed: the resources of the black people have to be increased, and the racial barriers have to be eliminated.

Discrimination and prejudice against blacks as blacks are not the only barriers to be removed. Blacks are now often discriminated against because they are "poor risks." And, in fact, they are more likely to be lower class, uneducated, ill, unstable, criminal, and otherwise "socially undesirable" in terms of middle-class standards than are whites. As a consequence, blacks are apt to be poorer risks as employees, tenants, borrowers, students, and law-abiding citizens. Employers, landlords, banks, stores, teachers, and the police—even if they are color-blind and acting solely in terms of economic self-interest—are inclined to discriminate against those they consider to be poor risks. Not to do so would place them at a competitive disadvantage. Moreover, others who are affected by the decisions—such as other employees, other tenants, and share owners—are likely to protest if the risks are taken, since they are predisposed to feel that they would be adversely affected. In addition, the American myth of equal opportunity provides a rationale for discriminating against those who are poor risks. In this land of "equal opportunity," poverty must be due to the deficient character and motivation of those who are poor. Thus self-interest, social pressure, and ideology combine to perpetuate the victimization of those who are poor risks.

Even if a white with a keen sense of injustice were able to perceive the "self-fulfilling prophecy" in discriminating against poor risks, he might nevertheless consider it a futile, hopeless gesture to disregard the common beliefs about the greater riskiness of transactions with blacks. Doing so would not make a significant impact upon the situation of the blacks unless many other whites were also engaged in similar actions. Moreover, an instance of failure—a housing development "tipping" so that it becomes all black, loans not being repaid, etc.—would make his action demonstrate to others that nondiscrimination is unwise.

It has long been recognized that without governmental action to pass and enforce laws to prohibit racial discrimination, the unbiased landlord or employer would find it difficult to survive unless he conformed to the practices of his business rivals and also discriminated. More recently, it has also begun to be recognized that if there is discrimination against the poor (as in the zoning regulations of many suburbs or the inadequately supported schools in poor districts) or against those who are poor risks (as in the case of inadequately prepared high school graduates seeking admission to college), then many blacks will remain disadvantaged despite strict enforcement of laws prohibiting racial discrimination.

This insidious form of color-blind racism is unlikely to disappear quickly. Its early demise would require governmental enforcement of racial quota systems in all areas of community life. It is obvious that there would be much resistance to the imposition of group quotas from those who would be displaced or disadvantaged by them and from many who feel that it would be counter to basic values in American society. Even without a quota system, much could be done to change the situation of the "poor risks" if we could achieve an expanding economy with full employment. Such an economy could find a place for even poor risks. And those who have a rewarding place are not likely to continue to be poor risks. The remedial programs for

the unskilled, the school dropout, the drug addict have often floun-
dered because an economy with considerable unemployment lacks positions even for those who are not considered to be poor risks. To succeed, such programs need a flourishing, receptive economy. However,
since much racism in the United States is not color-blind, a healthy
economy is not sufficient. There is also the need for vigorous enforcement of nondiscrimination laws to ensure that blacks as well as whites
will be actively recruited for positions at all levels. In addition, intense
effort is required to guarantee that they will not be barred from such
positions either by the lack of particularistic ties (such as those of
family, school, or neighborhood) to the controllers of such positions
or by irrelevant requirements such as credentials unrelated to job
competence.

It is evident that the pressure for improvement of the situation of
blacks will largely have to come from blacks. The problems facing a
low-power, minority group in bringing about social change are manifold. In the last section of chapter 13, the strategy and tactics available to low-power groups are discussed. Here, I wish to point out that
the power of a victimized minority to compel social change by itself is
limited. It cannot afford to be without allies. To be effective, it must
be for others as well as for itself. Being for oneself is the first responsibility of every person and every group: unless one is for oneself, others are not likely to be. However, one can define being for oneself so
that one is either for or against others. As a permanent definition of
self, the latter is inherently self-defeating for a group that needs allies.

*What generalized insights into the resolution of conflict can be
gained from the study of race relations?* After this extended discussion of interracial conflict, I turn to a consideration of some general
propositions that are suggested by our analysis of it. From the author's perspective, the basic fact about interracial conflict is that it
originated in the New World context of nearly complete opposition between the interests of the two parties involved, the white master and
the black slave. The prime shared interest was the survival of the slave
through his productive years, but some slaves were sufficiently de-
spondent about their circumstances to have little interest in survival.
Slavery was, thus, almost a pure case of competitive conflict in which
"cooperation" was coerced from the slave by the superior, indeed
overwhelming, power of the master.

Although there is considerable evidence indicating that the cooperation of slaves was minimal (Genovese 1965) and that passive resistance in such classical forms as laziness, slowness, ineptness, clumsiness, stupidity, inattentiveness, and misunderstanding was common, it is apparent that slavery and slave trading were initially profitable (Davidson 1961). Slavery's continued profitability depended upon several interrelated factors: the availability of a large supply of slaves or potential slaves so that the costs of acquiring or "growing" slaves were low; the availability of simple, profit-producing tasks, requiring neither special skills nor special equipment, that could be done by large numbers of unmotivated workers; a reasonably stable and assured market for the products of the slave labor; the ability to keep the costs of sustaining the productive slaves at a low level; the ability to keep the costs of supervision and coercion at a low level; and the lack of effective competition from well-motivated, skilled, and equipped workers producing rival products.

The large, single-crop plantations of the South were able to meet these conditions of profitability for many years but, in so doing, they gradually undermined their own economic position and the economy of the South, which they dominated politically. Slavery prevented significant technological and industrial progress; it led to agricultural methods that depleted the soil; it hampered the development of a home market for southern products; it made the South increasingly dependent upon the more industrialized and technologically advanced North; and it gave rise to an aristocratic style of life that concentrated power in the hands of relatively few large-plantation owners whose interests were antagonistic to those of the emerging industrial society (Genovese 1965).

As Genovese (1965, p. 16) points out: "Slave economics normally manifest irrational tendencies that inhibit economic development and endanger social stability." More generally, it seems reasonable to consider these propositions:

PROPOSITION 1. *Cooperation that is elicited by coercion is likely to be minimally productive and less economical as well as less reliable than cooperation that is self-chosen.*

Although there is no doubt that the powerful have often profited from the coercive exploitation of the less powerful, these gains occur only under conditions that are found less and less in complex, industrialized societies. To the extent that the required cooperation calls for skill, judgment, initiative, and a shared loyalty, it is not likely to be elicited successfully by force. On the other hand, constructing an economy that will permit the use of coerced labor produces systematic distortions in one's way of life and inefficiencies with respect to economic development that may far outweigh any immediate gains obtained from the exploitations. Genovese (1965) has made this point about the effects of slavery on the economy and society of the South. Myrdal (1944) and Clark (1967) have similarly shown how discrimination and segregation are not only a perversion of American ideals of liberty and justice but also a drag on American prosperity generally.

PROPOSITION 2. *More generally, any form of social relationship, as a function of its importance and duration, tends to influence and mold the characteristics of the participants.*

One develops attitudes toward himself, as well as toward the other, that reflect the typical interaction between oneself and the other. Whites who are used to interacting with blacks in inferior positions often think of themselves as superior to blacks. And it is not uncommon for blacks in such relationships to regard themselves as inferior. There is, of course, an asymmetry. People, in general, prefer to view themselves as superior rather than inferior. Thus people are more likely to seek explanations that will challenge a position of inferiority than they are to try to question a superior status. Hence it is not surprising that the subordinate often does not share a superior's exalted view of himself with its underlying condescension toward the subordinate. Nevertheless, when a subordinate group has little power and is very dependent upon a punitive superior, it may yield its self-esteem in order to ingratiate itself and to avoid the possibility of being brutalized for being "uppity." Not so long ago, Negro children in the South were trained by their parents to think of themselves as being inferior to whites in order to avoid trouble. A masochistic defense of this sort usually covers a great deal of rage, which is often expressed in a disguised form such as an exaggerated self-deprecation and submissiveness that subtly mocks the pretensions of those claiming superiority.

PROPOSITION 3. *Insofar as an interaction tends to develop habits, customs, institutions, attitudes, and ideologies in the interacting parties that are congruent with their positions in the interaction, there will be a tendency for the interaction to persist in its initial forms, despite objective changes in the situations of the interacting parties.*

People and groups get committed to, and invested in, the actions they have taken; the actions are rationalized and justified in the face of challenge or doubt; and the justifications are themselves supported and valued and become, in turn, the basis for further actions. We have seen how those who were exploiting the Africans developed a racist ideology to rationalize their exploitation and how this ideology served to support additional exploitation. This self-perpetuating, autistic cycle might not have persisted had it not been for the self-confirming effects of the actions taken on the basis of racist attitudes. Thus if, despite the degradation, exploitation, and discrimination to which they were exposed by whites, the blacks had been able to accumulate sufficient educational, economic, political, and community resources to become part of the "middle-class way of life"—if they had been able to achieve the upward social mobility of the European immigrant groups—it seems likely that the racist ideology, and the discrimination it justifies, would have largely faded away by now. Unfortunately, the relatively rigid color barriers, the handicaps deriving from the legacy of slavery, and the misfortune of entering the urbanized economy at a time when unskilled labor was not so much in demand —all these made middle-class respectability an elusive goal for most blacks.

In our earlier discussion of class conflict, it was pointed out that permeability of class boundaries served to discourage violence in class conflict. It is evident that the class boundaries are less permeable for blacks than for whites because of the relatively rigid color barriers to upward social mobility. As a consequence, race and class are intertwined in determining the attitudes of whites and blacks toward one another. Research (see Hyman 1969 for a summary) suggests that antipathy toward the lower class contributes substantially to prejudice against blacks and that the desired social distance from blacks decreases as the social status of blacks increases. These results suggest that if the color barrier to upward class mobility were somehow circumvented much white prejudice toward blacks would disappear. The common experience of middle-class blacks, however, is that they are not fully accepted and are repeatedly exposed to invisible barriers that constantly remind them of the existing distinctions between blacks and whites. Although it may be possible that color barriers would disappear if a sufficiently large percentage of the black population could escape from lower-class status, it is evident that the individual black person who improves his class status does not automatically find that his skin color is not a stigma. That is, the individual black cannot "make it" by himself; his group also has to "make it" before his skin color loses its stigmatizing quality.

Nor is it self-evident that, even if blacks do improve their social status, color will be eliminated as an impediment to natural, friendly social relations. So long as there is not an effective integration in neighborhoods, housing, school, work, leisure, and religion, then blacks and whites will not be able to relate to one another as individual human beings but only as members of different groups. This does not imply that integration should have priority as a goal for blacks over the accumulation of black power. It is evident that until the political, economic, community, and educational resources of the black population are increased, there can be no authentic cooperation between the two groups, and integration can only be partial and limited.

PROPOSITION 4. *The status of a subordinate ethnic, religious, or racial group is determined by the resources it has for adapting to and competing within the socioeconomic framework established by the dominant group.*

As Wagley and Harris (1958, p. 272) have suggested, ". . . minority groups with the greater measure of cultural preparedness have been the ones least subject to extreme forms of hostility and exploitation." The African slaves, who were stripped of their cultural, community, and family resources, were the most severely handicapped of all groups coming to the New World and were, as a consequence, the least able to resist the exploitation of the dominant group.

Racism was a particularly pernicious ideology because it assumed an inherent, irreversible difference in the value of different groups of human beings. It made it difficult for the dominant white group to recognize the legitimacy of organized black groups acting on behalf of the black population and mediating black grievances. This, in turn, has hampered the development of institutions and procedures for regulating interracial conflict and has reduced the possibilities of peaceful political bargaining between the conflicting racial groups.

PROPOSITION 5. *The claim to inherent superiority (whether it be of legitimacy, morality, authority, ability, knowledge, or relevance) by one or another side in a conflict makes it less likely that a conflict will be resolved cooperatively.*

If the "superiority" is mutually recognized, it need not be claimed; if it is not, the claim increases the scope of the issues in dispute. The mystique of superiority associated with various positions—"white," "employer," "faculty member," "president," "adult," "male," "under thirty"—is being questioned; the claim to inherent superiority is being rejected; and demonstrations of trustworthiness and competence are increasingly being called for instead.

6. Threats, Promises, and Influence

In chapters 9 and 10, a series of experiments are reported that indicate some of the harmful consequences of making threats. It would be a mistake, however, to conclude from these experiments, or from the ideas underlying them, that threat always or inevitably leads to a reaction of hostility and counterthreat. These experiments involved threats that were likely to be interpreted as making illegitimate claims and that would, as a consequence, be apt to induce or enhance competition between the threatened and the threatener. Although threat, as a form of social influence, is particularly susceptible to the interpretation of ill-intent upon the part of the threatener, a negative reaction to being threatened is by no means inescapable. It is the purpose of this essay to place threat in a broader perspective than the prevailing experimentation has done so far; in so doing, we shall compare promises and threats as forms of social influence.

Below is a list of the major characteristics of threats or promises; these are likely to affect the behavioral and attitudinal response of the person being subjected to the attempted influence. Similar characteristics play a role in determining whether a given method of influence, whether it be a promise or a threat, will be used. However, it is evident that the influencer and the influenced may perceive matters differently.

1. Legitimacy
2. Credibility
3. Magnitude
4. Kinds of values appealed to
5. Targets
6. Time perspective
7. Clarity and precision of the contingencies involved
8. Style
9. Costs and benefits to user

1. Legitimacy

Under what conditions is a person likely to agree that another has the right to threaten him in order to *compel* him to do something or *deter* him from doing something? [1] Is he more likely to feel that the other's influence attempt is legitimate if the other *encourages* him to do what the other wants or *deflects* him from doing what the other dislikes by a promise of reward rather than by a threat of harm? [2] Let us answer the second question first. Promises are more apt to be perceived as being legitimate than threats, since promises, more than threats, allow the decision about whether or not to act in a certain way to seem more under the voluntary control of the individual. Promises are less of an infringement upon one's freedom because a reward can rarely be inflicted without one's consent. One can refuse a reward, but one can be harmed despite one's opposition. In fact, a threat implies that the other will injure you despite your unwillingness. Thus threats are more likely than promises to be viewed as an infringement upon one's rights to autonomy and independence.

While it seems probable that freedom and autonomy are valued by individuals in most societies and in most relationships, it is not unknown for individuals in certain roles to view those things as inappropriate for themselves to have any voluntary control over. Under such circumstances, promises may be viewed as less proper than threats. Threat, then, may be perceived as being legitimate when the threatened individual makes no claim to the rights of free choice and self-determination. Similarly, threats from another may be viewed as legitimate if one grants the other superior rights with regard to setting the terms of the relationship between oneself and the other. Thus threats from a superior to a subordinate would not seem unsuitable in role relationships characterized by unquestioning obedience as a key value

---

1. "Compellance," which is aimed at eliciting something from the other, takes the form of "If you don't do X (which I desire) then I shall do—or continue to do—Y, which harms you"; while "deterrence," which is aimed at discouraging the other from doing something, takes the form of "If you do Z (which I dislike), I shall do —or continue to do—Y, which you dislike."

2. "Encouragement," which is like compellance in that it is aimed at eliciting something from the other, takes the form of "If you do X which I desire then I shall do Y, which benefits you." "Deflection" often takes the form of suggesting an alternative as well as encouraging an inhibition: "If you don't do Z (which I dislike) but do X instead (which does not bother me), I shall do Y which benefits you."

governing the subordinate's behavior. The reference here is to such relationships as father-child in an authoritarian family, master-slave in a traditional society, and captain-private in an old-fashioned army. On the other hand, when the other's superior rights are not acknowledged, his threats are not likely to be considered as legitimate forms of influence.

Threats may not be considered inappropriate if they are directed at deterring action that the actor acknowledges he has no right to perform. It is well to recognize, however, that most people are inclined to view their own actions as legitimate and well intentioned; hence they are not predisposed to respond favorably to behavior by the other which signifies that they have no right to do what they are doing. Nevertheless, there are situations in which (1) people are tempted to engage in actions that they consider illegitimate, and (2) people do things about which they feel ashamed or guilty. In such circumstances, a threat to deter such action or punishment as a response to such action—if appropriate in kind and magnitude—is likely to be considered legitimate. Promises and rewards, on the other hand, are likely to be considered inappropriate.

As Kelley (1965) has suggested, the perceived legitimacy of a threat may also be influenced by the legitimacy of the needs that are thought to give rise to it. A mother who threatens to harm anyone who disturbs the sleep of her critically ill child is more likely to be respected and obeyed than a woman who threatens to harm anyone who makes noise in the vicinity of her home. Just as superior status may legitimate superior rights and claims, so, too, may superior needs or even more intense needs. Thus the threats of a starving man, made to assert a claim for priority, will be viewed as more legitimate and acceptable than those of someone who merely has a good appetite. Under certain circumstances, a threat that is bizarre and seemingly inappropriate will be taken as a sign of desperate need and will be responded to sympathetically rather than antagonistically.

I have indicated that threats, compared with promises, are more likely to be considered illegitimate forms of influence, but when superior status or need justifies superior rights or claims, threats may become acceptable. The reactions to an influence attempt that is perceived to be illegitimate are likely to be negative. One may expect resistance to the influence attempt, rejection and refutation of the superior claims being made by the other, stronger assertion of one's own claims, and the development of negative attitudes toward the threatener.

Recent research by several students, as well as the studies described in chapters 9 and 10 (Hover, Garner, Kaplan, and Deutsch, in manuscript), is relevant to the foregoing assertions about illegitimate threat. Subjects were given four statements, each of which had presumably been made by a different person in the course of bargaining in a laboratory experiment. The four statements varied in terms of type of threat (norm-sanctioned, need, deterrent, and nonrationalized), in the magnitude of demand made upon the other (1, 3, or 5 points), and the duration of the consequences of the threat (for three trials or for the rest of the game). The different types of statements follow.

Norm-sanctioned. "Even though my independent values have been relatively high, I have consistently cooperated with you so that we can both get the most points. Because you took your independent value on the last trial, I got no points, and you have thus caused me to lose money. Unless you agree to give me (1, 3, or 5) more points than you get on the next three trials, which will (make up for what you caused me to lose), I will take my independent value (for three trials in a row or for the rest of the game)."

Need. "So far, we've been splitting the contract values evenly. However, I've been having a rough time financially, and it's really important that I earn quite a bit of money today. I'd really appreciate it if you would give me (1, 3, or 5) more points than you get on the next three trials. If you don't agree, I'll have to take my independent value (for three trials or for the rest of the game)."

Deterrent. "So far, we've been splitting the contract as evenly as possible. I think we should continue to cooperate and warn you ahead of time that if you fail to cooperate in the future, I will demand (1, 3, or 5) more points than you for three trials in a row. If you don't meet this demand, I will take my independent value (for three trials in a row or for the rest of the game)."

Nonrationalized. "So far, we've been splitting the contract values evenly. But I'm not satisfied with the amount that I'm earning. I've decided that unless you agree to give me (1, 3, or 5) more points than you get on each of the next three trials, I am going to take my independent values (for three trials in a row or for the rest of the game)."

The subjects were asked to predict how the person being threatened would rate the threatening action on such attributes as illegitimate-legitimate, good-bad, fair-unfair, ineffective-effective, reasonable-unreasonable, weak-strong, intelligent-stupid, just-unjust. The results indicate that none of the types of threats was viewed with any favor. The norm-sanctioned and need threats, however, were viewed with considerably less disfavor than the deterrent or nonrationalized threats, the latter being viewed with the most disfavor. The nonrationalized threat was not only viewed as most illegitimate but also as most bad, unfair, unreasonable, unjust, stupid, and ineffective; the norm-sanctioned threat was viewed as having the least of the foregoing characteristics and also as being the strongest. Generally, the longer the consequence of a threat endured (rest of the game rather than the next 3 trials), the less favorably was the threat viewed.

The subjects were also asked to predict how the person being threatened would feel about the threatener as a person. The threateners who employed nonrationalized or deterrent threats were viewed with more annoyance, coldness, unfriendliness, distrust, sadness, and lack of sympathy than those who used norm-sanctioned threats or ones based upon need. The most negative responses were to the threatener who did not rationalize his threat, while the least negative responses went to the threatener who based his threats upon need. The subjects thought compliance would be least to the nonrationalized and most to the norm-sanctioned threats. Little difference in compliance was expected to the deterrent and need threats. The larger the demand of points made by the threatener, the less compliant the threatened person was anticipated to be.

The research cited above supports the view that threats that are considered illegitimate are likely to produce rather negative reactions. It also suggests that even legitimate threats or threats based upon need are not viewed with favor or warmth. They are more palatable than illegitimate or deterrent threats, but they evoke no enthusiasm. Other research bears upon my assertion that promises will be more favorably regarded than threats.

Deutsch and Solomon (1959) and Deutsch (1960c, 1961) report strong evidence for a "positivity effect" such that praise is more commonly responded to favorably than is criticism—by observers as well as by those receiving one or the other. More recently, Cheney, Harford, and Solomon (1971), in a study employing a modified version of the Deutsch-Krauss trucking game, which is described in chapter 9, have demonstrated that the opportunity to send "positive messages" (e.g., "I'll let you use the road first this time, then you let me go through first next time") induces more cooperation than the opportunity to send "negative messages" (e.g., "If you don't let me use the one-lane road first this time, I will lower my gate and won't cooperate with you next time").

Heilman (1972), in a recently completed dissertation, directly compared responses to threats and promises and the reactions to threateners and promisers. She found that threats, in contrast to promises, were considered to be more inappropriate, more unfair, more bossy, and more fit for a child. Promisers, as compared with threateners, were thought to be wiser, more reasonable, more considerate, more easy-going, more gentle, more likable, less nasty, more friendly, and more trustworthy. Also, in a study that investigated reactions to eight different statements expressing an influence attempt, four of which employed threats of punishment for noncompliance and four of which promised a reward for compliance, Lewicki and Rubin (1971) found that promises were responded to much more favorably than threats. They compared such promises as "If you agree to work on my topic, I will write up the final report with "If you insist on working on your topic, you will have to write up the final report." Not only were promises viewed more favorably than threats, they were also rated as more likely to gain compliance and more likely to be employed, and their transmitters were liked more and seen as friendlier. Thus the evidence consistently indicates that threats are much more likely to be viewed negatively than are promises.

2. Credibility

It is obvious that you are bound to take more seriously a threat or promise that you think will be carried out than one whose implementation you doubt. In the discussion of trust in chapter 7, we shall consider in detail many of the factors that determine one's confidence in the trustworthiness of another's actions. That discussion is directly applicable to the credibility of a threat or promise. Thus a threat or a promise made by another will be credible as a function of the perceived strength and reliability of the other's desire to influence you (his determination), the perceived capability of the other to implement his threat or promise at an acceptable level of cost to himself (his power), his perceived commitment to implement it, and its appropriateness to what is being desired from you. Compare how much more credible a threat or a promise is when it is associated with a communication such as "I *very much* want you to do this" than "I don't care very much if you do this." Similarly, a threat or a promise that is in the other's power to implement is more apt to be viewed as genuine than one that is not. Further, a threat or a promise that is not excessively difficult, painful, or costly to carry out is inherently more believable than one that is burdensome, dangerous, expensive, or complicated to execute. Also, the commitment of honor, reputation, deposits, hostages, or the like to implementing a threat or a promise provides increased assurance that it will be implemented. In addition, a promise or a threat that is clearly inappropriate in magnitude or kind is less believable than an appropriate one because social restraints are more likely to inhibit the implementation of an inappropriate influence procedure.

Although a reputation of determination, power, and commitment enhance the credibility of threats and promises alike, the images of the "credible threatener" and the "credible promiser" are not likely to be identical. Heilman's previously cited dissertation is relevant. In her study, she compared the impressions that subjects formed of four types: threateners who carried out their threats; threateners who did not carry them out; promisers who fulfilled their promises; and promisers who did not fulfill them. Her results indicate that a threatener who fulfills his threat is evaluated with about the same degree of antipathy after making his threat as after carrying it out; a threatener who does not implement his threat is, as a result of his failure to do so, less negatively evaluated than he was immediately after making his threat. On the other hand, a promiser who does not fulfill his promise loses whatever positive regard he had and comes to be viewed as negatively as a threatener who implements his threat. A promiser who fulfills his promise remains very favorably evaluated. However, it is evident that a threatener who does not fulfill his threats loses a good deal of his credibility as a threatener; and similarly, a promiser who welshes loses almost all his credibility as a promiser: the nonfulfilling promiser loses more credibility as a promiser than the nonfulfilling threatener does as a threatener. It is interesting to note, though, that the welshing promiser has fairly high credibility as a subsequent threatener—almost as much credibility as the promiser who carries out his promise. On the other hand, the threatener, whether he implements his threat or not, has relatively little believability when he subsequently makes a promise. Thus a promiser who carries out his promises develops a reputation that makes credible his subsequent threats as well as his promises; in contrast, a threatener who implements his threats develops a reputation that makes credible his future threats but not his future promises.

3. Magnitude

As the magnitude of the threatened harm or promised reward increases, several different effects are possible. So long as it is perceived as credible and legitimate, a stronger rather than a weaker threat or promise could be expected to have greater influence on the behavior of the person being influenced. However, as dissonance theory would suggest and as research by Aronson and Carlsmith (1963) has demonstrated, when the external forces inducing behavior are more than the minimum required, the person being influenced is not as apt to develop the attitudes that will sustain the behavior after the external forces have been removed. A child who inhibits his desire to play with a desirable toy because of a mild threat is more likely to come to think of the toy as less desirable than a child who has been severely threatened.

Although the research has not yet been done, it seems probable that the credibility of a threat or a promise will decrease as its magnitude increases—particularly, if a threat or a promise of lesser magnitude is seen to be more than enough. The decrease in credibility is most apt to occur when the perceived difficulty or cost of implementing the more intense promise or threat increases more rapidly for the influencer than does the value of the promise or threat for the person who is the object of the influence. Thus the threats by the United States to increase the bombing of North Vietnam if the latter increased its rate of infiltration into South Vietnam may not have been credible to the North Vietnamese. They may have held the view that the perceived costs to the Americans (in terms of American pilots and planes lost and also in negative world opinion) of increasing the bombing would be greater than the expected gains. Similarly, if one is promised a costly reward, particularly if a less costly one would be an adequate incentive, doubt is thrown on the promise.

Not only does their credibility come into question as the magnitude of threats and promises increase but there is also a decrease in the marginal utility of the increases. The threat of being lashed twice is considerably greater than that of being lashed once, but the difference between twenty and nineteen lashes is small psychologically. Similarly, a reward of $2.00 is more different, perceptually, from a reward of $1.00 than $20.00 is from $19.00. Thus there is decreasing gain from increasing the magnitude of threats, and if there are increasing costs for so doing, then the incentive to resist a threat may increase as it gets stronger. That is, if I am convinced that it is really going to hurt you more than me if you carry out your overblown threat, I may attempt to provoke you to do so.

Threats or promises that are disproportionate in magnitude may be viewed as illegitimate or inappropriate even if credible. Thus if you are threatened with a fine of $100.00 rather than $1.00 for jaywalking, you may become indignant and defiant toward the punitive authority, whereas a smaller fine of $1.00 may be viewed as reasonable and elicit your willing compliance. Similarly, a promise of a disproportionate reward for compliant behavior may connote that the requested behavior is shady or disreputable and that you are being bribed rather than rewarded. In other words, the magnitude of a threat or a promise has expressive as well as instrumental significance. It communicates not only the economic consequences of complying or not but also something about the credibility of the communicator and the legitimacy of his attempted influence.

4. *Kinds of Values Appealed To*

Threats imply an attempt to reduce one's valued resources, while promises imply a readiness to augment them. Among the different types of valued resources that are the object of threats or promises are: affection, esteem, social status, coercive power, physical well-being, services, knowledge, material goods, and money. Many social science theories, particularly the social exchange ones, assume that distinctions in the types or kinds of resources can be safely ignored: namely, that a promise of health and a promise of wealth can be put on the same scale. This assumption is based upon the hope that each of the different resources can be expressed in terms of, or converted into, a common currency. This view supposes, for example, that a given quantity of affection is equal to a certain number of "utiles," which may, in turn, be equivalent to a specified amount of money. It also assumes that the existence of a common currency underlying different resources permits the ready exchange of different kinds of values.

The assumption that there is a ready exchange between all values seems dubious. If I do a favor for a friend and, in so doing, express my affection for him, I will be insulted if he offers me money in return. On the other hand, if I am in an economic transaction in which I put my house up for rent, I shall be rather annoyed if I am offered affection rather than money in exchange. While goods or services may be interchangeable with money, affection and money can rarely be used in exchange for one another. This is not to deny that by being affectionate toward your rich uncle he may become disposed to include you in his will. But this is not so likely if he thinks your affection was for his money rather than for him.

There has, as yet, been little research or theorizing which would specify how much exchangeability there is among the different types of resources in different kinds of social situations. Such research would help specify how compatible or incompatible a given type of request is with a given type of promise and would help, similarly, for a given type of demand and a given type of threat. Consider the childish promise "I'll give you my toy if you let me be your friend" or the childish threat "I won't love you if you don't buy me an ice cream." Perhaps these are considered childish because the child equates values (material goods and affection) that the adult distinguishes qualitatively or perhaps it is the discrepancy in magnitude between the demand (ice cream) and the threat (loss of love).

In any case, just as the disproportion in magnitude between what is being demanded or requested and the threat or promise may make the influence attempt seem incredible or illegitimate, so may differences in kind or quality. This probably happens when the resources are perceived to fall on different sides of the personal—impersonal and moral—immoral dichotomies than those being requested or demanded. One might also expect a negative response to a promise or a threat if it changes the arena of interaction from that involved in the request or demand. Thus if you are asked to do something for someone that implies a personal relationship between the two of you and he promises you something in return that has a very impersonal character (i.e., something that could be given to anyone, not something particularly related to you), your reaction is likely to be negative. Similarly, if someone asks you to do something that you believe is moral and you are promised something in return that is immoral to receive and that thereby implies that your behavior would be immoral, you are likely to reject the offer. Also, if someone wanting to prevent you from playing your radio too loudly threatens to throw mud on your window, you may become more perverse rather than compliant. Or if your wife threatens that she will not sleep with you unless you help with the dishes, she is enlarging the arena of conflict and, thereby, probably provoking a negative response.

In sum, the quality and the quantity of rewards and promises determine their effects. Despite the assumptions of social exchange theories, there is no evidence of a sufficiently inclusive market that would enable different qualities to be converted into a common currency and to be exchanged in terms of their values in this currency. It is, thus, important to know what and how to promise or threaten as well as "how much."

5. Targets

While it is obvious that a promise or a threat that is meant to influence a given decision should be formulated so as to influence those who have the power to determine the decision, it does not follow that it is always most effective to aim the harm or benefit directly at the decision maker. Thus a threat or a promise that is meant to influence you may be stated as a potential harm or benefit to a third party. Someone may threaten that your child will be harmed physically unless you do what is desired, or you may be promised that your son will be accepted as a student in a certain school if you contribute to its scholarship fund. Does it make any difference whether the target of influence is you or a third party? And how would your relationship to the third party be likely to affect your reaction?

Let us first consider these questions in relation to threat. It seems likely that if someone threatens to harm an innocent third party in order to get you to do something, you will be likely to view the threat as even less legitimate than a threat aimed at you directly. As a consequence of its lesser legitimacy, such a threat will have less credibility if one thinks that the threatener is unwilling to accept the loss of public reputation. On the other hand, if you think that the threatener is not bothered by questions of legitimacy and is willing to be viewed as an outlaw, such a threat may have enhanced credibility compared to a threat aimed directly at you. You may feel highly confident of your ability to defend yourself against the threatener, but you may feel that it will be much more difficult to defend members of your family or other innocent third parties from him without excessive cost. The nature of your relationship to the third party is obviously not insignificant in determining your reaction. The more important his welfare is to you and the more responsibility you have for assuring his welfare, the more vulnerable you will be to a threat directed against him.

The urban guerrillas in Latin America have effectively employed well-publicized threats against foreign diplomats to coerce their own governments. This, however, has often legitimated and aroused popular support for increased repressive action by the governments as a response to the tactics of the guerrillas. Thus it seems unlikely that such factors will in the long run promote the cause of the urban revolutionaries. Mafia members are also reputed to use threats against the families of potential witnesses as a means of persuasively silencing the witnesses. The reputation of determined ruthlessness makes the Mafia threats credible. The covertness of their action and the reluctance of the authorities to use repressive methods against them (since, unlike the urban guerrillas, they are not perceived as a threat to the state) enable the Mafia to "get away" with such tactics.

Promises to benefit third parties are likely to be more effective than promises to benefit you primarily when you cannot or should not receive the benefit or when the benefit would be valueless to you but of considerable significance to someone you like. Otherwise, it would seem that promises of direct personal benefit are likely to be more credible because their fulfillment or nonfulfillment can be checked directly. To illustrate, suppose someone promises to help you obtain a good apartment if you help him become a member of an exclusive club to which you belong. This may mean little to you since you already have a fine apartment. However, if the promise involved helping your aunt, who needs an apartment, it might influence you more. Suppose, on the other hand, that you need an apartment as well as your aunt and suppose that you have no preference about which of you should get the apartment. Under such circumstances, it would be less credible for the apartment to be promised as a benefit to her unless you were to make the decision that it is to be hers. If she is to benefit, you should bestow it, and the attempt to evade your part in the transmission of the benefit lessens its credibility.

6. Time Perspective

There are two aspects of time perspective that we will consider: at what point in time does the threat or promise get initiated, and how long do the consequences endure. It seems safe to assert that, for most people, consequences that are remote in time are less potent influences on their behavior than those that will occur in the near future. If promised benefits or threatened harms are expected to follow the present quickly, they are more likely to influence present behavior.

A threat or a promise can have a clearly limited duration in time or it can be indefinite and open-ended. If you threaten someone with "I won't speak to you unless you . . . ," there is no clear termination point to your silence if your threat fails. Boycotts, embargoes, and diplomatic nonrecognition also have no clear ending place once they are initiated. Out of inertia, they often persist past the time when it is evident that they are not achieving their objectives. Frequently, with regard to a limited, specific demand, a threat with time-limited consequences is more useful. Not only is it likely to be more palatable, but, in case it does not succeed, you are forced to reconsider how else you might achieve your objective, and thus you are prevented from trapping yourself in a deadlock out of sheer inertia.

Similarly, an open-ended promise ("If you pass the test, I'll let you use my car") without a qualifying adverb (such as "tonight") makes it difficult to withdraw the benefit without causing a grievance. It also makes it difficult to use the benefit as an incentive again.

7. Clarity and Precision of the Contingencies Involved

Your chances of influencing another to do what you want are considerably enhanced if the other clearly knows what you want him to do. Too often, particularly in situations of conflict, there is a tendency to express our attitudes toward the other or to state our own objectives rather than to indicate what we specifically want the other to do. The United States government, for example, has a negative attitude toward Castro's Cuban government, but there is little evidence to indicate that we have ever precisely formulated what it is that Castro's government could reasonably do to end our negative sanctions against it. As Fisher (1969) has pointed out, giving the other a "yessable proposition"—a proposal that unambiguously designates the action requested from him—focuses the other's decision on the specific behavior that is desired. To promise a child a reward if he is good, or to threaten him with punishment if he is bad, may give him little clue about what you want him to do. It may not be self-evident how to be good or how to avoid being bad.

One may argue that the ambiguity of what is expected from him may compel the child to be good or to avoid being bad in many ways. While this is a possibility, it also seems likely that his way may not be what you had in mind. If you then do not carry out your promise or remove your threat, the child's doubts about your credibility will be increased. Generally, one would expect that the effectiveness of threats or promises will be decreased if they are connected to vague, unclear proposals. Their credibility and legitimacy are impaired because the conditions under which they should be implemented are not adequately specified. Also, the attempt to comply with a vague proposal becomes more costly. Being good in every way that I can think of in order to have some chance of being good in the way that *you* are thinking of is likely to involve much more effort than doing something that is clearly defined as what you want, more effort than I may be willing to expend.

Even if you have clearly formulated what you want the other to do, you may be indefinite about the rewards to be given for his acquiescence or the costs to be inflicted for his noncompliance. Vagueness may be about the likelihood, magnitude, onset, duration, or target of the benefits or harms. On the face of it, ambiguity is only apt to be of sustained advantage when it leads to an overestimation of the potential costs of noncompliance. However, exaggeration of the expected benefits of agreeing may lead to resentment and accusations of bad faith when the actual rewards are received. On the other hand, if overestimation of a threat leads to compliance, the fact that the threat was misperceived may go undetected. However, if the threat has to be implemented because of noncompliance, it will look rather puny in comparison with what had been expected. As a result, the threatener will lose credibility despite his implementation of his threat.

Since vagueness in one's promises or threats is only of advantage when one has little power to deliver actual benefits or harms, it is likely that ambiguity in such matters creates the impression that one has little power or intent to deliver. After all, if one really has the determination and ability to benefit or harm the other sufficiently to motivate his compliance, why would one want to be vague about this?

8. Style

"Style" refers to the way in which something is said or done, as distinguished from its substance. The style of a threat or promise may markedly affect its interpretation in all its aspects, especially its legitimacy and credibility. A promise may be communicated in a manner that connotes that it is a bribe rather than a natural benefit; a threat may be expressed in a way that suggests blackmail rather than the appropriate, harmful consequences for defiant behavior. A hesitant and non-confident style may lead the other to doubt one's intentions or capabilities.

It is useful to recognize that the style of one's behavior is initially interpreted by the other in terms of his normative expectations, which are derived from his own personal and cultural background. Little difficulty due to misunderstandings of style may result when one is communicating with someone of a similar background. However, a woman who promises her date that she will be ready "in a minute" may be communicating in a style that is not meant to be taken literally. If her date is expecting a factual, precise communication, he will be misled. A man who tries to express his determination to carry out his threatened action by repeatedly jabbing his index finger at the other may communicate an unacceptable insult to someone who defines the immediate space surrounding him as very intimate and personal.

The style, as well as the substance, of a communication carries messages. Sometimes the messages disagree with one another. A mother who threatens her child with punishment if he disturbs his sleeping father may, by her manner, imply that that is precisely what she wants the child to do. An official who advocates "law and order" may contradict the meaning of his verbal statement by its belligerent, vigilant tone, which suggests a willingness to employ illegal methods against suspected criminals. Someone who proclaims his love for mankind may belie his words by labeling other humans "pigs." It seems reasonable to assume that when the substance and the style of a communication carry contradictory messages, the credibility of the substance will be impaired.

9. Costs and Benefits to the User

A major distinction between promises and threats is that their conditions of implementation differ. To maintain one's credibility, threats must be implemented when they fail rather than succeed in influencing the other; promises, on the other hand, must be carried out when they succeed rather than fail.

To implement a threat after it has failed to produce the desired effect, however, may have many disadvantages. One can generally assume that the costs of carrying out a threat will be more than those involved in making one. As Gumpert's experiment (see chapter 10) has demonstrated, this differential between the present cost of making a threat and the future cost of implementing it can seduce bargainers to start on the path that leads from threat to punitive action. Because of the ease of making a threat, the full costs of carrying it out may be underestimated.

In addition to the underestimation of the direct physical, economic, social, and psychological expenses of implementing a threat, there are other subtle, indirect disadvantages which are often not contemplated before a threat is made. These include the reality that the actions involved in implementing a threat are usually not the kinds of actions one would want to take were it not for the need to maintain one's credibility. As Fisher (1969, p. 38) has pointed out: ". . . since it is generally regarded as immoral to inflict pain simply to prove that you are willing and able to inflict it, we endanger our reputation and self-esteem. This immorality is so compelling that we always advance some other justification for an action threat: we refer to it as an interdiction, or retaliation, or even self-defense. Deliberate pain whose only justification is to extort a decision too closely resembles torture." The gap between the justification and the punitive actions undertaken to maintain the credibility of one's threatening power may create a "credibility gap" of its own in terms of one's judgment and morality.

There are other subtle costs of implementing a threat. The intended victim may not submit himself to it; he may resist and engage in counterpunitive action. If he does, the costs of carrying out one's original threat may multiply, and an escalating competition in punitive action may develop. The mounting costs of making one's future threats credible by implementing a past threat that has not been effective may, paradoxically, have the opposite effect from that intended. One's mounting costs of implementation may persuade the other that you have learned that it is too costly to repeat such a mistake. As Fisher (1969, p. 46) has suggested: "Looking at the difficulties in which the United States has found itself in Vietnam, would-be aggressors might conclude that the United States would be most reluctant to repeat such an experience and that they could now act with reduced fear of United States intervention."

Just as it does not automatically follow that one's credibility as a threatener will be enhanced by engaging in punitive action when one's threat has been unpersuasive, it also does not necessarily follow that the failure to take punitive, retaliatory action will suggest to the other that one will be soft the next time. He may think that having backed down once, you cannot afford to do so again. This was a lesson that Hitler failed to learn: namely, that the English-French capitulation in Munich would make further capitulation by them more rather than less difficult.

In general, the fulfillment of one's promise to another is less fraught with dangers than the implementation of a threat because reward is more likely to elicit positive attitudes and responses than punishment. However, if one's promises have been exorbitant, the costs of carrying them out may be clearly disproportionate to the gains obtained from the other's behavior. The fulfillment of foolish promises may simultaneously enhance one's reputation for both foolishness and honesty. Moreover, a promise that is honored reluctantly or begrudgingly because of its costs is less likely to elicit positive attitudes and responses than a reward that is bestowed enthusiastically.

THREATS AND PROMISES IN COMPARISON WITH OTHER FORMS OF INFLUENCE

Promises and threats are forms of social influence that attempt to affect another's behavior by altering the perceived gains and costs of his alternative courses of action through linking an externally imposed reward or punishment to his relevant alternatives. The use of promises and threats is often based upon the assumption that the other's own motivations are insufficient or not consonant with one's desires and that, hence, the other must be externally motivated to comply with one's wishes. In our discussion of threats, we have seen that the attempt to control the other through threat of punishment is likely to be resisted, especially when the other feels that it is demeaning to allow himself to be intimidated. Similarly, being rewarded may seem as demeaning as being punished if the rewarded behavior does not seem to be a freely chosen exchange for the reward.

There are other ways of attempting to influence another's behavior than the employment of externally imposed, positive or negative incentives. Essentially, these other ways either attempt to influence the other's subjective probability that a given course of action will lead to a given consequence, or they attempt to alter the other's appraisal or evaluation of the consequences that are expected to follow from the different courses of action.

Let us first consider affecting the other's subjective probabilities. There are a number of reasons why another might not do something that you want him to do, even though he might not be opposed to doing so: (1) it simply has never occurred to him to do it, i.e., the course of action does not exist psychologically for him; (2) he is aware of the possibility but does not know how to do it; (3) he knows what should be done but feels unable to do it successfully; or (4) he believes that the environmental obstacles are sufficient to prevent success. One can influence the other in such circumstances by (1) making him more aware of the behavioral possibility that was ignored or unsalient; (2) helping him learn to do it; (3) helping him build his skill and confidence through practice on tasks that start at a level within his skill range and gradually become more difficult; (4) helping remove some of the obstacles or persuading him that they are less difficult than he anticipates. Clearly, there are many ways of making a course of action seem more salient and more feasible and, thus, of encouraging the other to go ahead with it. All this can be done without increasing the other's external incentives. In an analogous way, one can make a given choice by another less likely if one (1) decreases its visibility and salience; (2) decreases the other's confidence about his relevant knowledge and skill; or (3) increases the external obstacles and enhances their visibility. There are, thus, many ways of discouraging a given behavior without threatening an arbitrary imposition of externally imposed costs or punishments.

Promises and threats influence behavior by altering the expected consequence of alternative actions via connecting them to arbitrary, externally imposed costs and gains. The expected consequences of action can be modified in other ways. For example, one can persuade the other that additional values, different from the ones initially considered, will be affected by the action. Thus opponents of the supersonic transport plane linked the plane to a possible increase in skin cancer as well as to faulty economic priorities. Advertisers traditionally try to associate their products with such positive values as sex appeal, popularity, and social status, even when the connection between these values and the make of one's car or soap may objectively seem remote.

It is evident that the power to reward or coerce is not the only type of power that can be used to influence another. As we pointed out in chapter 4, influence can derive also from expert power, ecological power, normative power, or referent power. Each of these types can affect the other's subjective probabilities or the other's evaluation of the consequences that are expected to follow from the different courses of action. The advantage of coercive power and ecological power over the other forms is that they can be applied without the consent of those being affected by them. The disadvantage of doing this is that power applied without one's consent is apt to be experienced as a violation of one's rights, especially the rights to autonomy and self-respect. To such use of power, one can expect a reaction of open resistance and anger from the strong and of inauthentic cooperation and resentment from the weak.

7. Trust and Suspicion: Theoretical Notes

As early as 600 B.C., Theognis in the *Sententiae* expressed a conviction that two of the concepts with which we shall be concerned in this text, trust and mistrust, are functionally interrelated. He wrote: "He who mistrusts most should be trusted least." John Florio in 1575 advanced a more detailed statement of the conditions of distrust. His *Firste Fruites* contained the admonition "Trust not to much foure things, that is, A strange dogge, an unknown horse, a talkative woman and the deepest place of a river." Shakespeare's list of the conditions for distrust in *King Lear* is similar to that of Florio. He warns, "He's mad that trusts in the tameness of a wolf, a horse's health, a boy's love, or a whore's oath." However, caution is not the only point of view expressed by the sages with regard to trust. Thus Samuel Johnson in *The Rambler* (1750) advised: "It is happier to be sometimes cheated than not to trust."

If we examine the writings of learned men throughout the ages, we find that, while they often disagreed about whether to trust or not, they did agree that the topic was important. We shall not attempt to make a systematic review of the past usages of these concepts. However, we shall attempt to portray the essence of past writings with illustrative quotations as a way of providing a guideline for our own theoretical constructions.

Nicolai Hartmann (1932), more than any other writer with whose works I am acquainted, has stressed the fundamental significance of trust or faith to human life. He wrote (2:294): "All human relationships, from external material 'credit' up to the highest forms of delegated powers in public life and of personal trust, are based upon faith.

This chapter is an extension of ideas first presented in *Conditions Affecting Cooperation*. Final Technical Report for the Office of Naval Research, Contract NONR-285(10), February 1957.

All the strength derived from cooperation consists in men's reliance upon one another. . . . It is preeminently a communal value; it is the most positive unifying force which welds together a variety of individual persons, with their separate interests, into a collective unit. . . . The distinctively moral value of life begins in the sphere of those who trust one another."

Despite the obvious significance of trust and other related phenomena, an examination of leading empirical and theoretical works reveals that these phenomena have been largely ignored by the social scientist. My work, much of which is presented in chapter 8, is among the first research investigations into these phenomena. In this chapter, we shall attempt to examine the concept of trust and other related concepts from a theoretical point of view and in such a way as to suggest feasible hypotheses for research in this area.

THE PSYCHOLOGICAL STATE OF TRUSTING

To illustrate this phenomenon, one can examine some everyday examples of the usage of the term *trust*.

1. "I couldn't trust my two-month-old infant with a ten-year-old babysitter, no matter how much I wanted to go to the New Year's Eve party!"
2. The lady who owns the grocery store said that she's going to trust me and let me borrow $100 till I get my first paycheck, so I gave her a big hug.
3. "Come on in. You can trust this dog; he won't bite."
4. "She wouldn't fly directly from Acapulco to Oaxaca on one of those nonscheduled airlines. She didn't trust it. So we had to fly back to Mexico City and then down again."

If we examine these different statements, we note that in each instance the person who has to choose whether to trust or not is faced with the possibility that, if he trusts, something detrimental may happen to him.[1] That is, the choice to trust may lead either to benefit or to harm, depending upon whether or not one's trust is fulfilled. It may

1. The closely allied concept of "hope" does not have this meaning. One is not necessarily worse off if one's hope is unfulfilled unless one has trusted one's hope sufficiently to invest in its fulfillment.

also be noted that the harm that may befall the trusting individual if his trust is unfulfilled is not a trivial harm in relation to the amount of benefit to be received from trusting and having his trust fulfilled.

The psychological situation facing the person who has to decide whether to trust or not is somewhat similar to that of the princess's suitor in *The Lady or the Tiger*. As you may recall, the suitor is discovered by the king, and as a punishment he is placed in an arena that has two doors. Behind one of the doors is a hungry tiger, and behind the other is a beautiful lady. The suitor has to choose to go through one door or the other, not knowing which one will lead to the tiger and which to the lady. Just as he is about to make his choice, he notices that the princess is subtly pointing to one of the doors, and he immediately chooses to go through that one. The story ends with the reader not knowing whether the suitor finds the tiger or the lady. The author leaves the reader puzzling over the intentions of the princess. Would she rather send her beloved to certain death or into the arms of a beautiful rival?

But a less obvious question is as interesting: Why is the suitor's choice so unhesitating? Has he no doubts about the intentions of the princess, or is it that he is willing to accept for himself whatever fate the princess wishes him to have?

Our discussion naturally leads to the question of why, or under what conditions, would anyone be willing to open an opaque door behind which may be either a tiger or a beautiful lady? Or more generally, why would anyone choose to do something that might have potential negative consequences that would outweigh the potential positive consequences? There are, I believe, several different types of circumstances that might lead a person to make this sort of choice.

1. *Trust as despair*. The negative consequences of remaining in the present situation or of not trusting may seem so great or so certain that one may choose to trust out of despair, as the lesser of two evils. It may be better to risk meeting the tiger than to face certain execution. Similarly, ordinarily one might not choose to jump off a roof into a fireman's net, trusting that he will be caught. However, if this is the only means of escape from a raging fire, one may jump in desperation. Some forms of the pathology of trust (i.e., of the tendency to be trusting where the circumstances, to the objective observer, do not warrant trust) appear to be a reflection of this. Thus the terror of

loneliness (which is unseen by the objective observer) may lead the individual who has a deep sense of his own unworthiness to reach out for social contact even with people who are untrustworthy.

2. *Trust as social conformity*. In many social situations, trust is expected, and violations of this expectation lead to social sanctions, which may be very severe. Here, too, the choice to trust may be the lesser of two evils. Thus one may risk meeting the tiger in order to avoid social ostracism or the label of "coward." Similarly, one may lend money to a friend even though one has little confidence that he will repay it because one cannot find any socially acceptable reason for refusing him. The open expression of lack of trust in his financial stability may destroy the friendship since lack of trust may be considered a serious violation of the ethics of personal relations. As Hartmann (2:291) points out, to be distrustful is morally far more flagrant than to be credulous. To sin is less virtuous than to be sinned against. Hence, to avoid being in the position of "sinning against another" by not trusting or to avoid the sanctions which may arise from the violation of social expectancies, one may choose to trust without expecting one's trust to be fulfilled.

3. *Trust as innocence*. In many situations the choice of a course of action that may lead to dangerous or negative consequences is based upon innocence or lack of appreciation of the dangerous possibilities. The innocence may reflect lack of adequate information, cognitive immaturity, or cognitive defect. Thus a trusting infant may choose the possibility of confronting the tiger, thinking that the tiger is a pet like his cat. Or a patient may trust his surgeon's advice because he lacks the information to appreciate the potential dangers involved.

4. *Trust as impulsiveness*. Cognitive immaturity or defect, or certain attitudes toward the future, may make it difficult for the individual to give appropriate weight to the future as compared with the immediate consequences of his behavior. An individual who is dominated by the pull of immediate gratification may disregard future consequences, no matter how objectively dangerous or unpleasant they are. Thus the immediate gratifications of the public gesture of courage when one impulsively commits himself to confront a potentially negative or dangerous situation may later be regretted as one faces the necessity of carrying out the commitment. Or if one generally feels that the future is unpredictable, that it may bring disaster no matter what he does, or that its unpredictability makes any specific fu-

ture event (whether desired or feared) improbable, he may disregard the future and act only in terms of the here and now. Thus why worry about getting lung cancer from smoking cigarettes in fifteen years if there may be an atomic war within ten years?

5. *Trust as virtue.* Cooperative action and friendly social relations are predicated upon mutual trust and trustworthiness. It is natural, then, that trust came to be a value in social life and that the ability to trust is considered a virtue. Trusting behavior may be an affirmation of this value and thus an expression of one's virtue. The affirmation may have the optimistic corollary of Emerson's "Trust men and they will be true to you," or it may center exclusively on the personal value of being trusting without regard to external consequences.

6. *Trust as masochism.* An individual may choose to open the opaque door because he expects the tiger rather than the lady! Pain, punishment, death, unfulfilled trust, or martyrdom may be preferred over pleasure. Punishment, etc., may relieve guilt, or it may be desired to confirm one's view that the world is hostile, untrustworthy, and unappreciative of one's virtues. As is expected, the virtue of trust, instead of being rewarded, is punished.

7. *Trust as faith.* One may have no doubt that a favorable outcome awaits him behind the opaque door because he has faith that the gods are with him. The faith may be specific in that one has no doubt that the lady rather than the tiger awaits. Or it may be more general: a belief that whatever awaits has been fated by the gods and is, therefore, to be welcomed. The possession of faith in a sense eliminates the psychological existence of the negative consequences.

Faith, from one point of view, may be considered an extreme form of trust. In everyday language, the two words are used interchangeably. Analogous psychological and social conditions give rise to both faith and trust. Thus faith, in the religious sense, is predicated upon individual virtue, while trust, in the interpersonal sense, is often based upon self-esteem. Socially, faith and interpersonal trust both appear in cohesive social systems. Yet, despite these similarities, there are important differences: faith is more blind than trust; trust is less certain than faith; faith is more closely linked to authoritarian values, while trust is more closely tied to equalitarian values.

8. *Risk-taking or gambling.* To the objective observer, the lady who may be behind the door may seem to be not uncommonly attractive, but the tiger's ferociousness may be of more focal significance.

To the participant, however, the lady may be a passionate love without whom life itself is of no value, and the tiger's significance is primarily as an indicator that the lady has not been obtained. In such circumstances, the participant can afford to risk going through the door—even though he feels that the chances that the lady awaits are very small. This situation is analogous to the gambler at the race track who bets on a 100 to 1 shot; he can afford to take a big risk (i.e., bet where there is a high probability of losing) if his potential gains from winning far outweigh his potential losses from losing. Sometimes, of course, people misjudge their own evaluations of the significance to them of losing and act as though they are gambling when, in fact, they are trusting ill-advisedly.

9. *Trust as confidence.* One may choose to go through the opaque door because he has confidence that he will find what is desired rather than what is feared. In other words, although one is cognizant of the possibility that he might encounter the tiger (whom he fears), he *expects* to find the lady and is sufficiently confident in his expectation that the effective fear of the tiger becomes small compared to the effective attraction of the lady.

We shall now formalize the preceding discussion by some definitions and a statement of some basic assumptions.

A THEORY OF TRUST

The rest of this essay is primarily concerned with trust as confidence. Much of the remainder is concerned with the development of hypotheses concerning trust that can be subject to experimental verification. Some of the hypotheses underlie the experiments on trust that are reported in the following chapter. In a final section, we discuss the pathology of trust in a less formalized manner. The intention is to give insight into the personality determinants of trust, which are less readily experimented with than the determinants that are the subject of the hypotheses.

Before developing hypotheses about trust, it is useful to define the basic terms that will be employed. Some of them are novel and some are in common use, but the latter are employed in rather specific ways that differ from their everyday uses. It is also necessary to define other terms that enter into the definition of the concepts with which we shall be most concerned. Following the definitions, some key psychological assumptions employed in various hypotheses are introduced. No claim to originality is made for them. This writer has borrowed freely from ideas expressed by theorists concerned with decision making, conflict, and dissonance. However, he has expressed these ideas in his own terms and has adapted them to suit the present purposes.

BASIC DEFINITIONS

DEFINITION 1. *An event is of positive motivational significance (has positive valence or utility) to an individual when he anticipates that its occurrence will increase, or prevent a decrease in, the well-being of anything or anyone (including himself) whose well-being is of positive interest to him.*

DEFINITION 2. *An event is of negative motivational significance (has negative valence or negative utility) when the individual anticipates that its occurrence will decrease, or prevent an increase in, the well-being of anything or anyone (including himself) whose well-being is of positive interest to him.*

DEFINITION 3. *The relative potency of an anticipated event is the relative power of that event to elicit behavior directed toward promoting or avoiding its occurrence as compared with behavior directed toward promoting or avoiding the occurrence of other events.*

DEFINITION 4. *A path that can lead to an event having positive motivational significance (Va^+) or to one having negative motivational significance (Va^-) is an ambiguous path.*

DEFINITION 5. *The choice of an ambiguous path, when Va^+ is less than Va^-, is a trusting choice; the choice of avoiding such a path is a distrusting choice. When the occurrence of Va^+ or Va^- is thought to be dependent upon another's purposed behavior, the choice of such a path is a socially trusting choice. Mutual trust exists when two people have complementary social trust with regard to each other's behavior.*

DEFINITION 6. *The choice of an ambiguous path, when Va^+ is greater than Va^-, is a risk-taking or gambling choice.*

DEFINITION 7. *The choice of avoiding a path which may lead to Va^- is a suspicious choice. Distrusting choices are, thus, types of suspicious choices. When the occurrence of Va^- is thought to be dependent upon another's purposed behavior, the avoidance of such a path is a socially suspicious choice. Mutual suspicion exists when*

*two people have complementary social suspicion with regard to
each other's behavior.*

DEFINITION 8. *Promotive behavior toward an event is behavior directed at increasing, or preventing a decrease in, the probability of
the event's occurrence; promotive behavior toward a person is behavior directed at increasing, or preventing a decrease in, that person's well-being.*

DEFINITION 9. *Contrient behavior toward an event is behavior directed at decreasing, or preventing an increase in, the probability of
the event's occurrence; contrient behavior toward a person is
behavior directed at decreasing, or preventing an increase in, that
person's well-being.*

DEFINITION 10. *Cognitions or evaluations are promotively interconnected with other cognitions or evaluations when an increase (decrease) in the strength of one produces an increase (decrease) in the
strength of another; they are contriently interconnected when an increase (decrease) in the strength of one produces a decrease
(increase) in the strength of another.*

DEFINITION 11. *An event is purposed if it is produced as a means of
influencing the well-being of something or somebody (including
that of the event's producer).*

BASIC PSYCHOLOGICAL ASSUMPTIONS

ASSUMPTION 1. *Individuals tend to behave promotively toward things
(including events, persons, and aspects of themselves) that are positively valent for them and contriently toward things that are negatively valent for them.*

ASSUMPTION 2. *The potency of the tendency to engage in promotive
or contrient behavior toward an anticipated event, at any given
time, is a positive function of (1) the strength of its valence; (2) the
perceived (i.e., subjective) increment in the probability of the
event's occurrence or nonoccurrence, which would result from engaging, rather than not engaging, in the promotive or contrient behavior; (3) the perceived probability level of the event's occurrence
or nonoccurrence after engaging in the promotive or contrient behavior; (4) the intrinsic valence of the activities involved in the promotive or contrient behavior; (5) the perceived immediacy of the
event's occurrence or nonoccurrence.*

ASSUMPTION 3. *The stronger the individual's positive evaluation of the relevant aspects of himself, the more likely he is to believe that events or persons having motivational significance for him can be influenced promotively by his behavior.*

ASSUMPTION 4. *The potency of a psychological conflict is a positive function of the potency of the weaker of the two conflicting behavioral tendencies and an inverse function of the size of the discrepancy in potency of the opposing tendencies.*

ASSUMPTION 5. *Whenever a state of intrapsychic conflict exists or impends, the individual will attempt to resolve it—or suppress it if he cannot resolve it.*

There are two basic modes of intrapsychic conflict resolution. First is the tendency to change the external reality so that the conflict between the behavioral tendencies no longer exists; the other is to change the cognitions and/or valences that determine the direction and potency of the conflicting behavioral tendencies. Whenever the conflict cannot be resolved externally, there will be a propensity to reduce the potency of the less potent tendency and increase the potency of the more potent one by changing the cognitions or evaluations that give rise to them. A cognition or evaluation will be more resistant to change when the other cognitions or evaluations with which it is promotively interconnected increase in number and/or grow stronger.

ASSUMPTION 6. *The more potent the conflict, the more the likelihood that it will be suppressed or the longer it will take to resolve and the more painful will be its experience if it cannot be externally resolved. The more potent a conflict has been, the more committed a person will be to maintaining whatever resolution he has made of it.*

ASSUMPTION 7. *Whenever an individual experiences a change in well-being that he attributes to a purposed event, he is more likely to perceive the event as being focused upon him the lesser its implications for others (the producer or others) are, relatively, to its implications for himself.*

ASSUMPTION 8. *People have a tendency to develop positive sentiments toward those whom they perceive as influencing their welfare promotively and negative sentiments toward those whom they perceive as influencing their welfare negatively; the strength of the sentiments will be a direct function of the perceived degree of influ-*

*ence on their welfare and of the perceived degree to which the in-
fluence was purposed by the other.*

ASSUMPTION 9. *People are, in their own ways, psychological theorists
and make psychological assumptions about others that are similar
to the ones advanced above.*

That is, people not only act as assumptions 1–8 suggest, but they
also think that other people will do likewise. They expect others to
help them if the others like them, and they expect others to like them
if they help the others.

BASIC HYPOTHESES CONCERNING THE OCCURRENCE
OF A TRUSTING CHOICE

A trusting choice has been defined as the choice of an ambiguous
path when the strength of Va^+ is less than that of Va^-. From the preceding definitions and from assumption 2, it is evident that such a
choice is more likely to occur if the subjective probability of the occurrence of Va^+ is higher than that of Va^-. More specifically, I propose the following basic hypothesis, which is a variant of the traditional "expected utility" formulation (Edwards 1954).

HYPOTHESIS 1. *Given that Va^- is stronger than Va^+, a trusting
choice will occur if: $Va^+ \times S.P.^+ > Va^- \times S.P.^- + K$.*

($S.P.^+$ refers to the subjective probability of attaining Va^+; $S.P.^-$ to
that of receiving Va^-; K is a constant referring to the "security level"
that the individual needs for action. It may differ for different individuals.) It is apparent that the stronger Va^- is relative to Va^+, the
higher must be one's confidence of getting Va^+ rather than Va^- before
he can make a trusting choice.

There are many factors that can affect one's subjective probability
or confidence that Va^+ rather than Va^- will occur. Some of these
have been discussed in chapter 4. Among the most important are
one's own past experiences in similar situations; the past experiences
of others; the opinions held by others whom one respects; one's personal assumptions about the benevolence-malevolence of the reality
one is in; and one's confidence about being able to influence the occurrence of Va^+ or the nonoccurrence of Va^- through one's own actions or through available help. To illustrate, consider the pleasant

prospect (Va^+) of taking a refreshing walk in Central Park on a warm summer evening and the frightening possibility (Va^-) that you might get mugged during that walk. Va^- is obviously stronger than Va^+; hence you are unlikely to go for the walk unless you are rather confident that you will not be mugged. You may be confident because you or others you know have walked in "dangerous areas" many times without incident; or because people-in-the-know have said that it is less dangerous to walk in Central Park than it is to ride in a taxi, and you ride taxis without concern; or because your daily horoscope has led you to assume that nothing but good things can happen to you during the next twenty-four hours; or because your training in jujitsu has led you to think "muggers beware"; or because you feel that help would be readily available if a mugging were attempted, since many people would be in the park attending the summer concerts.

Our first hypothesis indicates that a trusting choice would be made when the subjective probability of Va^-'s occurring is low in comparison to that of Va^+'s. Traditionally, such a hypothesis is formulated to deal with a situation in which the occurrence of Va^- precludes Va^+. However, suppose that both Va^+ and Va^- could occur if one took the ambiguous path, the only ambiguity being whether or not Va^- as well as Va^+ would occur. In such a situation, $S.P.^+$ and $S.P.^-$ could both be high and, if this were the case, one would not normally expect the ambiguous path to be chosen. However, as assumption 2 indicates, other factors than subjective probability may be influential. Among these other factors, I particularly wish to draw attention to the significance of time perspective.

HYPOTHESIS 2. *The more remote in time the possible occurrence of Va⁻ as compared with that of Va⁺, the more likely it is that a trusting choice will be made.*

A good deal of psychological research supports the proposition that the immediate present is a more potent influence upon behavior than the distant future. Rewards and punishments alike, if they are long delayed, are likely to have much less impact than those that occur soon. Thus one is more likely to trust when the pleasure (Va^+) is expected soon and the pain (Va^-) is not expected for a long time. Impulsive trust, as indicated earlier in the chapter, is based upon this minimization of future negative consequences. Similarly, the refusal to trust that present hard work will lead to a delayed reward reflects the lesser potency of future gratifications as compared to present pains. Usually, it is not the prospect of future reward that sustains present arduous efforts but rather the current rewards of social and self-approval that do so.

The first two hypotheses were concerned with the choice of the ambiguous path; our next centers on the consequences of the psychological conflict that is inherent in the ambiguous path. From our initial definitions and from assumptions 1, 2, and 6, one may hypothesize that:

HYPOTHESIS 3. *After an individual has chosen to be trusting or suspicious, he will seek additional reasons to support and strengthen his choice; his effort to do so will be greater, the more potent the conflict has been prior to his choice.*

This hypothesis is, of course, what one would expect from such consistency theories as the theory of cognitive dissonance (see chapter 3). There are many different ways of stregthening a choice to trust. One could increase the relative potency of Va^+ as compared to Va^-, or he might put Va^- into the remote future, and so on. The essential point is that choice is determining as well as determined. If one chooses to be trusting, he will relate to the world in such a way as to make the confirmation of his trust more likely; similarly, if one chooses to be suspicious, then he will act so as to have his suspicions justified.

Interpersonal Trust

Our initial hypotheses are formulated in general terms that cover an individual's relations with his inanimate as well as his social environment. One can make these hypotheses applicable to social situations by substituting for Va^+ some phrase such as "desired event produced by another person." Much of our subsequent discussion will be concerned with understanding the conditions that lead one to be trusting or not of the behavior of another person. Such factors as the perceived nature, strength, source, and focus of the other person's behavioral intentions as well as the perceived capabilities of the other person will be the center of our discussion. An important special case of interpersonal trust is concerned with the conditions under which the individual believes that he has the right to expect his trust to be fulfilled by the other and that, if the other does not fulfill his obligations, the trust has been violated, not merely unfulfilled. This is the important case of *reciprocal mutual trust* in a normatively regulated interaction system.

Trust and Perceived Intentions

To trust another person to produce a benevolent event (or to suspect that another person will produce a malevolent event), an individual must perceive that the other person has the ability (i.e., the power, skill, and/or resources) to produce it; has a reliable intention to produce it; and has the organized capability of applying his ability and his intention in specific circumstances in order to produce the event he intends. In this section, we shall be concerned with the perceptual elements affecting the perceived reliability of an intention.

The perceived reliability of an intention to perform a given behavior is a function of several main factors: (1) the perceived *strength* of the motivation underlying the intention; (2) the person's perceived *commitment* to the intention; (3) the perceived nature of the motivational *source* of the intention; and (4) the perceived *focus* of the intention.

HYPOTHESIS 4. *The stronger the perceived motivation underlying a given intention, the more reliable it will be perceived as being.*

Thus if I perceive that a friend has an intention to stop eating candies and other sweets, I will be more confident that he will do as he intends if I know that he has been told to lose the weight by his doctor, in order to avoid another heart attack, rather than by his dentist, purportedly to avoid some cavities in his teeth.

HYPOTHESIS 5. *The stronger a person's commitment to his intention is perceived to be, the more reliable it will be perceived to be.*

Essentially, commitment refers to the process whereby the conditions affecting the individual's motivations and opportunities to engage in certain behavior are arranged so as to leave him no other acceptable alternative except to do what he is committed to do. "Strength of an intention" refers to the desire to execute the intention, while "commitment" refers to the desire to avoid not doing what one intends. Thus an individual has committed himself to doing something to the extent that he has arranged circumstances (internally or externally) so that if he does not do it, he thinks he will suffer unacceptable negative consequences.

An intention to perform a given behavior may arise from any of a number of sources. The source of an intention determines its reliability. Suppose, for example, that a person expresses the intention to help a neighbor build a garage. This intention may derive from his desire to make his neighbor happy because he likes him, or it may come from his desire to have his neighbor help him build a porch. The source of the intention will, in part, determine how reliable it will be under changing circumstances. Thus if the person in our example decides not to build a porch or if he is offered help by another, his intention to help his neighbor build a garage may disappear. However, if the intention arises from his desire to make his neighbor happy, its persistence is not contingent upon circumstances that are irrelevant to the neighbor's welfare. Some of the possible sources of any given individual's behavioral intention with regard to another individual may include one or more of the following:

a. *an altruistic or malevolent intention*—an intrinsic desire to gratify (or harm) the other person;
b. *an exchange intention*—a desire to obtain (or avoid) something from the other person. One's own behavior is seen as a condition for this;
c. *an other-directed intention*—a desire to obtain (or avoid) something from others (i.e., not the other person). One's own behavior is seen as a condition for this;
d. *a conscience-directed intention*—a desire to obtain approval (or avoid disapproval) from oneself. One's own behavior in relation to the other is seen as a condition for this;
e. *an activity-directed intention*—a desire to obtain the satisfactions that are perceived to be intrinsically related to the experiences involved in producing the behavior;
f. a desire to obtain goals, other than those listed above, that are perceived to be mediated by the intended behavior per se.

If we examine sources *a* through *f*, we see that *a, d,* and *e* are sources that cannot be satisfied without producing the trusted behavior, while this is not necessarily so for *b, c,* and *f.* That is, one cannot gratify an intrinsic desire to please (or harm) another person, an intrinsic self-desire to be trustworthy (or sinister), or an intrinsic desire to engage in the activities that produce the trusted (or harmful) behavior by any other means except engaging in the trusted (or harmful) behavior. But a desire to obtain or avoid something that is not intrinsically related to the production of the trusted (or suspected) behavior may be frequently accomplished by other means. Thus we may state that:

HYPOTHESIS 6. *When an intention must persist over time, through changing circumstances, an individual is likely to perceive another's intention as more reliable if the source of the intention cannot be satisfied by means other than the production of the intended behavior than if it can be satisfied otherwise.*

In addition to the source of an intention, its focus is of importance. A person's intention may have as its terminal objective, or focus, the effect that his behavior produces upon the trusting or suspicious person, his own conscientiousness, or his own behavior. Thus suppose a messenger is entrusted with carrying a message to another person. The messenger may perceive that the desired reaction from others requires that he succeed in delivering the message, or that he try as hard as possible to deliver it, or that he follow the route he was told to take whether or not it enables him to deliver it. Clearly, an intention focused upon the effect it produces on the recipient of the behavior is likely to have a more reliable effect upon that recipient than behavior focused elsewhere.

HYPOTHESIS 7. *An intention that is perceived to be focused upon producing certain effects in another person will be perceived as being more likely to result in such effects than if the intention is focused elsewhere.*

From the preceding two hypotheses, it is evident that altruistic and malevolent intentions have reliability of both source and focus. A conscience-directed intention has reliability of source, but its focus may or may not be reliable; an activity-directed intention has reliability of source but little reliability in its focus. Exchange and other-directed intentions have little reliability of source but may or may not have reliability of focus, depending upon whether or not external arrangements are made such that the behavior receiver's experience of benefit (or harm) is a necessary condition for the behavior producer's gratifications.

So far, our discussion has indicated that the perceived reliability of another person's intention will be determined by how the four aspects of an intention are perceived: its motivational strength, the individual's commitment to it, the nature of its source, and its focus. But what determines how the individual will perceive these aspects of another's intention? A generalized answer to this question is that one's perception of another's intentions will be determined by what the other does in particular contexts, by one's source of information concerning what he does, and by one's characteristics (including one's relation to the other, which will predispose one to perceive what is consistent with one's other relevant perceptions, beliefs, and evaluations).

Conditions for the Perception of an Altruistic Intention

Let us make our discussion of the factors determining the perception of an intention more specific by considering the different sources of intentions. We shall start with a discussion of the conditions for the perception of an altruistic intention. From assumptions 1, 8, and 9 we may state that:

HYPOTHESIS 8. *An individual is more likely to perceive that another person has an altruistic intention to benefit him if he believes that the other person likes him than if he does not have this belief.*

It is now relevant to ask: Under what conditions will the acts performed by another person toward oneself be perceived as having this source in a positive sentiment? We assume that:

HYPOTHESIS 9. *When an individual perceives that another person's actions have resulted in a benefit for him, he will tend to perceive that the other person likes him. We also assume that this tendency will be enhanced according to the following:*

   a. *the strength of the benefit he has received;*
   b. *the frequency of his prior experiences of having been benefited by the other person and the diversity of the settings in which the benefits have occurred;*
   c. *the degree of confidence he has that the other person was able to avoid producing the actions that resulted in the benefit—i.e.,*

the knowledge that he was not required or forced to produce these actions;

d. *the degree of confidence he has that the other person was aware, before he produced the beneficial action, that it would have a beneficial consequence;*

e. *the amount of power that the other person has relative to his own, such that the other person had nothing to gain by doing it;*

f. *the smallness of the gain that others (including the benefit producer) are perceived to have as a result of the beneficial actions in comparison to the gains that the individual himself experiences;*

g. *the cost that the benefit producer is perceived to have incurred in producing the benefit.*

A person's perceptions of another will be determined not only by the information he receives from his direct experiences or from what others tell him but also by his need to absorb this information in such a way as to prevent disruption of the existing perceptions, cognitions, or evaluations to which he is strongly committed. If it is true that one's self-attitudes are deeply anchored, one's view of another person's attitude and behavior toward oneself would be very much influenced by whether one's own orientation toward himself were promotive or contrient. If one dislikes himself, it is difficult to accept affection from others. As Groucho Marx is reputed to have said in a humorous anecdote, "I won't accept membership in a club that would have me as a member." The following hypothesis, in its subcomponents, details the major possibilities.

HYPOTHESIS 10a. *If an individual is promotively oriented toward himself, he will tend to be promotively oriented toward others who are perceived to have characteristics or attitudes that are promotive (e.g., through similarity) to his own characteristics or attitudes, and he will also expect such others to be promotively oriented toward him; on the other hand, such an individual will tend to be contriently oriented toward others who are perceived to have characteristics or attitudes that are contrient (e.g., dissimilar) to his own, and he will also expect such others to be contriently oriented to him.*

HYPOTHESIS 10b. *If an individual is contriently oriented toward himself, he will tend to be promotively oriented toward others who are*

*perceived to have characteristics or attitudes that are contrient to
his own, and he will also expect such others to be contriently oriented toward him; on the other hand, such an individual will tend
to be contriently oriented to others whose characteristics or attitudes are promotive to his own, and he will expect such others to
be promotively oriented to him.*

Thus one can expect a person who likes what he has done to respond favorably to someone who also likes it but unfavorably to
someone who rejects it. However, if he dislikes what he has done,
praise will be regarded negatively, and criticism may elicit a positive
reaction (Deutsch and Solomon 1959; Deutsch 1961). Correspondingly, a neurotic woman who has contempt for herself may be attracted only to men who reject her or treat her as an inferior. Only if
a person has a positive regard for himself is he apt to admire those
who like him and who have likes and dislikes similar to his own. A
more detailed consideration of some of the consequences of negative
self-esteem is presented later in this chapter in the discussion of the
pathology of trust.

*Conditions for the Perception of a Reliable
Exchange Intention*

We are concerned here with the conditions under which an individual
will perceive that another person will perform certain activities that
he desires [2] when the only motivation that the other has for perform-
ing them is the other's expectation of getting something in return from
the individual who is benefited by his activities. In effect, we are assuming that the individuals involved are unconcerned with each other's welfare (and that they are aware that this is so) and that they
would each prefer to obtain what the other has to offer without recip-
rocating; moreover, we assume that they have no socialized motives
vis-à-vis each other that would make them feel guilty if they did not
reciprocate.

To illustrate, suppose that two strangers, Mr. Stanley and Mr. Murray, meet on a train. They strike up a conversation and find that Stanley owns a fishing rod that he rarely uses and Murray owns a tennis

2. Throughout the presentation, such terms as "desire," "gratification," and "advantage" will refer not only to the obtaining of something positive but also to the
avoidance of something negative.

racket that he rarely uses. Stanley would prefer to own the tennis racket and Murray the fishing rod; however, each would most like to own both the racket and the rod. Each would like to make an exchange with the other, but neither wants to be duped by the other. This situation is illustrated in figure 7.1.

From figure 7.1 it is apparent that receiving and not giving is preferable to reciprocal giving, which, in turn, is preferable to reciprocal not giving, which, in turn, is preferable to giving and not receiving (i.e., being duped). If this is so, how can an exchange be arranged? It is evident that an exchange will take place only under circumstances that will lead each person to believe that he will not be duped and

		Murray	
		Gives Racket	Retains Racket
Stanley	Gives Rod	+5, +5	0, +8
	Retains Rod	+8, 0	+3, +3

Figure 7.1. The trust problem in an exchange relationship.
This example assumes that Murray's racket is worth 5 units of pleasure to Stanley and only 3 such units to Murray. Similarly, Stanley's rod is worth 5 units to Murray and only 3 units to Stanley. The first numbers in the cells indicate what amount of value Stanley would have after he and Murray have made a given choice, the second numbers indicate what Murray would have.

that he will not be able to dupe the other. There are three fundamental ways to guarantee that an exchange will be reciprocated: (1) to employ arrangements that will make for simultaneity of giving and receiving in the exchange; (2) to use third parties; and (3) to use "hostages" or "deposits," which will enable each person to commit himself to the exchange and to be convinced that the other person has also committed himself.

Simple examples of simultaneity of giving and receiving are to be found in the actions of children exchanging toys. Typically, each child holds onto his own toy as he takes the toy of the other child. He releases his toy gradually (i.e., he can grab it again) as he feels the other child releasing his toy. The process is reversible until the exchange has been completed. When the objects to be exchanged are divisible, simultaneity of exchange is often achieved by exchange of one unit at a time.

HYPOTHESIS 11. *An exchange is made more likely by arrangements that enable each of the parties to the exchange to be aware that the other is making his contribution to the exchange simultaneously with his own contribution.*

Third parties may provide the arrangements by which simultaneity of exchange is achieved. The third party may, for example, serve as a transfer agent who receives the contributions and passes them on to the other person only *after* both parties have contributed. Or, a third party may function as an observer who is able to confirm for each party that the other is not attempting to dupe him. Moreover, the third party may be able to deter violations of an exchange by the penalties and punishments that he is able and willing to employ against a violator. It is evident that for a third party to play a facilitating role in an exchange, he must be viewed as neutral, competent, and motivated to facilitate the exchange.

HYPOTHESIS 12. *An exchange is made more likely by the availability of neutral, resourceful third parties who are motivated to facilitate the exchange.*

"Hostages" or "deposits of value" may be employed mutually by the parties to an exchange as tokens of good faith and as ways of committing themselves to carrying out their part of the exchange. If the hostages or deposits are sufficiently valued, the threat of their loss will be likely to deter temptations to be untrustworthy. However, the exchange of hostages or deposits often involves difficulties similar to those involved in any exchange: those related to the possibility of being duped. Thus if one of the parties obtains hostages from the other but the other does not do so from him, he may attempt to use the hostages as a basis for extorting an advantage. However, if arrangements can be made for the simultaneous exchange of hostages or deposits, or if they can be placed with a neutral, trusted third party, each party can be confident that the other is committed to the exchange.

Hostages or deposits are especially useful when the desired exchange between the parties cannot be simultaneous. Circumstances may require that one person's offering precede the other person's. Consider a situation in which you bring your shoes to a shop for repair. It will be impossible for the repair work and the payment in money to occur at the same instant in time. Usually, the repair work will be performed prior to the payment for it. The shoe repairman will commonly assume that you will pay for his work because he holds your shoes as "hostages"; thus he will not require a deposit. You will assume that the "hostages," your shoes, are not particularly valuable to the shoe repairman and that he has less incentive to abscond with your shoes than to return them and receive payment from you.

Now suppose that instead of bringing your shoes in for repair, you went to a shoemaker to ask him to make a pair of shoes for you. In this case, you would not be surprised if he were to ask for a deposit since you would not be leaving your shoes as hostages. It is frequently the case in buyer-seller transactions that are not immediately consummated that the buyer must give a deposit so that the seller can be assured that it is safe for him to run the risk of manufacturing, purchasing, or withholding from the market the item that the buyer wishes to purchase at some later date. In such instances, the seller is protected by the deposit (it lowers the risk of the buyer's reneging, and it lowers his cost if this happens), and the buyer is protected by third parties (the law); without such protection the buyer would be vulnerable to the expropriation of his deposit if it had any value to the seller.

Hostages and deposits are specific forms of the more general concept of *commitment*. As was indicated earlier in this chapter, a commitment to a particular course of action implies that unless the action is taken, the individual anticipates that he will suffer a sanction or loss greater than the gains he would accrue from not taking the action or from taking an alternative action. Offering a hostage or deposit is a way of committing oneself. Commitments, however, can also be made through less tangible commodities such as reputation, honor, and personal integrity. A person may arrange circumstances so that if he fails to do what he promises to do, he will clearly suffer either an external loss of reputation for trustworthiness or guilt and an internal loss of integrity. It is evident that an exchange is more likely if commitments can be made by the parties to an exchange in a manner that is convincing to both of them.

HYPOTHESIS 13. *An exchange is made more likely by conditions that enable the parties to commit themselves persuasively to carry out the exchange.*

"Commitment," as is indicated above, implies a loss if one does not fulfill one's part in an exchange; it is, in a manner of speaking, a negative incentive making for a reliable exchange intention. Positive incentives can serve a similar function.

HYPOTHESIS 14. *An individual is more likely to perceive that another will offer something in an exchange the greater the benefit he believes the other will obtain as a result of the exchange.*

Thus it is not only the strength of the need that he perceives the other to have for what is being offered but also the attractiveness that he perceives his own offering to have that will determine how much incentive he will perceive the other to have to participate in the exchange. One can suppose that a person with low self-esteem is inclined to devalue what he himself has to offer and is, therefore, less likely to expect the other to find an exchange with him worthwhile.

The Effects of Perceived Power

In preceding sections we have been concerned with perceived intentions as they relate to trust. Now we turn to a brief consideration of the effects of perceived power.

HYPOTHESIS 15. *The more power an individual attributes to another person, the more likely he is to be trusting (or suspicious) of the other person.*

That is, if you believe that another person is motivated to produce a benevolent event and is knowledgeable about the circumstances for producing it, then the more power (ability, skill, resources, etc.) that you believe him to have, the more likely you are to trust him to produce that event. On the other hand, the more power you attribute to another person to cause a malevolent event (assuming that he is motivated to produce such an event), the more likely you are to be suspicious if you feel that you can avert it and to be fearful if you feel that it cannot be averted. The perceived nature of the event to be produced will determine what the relevant dimensions of power are—e.g., intellectual ability, physical strength, social status, possession of equipment, wealth. Insofar as social status becomes a generalized indicator of power,[3] one would expect that the higher the social status an individual attributes to another person, the more likely he is to be trusting (or fearful) of the other.

In the preceding hypothesis, and in our discussion of the perception of altruistic intentions, we have discussed power from the point of view of the individual who is its object rather than its wielder. It is also relevant to consider the wielder of power. It is evident that one is less likely to perceive that an altruistic intention underlies a benefit from one who is dependent on you than from one on whom you are dependent.

HYPOTHESIS 16. *The more power an individual perceives himself to have over other individuals, the less likely he is to perceive that they have altruistic intentions when they benefit him and, hence, the less likely he is to trust them in situations where his power is irrelevant or cannot be applied.*

The Influence of Communication

From our discussion of the nature of mutual trust and mutual suspicion, we would expect that: there would be a smaller likelihood that the communications that occurred in a situation of mutual trust would be misleading or deceptive. That is, the function of communication in mutual suspicion would be to misinform rather than to inform the other person about one's activities and plans. This being the case, one could predict that:

HYPOTHESIS 17. *The correctibility of an individual's perceptions of the situation will be greater when the individual begins with the perception that the situation is one of mutual trust (and it is not) than when he begins with the perception that the situation is one of mutual suspicion (and it is not).*

---

3. Without going into extensive discussion of the conditions which determine the perception of power, one may say that the perception that another person is able to do something may result from: (1) the knowledge that he has been able to do it in the past and the belief that the achievement was not accidental and that the ability is not a transient one; (2) the inference from the knowledge that he can cause all the necessary conditions for producing the desired event or, more generally, the inference from the fact that he has been able to cause something which requires power which is equivalent to or greater than that necessary to producing the desired event; (3) the knowledge that others, in whose opinions he has confidence, believe that he can do it; (4) the wish that he be able to do it.

That is, it is easier to go from a situation of misplaced trust to one of justified suspicion than to go from a situation of misplaced suspicion to one of justified trust.

There is another aspect of communication that we wish to consider: communication as it relates to the development of trust. The question that should be raised is whether communication can be utilized to foster a mutually beneficial exchange in a situation where the people are individualistically oriented (i.e., only concerned with their own welfare) and where there is no possibility of internal or third-party sanctions if one is not cooperative. In effect, we are asking how communication opportunities can be used to raise the subjective level of probability concerning the occurrence of the desired event so that the individual can trust in its occurrence—and also how these opportunities can be used to elicit trustworthy behavior so that the trusting individual not only expects to receive cooperation but also wishes to give cooperation in return.[4]

One approach to answering this question is to rephrase it and ask: what are the minimum ingredients of a cooperative interchange? In essence, they are a complementarity of intention and expectation. That is, you intend to do what the other expects from you, and the other intends to do what you expect of him. However, for the cooperative interchange to be a stable, ongoing system, each person must have ways of reacting to violations of his expectation; this possibility of employing sanctions must be known to the other and must serve as an inhibitor of violation, since the frequent occurrence of violations will break down the system of interchange. Nevertheless, the nature of any ongoing system is such that, despite the probability of sanctions, violations of expectations are likely to occur, if only by chance. Hence, for the system to endure, there must be some way to avoid the following self-perpetuating cycle: violation on the part of one person, which leads to negative reactions by the other, which, in turn, leads to negative behavior from the first person, and so on. If it is to endure, a cooperative system must have some means of restoring complementarity once it has been violated. It must have, in effect, *a method of absolution* and of recognizing when a return to complementarity has occurred.

4. Another way of phrasing the question is: How can communication be utilized in a situation which is ambiguous as to whether the individuals are promotively or contriently interdependent in such a way as to turn it into one in which the individuals perceive themselves as promotively interdependent?

Let us assume that, in a situation that is ambiguous as to whether the individuals will interrelate themselves promotively or contriently, an individual's tendency to assume that another individual's communications are informative will be greater than his tendency to assume that they are misinformative. It seems probable that most societies would impose restraints upon using communication deliberately to misinform (i.e., to lie), and thus it is likely that internal restraints against lying would develop during the process of socialization. The strength of these internal restraints would, of course, vary from person to person and from situation to situation—hence the need to qualify our assumption. In some societies, "lying" might even be encouraged in certain types of situations—e.g., situations in which the truth is seen as painful. Most individuals are aware of the internal restraints against lying in themselves and implicitly assume that these restraints also exist in others.

With the preceding assumption, we can state that:

HYPOTHESIS 18. *The communication of any of the basic elements of a cooperative system of interaction (i.e., expectation, intention, reaction to violation, or method of absolution) will tend to increase the trust of the communicatee and the trustworthiness of the communicator. The increase will be greater as the number of basic elements that are incorporated into the communication increase.*

We would assume that a communication of "reaction to violation" implicitly communicates "intention" and "expectation" and that a communication of "method of absolution" also implicitly communicates all other elements.

The above hypothesis, in distinguishing between the effects of the communication upon the sender and its effects upon the receiver, assumes that sending a message is more "committing" to the contents of the message than receiving it. If this is so, and if both the sender and receiver experience it as so, then the receiver clearly has a better basis for trust than the sender, and the sender is more committed to being trustworthy than the receiver.

The Influence of Third Parties

At a number of points in previous sections, we have suggested that the relationship between any two people may be very much influenced by their relationships to a third person. In everyday life, we are aware of the tendency to dislike people who are disliked by people we like and, conversely, to like people who are liked by our friends.

In this section, we are again concerned with the conditions under which two individualistically oriented people can engage in a mutual exchange. Our interest here is in how a third party might influence the relations between two otherwise unrelated individuals in such a way as to promote the psychological conditions necessary for a mutual exchange. A third party may be another person, a group, a law-enforcing agent, Nature, etc.

Assuming that others who have sentiments similar to one's own are likely to act promotively toward the things one likes and contriently toward the things one dislikes (this follows from assumptions 1 and 9), it is possible (from assumption 8) to derive that one will be likely to develop positive sentiments toward others who have similar sentiments. From Heider's (1958) theory of cognitive balance, one would make the same derivation. By direct extension to third parties, we are able to predict that:

HYPOTHESIS 19. *If two people have similar sentiments (like or dislike) toward a third party and each is aware that this is so, they will tend to develop positive sentiments toward one another (provided that their relationship to the third party is not an exclusive one).*[5]

From our prior discussion of perceived intentions, one could predict that if two people have similar sentiments toward a third party and each is aware that this is so, they will be more likely to trust each other than if they do not. We would further expect that the tendency to trust each other would be enhanced if the two people with similar sentiments toward a third party each perceived that the second person's gains (or lack of losses) would affect the third party. That is to say, you would be likely to trust another person who felt that your gains would result in losses to his enemy, and he would be likely to trust you, if he thought you felt that his gains would result in losses to your enemy.

Essentially the same logic is involved when we consider the situation where you are not aware of the second person's sentiments to-

5. Hypothesis 19 does not hold for relationships between Person I and Person III which exclude the possibility of similar relationships between Person II and Person III. If you and I each want an exclusive relationship with the same person, our relationship would be one of contrient rather than promotive interdependence.

ward the third party but where you have a well-defined relationship to the third party and you are aware of the third person's sentiments toward the second person. Thus if you like the third party and you know that he will feel good if the second person is benefited, you are more likely to engage in trustworthy behavior than if you believe that the third party has no concern for the second person.

We shall not attempt to detail all the possible ways that a third-party relationship can influence the relationship between two people. In general, one can assert that if the relationship between two people affects the relationship between either of these people and a third party, then this will be a factor influencing the individual in his relationship to the second party.

SELF-ESTEEM AND SOME FORMS OF THE PATHOLOGY OF TRUST

For the most part, the formulations above have dealt largely with "situational" factors that might influence the relations between two people. However, it is clear that a person's attitude toward himself will very much influence his readiness to be trusting or suspicious in a specific set of external circumstances. Thus in the discussion of perceived intentions, the point was made that if a person dislikes, rather than likes, himself one would predict strikingly different reactions to being liked by another person than the customary ones. Similarly, we have seen how self-evaluations may influence the evaluation of one's potential offering to a cooperative endeavor and thus affect one's views of the likelihood that cooperation will occur. In this sense, self-esteem may tend to operate as a biasing factor, predisposing one individual to be more trusting or suspicious than another in essentially similar situations. However, there is reason to believe that self-esteem may affect trusting or suspicious tendencies in a more complex manner. We refer here to the fact that some people seem to show a more or less consistent pathology of trust or suspicion. There is reason to believe that such pathology is based on an underlying negative self-esteem.

The notion of a "pathology of trust" as well as a "pathology of suspicion" may sound somewhat strange since everyday usages of the terms *trust* and *suspicion* have the value connotation that "to be trusting" is good and "to be suspicious" is bad. For the recipient of behavior, it is obviously preferable to be the object of trusting or responsible behavior rather than of suspicious or malevolent behavior. However, from the point of view of the individual who initiates the behavior, can we hold that it is better to trust than to be suspicious?

It is evident that without knowledge of the specific circumstances, it is impossible to assert whether an individual will be better advised to be trusting or to be suspicious. The appropriatness of any behavior depends upon the characteristics of the situation in which the behavior is to take place. Thus it is appropriate to be suspicious rather than trusting if a bitter enemy offers to do you a favor by returning a precious manuscript that you have borrowed from the library. On the other hand, if a conscientious friend were to make the same offer, trusting rather than suspicious behavior would be more in order.

Take an extreme example, that of an individual who is always trusting, without regard to the nature of the situations in which he displays trusting behavior; it is evident that there will be occasions when his trust will be fulfilled and other occasions when his trust will be violated. The proportions of fulfillment and of violations will depend, in a sense, upon chance—i.e., upon whether the environment of the individual has a high or low proportion of trustworthiness. For example, if an individual trusts indiscriminately all the people who ask to borrow money from him, the proportion of people who repay him will vary considerably depending upon whether the people who borrow at any given time are millionaires or paupers, conscience-ridden or conscienceless. Indiscriminate suspicion will likewise be accidentally appropriate on some occasions and inappropriate on other occasions.[6]

The essential feature of nonpathological trust or suspicion is that it is flexible and responsive to changing circumstances. Pathological trust or suspicion, on the other hand, is characterized by an inflexible, rigid, unaltering tendency to act in a trusting or suspicious manner ir-

6. It is possible to defend the notion that, as long as an individual reacts indiscriminately, he is better off if he reacts with trust than with suspicion. This notion can be defended by making any of the following assumptions: (1) reality is composed of more benevolent than malevolent events; e.g., such that most people can be trusted; (2) trusting behavior tends to induce trustworthiness in others while suspicious behavior tends to induce malevolence; (3) the emotional concomitants of trusting are more pleasant and more beneficial than the emotional concomitants of suspicion.

respective of the situation or of the consequences of so acting. The pathology is reflected in the indiscriminateness and incorrigibility of the behavior tendency.

Although it is evident that internal conflict is not sufficient to explain behavior pathology, it is well established that such internal conflict is a necessary condition for those forms of pathology not based upon defect, deficiency, or impairment. Apart from internal conflict, the conditions required for these common forms of behavior pathology are not clearly known. They tend to be subsumed under the general concept of *ego strength* or self-esteem, it being assumed that people with high ego strength are more able to resolve internal conflict or tolerate it without having it involve areas of the personality that are not immediately germane to the factors in conflict. However, even when ego strength is high, situational factors may make it difficult to either resolve or tolerate a conflict. In essence, an internal conflict is likely to be pathological to the extent that the behavior of the individual in conflict produces consequences that will perpetuate or enhance rather than resolve or diminish the conflict.

What is the nature of the internal conflict that reflects itself in pathological trust or suspicion? In essence, it is a conflict between being trusting and being suspicious. The object of trust or suspicion may be oneself or others. That is, just as one may have trust or suspicion with regard to the behavior of another, this is also possible with regard to one's own behavior.

It is to be expected that, wherever there is pathology of trust or suspicion with regard to others, there is an accompanying pathology with regard to oneself. Similarly, the ability to react with appropriate trust or suspicion to others implies that one is appropriately trusting or suspicious of oneself. Pathological overtrust of the other (gullibility) is usually accompanied by pathological undertrust of oneself; pathological oversuspicion of others (paranoia) is usually accompanied by pathological undersuspicion with regard to oneself.

The specific *manifestations* of pathological trust or suspicion are diverse and manifold. They are determined by the ego strength and character structure of the individual as well as by the characteristics of the situations in which the individual finds himself. However, certain general statements can be made.

First, let us elaborate some of the *consequences* that follow from the pathology of trust or suspicion. Pathology of trust or suspicion implies *ambivalence* between relatively extreme trust and relatively extreme suspicion. Hence, if an individual is inflexibly trusting or suspicious in his overt behavior and attitude, then he is at the same time covertly the opposite. Various defense mechanisms—e.g., projection, isolation—may be employed to keep the covert side of an ambivalent structure dissociated from behavior. The defenses, in addition to dissociating the covert side of the ambivalent structure, make the overt side more rigid, inflexible, and unvarying in expression. However, since defenses are rarely completely effective, it is not unusual for the ambivalence between trust and suspicion to be expressed through alternation or oscillation between extreme trust and extreme suspicion so that, behaviorally, the individual seems markedly variable or inconsistent in his orientation. A further possibility, which is probably the most common, is that an individual will express his conflict by segregating the conflicting orientations so that in reference to certain people or in certain situations he exhibits pathological trust, while in reference to others his orientation is inflexibly suspicious.

Although pathological trust and pathological suspicion both imply an internal conflict and have the characteristics of pathology in common, there are important differences between them. From our definitions of "trust" and "suspicion," it is apparent that trust with regard to another person is conducive to the establishment or continuation of a relationship, and suspicion is conducive to the avoidance or breaking off of a relationship. In other words, trust is promotive, and suspicion is contrient or alienative with respect to social relations.

Thus one would expect that, where the conflict between trust and suspicion is expressed in the form of pathological trust, the individual is more likely to be oriented toward others, while the individual who expresses his conflict in the form of pathological suspicion is more likely to be oriented away from or against others. These differences in expression of the underlying conflict reflect themselves in differences in conscious striving toward others, in perceptions and evaluations of others and of oneself, and in overt behavior.

Because the manifestations of the pathology of suspicion have been discussed extensively in the psychopathological literature dealing with paranoia and related conditions, this discussion will be confined to the *manifestations of pathological trust*. One indication of pathological trust is a tendency for the individual to confuse risk-taking and trusting situations. When the situation calls for a risk-taking or gambling orientation, he acts as though he requires a high level of confidence, and when the situation calls for a trusting orientation, he acts as though a high level of confidence is irrelevant. *Pathological trust may be expressed as an optimistic overestimate of the probability of getting what one wants.* A familiar example is the gambler who, despite repeated losses, expects Mother Nature to bestow her bounty upon him when he bets his fortune. *Pathological trust may also appear as an underestimation of the negative consequences of not obtaining what one wants.* A situation in which one may suffer much by trusting unwisely is experienced as one in which it is safe to gamble because the losses will not be bothersome. For example, the drug user, who is often well aware of his chances of being caught if he commits a crime, frequently underestimates the social-emotional consequences for him if he is arrested. Consequently, he may have a "so what" attitude toward the possibility of imprisonment, even though the actuality of imprisonment may have great emotional impact. Although both forms of pathological trust are characterized by the individual's responding as though there is little danger in acting on the assumption that the event he desires will occur, they have little in common otherwise. Let us consider the manifestations and concomitants of each of these two forms separately.

There are two major forms of the overoptimistic variety of pathological trust—the "gullible" or dependent form and the "omnipotent" or dominant form. The *gullible form of overoptimistic trust* implies an overestimation of the benevolence and power of the object of trust. That is, we would expect the gullible individual consciously to view others (toward whom he displays pathological trust) in a naive and exaggerated positive way that excludes negative characteristics. The object of trust is all good and all powerful; it has no defects or weaknesses that cannot be explained away or turned into graces. Accompanying this undifferentiated positive view of the object of trust is a view of the self as weak, helpless, and, when frustrated, bad. The gullible person, in effect, sees himself as dependent upon the more powerful, more knowing, more capable object of trust and maintains an attitude of compliance, submissiveness, and ingratiation in order to insure the benevolence of the object of trust.

Since the trust of the gullible person is often unwarranted, he is bound to have many experiences in which his trust is unfulfilled or violated. Ordinarily, when trust is not pathological, repeated experiences of nonfulfillment would lead to a less positive view of the object of trust and less optimism with regard to trust fulfillment. This correction of perception as a result of experience does not occur in the gullible person because, viewing himself as weak and helpless, he has no feasible alternative to that of continued reliance on the object of trust. He protects his image of his protector in order to feel protected. Since he feels he cannot depend upon himself, he is more apt to blame himself when he is frustrated because of the violation of his trust, than he is to blame the one upon whom he feels dependent. Consciously, he experiences a nonfulfillment of trust as a confirmation of his helplessness and worthlessness rather than as an indicator of the unreliability (due to powerlessness or malevolence) of his object of trust. He becomes depressed and self-pitying rather than angry, contemptful of himself rather than of the other, more compliant rather than less.

Overtly, then, we would expect the gullible person, in situations where he is characteristically gullible, to be characterized as follows: perception of himself as weak, helpless, inadequate; perception of others in whom he trusts as benevolent, powerful, reliable; perception of him by others as dependent, docile, compliant, ingratiating, lacking in self-confidence. We might anticipate that the gullible person's covert or unconscious perceptions of himself and of others would be rather different from his conscious perceptions. One would expect him to view those whom he overtly trusts with considerable suspicion covertly, perceiving them as powerful but malevolent. Unconsciously, the gullible person perceives that the powerful, malevolent other is converted from an object of suspicion into an object of trust by his own power to control and manipulate the other surreptitiously through his dependency. That is, he perceives that the malevolence of the powerful other is controllable by his own weakness and ineffectuality. Unconsciously, his overt ineffectuality is perceived as a source of strength not only because it controls the other, but also because it prevents or wards off demands by others upon him—i.e., if he is ineffectual no one can expect anything from him. Further, an overt pose of ineffectuality serves to prevent a covert self-conception of power and grandiosity from being exposed to contradiction by experience. If one does not try, one can never fail; lack of success under such conditions does not contradict the self-conception that one could have been successful if one wanted to.

The *omnipotent form of overoptimistic trust* implies an overestimation of one's own power to influence or control the object of trust. Everyday examples are to be found in street traffic when the omnipotent pedestrian or motorist will blithely or arrogantly ignore cars or traffic lights, assuming that he can disregard onrushing cars without being involved in an accident. In effect, the omnipotent individual feels that his wish, even though unexpressed, is enough to produce the desired behavior from the object of trust. The object of trust is, in other words, viewed as a servant of the omnipotent person's wishes. The omnipotent person may view his power to evoke service as emanating from his ability to compel service or from his ability to compel the feelings of love or duty that then, in turn, stimulate the desire to serve. The perceived source of his power over the object of trust will, of course, very much influence his reaction to the latter. However, despite important differences, there are basic similarities. Consciously, the object of trust is viewed as controllable, and the self is viewed as having the characteristics that enable control; the other is weak, the self is strong. To the observer, the omnipotent truster is likely to be perceived as authoritative, dominating, arrogant, imperious, lordly, or demanding—if his behavior is seen out of context; in context, his behavior is more likely to be perceived as pompous, blustering, or as an expression of bravado.

The overt feelings of omnipotence would, one could predict, be linked with covert feelings of lack of self-trust and inability to function without the help of the objects of trust. Covertly, one would anticipate that the objects of trust would be viewed as irresponsible and as entities whose help would be available only if their antipathy could be overcome.

The type of pathological trust wherein the individual distorts the significance to him of the consequences of having his trust violated may be labeled the *impulsive* or *nonchalant*. Whereas the overoptimistic person distorts *external* reality in the direction of assuming that it will be favorable to him, the impulsive or nonchalant person distorts *internal* reality in the direction of assuming that he does not care about or cannot be hurt by an unfavorable future external reality. His behavior is heedless of, indifferent to, or unconcerned about the consequences of not having his trust fulfilled. His lack of concern may reflect either an overemphasis of the momentary situation, an exclusive living in the present so that the future consequences of his behavior are neglected, or a tendency to think of himself as immune to the unpleasant. In either case, the impulsive or nonchalant person's behavior has the appearance of being impulse-dominated; it is heedless to the cognized reality and / or unresponsive to the anticipated negative consequences of seeking impulse gratification under conditions that call for restraint or postponement.

There are many factors that may lead one to neglect the future consequences of one's behavior. First, there are deficiencies or immaturities of the intellectual apparatus, which may lead to an inability to perceive time as extending into the future. The immature cognitive apparatus of the infant makes it difficult for him to cognize that there is anything but the here and now. Second, the momentary situation may be so compelling emotionally that the future becomes relatively insignificant. Thus if one is in a burning plane, one may parachute into the ocean to avoid being burned to death, knowing that the chances of being picked up are very small. In general, if the present situation is perceived to be so bad that nothing could make it any worse, one can act without regard to the possibility of future harm. If this basic condition exists, the clutching at a momentary pleasure or an improbable future gain, no matter how disastrous the possible future consequences of so doing may be, is understandable. Third, if the individual perceives himself to be a victim of fate, circumstance, or personal defect, the possibility of future harm may be accepted as inevitable (and hence unavoidable) and may even be desired as a confirmation of his perception of himself as victimized.

The impulsive or nonchalant type of pathological trust requires no overestimation of the benevolence and power of the object of trust, since little reliance is placed upon him. In fact, one might say that this type perceives that the object of trust is irrelevant to his actions or that it has to be outwitted, seduced, or deceived into allowing his actions to be successful. Hence, one would expect him to be either indifferent to, or manipulative of, his object of trust.

In the preceding pages, I have described three varieties of pathological trust. There may well be additional types; I make no claim to have exhausted the possibilities. My purpose in making this description is to emphasize that trust as well as suspicion can be irrational. The choice to trust or not does not always result from a realistic appraisal of probabilities and valences. It is often a reflection of personality tendencies that have their roots in a dimly remembered past.

PART TWO: RESEARCH PAPERS

8. Experimental Studies of Trust and Suspicion

Several of the studies to be reported in this chapter were among the earliest, and possibly the earliest, ones to employ the Prisoner's Dilemma game (to be described below) in psychological research. I take no credit (or blame) for spawning the enormous research literature that has utilized this game since these initial studies. For summaries of this literature, the reader is referred to Gallo and McClintock (1965), Swingle (1970), and Wrightsman, O'Connor, and Baker (1972). My interest in the game has not been in it per se but in the substantive psychological issues that can be explored with its use. The substantive findings of the studies reported in this chapter have not been negated by the subsequent research of others who have experimented with the Prisoner's Dilemma.

THE EXPERIMENTAL SITUATION

In our experimental studies of trust and suspicion, we utilized a two-person, non-zero-sum game in which the gains or losses incurred by each person are a function of the choices made by one's partner as well as of those made by oneself.

The game we employed is a version of the Prisoner's Dilemma, which Luce and Raiffa (1957, p. 95) have described as follows:

Two suspects are taken into custody and separated. The district attorney is certain they are guilty of a specific crime, but he does not have adequate evidence to convict them at a trial. He points out to each prisoner that each has two alternatives: to confess to the crime the police are sure they have done or not to confess. If they both do not confess then the district attorney states that he will book them on some very minor trumped-up charge . . . ; if they both confess,

179

they will be prosecuted, but he will recommend less than the most severe sentence; but if one confesses and the other does not, then the confessor will receive lenient treatment for turning state's evidence whereas the latter will get the "book" slapped at him.

The game, in its abstract form, is illustrated in Figure 8.1. Person I has to choose between rows X and Y; Person II has to choose between columns A and B. The amount of (imaginary) money each person wins or loses is determined by the cell he gets into as a result of his respective choices. For example, if Person I chooses row X and Person II chooses column A, they both get into the AX cell, and they each wins $9.00.

$$
\begin{array}{ccc}
 & A & B \\
X & +9, +9 & -10, +10 \\
Y & +10, -10 & -9, -9
\end{array}
$$

Figure 8.1. The trust problem (the Prisoner's Dilemma) used in several of our experiments. Person I chooses between rows X and Y. Person II between columns A and B. Person I's payoffs are the first numbers in the cells, Person II's are the second numbers.

If you examine the possibilities of choice for Person I, you will notice that he can win most and lose least by choosing Y. Similarly, Person II can win most and lose least by choosing B. However, if I chooses Y and II chooses B they both lose $9.00. Both can win only if they end up in the AX cell. If I is reasonably sure that II is going to choose A, he can win more by choosing Y. Analogously, if II is confident that I is going to choose X, he can win more by choosing B rather than A!

In playing the game, the subjects, who were all college students, knew exactly what the situation was and understood the implications of any combination of choices that they and other persons might make. In one set of experiments, the game was a one-trial game; in another set of experiments, it was a ten-trial game. The data obtained from each subject included, in addition to his choice, what he thought the other person would choose and what he thought the other person expected him to choose.

The essential psychological feature of the game is that there is no possibility for "rational" individual behavior in it unless the conditions for mutual trust exist. If each player chooses to obtain either maximum gain or minimum loss for himself, he will lose. But it makes no sense to choose the other alternative, which could result in maximum loss, unless one can trust the other player. If one cannot trust, it is, of course, safer to choose so as to suffer minimum rather than maximum loss, but it is even better not to play the game. If one cannot avoid playing the game and if one cannot trust, there may be no reasonable alternative except to choose "the lesser of two evils" and / or attempt to develop the conditions that will permit mutual trust.

There are, of course, many social situations that are like that of the game, in the sense that they do not permit rational individual behavior unless the conditions for mutual trust exist. Any social situation in which an individual may enhance his own satisfactions to the disadvantage of another by not adhering to the normalized expectations or social rules governing the situation is of this sort—e.g., buyer-seller transactions, husband-wife relationships, pedestrian-driver interactions, a crowd in a theater when there is a fire. In everyday situations, mutual trust is predicated upon the existence of socialized motives (e.g., an interest in the welfare of others, a desire for social approval), conscience, external authority, or arrangements that will provide the participants with an incentive for adhering to the rules. Generally, if people who are willing to adhere to the rules cannot trust that other participants in the situation will also adhere to the rules, there is little possibility for rational behavior except to attempt to develop the conditions under which mutual adherence to the rules will occur.

The experiments described below were conducted to see whether the experimental game would, in fact, elicit the phenomena of trust and suspicion and to study some of the conditions that might affect the individual's willingness to trust or not. Observation of the subjects as they played and interviews with them afterward make it quite clear that, despite the highly artificial nature of the game situation, they became intensely involved and felt double-crossed, cheated, and exploited and experienced other emotions appropriate to their activities while playing.

THE EFFECTS OF MOTIVATIONAL ORIENTATION [1]

My research on interpersonal trust began with the assumption that there were three basic types of motivational orientations that an indi-

1. The research presented in this section is presented more fully in Deutsch (1958; 1960a).

vidual would be likely to have in an interpersonal situation: *cooperative*—the person has a positive interest in the welfare of the others as well as his own welfare; *individualistic*—the person has an interest in doing as well as he can for himself and is unconcerned about the welfare of the others; and *competitive*—the person has an interest in doing better than the others as well as in doing as well as he can for himself.[2] It seemed reasonable to hypothesize that mutual awareness of a shared cooperative orientation would be very likely to help establish a relationship of mutual trust, while mutual awareness of a shared competitive orientation would be very likely to lead to a relationship of mutual suspicion. More generally, one could assume that any factors that would facilitate the development of a shared cooperative orientation would increase the likelihood of mutual trust. Such factors might include bonds of friendship, awareness of similarity in values, common group membership and allegiance, normative pressures to be cooperative in the broader culture or in the experimental situation, and personality predispositions favoring cooperation. Similarly, any factors that would stimulate the development of a competitive orientation would decrease the chance of developing a mutually trusting relationship. Such factors might include negative attitudes toward one another, awareness of dissimilarity in values or

---

2. There are other possible types. The theoretical possibilities can be evoked by considering that an individual can be oriented toward what happens to himself (S), what happens to the other (O), or what happens to himself and the other in relation to one another. Using "max" and "min" as abbreviations for "maximum" and "minimum," the following ten elementary orientations are possible: (1) *individualistic*— max S (S is concerned with maximizing his own satisfactions); (2) *masochistic*—min S (S is concerned with minimizing his own satisfactions); (3) *altruistic*—max O (S is concerned with maximizing O's satisfaction); (4) *hostile*—min O (S is concerned with minimizing O's satisfaction); (5) *collectivistic*—max S and O (S wishes to maximize the total satisfactions received); (7) *rivalrous*—max S−O (S wishes to maximize the differences between what he and O get in his own favor); (8) *egalitarian*— min S−O (S wishes to minimize the difference in his favor between what he and O get); (9) *self-abasing*—max O−S (S wishes to maximize the differences between O and S, in O's favor); and (10) *defensive*—min O−S (S wishes to prevent O from doing better than S). It is evident that a rivalrous orientation will often require S to try to maximize S, minimize O, and minimize O−S. Similarly, a collectivistic-egalitarian orientation will often oblige S to maximize S and O. A self-abasing orientation will require S to minimize S and maximize O; a nihilistic orientation will entail a minimization of both S and O. Thus, the cooperative orientation is typically an amalgam of the "individualistic," "altruistic," "collectivistic," and "egalitarian" elementary orientations; the competitive orientation is usually a composite of the "individualistic," "hostile," "rivalrous," and "defensive" elements.

opposition of interest, normative pressures for competition, and personality pre-dispositions favoring competition.

By definition, the person with an individualistic orientation obtains no intrinsic satisfaction from the other's gains or losses. The character of the relationship does not predispose the individualistic person to be either trustworthy or untrustworthy. Under what circumstances can a person with this orientation be trusted to fulfill his part of an implicit or explicit contract? Clearly, one such circumstance is when the contract or exchange is *enforceable* by the superior power that one possesses or by third parties such as the police, the courts, or one's allies. Another circumstance is when the individualistic person has *committed* himself to the contract by allowing something that is valuable to him, such as his reputation, a deposit, or a hostage of some sort, to be lost if he does not fulfill his trust. But there are many circumstances in which neither binding commitments nor enforcement of agreements can be arranged. In such circumstances, one can trust the individualistic other if one can control the timing of the exchange between oneself and the other so that the other gets what he wants from you only as or after he gives you what you want. The problem is somewhat more complicated when both parties to an exchange see the other as being individualistically oriented. In this case, to engage in an exchange each party must be in the position of knowing that the other is making his contribution to the exchange simultaneously with his own contribution. "Physical simultaneity"—i.e., the occurrence of the decisions at the same physical time—is not crucial; what is required is "psychological simultaneity"—the mutual awareness of what the other is doing as each decides what to do.

The implication of the above reasoning is that trusting behavior can occur, even when the participants are solely interested in their own welfare, if their trustworthiness can be enforced or guaranteed by third parties, if commitments can be made that make untrustworthiness too costly, or if the timing of an exchange permits each party to withhold or withdraw his contribution provided the other does likewise. In other words, one can expect that a trusting relationship can be developed under an individualistic orientation only if external circumstances provide the support for it. Without such external support, there is little basis for trust between those who are concerned only with their own welfare.

To test some of the ideas advanced in the preceding pages about the effects of the different motivational orientations upon the development of trust or suspicion, subjects (Ss) participated in the experimental game described earlier under the three different types of orientation. The various motivational orientations were created by inserting different paragraphs at the end of the instructions explaining the mechanics of the game. The instructions for the *cooperative motivational orientation* were:

> Before you start playing the game, let me emphasize that in playing the game you should consider yourself to be partners. You're interested in your partner's welfare as well as in your own. You do have an interest in whether your partner wins or loses. You do care how he does, and he does care how you do. His feelings make a difference to you, and your feelings make a difference to him. You want to win as much money as you can for yourself, and you do want him to win. He feels exactly the same way; he wants you to win, too. In other words, you each want to win money, and you also want your partner to win, too.

The *individualistic motivational orientation* was created by the following instructions:

> Before you start playing the game, let me emphasize that in playing the game your only motivation should be to win as much money as you can for yourself. You are to have no interest whatsoever in whether the other person wins or loses or in how much he wins or loses. This is not a competitive game. You both can win, you both can lose, or one can win and the other can lose. You don't care how he does, and he doesn't care how you do. Assume that you don't know each other and that you'll never see each other again. His feelings don't make any difference to you, and your feelings don't make any difference to him. You're not out to help him and you're not out to beat him. You simply want to win as much money as you can for yourself, and you don't care what happens to him. He feels exactly the same way.

The instructions for the *competitive motivational orientation* were:

> Before you start playing the game, let me emphasize that in playing the game your motivation should be to win as much money as you can for yourself and also to do better than the other person.

You want to make rather than lose money, but you also want to come out ahead of the other person. Assume that you don't know each other and that you'll never see each other again. His feelings don't make any difference to you. He feels the same as you.

The effects of several other variables, in addition to motivational orientation, were investigated. These were:

I. *Psychological simultaneity of choice.* Three degrees of simultaneity of choice were created:
   A. Full psychological simultaneity of choice was created in the *reversibility* treatment. Here the Ss were allowed to change their choices, after they had both chosen secretly and simultaneously (without prior communication), once their choices had been announced to them by the experimenter. Either one or both of them could change their choices. They were allowed to continue changing choices as long as they wanted to. They were told, however, that if no one changed his choice during a thirty-second interval, this would be taken to indicate that neither wanted to change. Thus at the end of the thirty-second interval, as each S made the decision not to change his choice, each S was fully aware of the other's choice.
   B. In the *simultaneous choice* conditions, the Ss made their choices at the same time, secretly, without knowledge of the other person's choice.
   C. In the *nonsimultaneous choice* conditions, Person I made his choice first and it was announced to Person II before he made his choice; Person I was aware that this would be done when he made his choice.

I assumed that mutual cooperation would be greatest in the reversibility condition and least in the nonsimultaneous choice condition. Moreover, I anticipated that the effects of this variable would be most pronounced under the individualistic motivational orientation.

II. *Communication versus no communication.* In the *communication* conditions, the Ss were allowed to communicate with each other before making their choices by writing notes to each other; in the *no communication* conditions, the Ss were not allowed to communicate with each other before making their

choices. My assumptions were that communication would permit the individualistically oriented Ss to commit themselves
and that doing so would facilitate the development of trust.

III. *One-trial versus ten-trial games.* Some of the games were of
one-trial length, others lasted ten trials. In the ten-trial game
(which always had the Ss choosing simultaneously in secret),
the choices made by the Ss were announced to each other after
each trial so that the Ss could figure their gains or losses on
that trial. Although none of the hypotheses relates to the number of trials in the game, I was interested in seeing if choice behavior would be influenced by the length of the game.

Results

Table 8.1 presents data indicating the effects of the motivational orientation upon the choice to cooperate (recall that a choice of A or X
is a cooperative choice) under the various experimental conditions.
The data give clear support to the hypotheses. They indicate that in
all experimental conditions, a cooperative orientation primarily leads
the individual to make a cooperative choice that results in mutual
gain, whereas a competitive orientation primarily leads the individual
to make a noncooperative choice that results in mutual loss. In contrast, for the individualistic orientation the choice to cooperate or not
is very much a function of the specific experimental treatments.

Table 8.2 presents data indicating the choices made by the Ss in
conjunction with their expectations concerning the choices of the
other persons. It is evident that, in all experimental treatments, the cooperatively oriented Ss predominantly expected as well as chose cooperation, whereas the competitively oriented Ss primarily expected as
well as chose noncooperation. Again, the choice-expectation patterns
of the individualistically oriented Ss are much more influenced by the
specific experimental treatments. It is interesting to note that in all
three motivational orientations, but particularly in the competitive
and individualistic ones, there is a tendency for the S to expect more
cooperation from the other person than he is willing to offer the
other. This tendency is reflected in the preference for double-crossing
the other (i.e., choosing noncooperatively when he knows or expects
that the other person will choose cooperatively) rather than being
double-crossed by the other. Essentially, the S appears to think that
the other person is more likely to be a sucker, and allow himself to be
double-crossed, than the S is himself.

TABLE 8.1. Percentage of Cooperative Choices by Individuals and by Pairs for Different Motivational Orientations and Different Experimental Conditions

Condition	N[1]	Individuals Who Chose Cooperatively[2]	Pairs in Which Both Chose Cooperatively	Pairs in Which Both Chose Noncooperatively
A. *No Communication, Simultaneous Choice*				
Cooperative	46	89.1	82.6	4.3
Individualistic	78	35.9	12.8	41.0
Competitive	32	12.5	6.3	81.3
B. *No Communication, Nonsimultaneous Choice*				
Cooperative	48	79.3	73.9	17.4
Individualistic	48	18.8	4.2	62.5
Competitive	30	16.7	6.7	73.3
C. *Communication, Simultaneous Choice*				
Cooperative	32	96.9	93.8	
Individualistic	34	70.6	58.8	17.6
Competitive	48	29.2	16.7	58.3
D. *Communication, Nonsimultaneous Choice*				
Cooperative	32	84.4	81.3	12.5
Individualistic	42	52.4	38.1	33.3
Competitive	44	34.1	27.3	59.1
E. *Reversibility*				
Cooperative	74	94.6	94.6	5.4
Individualistic	70	77.1	77.1	22.9
Competitive	62	36.1	36.1	63.9
F. *Ten Trials, No Communication, Simultaneous Choice*				
Cooperative	34	70.9	55.5	15.0
Individualistic	34	35.6	13.5	43.2
Competitive	42	25.3	3.9	52.9

[1] N refers to the number of individuals in the given experimental treatment; no individual was used in more than one treatment. The number of pairs (i.e. Person I and Person II who played the game together) is $N/2$. The individual percentages are based upon N, the pair percentages are based upon $N/2$.

[2] The statistical significances ($p < .05$) within the table may be summarized as follows: Within every experimental condition (i.e., A through F) the cooperative orientation results in significantly more cooperative choices than do either the individualistic or competitive orientations; within every condition except the *no communication-nonsimultaneous choice* condition and the *ten-trial game,* the individualistic orientation results in significantly more cooperative choices than does the competitive orientation. Comparing the cooperative orientation across experimental conditions A through E, none of the comparisons are statistically significant; the competitive orientation in E results in more cooperative choices than it does in A, otherwise there are no significant differences among the competitive orientations; for the individualistic orientation, communication (i.e., C vs. A, D vs. B) results in a significant increase in cooperative choices as does "reversibility" (i.e., E vs. A).

TABLE 8.2. Percentage of Ss Who Made Cooperative (C) or Noncooperative (K) Choices in Conjunction with Cooperative (CE) or Noncooperative (KE) Expectations Concerning the Other Person's Choices

			C		K	
Condition	N	Choice Expect [1]	CE	KE	CE	KE
A. *No Communication, Simultaneous Choice*						
Cooperative	46		84.8	4.3	6.5	4.3
Individualistic	39 [2]		33.3	5.1	25.6	35.9
Competitive	32		3.1	9.4	12.5	75.0
B. *No Communication, Nonsimultaneous Choice* [3]						
Cooperative I	24		83.3	0	0	16.6
Cooperative II	24		75.0	0	8.3	16.7
Individualistic I	24		29.2	0	0	70.9
Individualistic II	24		8.3	0	20.8	70.8
Competitive I	15		26.7	0	0	73.3
Competitive II	15		6.7	0	20.0	73.3
C. *Communication, Simultaneous Choice*						
Cooperative	32		90.6	6.2	3.1	0
Individualistic	34		61.8	8.8	2.9	26.5
Competitive	48		20.8	8.3	18.8	52.1
D. *Communication, Nonsimultaneous Choice* [3]						
Cooperative I	16		87.5	0	0	12.4
Cooperative II	16		81.2	0	6.2	12.5
Individualistic I	21		66.6	0	0	33.4
Individualistic II	21		38.1	0	28.6	33.3
Competitive I	22		40.9	0	0	59.1
Competitive II	22		27.3	0	13.6	59.1
F. *Ten Trials, No Communication, Simultaneous Choice*						
Cooperative	34		62.3	8.7	15.0	14.4
Individualistic	34		27.3	8.1	31.2	34.5
Competitive	42		17.8	7.5	26.6	47.4

[1] The statistical significances (p<.05) with regard to the frequency of cooperative expectations may be summarized as follows: within every experimental condition except F, the cooperative orientation results in significantly more cooperative expectations than does the individualistic orientation. Within every treatment, the cooperative orientation differs significantly from the competitive orientation. The individualistic orientation, compared with the competitive, results in significantly more cooperative expectations for all conditions but B and F. For the cooperative orientation, there are no significant differences between any of the experimental conditions; for the competitive orientation, the only significant comparisons are A vs. C, A vs. D, A vs. F; for the individualistic orientation, the only significant comparisons are A vs. B, B vs. C, B vs. D, and B vs. F.

[2] The discrepancy in N between tables 8.1 and 8.2 is due to the fact that a folder of data was lost after table 8.1 and before table 8.2 were tabulated.

[3] I refers to Person I, who chose and announced his choice before Person II

The Effects of Simultaneity of Choice

An implication of the simultaneity hypothesis is that mutual cooperation would be likely to result if the conditions permit each of two individualistically oriented Ss to be simultaneously aware that the other
is choosing to cooperate as he makes his own choice to cooperate. The
experimental treatments offer three degrees of simultaneity of choice.
The reversibility treatment has full psychological simultaneity of
choice; each S is aware of the other person's choice as he and the
other make the mutual decision not to change their choices. The no
communication-simultaneous choice treatment (where both Ss choose
in secret at the same time) has physical simultaneity of choice but
lacks psychological simultaneity. The no communication-nonsimultaneous choice treatment (where one S makes his choice and announces
it before the other S makes his choice) has neither physical nor psychological simultaneity. The results (see table 8.1) clearly support the
hypothesis. Under conditions of full psychological simultaneity (the
reversibility treatment), the individualistically oriented Ss mostly
choose to cooperate, and thus they react quite differently from the
competitively oriented Ss but somewhat similarly to the cooperatively
oriented ones. In contrast, under conditions of complete lack of simultaneity (the no communication-nonsimultaneous choice treatment), they react very similarly to the competitively oriented Ss and
very differently from the cooperatively oriented Ss. Under conditions
of physical but not psychological simultaneity of choice, they choose
somewhat more cooperatively than when there is complete lack of simultaneity, but their choices are still predominantly noncooperative.

Another perspective on the effects of variations in psychological simultaneity is obtained by examining the tendency of an S to double-
cross the other in the three experimental treatments we have been
considering. In the reversibility treatment, there was no possibility for
double-crossing the other, since he could always change his choice. In

---

(*Table 8.2, note 3, continued*)
chose. II refers to Person II. In the Nonsimultaneous treatments, we had no data on
Ss' expectations before they made their choices so we have assumed that Person I
expected Person II to reciprocate (i.e. if Person I chose cooperatively he expected
Person II to choose cooperatively). Person II knew Person I's choice before he made
his choice, so we have equated his knowledge with his expectation (i.e. if Person II
knew Person I chose cooperatively, he "expected" that Person I chose cooperatively).

the no communication-simultaneous choice treatment, of the Ss who expected the other person to cooperate, 80 percent of the competitively oriented, 43 percent of the individualistically oriented, and 7 percent of the cooperatively oriented chose not to cooperate. In the no communication-nonsimultaneous choice treatment, of the opportunities for double-crossing the other, 75 percent were used by the competitively oriented, 71 percent by the individualistically oriented, and only 10 percent by the cooperatively oriented Ss.

The Effects of Communication

In the theoretical section, I hypothesized that if two individuals were individualistically oriented, mutual cooperation would occur if each could commit himself, and be convinced that the other person had also committed himself, to the choice of cooperation. I suggested that the opportunity to communicate would enable individualistically oriented Ss to commit themselves (and be assured that the other had also committed himself) to choosing cooperatively by making a promise that it would be difficult to break because of guilt or fear of social disapproval. If we contrast the communication treatments (where two-way communication by notes was permitted between the two players) with the no communication treatments, we see that the opportunity to communicate does increase the tendency to choose cooperatively. The increase is greatest and is only significant for the Ss with the individualistic orientation. The Ss with the cooperative orientation do not, in effect, need the opportunity to communicate to choose cooperatively, whereas the Ss with the competitive orientation have motives and expectations that make it difficult for them to engage in or expect trustworthy communication. Thus table 8.3, which indicates what the Ss did with their communication opportunity, reveals that (for the simultaneous choice condition) more than half of the competitively oriented pairs did not use their opportunities to communicate about the game (though about one-third of these pairs did communicate about irrelevant matters). This is true for none of the individualistically or cooperatively oriented Ss. Almost two-thirds of the cooperative agreements reached through communication in the competitively oriented pairs were misleading, in the sense that at least one member of the pair violated them in his game-playing behavior. This was true for 17 percent of the cooperative agreements reached by individualistic pairs and for none of the agreements of the cooperatively oriented pairs.

The results for the nonsimultaneous choice treatment are similar to the foregoing. However, the differences between the individualistically and competitively oriented Ss are not quite so striking in the nonsimultaneous choice treatment as they are in the simultaneous choice treatment.

TABLE 8.3. Percentage of Pairs with Different Motivational Orientations That Engaged in Various Types of Communication

	Simultaneous Choice			Nonsimultaneous Choice		
	Coop. (16)[1]	*Indiv.* (17)	*Comp.* (24)	*Coop.* (16)	*Indiv.* (21)	*Comp.* (22)
No Comm.	0	0	38	0	5	23
Irrelevant Comm.	0	0	17	6	0	14
Comm. of Noncoop.	6	18	8	6	10	14
No Agreement	0	12	4	13	29	5
Misleading Comm.	0	12	21	0	19	18
Comm. of Coop.	94	59	13	75	38	27

[1] Figures in parentheses indicate the number of pairs in the given experimental treatment upon which the percentages are based. The differences among the three orientations are statistically significant ($p<.05$). The test of significance was a chi-square based upon a collapsed version of the table. (Simultaneous choice and nonsimultaneous choice were collapsed; the two top rows were collapsed, and so were the third, fourth, and fifth rows.)

The Ten-Trial Game

Figure 8.2 presents data for the ten-trial game, indicating the percentage of Ss in each motivational orientation that made cooperative choices and the percentage that had cooperative expectations in each of the ten trials. The ten-trial game was similar to the no communication-simultaneous choice one-trial game, except that the choices of the Ss were made known to all by the experimenter after each trial. From tables 8.1 and 8.2, it is apparent that an extended series of trials did not significantly increase the likelihood or the expectation of a cooperative choice (except for the competitively oriented) averaged over the ten trials as compared with the similar one-trial game.[3]

A comparison of the results on the first trial in the ten-trial game

3. It may be noted that in our exploratory research we had several pairs play the game for 5 trials and several play it for 100 trials and several more play it with no definite limit of trials. My impression is that the results were essentially the same as for the ten-trial game, except that the monotony of extended repetition of the same choices led some of the Ss to choose frivolously as a means of distraction.

(see figure 8.2) with the results for the similar one-trial game (see tables 8.1 and 8.2) also indicates that the anticipation of an extended series of trials did not significantly increase the likelihood or the expectation of a cooperative choice (except for the competitively oriented). Moreover, for the Ss with an individualistic or competitive orientation, the percentage of cooperative choices tended to decrease somewhat on the last trials; this was not the case for the cooperatively oriented Ss. Further light is shed on these results by the data concern-

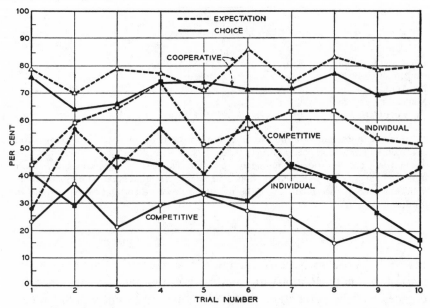

Figure 8.2. Percentage of cooperative choices and of cooperative expectations for the three motivational orientations in the ten-trial game.

ing the confirmation or disappointment of the Ss' expectations with regard to the others' choices. These data (see table 8.4) indicate that expectations of cooperation from the other person were very likely to be confirmed for Ss with a cooperative orientation but were very likely to be disappointed for those with an individualistic or competitive orientation. The opposite was true for expectations of noncooperation from the other person. It is interesting to note that the expectation of a cooperative choice from the other person did not decrease as much as one might have expected from its rate of disappointment in the individualistic and competitive orientations. Apparently, the Ss with the individualistic and competitive orientations were more loath to expect realistically that they would end up losing no matter what they did (i.e., to expect a noncooperative choice) than to expect that they could outwit the other person so that the other person would end up at a disadvantage. The competitively oriented, as compared with the individualistically oriented, Ss were evidently less optimistic about outwitting the other person, since a smaller percentage of their non-cooperative choices was accompanied by an expectation that the other player would choose cooperatively (see table 8.2).

TABLE 8.4. Percentage of Cooperative and Noncooperative Expectations Confirmed or Disconfirmed for the Different Motivational Orientations in Ten-Trial Game

| | Cooperative Expectation | | Noncooperative Expectation | |
	Confirmed	Disconfirmed	Confirmed	Disconfirmed
Cooperative	72.0(261) [1]	28.0(261)	41.6(77)	58.4(77)
Individualistic	36.4(195)	63.6(195)	65.5(142)	34.5(142)
Competitive	27.6(185)	72.4(185)	76.7(228)	23.3(228)

[1] The figures in parentheses indicate the number of expectations upon which the percentage is based. Apart from some incompletions in filling out the forms, each S indicated ten times what he expected the other person to choose; i.e., before each one of the ten trials. The differences between the cooperative and either of the other two orientations are statistically significant ($p < .05$), but the differences between the individualistic and competitive orientations are not.

If we consider the choice behavior of the Ss over the ten trials as a form of communication to the other player, it is quite evident that it was relatively ineffective in comparison with the more explicit communication of the notes in inducing mutual cooperation among the individualistically oriented. My impression was that, without explicit communication, once the two players' choices were out of phase— e.g., one choosing cooperatively and the other not—it was extremely difficult for them to get together again. Thus if Person I chose cooperatively and Person II chose uncooperatively, Person I might get angry and choose uncooperatively while Person II would choose cooperatively, but this would then lead Person II to feel that his "virtuous reform" had gone unrewarded, and the vicious cycle would be perpetuated, ending in a frustrating, mutually self-defeating stalemate.

Summary and Conclusion

Taken together, the results clearly support the hypotheses concerning the effects of motivational orientation. It is evident that a cooperative orientation will produce trusting (and trustworthy) behavior even when the situational facilities do not encourage it—e.g., when no communication is permitted and when one has to choose without knowledge of the other person's choice. On the other hand, even when situational facilities are encouraging, a competitive orientation will result in suspicious and/or untrustworthy behavior rather than in trust and trustworthiness. In contrast to both the cooperative and the competitive orientations, the behavior resulting from an individualistic orientation is very much influenced by situational determinants. The opportunity to commit oneself to a cooperative agreement through communication and the opportunity to know what the other is doing as one decides what to do facilitate considerably the development of mutual cooperation between individualistically oriented subjects. The implication of these results is important and is worth emphasizing because of the common assumption that mutual trust is possible only when people are oriented to each other's welfare. These results suggest that trust in cooperative behavior from another can reside in the situational determinants of the other's behavior rather than in his character.

It should be noted that, in my initial study, the subjects knew that they were paired with someone whose orientation was similar to their own. What would have happened if the paired subjects had had different orientations, such, for example, that one in each pair was cooperatively oriented and the other competitively oriented? It seems reasonable to assume that a competitive subject would be tempted to exploit the cooperative subject and that the latter would, as a result, be forced into defensive, competitive response. The end result of such a pairing would much more likely be mutual competition than mutual cooperation. The choice-expectation data of table 8.2 are consistent with our assumption. Competitively oriented subjects would be unlikely to make a cooperative response even when they expected the other to be cooperative, while cooperatively oriented subjects would be likely to defend themselves by choosing noncooperatively when they expected an uncooperative response from the other. The findings of this and subsequent research by Kelley and Stahelski (1970) suggest that *trust, when violated, is more likely to turn into suspicion than negated suspicion is to turn into trust. If this is so, it should be easier to move from cooperation to competition than from competition to cooperation.*

Recent research by Garner and Deutsch (1973) indicates that the pessimism of the preceding statement needs qualification. The deterioration of cooperation is most likely to occur when paired subjects, who in fact have different orientations from one another, are each expecting the other to be similar to himself. If one's initial expectation that the other has a different orientation from his own is correct and thus confirmed rather than disconfirmed, cooperation does not deteriorate. The cooperatively oriented subject in this latter situation may choose cooperatively, despite his belief that the other will choose competitively, in an attempt to change the other so that the other is less competitive; in so doing, he may meet with a measure of success.

THE INFLUENCE OF COMMUNICATION [4]

My initial study of the influence of communication indicated that subjects with an individualistic orientation were more likely to trust each other if they could communicate freely before they made their choices. However, it was evident that a sizable percentage of these subjects did not utilize the communication opportunity effectively. It was also apparent that the notes of the subjects who established mutual trust were different in a number of respects from the notes of the subjects who did not succeed in this. These results suggested the general question: How can communication opportunities be used to raise the individual's confidence that his trust will be fulfilled and also to elicit trustworthy or responsible behavior?

One approach to answering this question is to rephrase it and ask what the minimum ingredients of a cooperative interchange are. In essence, they are a complementarity of intention and expectation. That is, Person I expects Person II to perform certain activities that are

4. The research reported here was conducted by Dr. James L. Loomis and is presented more fully in his article (Loomis 1959). Dr. Loomis also employed the Prisoner's Dilemma game. The payoffs values he employed increased the likelihood of suspicion and/or untrustworthy behavior. His matrix was:

$$+10, +10 \qquad -20, +20$$
$$+20, -20 \qquad -10, -10$$

necessary to I's gratifications, and I, in turn, intends to perform certain activities that are necessary to II's gratifications; a complementary situation exists for II vis-à-vis his intentions and expectations. However, for the cooperative interchange to be a stable, ongoing system, each person must have a way of reacting to violations of his expectations, a way that is known to the other and that can serve as an inhibitor of violation. The frequent occurrence of violations will usually break down the system of cooperative interchange. However, the nature of any ongoing system is such that violation is likely to occur, if only by chance. Hence, for the system to endure, there must be some way of avoiding the following self-perpetuating cycle: violation on the part of Person I, leading to a reaction to I's violation on the part of Person II, leading to expectation of distrust from II and, hence, to repeated violation by I, leading to a reaction to I's violation on the part of II, etc. That is, the system must have some means of restoring complementarity, once it has been violated. It must have, in effect, a method of absolution and of recognizing when a return to complementarity has occurred. In sum, the following elements appear to be involved in a stable cooperative system: cooperative expectation, cooperative intention, sanctions for violations, and absolution.

An experiment in which prepared notes were constructed using one or more of these four elements was designed by James Loomis as his dissertation research. There were five different notes in all. The simplest note (which stated the note writer's expectation) said, in effect, "I would like you to cooperate so that I can win." The most complete note included all four elements. It stated, "I will cooperate, and I would like you to cooperate. That way we can both win. If you don't cooperate, then I will choose so that you can't win. If you decide to cooperate and make a cooperative choice after first not doing so, then I will cooperate." The intermediate notes contained one, two, or three of these elements. Some of the subjects received notes and others sent notes; but there was never any two-way communication. As a control, one group of subjects played the game without any opportunity to communicate.

The experiment proceeded as follows. The game was explained. It was indicated that there would be five trials during the game. Then, the subjects were tested to see whether they understood the implications of the various combinations of choices. The subjects were all given the individualistic orientation. Next, the subjects either sent or received a note. The subjects were induced to send a note of a given type by instructions and by the message form on which they were asked to write. Thus if a subject was a "sender" and was assigned to communicate his intention only, he got a note form which read: "I am going to choose————." If he was assigned to communicate expectation only, his note form read: "I would like you to choose————." And so on.

After the note writing and reading was completed, the game began. The subject and the other person, without knowledge of what each other's choice would be on that trial, made their choices. After the choices were made on each trial, they were announced.

Results

We expected that trust and cooperation would increase as a function of the completeness of the communication. Results on the first trial (see table 8.5), where the subjects had not yet experienced how the other persons would play, indicated that 11 percent of the control subjects who received no communication, 31 percent of the subjects who received a note indicating only what choice they were expected to make, and 80 percent of the subjects who received the full communication treatment trusted the other person and made cooperative choices (i.e., they were trustworthy as well as trusting). The results at the intermediate levels were consistent with this trend.

The subject's communication position did have differential effects. The note receivers more frequently tended to expect the other person to be trusting and trustworthy than did the note senders. (The excep-

TABLE 8.5. Percentage of Subjects Who Expected Cooperation and Also Chose Cooperatively by Level of Communication and by Communication Position (On first trial)

Communication Level	Receiver [1]	Sender [1]	Total [2]
No communication	11	11	11
Expectation only	22	39	31
Intention only	39	39	39
Expectation and intention	56	39	47
Sanction	67	56	61
Absolution	89	72	80

[1] Each percentage is based on an N of 18.
[2] Each percentage is based on an N of 36.

tion occurred when the note receiver was given a note containing only the note sender's expectation of cooperation from the receiver.) On the other hand, the note receiver was more likely than the note sender to violate the trust he perceived the other person to have, even when he expected the other person to be trustworthy as well as trusting. In other words, there was a clear tendency for the note receiver to expect more trustworthiness but to be less trustworthy, despite this expectation, than the note sender. In considering these results, one should keep in mind that the notes that were sent or received were always cooperatively oriented.

A possible explanation for the differences due to the communication position of the subject may be found in terms of commitment. The note sender had, by sending the note, committed himself to cooperation and hence was more likely to choose cooperatively. The note receiver, as a result of the note and its implicit commitment, had a better basis for expecting the other person to be trusting and trustworthy, but since he had not written a note, he had not committed himself to choose cooperatively.

What are the conditions under which a person will be committed to what he communicates? This study throws no light upon this question. However, our earlier studies of two-way communication suggest that, when subjects are competitively oriented, there is little commitment to what one communicates and hence little basis for trust as a result of the communication one receives. It would seem that the situation has to be ambiguous, rather than clearly competitive, as to whether the individuals will interrelate themselves cooperatively or competitively before an individual will assume that communications are informative rather than misleading. The greater trustworthiness of communications in an individualistic as compared with a competitive situation possibly reflects the greater social restraints against deception in the individualistic situation. Customarily, "anything goes" under intense competition.

Summary

To sum up our research on the influence of communication, it is evident that mutual trust can be established in people with an individualistic orientation through communication. Communication is likely to be effective in this area to the extent that the basic features of a cooperative interrelationship are made explicit in what is communicated.

These basic features are (1) expression of one's cooperative intention; (2) expression of one's cooperative expectation; (3) expression of one's planned reaction to violations of one's expectation; and (4) expression of a means of restoring cooperation after a violation of one's expectation has occurred.

THE INFLUENCE OF SOME TYPES OF POWER RELATIONSHIPS AND GAME STRATEGIES UPON THE DEVELOPMENT OF INTERPERSONAL TRUST [5]

In this dissertation experiment designed by Leonard Solomon, we were interested in studying whether an individualistically oriented subject would be more trusting when the other's temptation to be untrustworthy was low rather than high and when the subject had more rather than less power to affect the outcomes of the other. In addition, we were concerned with studying the effects of three different strategies upon the subject's trust and trustworthiness. These were: *unconditionally cooperative,* in which the other (who was an accomplice of the experimenter) chose cooperatively no matter how the subject chose; *conditionally cooperative,* in which the other matched the subject's choice, choosing cooperatively only when the subject chose cooperatively; and *unconditionally noncooperative,* in which the other chose noncooperatively no matter how the subject chose.

We reasoned that since an individualistically motivated subject is utilitarian in perspective, he would attribute a similar orientation to the other. Moreover, he would expect the other, if tempted, to yield to the temptation to be untrustworthy. Thus the subject would be suspicious when the other could profit more from noncooperative than from cooperative behavior. Similar reasoning would suggest that if the subject were more able to control the outcomes of the other, and thus to reward or punish him, he would be more likely to trust the other. Also, one would expect the subject to be most trusting of an unconditionally cooperative other, less trusting of a conditionally cooperative other, and least trusting of an unconditionally competitive other.

Four different matrices were used in this study (see figure 8.3), of which only one (matrix *iii*) is a true Prisoner's Dilemma game. The subjects were all in position I for the first six trials of the game and in

5. The research reported here was conducted by Dr. Leonard Solomon and is reported more fully in his paper (Solomon 1960).

position II for the final trial. Position I chose first and announced his choice before position II chose. No other communication was allowed between the players. The subjects were all individualistically oriented. Unknown to the subjects, the other players (i.e., the occupant of position II on the first six trials and position I on the last trial) were always accomplices of the experimenter. The accomplice on the first five trials always chose according to one of the following three strategies: *unconditionally benevolent*—i.e., no matter what the subject chose, he always chose column A, which made the subject experience a gain; *conditionally benevolent*—i.e., he chose column A only when the subject chose row X (which enabled maximum mutual gain but which had the potential of maximum loss for the subject); *unconditionally malevolent*—i.e., no matter what the subject chose, he always chose column B, which made the subject suffer a loss.

i	A	B	ia	A	B
X	+30, +30	−30, +30	X	+30, +30	−30, +40
Y	+20, +30	−10, +30	Y	+20, +30	−10, +40

ii	A	B	iii	A	B
X	+30, +30	−30, +40	X	+30, +30	−30, +40
Y	+20, +10	−10, +20	Y	+40, −30	−20, −20

Figure 8.3. The matrices used in Solomon's experiment (Experiment III).

Matrices *i* and *ia* are similar in that the subject's possibility of gain or loss is completely dependent upon his partner's choice, but they differ in that the partner has nothing to gain by choosing column B rather than column A in matrix *i* but can gain by choosing B in matrix *ia*.

Results

The results indicate that the subject is more likely to expect his partner to choose column A (i.e., to make a benevolent or trustworthy choice) in matrix *i*, where his partner has nothing to gain by choosing column B, than in matrix *ia*. The subject expecting trustworthy behavior is also more likely to make a trusting choice (i.e., to choose row A). A comparison of the results for matrices *ia* and *ii* indicates that when the subject has some power, rather than none, to influence the outcome of his partner, he is more likely to expect trustworthy behavior and to make a trusting choice. Comparison of matrices *ii* and *iii* suggests that a further increase in power to influence the other person's outcome does not necessarily lead to an increase in trust on the part of the subject if he himself feels an incentive to engage in untrustworthy behavior (i.e., in matrix *iii,* the subject would prefer the payoffs in the AY cell to those in the AX cell).

The three types of motivational strategies followed by the accomplices produced clear differences. For matrix *iii* (the only matrix in which the subject has an incentive not to cooperate even when he is assured of the other's cooperation) the conditionally benevolent strategy evoked an average of 3.47 row X choices out of 5 possible choices; the unconditionally benevolent strategy evoked an average of 1.43; and the unconditionally malevolent produced an average of 1.00 row X choices. It should be noted that, although the unconditionally benevolent and unconditionally malevolent conditions did not differ significantly in the number of cooperative choices, the subject's choice of noncooperation (i.e., of row Y) in the former treatment was frequently based on an expectation of cooperation (i.e., it was exploitative), while in the latter treatment it was most commonly based on an expectation of noncooperation. Further data indicate that, in the equal power condition, the accomplices who used a conditionally, rather than an unconditionally, benevolent strategy were liked more; the reverse was true in the unequal power condition. The unconditionally malevolent accomplices were liked the least in all conditions. The subjects found it difficult to understand the motivation of the unconditionally benevolent accomplices.

In the last trial, the trial in which the subject and the accomplice reversed positions so that the subject chose last, the accomplice always made a trusting choice (i.e., he chose row X). The data indicated that the subjects who had experienced a conditional or unconditional benevolence were about equally trustworthy (i.e., they chose column A); both were more trustworthy than the subjects who had experienced unconditional malevolence.

Summary

The results of this study indicate that an individual is more likely to trust another (1) if he believes that the other person has nothing to gain from untrustworthy behavior and (2) if he perceives that he is able to exert some control over the other person's outcome. Further, an individual who is individualistically oriented is more likely to respond to another person's trustworthiness with nonexploitative behavior and positive feelings if he perceives that the other person's behavior is conditional upon the existence of mutual trustworthiness. Finally, an individual who experiences benevolent rather than malevolent treatment from another is more likely to respond benevolently when he has the power to determine the outcome of the other.

6. THE INFLUENCE OF THIRD PARTIES [6]

In everyday life we are aware that the relations between two people can be very much influenced by their relationships to a third party. A third party may be another person, a group, a law-enforcing agent, nature, etc. Thus if two people are both in the same relationship to a third party, a bond may be established between them that might not otherwise exist. For example, if two adolescents like "rock and roll," two employees resent their boss, or two people are victims of a tornado, they may develop friendly feelings toward one another that might not develop otherwise. Margolin (1954) has demonstrated this experimentally. He showed that if a subject is in a hostile relationship to a third person and he perceives that another person is also in a hostile relationship to the third person, the subject will develop a friendly relationship to the other person. He obtained parallel results when the relationships with the third person were friendly rather than hostile.[7]

The experiment reported here was an attempt by James Farr and myself to see whether two individualistically oriented players in our game situation would trust each other more if they each knew that they both disliked a third person. The experimental procedure was to have three people meet in the same room to take individual "intelligence" tests. One of the people was an accomplice of the experimenter; he was instructed to act in a conspicuously obnoxious and irritating manner.

6. The research described in this section was conducted by Dr. James N. Farr.
7. These results are derivable from Heider's theory of cognitive balance, which, in effect, asserts that the individual attempts to cognize the various aspects of his environment and of himself in such a way that the behavioral implications of his cognitions are not in contradiction. The existence of such contradictory implications produces a state of imbalance which gives rise to forces to remove the imbalance.

It was then arranged that the two naive subjects would play the game. They played the game for ten trials, without any communication being allowed between them, choosing simultaneously and in secret. In one of the experimental conditions, the accomplice's role was simply that of an observer who kept track of the player's scores. He was not involved in the game; the players' behavior did not affect him. In the other experimental condition, the accomplice had the task of predicting the choices of the two players. If he predicted correctly for a given trial, he could collect whatever was lost by the players on the trial; if he predicted correctly but there were no losses, he did not collect anything. If he predicted incorrectly, he did not collect anything. As a control group in which no third person was present, we used the results of the previously described ten-trial game, which was identical with the two experimental conditions except that there was no third person present (see the first experiment described in this chapter).

Results

The results indicate that the introduction of a disliked third person increases the tendency to make trusting (and trustworthy) choices. Where the disliked third person's outcome is interdependent with the choices of the two players, the highest percentage of trusting choices occurs; the next highest occurs where the disliked person is present merely as an observer; the least amount occurs when there is no third party present. The differences between the three-person-interdependent and the two-person conditions hold for each of the ten trials; the differences between the observer and the two-person conditions occur only for the initial and final trials. These results indicate that awareness of mutual opposition to a third party may lead the individualistically oriented players to have a greater motivation to be trustworthy and/or to believe that the other person's motivation to be trustworthy will be greater.

TRUST TRUSTWORTHINESS, AND THE *F* SCALE [8]

In the study reported here, Ss were drawn from an introductory psychology course at a local university. Several weeks prior to the experi-

8. The research reported here was conducted by Morton Deutsch with the assistance of Leonard Solomon. It is more fully reported in Deutsch 1960.

ment, they had filled out the *F* scale.[9] During the experiment, the instructions to the Ss about the game (see figure 8.1) were such that they fully understood the implications of any combination of choices that they and the other persons might make, and they knew that the other persons had a similar knowledge of the game. Unlike some of our other experiments (in which the Ss were induced to assume a cooperative, individualistic, or competitive orientation), the Ss were given no motivational orientation. They were allowed to assume whatever orientation they wished to assume vis-à-vis the other persons, about whom they were given no information. The S did not know the identity of the other person, and he knew that the other person did not know his identity (except that each S knew that the participants in the experiment were all students in the same psychology course).

Ss played the game twice, each time in a different "position" and each time, presumably, with a different person. In the first position, S made his choice first, and his choice was presumably announced to the other person before the other made his choice. In fact, the other person was fictional, hence, the S was not informed what the "other person" chose after the S had made his choice. In the first position the S was faced with the decision of trusting the other person or not. In the second position, the S chose second, after he knew the choice of the other person. Here, too, the other person was fictional, and the actual S was always informed that the "other person" had chosen row X (i.e., had trusted). Hence, in the second position, the S was faced with the decision of being trustworthy or not.

Results

Table 8.6 presents the data concerning the relationship between choices in the two positions. It is clear that the Ss who were trusting when they chose first tended to be trustworthy when they chose last; on the other hand, the Ss who were suspicious when they chose first tended to be untrustworthy when they chose last.

Before the Ss made their choices in the first position, they were asked to indicate what they expected the other persons to choose. Of the twenty-four Ss who chose row X in the first position and column A in the second position, twenty-one indicated that they expected the other persons in the second position to choose column A; of the

9. See Adorno et al. 1950, p. 260.

twenty-two persons who chose row Y in the first position and column B in the second position, seventeen indicated that they expected the others in the second position to choose column B. Thus a choice of row X was predominantly a trusting rather than a masochistic choice, and a choice of row Y was correlated with an expectation of untrustworthiness rather than of masochism from the other person.

When the Ss were in the second position, they were asked to indicate what they thought the other persons (who were then in the first position) expected them to choose. The results indicate that 95 percent of the Ss who were trusting and trustworthy in their own choices and who had also expected trustworthy choices from the others (i.e., a choice of column A) thought that the other person would be trusting (i.e., would expect a choice of column A from the S); only 35 percent of the Ss who were suspicious and untrustworthy in their own

TABLE 8.6. Relationship between Choices
in the First and Second Positions

	Second Position Choice	
First Position Choice	*Trustworthy* (A)	*Untrustworthy* (B)
Trusting (X)	24	5
Suspicious (Y)	4	22

choices and who had also expected untrustworthy choices from the others (i.e., a choice of column B) thought that the other persons would be suspicious (i.e., would expect a choice of column B from the S). This finding suggests that the Ss who were trusting and trustworthy expected trustworthiness and trusting from the others, while the Ss who were suspicious and untrustworthy predominantly expected an exploitative orientation from the others (i.e., they expected the other persons to be trusting but not trustworthy). Hence, it is not surprising that, in the second position, these latter Ss would respond to a trusting choice on the part of another by taking advantage of the other.

The data presented in table 8.7 indicate a significant relationship between the S's game behavior and his score on the F scale.[10] Almost

10. The point biserial correlation between the scores on the F scale and the two most frequent categories of game behavior indicated on table 8.7 is .50 (p < .001). The mean of the F scores for the Trusting and Trustworthy Ss was 2.38; the mean for the Suspicious and Untrustworthy Ss was 3.37.

all the Ss with relatively low scores made trusting and trustworthy choices; almost all the Ss with relatively high scores [11] made suspicious and untrustworthy choices; and the Ss with medium scores tended to choose one way or the other equally often. It is interesting to note that seven of the nine Ss who were inconsistent in their choices in the two positions (i.e., they were trusting but untrustworthy or suspicious but trustworthy) were in the medium range of the *F* scale for their class.

TABLE 8.7. Relationship between Behavior in the
Game Situation and F Scale

	F Scale Score			
	Low	*Medium*	*High*	
Game Behavior	(1.2–2.2)	(2.3–3.3)	(3.4–4.4)	N
Trusting and Trustworthy	12	10	2	24
Suspicious and Untrustworthy	0	13	9	22
Suspicious and Trustworthy	0	4	0	4
Trusting and Untrustworthy	2	3	0	5

Discussion

The data of table 8.6 provide a striking demonstration of the symmetry of the S's behavior in his two complementing roles vis-à-vis the other person. *His behavior toward the other is congruent with what he expects from the other, and what he expects from the other is congruent with his behavior toward the other.*[12] The Ss tend to be trusting and trustworthy or suspicious and untrustworthy in this essentially ambiguous situation with unknown others. This result suggests that the personality predispositions tapped by the experimental game are not simply one-sided internalized orientations toward another or internalized expectations from another but are instead internalizations of a *reciprocal* pattern of interrelationships with another. In other words,

11. It is evident that the "highs" are high only in comparison with the other Ss in their class; the high scores in this group are similar to the mean scores reported in other groups (Adorno, Frenkel-Brunswik, Levinson, and Sanford 1950, p. 266). When using the *F* scale as a personality measure, we believe it makes most sense to consider the individual's score in relation to the scores of others within his cultural milieu.

12. It is apparent that the Ss were not behaving in accordance with the ethical injunction of "do unto others as you would have others do unto you," but were rather guided by the dictum of cognitive consistency, "do unto others as you expect others to do unto you and expect others to do unto you as you do unto them."

what appears to be internalized is a *system* of interrelations between oneself and the other, including the norms that prescribe *both* what to expect from the other and how to act toward the other. A similar conception of the nature of personality predispositions is advanced more fully by such authors as Mead (1934) and Parsons and Bales (1955).

The F scale data indicate that the game behavior was related to personality predispositions and not determined by accidental orientations assumed during the course of the experiment, except in the special sense that vulnerability to accidental factors was itself influenced by the personality predispositions measured by the F scale.

The mass of research on the F scale, surveyed in Christie and Cook (1958), indicates that there are consistent differences between low and high scorers in their behaviors in social situations and in their responses to various questionnaires. The high, as compared with the low, scorers tend to be more authoritarian, less intellectually sophisticated, less liberal in their political views, more cynical concerning human nature, more prejudiced toward minority groups, and to have experienced and to favor stricter child-rearing practices. The present results suggest that, in addition, one may say that, in an ambiguous situation involving the choices of trusting or not and of being trustworthy or not, low scorers are more likely to be trusting and trustworthy while high scorers are more likely to be suspicious and untrustworthy (exploitatively oriented).

These results are obviously in accord with the description of what the F scale was intended to measure and with the conception of the "antidemocratic personality" as advanced in *The Authoritarian Personality* (Adorno et al. 1950). However, it is not necessary to posit, as do the authors (Adorno et al. 1950), that the characteristics of the authoritarian personality are to be

> understood as expressions of a particular kind of personality structure within the personality. The most essential feature of this structure is . . . that the conscience or superego is incompletely integrated with the self or ego. . . . There is some reason to believe that a failure in superego internalization is due to weakness in the ego, to its inability to perform the necessary synthesis. . . . (p. 234)

An alernative viewpoint would be that the personality differences between high and low scorers on the F scale do not necessarily reflect *structural* differences in personality so much as *content* differences in the values that have been internalized as a result of the individual's reaction to his socialization experiences in a particular social milieu, characterized by a given value pattern. This latter viewpoint suggests that highs and lows, suspicious people and trusting people, do not necessarily differ in superego integration or in ego weakness (a common synonym for psychopathology). As has been indicated more fully in an earlier chapter, there are characteristic forms of pathological trust (e.g., gullibility) as well as of pathological suspicion (e.g., paranoia). Presumably, the pathologies of trust and suspicion reflect internal conflict and ego weakness, both of which may be found in individuals who have internalized widely differing values.

Summary

Ss played an interpersonal game that, in one position, required them to choose between being trusting or suspicious of another and, in a second position, required them to choose between being trustworthy or untrustworthy toward another. There was a striking tendency for Ss who were suspicious to be untrustworthy. *F* scale scores correlated significantly with game behavior; Ss with low scores tended to be trusting and trustworthy while Ss with high scores tended to be suspicious and untrustworthy in their game choices.

THE EFFECT OF INCENTIVE MAGNITUDE ON COOPERATION
IN THE PRISONER'S DILEMMA GAME [13]

In recent years the Prisoner's Dilemma (PD) has come to be widely used in the investigation of various factors contributing to the cooperative or competitive resolution of human conflict. Aspects of communication, decision making, motivation, person perception, and personality have been studied by means of the PD game; data collected in this format have been used to support a considerable number of propositions about conflict resolution (see a review by Gallo and McClintock 1965).

Typically, PD research in which pairs of subjects make several successive game choices has shown a dramatic decrement in the amount of mutual cooperation over trials; subjects generally have great diffi-

13. This study was done in collaboration with Peter Gumpert and Yakov Epstein. It is more fully reported in Gumpert, Deutsch, and Epstein (1969).

culty maintaining cooperation and thus realizing maximum joint earning. PD researchers have generally interpreted these results as indicating that players are tempted, at least from time to time, to try to maximize their own short-term gains at the expense of the other by making the competitive choice. Thus they tend to perceive the other players as similarly tempted and may begin to choose competitively out of a desire to defend against loss at the hands of the other and a desire to maximize their own gain. As we suggested at the beginning of this chapter, the essential psychological feature of the game is that unless the conditions for mutual trust exist for the players, their behavior will tend to stabilize in the mutually competitive cell of the PD matrix.

Gallo and others (Gallo 1966; Gallo and McClintock 1965; Kelley 1965; McClintock and McNeel 1966b) have proposed, on the other hand, that since previous research within the framework of the PD game has typically been conducted using very small or imaginary incentives for play, the research is subject to two alternative interpretations. One interpretation suggests that subjects become bored with making long sequences of mutually cooperative choices for rewards of only trivial value and, therefore, convert the game to a more challenging one in which the object is to maximize the difference between their own payoffs and those of their opponents. The second interpretation suggests that at the beginning of the game experimental subjects fail to understand fully the consequences of their choices and thus begin by experimenting with various strategies. "By the time the subject learns the implication of what he is doing, if he ever does, it is probably too late to break out of the competitive pattern that has been established, particularly if motivation to do so is minimal or entirely lacking" (Gallo and McClintock 1965, p. 76).

We are particularly concerned here with the first of these interpretations. It suggests that an implicit assumption of most researchers who have used the PD game—that experimental subjects take the game and the experimenter's instructions seriously—may not be tenable where monetary-incentive magnitude is low or imaginary. Since this interpretation has received some measure of empirical support, it is particularly damaging to much previous PD research. The empirical support comes from the study by Gallo (1966) in which subjects played a game similar in some respects to both the PD game and the trucking game devised by Deutsch and Krauss (see chapter 9). In Gallo's experiment, subjects who played for imaginary money behaved in typically competitive fashion, while subjects who played for a sizable amount of real money played the game far more cooperatively. Gallo interpreted his results as calling into question the interpretation by Deutsch and Krauss of their experiments on the effects of threat availability on the outcome of interpersonal bargaining. Although subsequent research using the trucking game with moderately large monetary incentives has failed to support Gallo's alternative interpretation (see chapters 10 and 11), the PD research remains open to this question.

Previous researchers have asserted that the basic problem preventing cooperation between players in the PD game is that the temptation to maximize outcomes by defecting from mutual cooperation is highly salient. If this is so, one could argue that the temptation might become even more salient if the stakes were made higher, thus leading to less, rather than more, cooperation. Clearly, an experiment systematically varying incentive size is called for.

In the experiment of Gumpert, Deutsch, and Epstein reported here, subjects played the PD game illustrated in figure 8.4 under five incentive conditions. In one condition, the numbers in the matrix represented imaginary dollars (ID). In another condition, the numbers represented real dollars (RD). In the other three conditions, the matrix values represented (real) cents and were multiplied by 1, 5, and 10, respectively.

$$
\begin{array}{ccc}
 & b_1 & b_2 \\
a_1 & +1, +1 & -2, +2 \\
a_2 & +2, -2 & -1, -1 \\
\end{array}
$$

Figure 8.4. The matrix employed in the experiment of Gumpert, Deutsch, and Epstein (Experiment VI).

Subjects in the ID conditions were given $4.00 in real money before the instructions were delivered. In the instructions they were told that they would keep this money regardless of the outcome of the game. They were also given a credit of $10.00 in imaginary money and instructed to "play as though you felt real money was at stake." They were told to "feel that whether you win or lose, the imaginary money is very important to you." Subjects in the RD condition were given a credit of $10.00 in real money and asked to attach great importance to winning or losing this money. In order to increase the credibility of the large sum of money involved, these subjects were given ten $1.00 bills, which they placed in their pockets at the beginning of the experiment. Subjects in the 1, 5, and 10 conditions were given a stake of $2.00 in real money before the game and, as in the RD condition, were asked to attach great importance to winning or losing this money.

At the conclusion of the game subjects were paid, carefully debriefed, and asked not to discuss the nature of the experiment with anyone.

Twenty-Trial Results

Table 8.8 presents the mean number of cooperative choices made by dyads in the five conditions in each of the four trial blocks. Inspection of table 8.8 suggests that subjects in the ID condition were more cooperative than were subjects in the various real money conditions. Indeed, statistical analyses indicate that the game behavior of subjects in the four real money conditions was similar and that subjects in the RD condition behaved quite differently from subjects in the ID condition.

Analysis of the number of cooperative choices in the four real money conditions reveals no condition differences and a highly significant overall decrement in cooperation over trial blocks in all conditions. Comparison of the ID and RD conditions yields a significant condition effect and a significant decrement in cooperation over time for both conditions.

TABLE 8.8. Mean Number of Cooperative Choices
Made by Both Players

	Trial Block			
Experimental Condition	*I* (1–5)	*II* (6–10)	*III* (11–15)	*IV* (16–20)
Imaginary dollars	5.7	4.2	3.8	4.7
$.01–$.02	5.0	4.2	3.7	2.7
$.05–$.10	2.6	3.9	3.3	2.4
$.10–$.20	3.6	3.3	2.5	3.2
Real dollars	4.7	3.1	2.6	2.2

NOTE: The maximum number of cooperative choices in a five-trial block is, of course, 10.

Our data, then, indicate that subjects in the ID condition were choosing cooperatively about one-half (46 percent) of the time; this proportion is consistent with previous PD findings. As monetary incentives became strong, on the other hand, subjects chose cooperatively less frequently—about 38 percent of the time in the condition involving the least money and about 31 percent of the time in the other three. The mean total outcome of the dyads in the RD condition was −$14.80, as compared with −$3.00 in the ID condition. Clearly, Gallo and McClintock's (1965) fears about the PD game are not borne out in this experiment.

Discussion

In view of the unambiguous results obtained in the present research, it becomes necessary to attempt to account for the markedly different results obtained by Gallo (1966) in his trucking game experiment. A close reading of Gallo's experimental procedure suggests some differences in the two experiments that could account for the differences in their results. In Gallo's experiment, the experimenter took great pains to convince subjects in the real money conditions that they could keep all the money they earned; in his imaginary money conditions, subjects were urged to play as though real money was at stake. It does not seem unreasonable to suggest, therefore, that Gallo's instructions made his subjects sensitive to the criteria by which the experimenter might judge their performance—and that these criteria might have appeared different in the two incentive conditions. The instructions in the real money conditions might have made profit maximization particularly salient to the subjects as the experimenter's criterion for good performance, while the imaginary money instructions seem more ambiguous and could have allowed some of the subjects, especially those under Gallo's relative value (competitive) instructions, to believe that they might be judged by the degree to which they earned more than their opponents.

In our experiment, it was rather easy to assure subjects that they would keep what they earned, since they were publicly recruited for money; the relevant instructions were minimal. Our imaginary money instructions, however, might be viewed as making profit maximization particularly salient for the subjects as the experimenter's criterion for good performance. Thus we must be willing to admit that the differences observed between the ID condition and the RD condition could be due to artificially inflated cooperation in the ID condition. However, the results for the ID condition are reasonably similar to those obtained in the "least money" condition, so we do not take this possibility very seriously. Even if it were true, however, there is no evidence in our data to support the contention that subjects in the RD condition behaved *more* cooperatively than did subjects in the other conditions.

We should note that McClintock and McNeel (1966a) have also reported research that they interpret as indicating that cooperation in the PD game increases as payoff magnitude increases. Their data, however, were collected using the Maximizing Difference game rather than the PD game. In the Maximizing Difference game, the mutual choice yielding the greatest joint payoff also yields the greatest payoff to each individual on any trial, and a player highly motivated to earn money has every reason to trust that his similarly motivated opponent is unlikely to defect from the most lucrative choice (which happens to be cooperative) to a less attractive one. In the Maximizing Difference game, then, the problem of trust as an obstacle to achieving cooperation is alleviated, rather than exacerbated, by an increase in the strength of the players' motivation to maximize their own gains.

Our results have indicated that markedly increasing the payoff magnitude in the PD game does not lead to an increase in cooperation, it may be, in fact, that cooperation decreases with an increasing payoff magnitude. Though the loopholes are certainly not all closed by the present results, we feel somewhat reassured about the meaning of previous research using the PD game.

SUMMARY AND CONCLUSIONS

In the preceding chapter I attempted to define trust and other related concepts in a way that does not violate everyday usage and yet is sufficiently precise to permit theoretical and experimental work. In the present one, I have described both the experimental situation we have used and some of our research results. I draw the following implications from our results:

1. It is possible to capture in the laboratory the phenomena of trust and to study experimentally some of the variables that influence the tendency to engage in trusting and responsible behavior.

2. There are social situations that, in a sense, do not allow for the possibility of rational individual behavior as long as the conditions for mutual trust do not exist.

3. Mutual trust is most likely to occur when people are positively oriented to each other's welfare and least likely to occur when they are negatively oriented to each other's welfare.

4. Mutual trust can occur even under circumstances in which the people involved are clearly unconcerned with each other's welfare, provided that the characteristics of the situation are such that they lead one to expect one's trust to be fulfilled. Some of the situational characteristics that may facilitate the development of trust appear to be the following:

a) The opportunity for each person to know what the other person will do before he commits himself irreversibly to a trusting choice.

b) The opportunity and ability to communicate fully a system for cooperation that defines mutual responsibilities and also specifies a procedure for handling violations and returning to a state of mutual cooperation with minimum disadvantage if a violation occurs.

c) The power to influence the other person's outcome and hence reduce any incentive he may have to engage in untrustworthy behavior. It is also apparent that exercise of that power, when the other person is making untrustworthy choices, may elicit more trustworthiness.

d) The presence of a third person whose relationship to the two players is such that each perceives that a loss to the other player is detrimental to his interests vis-à-vis the third person.

5. The experimental work that we have done on trust should be viewed as an opening wedge rather than as a thorough or comprehensive study of this phenomenon. Our research, so far, has concentrated largely on trust in two-person, transient situations. There is an obvious need to investigate the development of trust in more complex social situations involving more people. In addition, it would be worthwhile to investigate trust in less ephemeral relations, to study trust and trustworthiness as properties of particular types of social relations.

9. The Effects of Threat and Communication upon Interpersonal Bargaining: Initial Studies

INTRODUCTION

A *bargain* is defined in Webster's Unabridged Dictionary as "an agreement between parties settling what each shall give and receive in a transaction between them"; it is further specified that a bargain is "an agreement or compact viewed as advantageous or the reverse." When the term *agreement* is broadened to include tacit, informal agreements as well as explicit agreements, it is evident that bargains and the processes involved in arriving at bargains (bargaining) are pervasive characteristics of social life.

The definition of bargain fits under sociological definitions of the term *social norm*. In this light, it may be seen that the experimental study of the bargaining process and of bargaining outcomes provides a means for laboratory study of the development of certain types of social norms. It is well to recognize, however, that bargaining situations have certain distinctive features which, unlike those involved in many other types of social situations, make it relevant to consider the conditions that determine both whether or not a social norm will develop and its nature if it does develop. Bargaining situations highlight for the investigator the need to be sensitive to the possibility that, even where cooperation would be mutually advantageous, shared purposes may not develop, agreement may not be reached, and interaction may be regulated antagonistically rather than for mutual gain.

The essential features of a bargaining situation exist when:

The research reported here was done in collaboration with R. M. Krauss and is reported in Deutsch and Krauss (1960, 1962).

1. both parties perceive that there is the possibility of reaching an agreement in which each party would be better off, or no worse off, than if no agreement is reached;
2. both parties perceive that there is more than one such agreement which could be reached; and
3. each party perceives the other to have conflicting preferences or opposed interests with regard to the different agreements that might be reached.

Everyday examples of a bargaining situation include such situations as: the buyer-seller relationship when the price is not fixed; the husband and wife who want to spend an evening out together but have conflicting preferences about where to go; union-management negotiations; drivers who meet at an intersection where there is no clear right of way; disarmament negotiations.

From our description of the essential features of a bargaining situation, it can be seen that, in terms of our prior conceptualization of cooperation and competition (see chapter 2), it is a situation in which the participants have mixed motives toward one another. On the one hand, each has an interest in cooperating so that they can reach an agreement; on the other hand, they have competitive interests with regard to the nature of the agreement that they reach. In effect, to reach agreement the cooperative interest of the bargainers must be strong enough to overcome their competitive interests. However, agreement is not only contingent upon the *motivational* balances of cooperative and competitive interests but also upon the situational and *cognitive* factors that would facilitate or hinder the recognition or invention of a bargaining agreement that would reduce the opposition of interest and enhance the mutuality of interest.[1]

The discussion in the preceding paragraph leads to the formulation of two general, closely related propositions about the likelihood that a bargaining agreement will be reached:

1. The stronger the cooperative interests of bargainers are in comparison with their competitive interests in relationship to each other, the more likely they are to reach an agreement.
2. The more resources that bargainers have available for the recog-

1. Schelling, in a series of stimulating papers on bargaining (1957, 1958), has also stressed the "mixed motive" character of bargaining situations and has analyzed some of the cognitive factors that determine agreements.

nition or invention of potential bargaining agreements and the more resources they have for communicating to one another once a potential agreement has been recognized or invented, the more likely they are to reach an agreement.

From these two basic propositions and additional hypotheses concerning the conditions that determine the strengths of the cooperative and competitive interests and the amount of available resources, we believe that it is possible to explain the ease or difficulty of arriving at a bargaining agreement. We shall not present a full statement of these hypotheses here but shall instead turn to a description of a series of experiments that relate to proposition 1 above. These experiments were done in collaboration with Robert M. Krauss.

Experiment I: The Effects of Threat

This experiment was concerned with the effect of the availability of threat upon bargaining in a two-person experimental bargaining game that we devised. *Threat* is defined as the expression of an intention to do something that is detrimental to the interests of another. Our experiment was guided by two assumptions about threat:

1. If there is a conflict of interest and a means of threatening the other person exists, there will be a tendency to use a threat in an attempt to force the other person to yield. The more irreconcilable the conflict is perceived to be, the stronger this tendency will be.

2. If threat is used in an attempt to intimidate another, the threatened person (if he considers himself to be of equal or superior status) will feel hostility toward the threatener and will tend to respond with counterthreat and/or increased resistance to yielding. We qualify this assumption by stating that the tendency to resist will be greater, the greater the perceived probability and magnitude of detriment to the other and the lesser the perceived probability and magnitude of detriment to the potential resistor from the anticipated resistance to yielding.

The second assumption is based upon the view that to allow oneself to be intimidated, particularly by someone who does not have the right to expect deferential behavior, is (when resistance is not seen to be suicidal or useless) to suffer a loss of social face and, hence, self-esteem; this further depends upon the view that the culturally defined way of maintaining self-esteem in the face of attempted intimidation is to engage in a contest for supremacy vis-à-vis the power to intimidate or, minimally, to resist intimidation. Thus it can be seen that the use of threat (and if it is available to be used, there will be a tendency to use it) should, in effect, strengthen the competitive interests of the bargainers in relationship to one another by introducing or enhancing the competitive struggle for self-esteem. Hence it follows from proposition 1 above that the availability of a means of threat should make it more difficult for the bargainers to reach agreement (providing that the threatened person has some means of resisting the threat). The preceding statement is relevant to the comparison of our experimental conditions (described below) of threat, *bilateral* and *unilateral,* with our experimental condition of *nonthreat.* We are hypothesizing that a bargaining agreement is more likely to be achieved when neither party can threaten the other than when one or both parties can threaten the other.

It is relevant now to compare the situations of bilateral threat and unilateral threat. For several reasons, it seems likely that a situation of bilateral threat is less conducive to agreement than a condition of unilateral threat. First, the sheer likelihood that a threat will be made is greater when two people, rather than one, have the means of making the threat. Second, once a threat is made in the bilateral case, it is likely to evoke counterthreat. Withdrawal of threat in the face of counterthreat probably involves more loss of face (for reasons analogous to those discussed above in relation to yielding to intimidation) than does withdrawal of threat in the face of resistance to threat. Finally, in the unilateral case, although the person without the threat potential can resist and not yield to the threat, his position vis-à-vis the other is not as strong as the position of the threatened person in the bilateral case. In the unilateral case, the threatened person may have a worse outcome than the other whether he resists or yields; in the bilateral case, the threatened person is sure to have a worse outcome if he yields, but he may insure that he does not have a worse outcome if he does not yield.

Method

Subjects were asked to imagine that they were in charge of a trucking company that carried merchandise over a road to a destination. For each trip they completed they made sixty cents minus their operating expenses. Operating expenses were calculated at the rate of one cent per second. So, for example, if it took thirty-seven seconds to complete a particular trip, the player's net profit would be sixty cents minus thirty-seven cents, or twenty-three cents, for that particular trip.

Each subject was assigned a name, Acme or Bolt. As the road map (see figure 9.1) indicates, both players start from separate points and

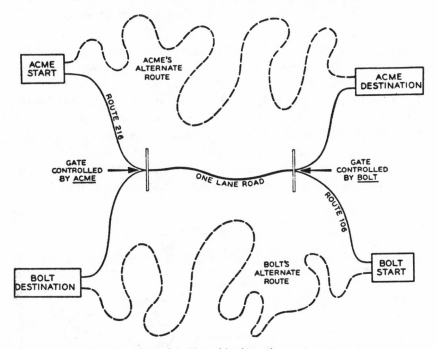

Figure 9.1. The subject's road map.

go to separate destinations. At one point their paths coincide. This is the section of road labeled *one-lane road*. This section of road is only one lane wide; this means that two trucks, heading in opposite directions, cannot pass each other. If one backs up, the other can go forward, or both can back up, or both can sit there head-on without moving.

There is another way for each subject to reach the destination on the map, and this is labeled the *alternate route*. The two players' paths do not cross on this route, but the alternate is 56 percent longer than the main route. Subjects were told that they could expect to lose at least ten cents each time they used the alternate route.

At either end of the one-lane section, there is a gate that is under the control of the player to whose starting point it is closer. By closing the gate, one player can prevent the other from traveling over that section of the main route. It is the use of the gate that we will call the threat potential in this game. In the bilateral threat potential condition (two gates), both players had gates under their control. In a second condition of unilateral threat (one gate), Acme had control of a gate but Bolt did not. In a third condition (no gates), neither player controlled a gate.

Subjects played the game seated in separate booths positioned so that they could not see each other but could both see the experimenter. Each S had a control panel mounted on a $12'' \times 18'' \times 12''$ sloping-front cabinet (see figure 9.2). The apparatus consisted essentially of a reversible impulse counter which was pulsed by a recycling timer. When the S wanted to move her truck forward, she threw a key which closed a circuit pulsing the "add" coil of the impulse counter that was mounted on her control panel. As the counter cumulated, the S was able to determine her position by relating the number on her

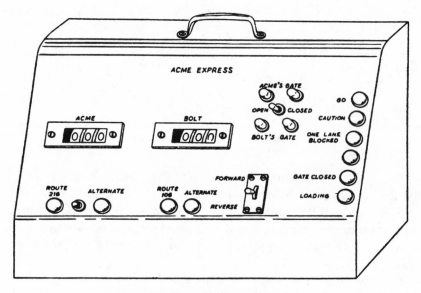

Figure 9.2. The subject's control panel.

counter to reference numbers that had been written in on her road map. Similarly, when she wished to reverse, she would throw a switch that activated the "subtract" coil of her counter, thus subtracting from the total on the counter each time the timer cycled.

S's counter was connected in parallel to counters on the other S's panel and on E's panel. Thus each player had two counters on her panel, one representing her own position and the other representing the other player's. Provision was made in construction of the apparatus to cut the other player's counter out of circuit, so that each S knew only the position of her own truck. This was done in the present experiments.

The only time that one player definitely knew the other player's position was when they met head-on on the one-way section of road. This was indicated by a traffic light mounted on the panel. When this light was on, neither player could move forward unless the other moved back. The gates were controlled by toggle switches; panel-mounted indicator lights showed, for both subjects, whether each gate was open or closed.

The following rules of the game were stated to the Ss:

1. A player who started out on one route and wished to switch to the other route could do so only after first reversing and going back to the start position. Direct transfer from one route to the other was not permitted except at the start position.
2. In the conditions where the Ss had gates, they were permitted to close the gates only when they were traveling on the main route. (That is, they were not permitted to close the gates while they were on the alternate route or after having reached their destination.) However, the Ss were permitted to open their gates at any point in the game.

The Ss were allowed a number of practice exercises to familiarize themselves with the game. In the first trial, they were made to meet head-on on the one-lane path; Acme was then told to back up until she was just off the one-lane path, and Bolt was told to go forward. After Bolt had gone through the one-lane path, Acme was told to go forward. Each continued going forward until she arrived at her destination. The second practice trial was the same as the first except that Bolt rather than Acme backed up after meeting head-on. In the next practice trial, one of the players was made to wait just before the one-way path while the other traversed it, and then he was allowed to continue. In the next practice trial, one player was made to take the alternate route, and the other was made to take the main route. Finally, in the bilateral and unilateral threat conditions, the use of the gate was illustrated (by having the player get on the main route, close the gate, and then go back and take the alternate route). The Ss were told explicitly, with emphasis, that they did *not* have to use the gate. Before each trial in the game, the gate or gates were placed in the open position.

The instructions stressed an individualistic motivational orientation. The Ss were told to try to earn as much money for themselves as possible and to have no interest in whether the other player made or lost money. They were given $4.00 in poker chips to represent their working capital and told that after each trial they would be given money if they made a profit or that "money" would be taken from them if they lost (i.e., took more than sixty seconds to complete their trip). The profit or loss of each S was announced so that both Ss could hear the announcement after each trial. Each pair of subjects played a total of twenty trials; on all trials, they started off together. In other words, each trial presented a repetition of the same bargaining problem. In cases where subjects lost their working capital before the twenty trials were completed, additional chips were given them. Subjects were aware that their monetary winnings and losses were to be imaginary and that no money would change hands as a result of the experiment.

Sixteen pairs of subjects were used in each of the three experimental conditions. The Ss were female clerical and supervisory personnel of the New Jersey Bell Telephone Company who volunteered to participate during their working day.[2] Their ages ranged from 20 to 39, with a mean 26.2 All were naive to the purpose of the experiment. By staggering the arrival times and choosing girls from different locations, we were able to insure that our subjects did not know with whom they were playing.

Results

The best single measure of the difficulty experienced by the bargainers in reaching an agreement is the sum of each pair's profits (or

2. We are indebted to the New Jersey Bell Telephone Company for their cooperation in providing subjects and facilities for this experiment.

losses) on a given trial. The higher the sum of the payoffs to the two players on a given trial, the less time it took them to arrive at a procedure for sharing the one-lane path of the main route. (It was, of course, possible for one or both players to decide to take the alternate route in order to avoid a protracted stalemate during the process of bargaining. This, however, always resulted in at least a twenty-cent smaller joint payoff, if only one player took the alternate route, than an optimally arrived-at agreement concerning the use of the one-way path.) Figure 9.3 presents the medians of the summed payoffs (i.e.,

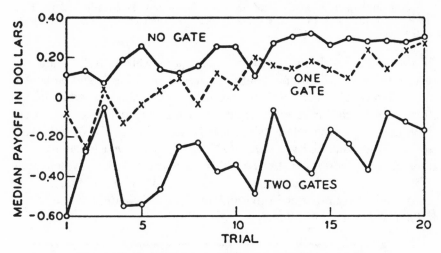

Figure 9.3. Median joint payoff (Acme and Bolt) over trials.

Acme's plus Bolt's) for all pairs in each of the three experimental conditions over the twenty trials.[3] These results indicate that agreement was least difficult to arrive at in the no threat condition, more difficult to arrive at in the unilateral threat condition, and exceedingly difficult or impossible to arrive at in the bilateral threat condition. (See also table 9.1).

Figure 9.4 compares Acme's median profit in the three experimental conditions over the twenty trials; figure 9.5 compares Bolt's profit in the three conditions. (In the unilateral threat condition, Acme controlled a gate and Bolt did not.) It is evident that Bolt's as well as Acme's outcome was somewhat better in the no threat condition than

3. Medians are used in graphic presentation of our results because the wide variability of means makes inspection cumbersome.

TABLE 9.1. Mean Payoffs Summated over the Twenty Trials

Variable	*(1)* No Threat	*(2)* Unilateral Threat	*(3)* Bilateral Threat	*Overall*	*(1)* vs. (2)	*(1)* vs. (3)	*(2)* vs. (3)
	Means			*Statistical Comparisons: p Values* [1]			
Summed Payoffs (Acme + Bolt)	203.31	−405.88	−875.12	0.01	0.01	0.01	0.05
Acme's Payoff	122.44	−118.56	−406.56	0.01	0.10	0.01	0.05
Bolt's Payoff	80.88	−287.31	−468.56	0.01	0.01	0.01	0.20

[1] Evaluation of the significance of overall variation between conditions is based on an *F* test with 2 and 45 df. Comparisons between treatments are based on a two-tailed *t* test.

in the unilateral threat condition; Acme's as well as Bolt's outcome was clearly worse in the bilateral threat condition. (See table 9.1 also.) However, figure 9.6 reveals that Acme did somewhat better than Bolt in the unilateral condition. Thus if threat potential exists within a bargaining relationship, it is better to possess it oneself than to have the other party possess it. However, it is even better for neither party to possess it. Moreover, from figure 9.5, it is evident that Bolt was better off not having a gate, even when Acme had a gate. Bolt tended to do better in the unilateral threat condition than in the bilateral threat condition.

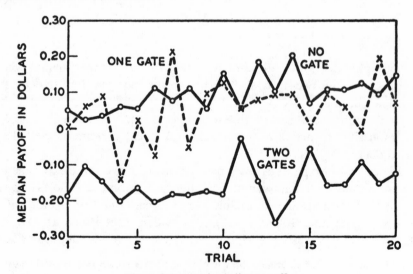

Figure 9.4. Acme's median payoff.

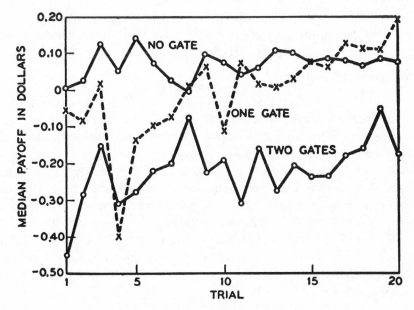

Figure 9.5. Bolt's median payoff.

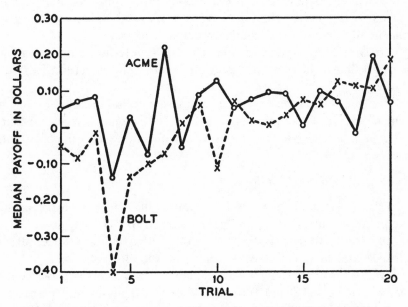

Figure 9.6. Acme's and Bolt's median payoff in Unilateral Threat condition.

To provide the reader with a more detailed description of what went on during the bargaining game, a synopsis of the game for one pair in each of the three experimental treatments is presented below.

No Threat Condition

Trial 1. The players met in the center of the one-way section. After some back-and-forth movement, Bolt reversed to the end of the one-way section, allowing Acme to pass through, and then proceeded forward herself.

Trial 2. They again met at the center of the one-way path. This time, after moving back and forth deadlocked for some time, Bolt reversed to the start position and took the alternate route to her destination, thus leaving Acme free to go through on the main route.

Trial 3. The players again met at the center of the one-way path. This time, however, Acme reversed to the beginning of the path, allowing Bolt to go through to her destination. Then Acme was able to proceed on the main route.

Trial 5. Both players elected to take the alternate route to their destinations.

Trial 7. Both players took the main route and met in the center. They waited, deadlocked, for a considerable time. Then Acme reversed to the end of the one-way path, allowed Bolt to go through, and finally proceeded through to her destination.

Trials 10–20. Acme and Bolt fall into a pattern of alternating who is to go first on the one-way section. There is no deviation from this pattern.

The only other pattern that emerges in this condition is one in which one player dominates the other. That is, one player consistently goes first on the one-way section, and the other player consistently yields.

Unilateral Threat Condition

Trial 1. Both players took the main route and met in the center. Acme immediately closed the gate, reversed to start, and took the alternate route to her destination. Bolt waited a few seconds at the closed gate; then she reversed and took the alternate route.

Trial 2. Both players took the main route and met in the center. After moving back and forth deadlocked for about fifteen seconds, Bolt reversed to the beginning of the one-way path, allowed Acme to pass, and then proceeded to her destination.

Trial 3. Both players started out on the main route, meeting in the center. After moving back and forth deadlocked for a while, Acme closed her gate, reversed to start, and took the alternate route. Bolt, meanwhile, waited at the closed gate. When Acme arrived at her destination, she opened the gate, and Bolt went through to complete her trip.

Trial 5. Both players took the main route, meeting at the center of the one-way section. Acme immediately closed her gate, reversed, and took the alternate route. Bolt waited at the gate for about ten seconds, then reversed and also took the alternate route to her destination.

Trial 10. Both players took the main route and met in the center. Acme closed her gate, reversed, and took the alternate route. Bolt remained at the closed gate. After Acme arrived at her destination, she opened the gate, and Bolt completed her trip.

Trial 15. Acme took the main route to her destination, and Bolt took the alternate route.

Trials 17–20. Both players took the main route and met in the center. Bolt waited a few seconds and then reversed to the end of the one-way section, allowing Acme to go through. Then Bolt proceeded forward to her destination.

Other typical patterns that developed in this experimental condition included an alternating pattern similar to that described in the no threat condition, a dominating pattern in which Bolt would select the alternate route and leave Acme free to use the main route unobstructed, and a pattern in which Acme would close her gate and then take the alternate route, also forcing Bolt to take the alternate route.

Bilateral Threat Condition

Trial 1. Acme took the main route, and Bolt took the alternate route.

Trial 2. Both players took the main route and met head-on. Bolt closed her gate. Acme waited a few seconds, then closed her gate, reversed to start, and went forward again to the closed gate. Acme reversed and took the alternate route. Bolt again reversed, then started on the alternate route. Acme opened her gate, and Bolt reversed to start and went to her destination on the main route.

Trial 3. Acme took the alternate route to her destination. Bolt took the main route and closed her gate before entering the one-way section.

Trial 5. Both players took the main route and met head-on. After about ten seconds of backing up and going forward, Acme closed her gate, reversed, and took the alternate route. After waiting a few seconds, Bolt did the same.

Trials 8–10. Both players started out on the main route, immediately closed their gates, reversed to start, and took the alternate route to their destinations.

Trial 15. Both players started out on the main route and met head-on. After some jockeying for position, Acme closed her gate, reversed, and took the alternate route to her destination. After waiting at the gate for a few seconds, Bolt reversed to start and also took the alternate route to her destination.

Trials 19, 20. Both players started out on the main route, immediately closed their gates, reversed to start, and took the alternate route to their destinations.

Other patterns that emerged in the bilateral threat condition included alternating first use of the one-way section, one player's dominating the other on first use of the one-way section, and another dominating pattern in which one player consistently took the main route while the other consistently took the alternate route.

Discussion

The results of experiment I clearly indicate that the availability of a threat potential in our experimental bargaining situation adversely affected the player's ability to reach effective agreements. In terms of our introductory analysis of bargaining as a mixed-motive situation (i.e., one in which both competitive and cooperative motivations are acting upon the participants), we can interpret these results as indicating that the existence of threat enhances the competitive aspects of interaction.

These results, we believe, reflect psychological tendencies that are not confined to our bargaining situation: the tendency to use threat (if a means for threatening is available) in an attempt to force the other person to yield when he is seen as an obstruction; the tendency to respond with counterthreat or increased resistance to attempts at intimidation. How general are these tendencies? What conditions are likely to elicit them? Answers to these questions are necessary before our results can be generalized to other situations. However, we will postpone consideration of the psychological processes that operate in bargaining until we have had an opportunity to examine the results of some further experiments.

EXPERIMENT II: THE EFFECTS OF
PERMISSIVE COMMUNICATION

Our discussion thus far has suggested that the psychological factors that operate in our experimental bargaining game are to be found in many real-life bargaining situations. However, it is well to point out an important unique feature of our experimental game: namely, that the bargainers had no opportunity to communicate verbally with one another. Prior research on the role of communication in trust (see chapter 8) suggests that the opportunity for communication would ameliorate the difficulty that bargainers experience in reaching agreement. This possibility was expressed spontaneously by a number of our subjects in a postexperimental interview. It should be noted, however, that the same research indicates that communication may not be effective between competitively oriented bargainers.

To test the effect of communication upon bargaining, we undertook an experiment in which subjects were permitted to talk over an intercom hookup. It was further decided to differentiate bilateral communication (both parties permitted to talk) from unilateral communication (only one party permitted to talk).

Method

The experimental apparatus, instructions to the Ss, and training procedures were the same as those described in experiment I. In addition, each S was equipped with a headset (earphones and microphone) hooked into an intercom system. The intercom was so constructed that the experimenter (E) could control the direction of the Ss' communication. This was necesary so that in the unilateral communication one S was prevented from talking to the other, but both were able to talk to E when necessary. A filter, built into the intercom's amplification system, distorted voice quality sufficient to make it unlikely that the Ss would recognize one another's voices, even if they were previously acquainted, without significantly impairing intelligibility.[4] The Ss received the following instructions regarding communication:

During the game, when your trucks are enroute, you may communicate with each other. . . . (Here the Ss received instructions

4. In only one group did an S recognize her partner's voice; this group was discarded.

on operating the intercom system.) In talking to the other player, you may say anything you want; or if you don't want to talk, you don't have to. You may talk about the game, about what you'd like to happen in the game, what you're going to do, what you'd like the other player to do, or anything else that comes to mind. What you talk about—or whether you decide to talk—is up to you.

These instructions were modified in the unilateral communication condition to indicate that only one player (Acme) would be permitted to talk. Communication was not allowed between trials; only during the actual trip were the Ss permitted to talk.

The two levels of our communication variable (bilateral and unilateral) were combined with the three levels of threat employed in the previous study to produce a 2×3 factorial experiment. It was necessary to employ such a design to test the possibility that communication might be differentially effective under different conditions of threat.

Five pairs of Ss were entered randomly into each of six treatment conditions. All were female clerical and secretarial employees of the Bell Telephone Laboratories and were, in most respects, comparable to the New Jersey Bell Telephone employees used in experiment I. Again, the Ss were selected from different work areas and arrival times were staggered to prevent the Ss from knowing their partner's identity.

Results

An analysis of variance of experiment II indicates that our communication variable had no effect on the players' ability to reach effective agreements; however the threat variable, as in the first experiment, had a significant effect. It should also be noted that the results of this experiment are not significantly different from the findings of experiment I, where no communication was permitted. For economy of presentation, these cross-experiment comparisons will be included with the results of experiment III given below.

Product-moment correlations were computed between frequency of communication for each pair (the number of trials out of twenty in which one or both Ss spoke) and joint payoff. Both overall and within the threat conditions, no significant relation was observed between frequency of communication and payoff. As will be discussed below, only a minimum of communication did occur and quite likely frequency of communication in this situation was determined by characteristics of the Ss that were irrelevant to the achievement of agreement in the bargaining situation.

There is an additional finding of interest. It will be recalled that in the unilateral threat condition, Acme was the player possessing the threat potential. Similarly, in the unilateral communication condition, it was Acme who was allowed to talk. To ascertain the effect of this double asymmetry, we ran an additional five pairs of Ss in a unilateral threat-unilateral communication condition in which Bolt was given the opportunity to talk but Acme still possessed the threat potential. A comparison of this group with the standard unilateral threat-unilateral communication condition revealed no significant differences between them.

We can also examine the gross frequency of talking in the three threat conditions. Each pair of Ss received a score based upon the number of trials in which one or both players spoke to the other. The mean frequency of communication in the three threat conditions is presented in table 9.2. Most talking occurs in the no threat condition; the rate of talking in the unilateral and bilateral threat conditions is approximately equal. However, these differences, when tested by a one-way analysis of variance, are not large enough to permit a rejection of the null hypothesis.

TABLE 9.2. Frequency of Talking in the Three Threat Conditions

	No Threat	Unilateral Threat	Bilateral Threat
Mean number of trials on which talking occurred	5.7	3.9	3.3

If we examine frequency of talking in the unilateral versus bilateral communication conditions we find that, in accordance with expectation, significantly more talk occurs in the bilateral condition. These means are presented in table 9.3.

TABLE 9.3. Frequency of Talking in the Bilateral vs.
Unilateral Communication Conditions

	Bilateral Communication	Unilateral Communication
Mean number of trials on which talking occurred	5.8	2.7

We had intended to record our Ss' communications and preserve them for a subsequent content analysis. Unfortunately, breakdowns of the recording equipment and electrical distortions introduced by the bargaining game apparatus rendered this impossible. Thus, except for the impressions gained by E who monitored all communication, these data are lost, and any discussion of communication content must necessarily be impressionistic.

In a postexperimental questionnaire and interview, we questioned the Ss closely in an attempt to ascertain the reason for the paucity of communication. Most of our Ss were at a loss to explain why they did not talk, although almost all acknowledged that they were less than normally talkative. With some probing on E's part, a frequent comment concerned "the difficulty of talking to someone you don't know." Possibly, the communication process normally involves a system of reciprocal expectations whereby a speaker has some idea of the effect that his words will have on a listener. Even in an encounter between strangers, these expectations may be partly derived from such visual cues as appearance, dress, facial expression, etc. All these cues were absent in the communication between our Ss. Interestingly enough, when the Ss were introduced after the experimental session, a great deal of spontaneous talking ensued. This was true even of the Ss who had not spoken at all during the experimental session.

Discussion

It is obvious from the results of experiment II that the opportunity to communicate does not necessarily result in an amelioration of conflict in our experimental bargaining situation. Indeed, it should be stated that the *opportunity* to communicate does not necessarily result in communication at all. Actually, little communication occurred; most of our Ss did not utilize their opportunity to communicate.

The results of experiment II are in line with the finding reported in the first experiment of chapter 8. Apparently, the competitive orientation induced by the threat potential in our situation was sufficiently strong to overcome any possible ameliorating effects of communication. In the no threat condition, where competitiveness is at a minimum, the advantage gained by the use of communication to coordinate effort was offset by the time consumed by talking. It would seem that the coordination problem posed for the Ss by our experimental game was sufficiently simple to be soluble without communication, given the existence of an appropriate motivational orientation. This will be considered further in our discussion of experiment III.

EXPERIMENT III: THE EFFECTS OF COMPULSORY COMMUNICATION

Any straightforward interpretation of the effects of communication upon interpersonal bargaining is difficult to make based on the results of experiment II. This is particularly true in view of the fact that the majority of our Ss did not use the opportunity to communicate that was presented to them. Thus one may speculate that had our Ss in fact communicated, the outcome of experiment II might have been quite different.

Studies of collective-bargaining procedures suggest that one of their important values lies in their ability to prevent disputants from breaking off communication (Douglas 1962). Newcomb (1948) has used the term *autistic hostility* to denote a situation in which a breakdown, or absence, of communication leads to the exacerbation of interpersonal conflict. Rapoport (1960) has stressed the importance of continued communication in resolving international conflict.

Experiment III was undertaken to test the effect of forced, or compulsory, communication.

Method

The experimental apparatus, instructions to the Ss, and training procedures employed here were the same as in experiment II. The Ss received the following instructions on communication (the italicized portions differ from the instructions used in experiment II):

> During the game, when your trucks are enroute, you *both will be required* to communicate with each other. . . . (Here the Ss received instructions on operating the intercom system.) In talking to the other player, you may say anything you want. You may talk about the game, about what you'd like to happen in the game, what you're going to do, what you'd like the other player to do, or anything else that comes to mind. What you talk about is up to you. *But remember, you must say something to the other player on every trip.*

In experiment III, only a bilateral communication condition was run, again under three levels of threat potential. On trials where both Ss failed to talk, they were reminded by E at the conclusion of the trial of the requirement that they talk to the other player on every trial. In no group was it necessary to make this reminder on more than four trials.

Ten pairs of Ss were entered randomly into each of the three treatment conditions. Ss were drawn from the same pool used in experiment II; however, none of the Ss in this experiment had served in the previous one.

Results

We will refer to the form of communication utilized in experiment II as *permissive communication;* communication in experiment III will be called *compulsory communication;* in experiment I, a condition of *no communication* was involved. Since in experiment II no differences were found between our bilateral and our unilateral communication treatments, we have combined these two categories to increase the *N* of the permissive communication group.

Figure 9.7 presents the mean joint payoffs (summarized as the averages of four-trial blocks for convenience) for all three experiments. (See also table 9.4). The effectiveness of the compulsory communication variable is seen in the comparison of groups in the unilateral

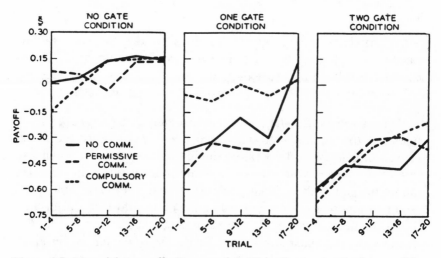

Figure 9.7. Mean joint payoffs (Acme and Bolt) in the communication conditions across the three threat conditions.

threat condition. Here alone, of all the conditions in which gates are present, does performance approach that of the Ss in the no threat condition. In the bilateral threat condition, the competitive motivation present seems too great to be overcome, even by the compulsory communication treatment. As was noted above, in the no threat condition, coordination was sufficiently simple that communication failed to produce any visible effect.

TABLE 9.4. Mean Joint Payoffs (Acme + Bolt) Per Trial

	No Threat	N	Unilateral Threat	N	Bilateral Threat	N
Compulsory Communication	6.09	(10)	−5.14	(10)	−41.73	(10)
Permissive Communication	8.54	(10)	−34.58	(15)	−41.32	(10)
No Communication [1]	10.41	(16)	−22.13	(16)	−47.44	(16)

NOTE: In an analysis of variance, significant ($p < .01$) F ratios were found for the "threat" and "communication" main effects and for the "threat × communication" interaction. Additionally, analysis of trend discloses a significant linear effect over trials ($p < .01$) for all groups, with no differences between group trends present.

[1] Discrepancies between these means and means computed from table 9.1 may be attributed to different methods of averaging.

We might examine more closely performance in the unilateral threat condition. For example, it is possible that the effectiveness of compulsory communication, as reflected in the joint payoff data, is due to an increase in the payoff to Acme (the player possessing a threat potential) without a corresponding increase in Bolt's payoff. In other words, it is possible that compulsory communication acts to increase the advantaged player's bargaining power in an asymmetrical situation. Figure 9.8 breaks down the payoffs of Acme and Bolt in the three communication conditions. Although in all conditions Acme does better than Bolt, the margin of discrepancy does not vary substantially in the three conditions.

An analysis of trend over trials (Grant 1956) was performed on the data of the three experiments. Overall, a significant linear component was present, revealing an improvement in outcomes over the course of the trials (see figure 9.7); however, no differences in trend resulted from a partitioning of the Ss by the two independent variables or their interactions. This result held true when the analysis was based on the joint payoff scores and on Acme and Bolt's scores analyzed separately.

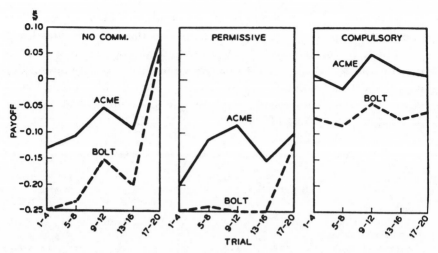

Figure 9.8. Acme's and Bolt's mean payoffs in the Unilateral Threat condition across the three communication conditions.

Again, we had intended to record our Ss' conversations for later content analysis, but the same technical difficulties discussed above continued to plague us. However, in experiment III we were somewhat more successful in obtaining complete recordings of a small number of our Ss' conversations. In order to give the reader some notion of the sort of conversations that did take place, we present below a transcript for selected trials of three pairs of Ss, one in each of the threat conditions; these trials were judged to be relatively typical. The numbers in parentheses below each conversation represent the payoff to each player on that trial (in imaginary dollars). Positive numbers represent winnings, and negative numbers are losses.

No Threat Condition

Trial	*Acme*	*Bolt*
1.	I'll stop at 5 so you can go through first. . . . I'm backing up for you.	
	(0.01)	(0.19)
2.		I'll wait for you at 5.
	Okay, wait 6 seconds because I had to back up last time.	
	(0.26)	(0.10)

No Threat Condition (Continued)

Trial	Acme	Bolt
6.	(0.27)	I'll wait at 5 this time. (0.09)
7.	I'll wait for you at 4 or 5. We might as well alternate, 'cause I don't see how we'll make any money any other way. (0.03)	Okay, that's true. (0.25)
12.	Is it my turn to wait for you? Okay, I couldn't remember whose turn it was. (Counting) 13, 14, 15. (0.27)	I'll wait for you this time at 5. Let me know when you reach 15. (0.09)
13.	I'll wait for you. Okay. I didn't go on break this morning; and boy, am I hungry! I'll make 9 cents, and you'll make 27. I started a few seconds too late. (0.07)	All right. I'll let you know at 15. You can start now. (0.26)
16.	Okay. I'll count up so you know. 13, 14, 15. There's no way to make money except by compromising this way. Except for the first few times. (0.27)	I'll wait at 5 this time, and let me know at 13 also. Okay. Thank you. No, that's the only way, and it comes out even that way, usually. Yuh. (0.09)

No Threat Condition (Continued)

Trial	Acme	Bolt
1.	I'll wait at 5.	Okay. You'll make 9 cents, I'll make 27.
	Yeah. Are you from around here?	Yuh, Summit (a local town). . . .
	Thank you. I won't ask you any more because I don't know you.	(Counting) 13, 14, 15. Okay. No.
	(0.08)	(0.26)
20.		I'll wait for you this time.
	Okay. Do you have a watch on?	Yeah.
	What time is it?	11:25 A.M. What number are you on now?
	12.	Okay. (Counting) 13, 14.
	(Counting) 14, 15. You're such a cooperative partner.	What?
	Nice working for such a cooperative partner.	Oh, nice to work with you, too.
	(0.26)	(0.09)

Unilateral Threat Condition

Trial	Acme	Bolt
1.	Do you intend to take the main route?	Um . . . I'm taking it, but I've stopped. Are you going to close the gate?
	I've closed it already. I'm going to open it.	You finish yet?
	Yes, I have.	
	(0.26)	(0.05)
2.		Are you on the main road?
	Yes, I am. I think we're going to meet again. I guess we've met, uh, I'm going to back up.	Where are you?
	I'm backing up.	What number are you on?
	Now I'm on 4.	Oh, all right. I'll go forward.
	I think we met again.	
	(−0.17)	(0.00)

Unilateral Threat Condition (Continued)

Trial	Acme	Bolt
5.	My gate's closed. It's open now. Oh, we met? I'm going to reverse. Yes. I can go? No. Wait a sec. I'll back up some more. Okay. You must almost be there. (-0.12)	Uh huh. I noticed. Yes. We met? Go now. We'll try. No? (Laughs) (0.06)
6.	My gate's closed. No, it's open now. You go. . . . Oh. Oh, we met. Okay. Okay, I'm there already. (0.21)	Uh huh. Are you gonna leave it closed? I'll go back. Try it now. (-0.03)
9.	I'll back up. Oh, you're there? You beat me by a hair. I'm only halfway there. Oh. (-0.06)	Okay. I'm there. I keep forgetting to push this thing down (probably a reference to switch on intercom). (0.11)
10.	My gate's closed. Yes. (0.26)	Are you there? All right. You beat me by seven, eight. (0.10)
13.	 Yeah. It's open. (0.26)	Are you there? Are you gonna . . . oh, it's open. (0.05)

Unilateral Threat Condition (*Continued*)

Trial	Acme	Bolt
14.	I'll back up.	Try going forward.
	Okay. No.	Not yet?
	You keep coming now.	What, go forward?
	Yeah.	On 15, 16, okay.
	I wonder how many times we're going to play this.	
	(−0.07)	(0.09)
19.		Are you going back?
	Yes, are you going forward?	Yes.
	I'm back. There.	Um, no.
	Oh.	
	(0.01)	(0.18)
20.		You going forward?
	Uh huh.	What number are you on?
	(Counting) 10, 11.	10?
	Okay.	You there?
	Yeah, no, we're blocked.	Oh, I'll go back.
	Are you stopped or going back?	I'm going forward.
	Oh, now you're going forward.	
	Oh, I guess we're okay now.	I'm on 9; are you there?
	Yeah.	I think I'm glad I'm not a truck driver.
	(0.20)	(−0.01)

Bilateral Threat Condition

Trial	Acme	Bolt
1.	You decide on your route? I am, too.	I'm taking the main route. Oh, we're stopped. What happens now? Did you stop?
	What did you say? Yeah, the lane is blocked completely.	
		Well, who's going to back up?
	Well, I don't know. You gonna back up this time? All right. I know it's locked. Anything's fair.	All right. I'll back up. Your gate is locked. That wasn't very fair. Well, what are you going to do?
	I don't have to do anything. I'm going to my destination. (Laughs)	
		This is not funny. At your destination?
	No!	I'll never reach mine at this point.
	I've reached mine. Sit tight. No, have you? Thanks a lot. (Laughs)	Well? Planned your next route? I've got some ideas. I'm getting there slowly but surely.
	(-0.95)	(-1.87)
2.		I've got my plan. How're you doing?
	I've got mine too. Fine. How are you doing?	Oh, I'm fine. I'm not getting any place fast, though.
	This doesn't move very quick. That makes two of us. Twenty-seven (on alternate route). Where are you?	Slow trucking. Where are you now?
		Twenty-four. (Both laugh) Looks like we both don't trust each other. I'll lose money this game.
	(-0.44)	(-0.54)

Bilateral Threat Condition (*Continued*)

Trial	Acme	Bolt
5.	We're stopped. What are we going to do now?	Oh, I backed up the first time. Now it's your turn.
	All right. What are you going to do?	I'm going to take the alternate route.
	Go right ahead.	Are you going to open your gate?
	No.	What are you going to do now?
	I've got to at least make the loss even.	I hear only one ticking (a reference to noise made by the apparatus).
	(−1.02)	(−0.75)
7.		You've got yours closed, too.
	We're both stopped.	Are you going to open your gate?
	Why should I?	I'll do the same next time.
	Is that a threat?	You playing tricks?
	No.	I'll lose five dollars this trip because of you.
	(−1.33)	(−0.75)
9.	I see you've got your gate closed. What route are you on? Okay, if that's the way you want to play.	Why should I tell you?
	I asked you first.	No, I'll tell you where I am if you tell me where you are. So am I (*sic*) . . . at 17. . . . How far are you?
	I don't believe you.	Have it your way.
	(−1.33)	(−0.75)

Bilateral Threat Condition (Continued)

Trial	Acme	Bolt
13.	(Unintelligible) I think that's my business. Don't have time. (-0.60)	You had yours closed. Why don't you open your gate? I'm not getting any place. (-0.23)
14.	You have yours shut, too. You never let me through. I know you are (sarcastically). (-0.20)	What? Let's both open our gates as long as we're going the other way. (-0.22)
18.	What route are you taking? I think we both are going bankrupt. (-0.39)	(no answer) They (*sic*) just don't trust each other, right? (-0.50)
20.	 So is yours, so that means you must have taken the alternate route. Well, you wouldn't be crazy enough to go to the main route with my gate closed. You know better than that. If I go into the trucking business I'm not going to have gates. (-0.21)	Your gate's closed again. Why? What gives you that idea? Well, maybe I think I can persuade you to open it. Do I? . . . I get the use of these gates all mixed up. I shut mine when I don't want to and, oh, . . . (-0.22)

Discussion

In the introduction, we presented our view of bargaining as a situation in which both cooperative and competitive tendencies are present and acting upon the individual. From this point of view, it is relevant to inquire as to the conditions under which a stable agreement of any form will develop. However, implicit in most models of bargaining (e.g., Zeuthen 1930; Stone 1958; Cervin 1961; Suppes and Carlsmith 1962) is the assumption that the cooperative interests of the bargainers will be sufficiently strong to insure that some form of mutually satisfactory agreement will be reached. For this reason, such models have focused upon the form of the agreement reached by the bargainers. Siegel and Fouraker (1960) report a series of bargaining experiments quite different in structure from ours; in their experiments, only one of many pairs of subjects was unable to reach agreement. Siegel and Fouraker explain this rather startling statistic as follows:

> Apparently the disruptive forces which lead to the rupture of some negotiations were at least partially controlled in our sessions. . . .
>
> Some negotiations collapse when one party becomes incensed at the other, and henceforth strives to maximize his opponent's displeasure rather than his own satisfaction. . . . Since it is difficult to transmit insults by means of quantitative bids, such disequilibrating behavior was not induced in the present studies. If subjects were allowed more latitude in their communications and interactions, the possibility of an affront-offense-punitive behavior sequence might be increased (p. 100).

In our experimental bargaining situation, the availability of threat clearly made it more difficult for the bargainers to reach a mutually profitable agreement. Indeed, bilateral threat presents a situation so conflict-fraught that no amount of communication seems to have an ameliorating effect. These tendencies, we believe, are not confined to our experimental situation. The affront-offense-punitive behavior sequence to which Siegel and Fouraker refer, and which we have observed in our experiment, is a common attribute of everyday interpersonal conflict. The processes that underlie this sequence have long been of interest to social scientists, and an imposing set of theoretical constructs have been employed to explain it.

Dollard et al. (1939) cited a variety of evidence to support the view that aggression and the use of threat are common reactions to a person who is seen as the agent of frustration. There seems to be little reason to doubt that the use of threat is a frequent reaction to interpersonal impasses. However, everyday observation indicates that threat does not inevitably occur when there is an interpersonal impasse. We would speculate that it is most likely to occur when the threatener has no positive interest in the other person's welfare (he is either egocentrically or competitively related to the other); when the threatener believes that the other has no positive interest in the former's welfare; and when the threatener anticipates either that his threat will be effective or, if ineffective, that it will not worsen his situation —because he expects the worst to happen if he does not use his threat. We suggest that these conditions were operative in our experiment; the subjects were either egocentrically or competitively oriented to one another,[5] and they felt that they would not be worse off because of the use of threat.

Everyday observation suggests that the tendency to respond with counterthreat or increased resistance to attempts at intimidation is also a common occurrence. It is our belief that the introduction of threat into a bargaining situation affects the meaning of yielding. Although we have no data to support this directly, we will attempt to justify it on the basis of some additional assumptions.

Goffman (1955) has pointed out the pervasive significance of "face" in the maintenance of the social order. In this view, self-esteem is a socially validated system that grows out of the acceptance by others of the claim for deference, prestige, and recognition that one presents in one's behavior toward others. One may view the behavior of our subjects as an attempt to make claims upon the other, an attempt to develop a set of shared expectations as to what each was entitled to. Why, then, did the subjects' reactions differ so markedly as a function of the availability of threat? The explanation for this lies, we believe, in the cultural interpretation of yielding (to a peer or subordinate) under duress as compared to giving in without duress. The former, we believe, is perceived as a negatively valued form of behav-

---

5. A postexperimental questionnaire indicated that, in all three experimental conditions, the Ss were most strongly motivated to win money, next most strongly motivated to do better than the other player, next most motivated to "have fun," and were very little or not at all motivated to help the other player.

ior, with negative implications for the self-image of the individual who so behaves. This is at least partly so because the locus of causality is perceived to be outside the voluntary control of the individual. No such evaluation, however, need be placed on the behavior of one who "gives in" in a situation where no threat or duress is a factor. Rather, we should expect the culturally defined evaluation of such an individual's behavior to be one of reasonableness or maturity. Again, this may be because the cause of the individual's behavior is perceived to lie within the individual.

One special feature of our experimental game is worthy of note. The passage of time, if no agreement is reached, is costly to the players. There are, of course, bargaining situations in which the lack of agreement may simply preserve the status quo, without any worsening of the bargainers' respective positions. This is the case in the typical bilateral monopoly case, where the buyer and seller are unable to agree upon a price (e.g., see Siegel and Fouraker 1960; Cervin and Henderson 1961). In other sorts of bargaining situations, however (e.g., labor-management negotiations during a strike; internation negotiations during an expensive cold war), the passage of time may play an important role. In our experiment, we received the impression that the meaning of time changed as time passed without the bargainers reaching an agreement. Initially, the passage of time seemed to cause pressure on the players to come to an agreement before their costs mounted sufficiently to destroy their profits. With the continued passage of time, however, their mounting losses strengthened their resolution not to yield to the other players. They comment: "I've lost so much, I'll be damned if I give in now. At least I'll have the satisfaction of doing better than she does." The mounting losses and continued deadlock seemed to change the game from a mixed-motive into a predominantly competitive situation.

The results of experiments II and III justify, we believe, a reconsideration of the role of communication in the bargaining process. Typically, communication is perceived as a means whereby the bargainers coordinate effort (e.g., exchange bids, indicate positions, etc.). Usually, little emphasis is given to interaction of communication with motivational orientation. Certainly, the coordination function of communication is important. However, as Siegel and Fouraker point out, free communication may also be used to convey information (e.g., threats, insults, etc.) that may intensify the competitive aspects of the situation.

It should be emphasized here that the solution to our bargaining problem (i.e., alternating first use of the one-lane section of the main route) is a simple and rather obvious one. Indeed, the sort of coordination of effort required by the game is sufficiently simple to be readily achievable without the aid of communication. (Note that the Ss in the no threat-no communication conditions did as well as the Ss in the two no threat conditions with communication.) More important than this coordinating function, however, is the capacity of communication to expedite the development of agreements. In this context, agreements serve a function similar to that ascribed by Thibaut and Kelley to the social norm; that is, ". . . they serve as substitutes for the exercise of personal influence and produce more economically and efficiently certain consequences otherwise dependent upon personal influence processes" (1959, p. 130). Effective communication, by this line of reasoning, would be aimed at the development of agreements or, to state it another way, at a resolution of the competitive orientation that produces conflict in the bargaining situation.

One must grant that our Ss were relatively unsophisticated in the techniques of developing agreements under the stress of competition. Possibly, persons who deal regularly with problems of conflict resolution (e.g., department heads, marriage counselors, labor-management arbitrators, diplomats, etc.) would have had little difficulty reaching agreement, even under our bilateral threat condition.

Another barrier to effective communication lies in the reticence of our Ss. As we noted above, our Ss found talking to an unknown partner a strange and rather uncomfortable experience. This factor alone would limit the possibility of any communication, let alone communication that was effective.

It is, of course, hazardous to generalize from a set of laboratory experiments to the problems of the real world. But our experiments and the theoretical ideas that underlie them can perhaps serve to emphasize some notions that even by themselves have some intrinsic plausibility. In brief, these are the following:

1. There is more safety in cooperative than in competitive coexistence.

2. The mere existence of channels of communication is no guarantee that communication will indeed take place; and the greater the competitive orientation of the parties vis-à-vis each other, the less likely will they be to use such channels as do exist.
3. Where barriers to communication exist, a situation in which the parties are compelled to communicate will be more effective than one in which the choice to talk or not is put on a voluntary basis.
4. If the bargainers' primary orientation is competitive, communication that is not directed at changing this orientation is unlikely to be effective.
5. It is dangerous for bargainers to have weapons at their disposal.
6. It may be more dangerous for a bargainer to have the capacity to retaliate in kind than for him not to have this capacity when the other bargainer has a weapon.

This last statement assumes that the one who yields has more of his values preserved by accepting the agreement preferred by the other than by extended conflict. Of course, in some bargaining situations in the real world, the loss incurred by yielding may exceed the loss due to extended conflict.

10. Further Studies of the Effects of Threat

EXPERIMENT IV: TUTORED COMMUNICATION [1]

The previous studies by Krauss and this writer suggested quite strongly that the mere existence of a communication channel would not guarantee its effective utilization, even when subjects were compelled to use it. This reasoning led us to compare the effects of two orientations to communication. One orientation (untutored pretrial communication—UPC) stressed the importance of communicating but did not attempt to specify the content of the communication. The other (tutored pretrial communication—TPC) involved instructing the subjects to center their discussion on negotiating a fair solution to the bargaining problems.

Another aspect of communication in bargaining seems worthy of note. Bargainers can either negotiate agreements that specify a principle for the resolution of conflict, or they can reach accords that are ad hoc, that is, applicable only to a particular case or instance. It is to be expected that ad hoc agreements are critically dependent upon the availability of communication, while general agreements, because of the broader applicability of the principle they specify, are not so dependent. We attempted to examine this factor by manipulating the *future perspective* of our subjects. The specific induction is described below under *method*.

As is noted above, in our previous studies the bilateral threat condition was found to be the most difficult in which to achieve a constructive resolution of conflict. For this reason we decided to focus our attention on this condition, and in the experiments to be reported here, all subjects bargained under bilateral threat.

1. Experiments IV and V were done in collaboration with R. M. Krauss and were first reported in Krauss and Deutsch (1966).

Method

Subjects. Seventy-six experimentally naive female clerical employees of the Bell Telephone Laboratories served as subjects. Their ages ranged from eighteen to thirty-two years. All were high school graduates. Subjects were assigned randomly to their treatments, with the restriction that the members of a pair had to come from different offices. This was necessary to prevent a subject from discovering her partner's identity. To further insure anonymity, the subjects' arrival times were staggered by about five minutes. The subjects were all volunteers and participated during their regular working hours.

Procedure. The game instructions and the practice routine were the same as those employed in the experiments described in the preceding chapter. Following the practice trials, the instructions that established the communication orientation were administered. Subjects in the UPC condition were told that they would be required to talk to each other before each trial. They were also told that they could talk about anything they wanted but that it would be necessary to say *something* to each other before every trial.

Subjects in the TPC condition were also told that they must communicate before each trial; however, their instructions specified the content of their pretrial communication. They were told to use this opportunity to make a proposal to the other player regarding a method of conducting the forthcoming trial. Moreover, they were instructed to try to make proposals that were fair to both themselves and to the other players. (". . . Make a proposal which you think is reasonable and acceptable both to yourself and to the other person. Try to make a proposal which is both fair to yourself and which you would be willing to accept if you were in her shoes.")

After these instructions, the subjects proceeded to play the bargaining game, communicating before the start of each trial. After each trial, the experimenter announced the amount won or lost by each subject so that both could hear it. Though the subjects were not aware that this was to be the case, our procedure called for pretrial communication before trials 1–7 only. Prior to the seventh trial, subjects in the no future perspective (NFP) condition were simply told that this was to be the last time they could talk *before* the trial, although they would still be allowed to talk *during* it. Subjects in the future perspective (FP) condition were told, in addition, that they could, if they wished, use this final opportunity to discuss future trips as well as the one immediately to follow. On all twenty trials, the subjects were permitted to communicate during the trial.

Nine pairs of subjects were run in each of the UPC conditions (UPC-FP and UPC-NFP) and ten pairs in each of the TPC conditions (TPC-FP and TPC-NFP).

Results

The subjects' joint payoff was taken as the measure of their ability to conclude bargaining agreements. Statistical analysis reveals that subjects in the TPC condition, who were trained to communicate fair proposals, achieved significantly better payoffs than did subjects in the UPC treatment. Neither the effect of the future perspective manipulation nor the interactions were significant.

Our speculation had been that the agreements reached under TPC might erode when the opportunity for pretrial communication was withdrawn, due either to the minor harassments of inadequate coordination or to adventurism on the part of one or the other player. However, the agreements apparently were sufficiently stable to be maintained over a series of subsequent trials. It seems likely that, given the simplicity of the bargaining situation, communication *during* the trial (which was permitted) enabled the players to handle such potentially erosive effects. With a more complex bargaining situation, or with greater restriction on communication, our speculations might have some merit.

The mean transformed values for the two communication orientations in three trial blocks are plotted in figure 10.1. In addition, we have plotted values for the permissive communication-bilateral threat condition taken from a previous experiment (see chapter 9) and appropriately transformed. Although TPC pairs ended up with a positive joint outcome (untransformed) that averaged fifty cents for the twenty trials, which is significantly better than the average *loss* of $8.26 in the permissive communication condition, the difference between UPC and permissive communication is not statistically significant. Thus the requirement that the subjects communicate before the trial did not result in a significant improvement in bargaining outcomes unless subjects also received tutoring.

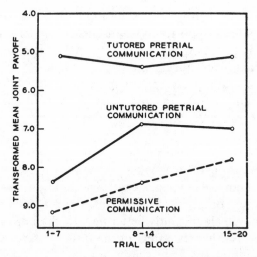

Figure 10.1. Transformed mean joint payoff in the three trial blocks (the lower the value of the transformed payoff, the better the outcome for the players).

EXPERIMENT V: THE TIMING OF COMMUNICATION

The results of experiment IV indicate that subjects who have been in-duced to communicate fair proposals can resolve a good part of the conflict of interest implicit in the bargaining situation. Our next experiment was directed at determining if the effectiveness of pretrial communication is affected by the period of time in which the communication occurs. That is, is there a difference between the effectiveness of communication introduced at the very beginning of the game (before the subjects have had any experience together) and that of communication introduced after the subjects had played the game for several trials?

Two possibilities occurred to us. First, it could be argued that subjects who played the game under bilateral threat and experienced the customary sequence of deadlock and retaliation would develop mutually negative attitudes. These attitudes, once developed, would impose barriers to communication when the opportunity to communicate was later introduced. On the other hand, it could also be argued that the experience of unsuccessful outcomes would make the subjects more receptive to innovations that would have some potential for conflict resolution. That is to say, knowing how bad things could get without communication, they might be more likely to make effective use of a communication channel when the opportunity presented itself.

Method

Based on our prior experiments with the bilateral threat condition, it was reasonable to expect that the subjects would routinely be using their gates by the seventh trial. Thus we were able to set up a postdeadlock communication condition by permitting pretrial discussion on trials 8–14 but not on trials 1–7. We ran ten new pairs of subjects under postdeadlock-UPC and ten pairs under postdeadlock-TPC. Both groups ran under the FP treatment. In all other respects the procedure of experiment IV was paralleled. Again, communication was permitted during all the trials.

Results obtained from these treatments will be contrasted with those obtained in experiment IV. It will be remembered that, in the earlier experiment, pretrial communication was permitted on trials 1–7 only, and, hence, subjects in this experiment may be thought of as having undergone predeadlock communication. Thus our analysis will consist of four treatment conditions: predeadlock-TPC-FP, predeadlock-UPC-FP, postdeadlock-TPC-FP, postdeadlock-UPC-FP.

Results

The means for the three trial blocks (trials 1–7, 8–14, and 15–20) and for the different experimental conditions appear in table 10.1. Statistical analysis indicates that postdeadlock communication was more effective than predeadlock communication. And, as in experiment IV, there was an overall superiority of tutored versus untutored communication. However, it should be noted that the effectiveness of untutored communication was enhanced by the postdeadlock procedure. The average payoff under postdeadlock-UPC was almost as good as under post-deadlock-TPC for these seven trials.

But it can be contended that these results are misleading. The payoffs in the postdeadlock conditions are from trials 8–14, while the predeadlock payoffs are from trials 1–7. It is possible that subjects in the postdeadlock treatments simply developed greater skill in the game because they had more practice than subjects in the predeadlock condition. However, for all subjects, in both the pre- and postdeadlock treatments, no pretrial communication was permitted on trials

15–20. Hence, group differences in performance on these trials must reflect the effects of prior experimental inductions. In addition, all the subjects had equivalent amounts of practice in this trial block. From the results of an analysis of variance of summed joint payoff on trials 15–20 (the "criterion" trials), it is still clear that postdeadlock communication produced better outcomes than predeadlock communication. Similarly, outcomes under TPC were greater than under UPC. Once again, it is noted that the effectiveness of untutored communication was greatly enhanced by the postdeadlock procedure: on the six criterion trials, subjects in postdeadlock-UPC did slightly better than those in predeadlock-TPC. However, the improvement in outcomes

TABLE 10.1 Transformed Mean Joint Payoffs (Acme + Bolt) under Different Communication Conditions in Bilateral Threat Situation

	Trials 1 through 7	Trials 8 through 14	Trials 15 through 20
Tutored and Untutored Communication Combined			
Predeadlock	6.216	5.318	5.376
Postdeadlock	7.763	4.450	3.656
Tutored Communication			
Predeadlock	4.719	4.609	4.178
Postdeadlock	8.778	4.256	3.213
Untutored Communication			
Predeadlock	7.713	6.027	6.573
Postdeadlock	6.747	4.644	4.099

NOTE: Payoffs have been transformed so that $x' = \sqrt{k-x}$, with k equal to the highest score in any single analysis plus 1.0; x is the untransformed score. The lower the score, the better the outcome for the players.

from the initial to the final block of trials was markedly better in the postdeadlock conditions for the pairs who were tutored as compared with those who were not tutored in how to communicate.

Discussion of Experiments IV and V

It seems clear that communication that takes place prior to bargaining is no more effective than communication that goes on during bargaining in the resolution of the bargainers' conflict. It is not the reduction of the pressure of time on communication but rather the provision of a strong incentive to utilize the opportunity to communicate to engage in fair bargaining that is central to the economical resolution of conflict.

It is clear that the incentive to make fair proposals is derived from the instructions of the experimenter in the tutored communication condition. When the experimenter, a figure not without prestige and authority for them, instructs the subjects to use the communication channel to exchange fair proposals, he is doing more than simply suggesting the content of communication. He is, in effect, establishing a social norm of fairness or equity as part of the context of the experiment. For a subject in these circumstances to attempt to secure more than his fair share violates the cultural standard of reasonable or sportsmanlike behavior. But when no such restrictions are present, as in the UPC condition, the subject is free to respond to the competitive aspects of the bargaining situation, and this is reflected in his communication behavior as well as in his bargaining.

Why, then, did the untutored communication treatment prove effective in the postdeadlock condition, when it had so negligible an effect with the predeadlock procedure? To begin with, subjects in the postdeadlock condition have experienced the frustrating and unproductive course of events typical of behavior under bilateral threat. Presumably, such experience served as an incentive for them to seek some means of resolving their conflict. But experience by itself is not enough. It must be supplemented by some strong prod to reconsider the situation. This was implicit in the experimenter's action of interrupting the progress of the game and giving the subjects an opportunity to communicate before the trial. We assume that the experimenter's intervention was interpreted by the subjects as both a pressure and an opportunity to improve their bargaining outcomes. But it is also clear that, where the lessons of experience are drawn explicitly for the subjects, they are utilized more aptly.

EXPERIMENT VI: MAGNITUDE OF THREAT AND EQUALITY OF THREAT [2]

This experiment, which was Harvey Hornstein's dissertation, focused upon the effects of different magnitudes of threat under conditions where the bargainers have equal or unequal threat potentials. A bargaining game modeled after the one developed by Siegel and Fouraker was employed.

2. This study was conducted by Harvey A. Hornstein and is reported more fully in Hornstein (1965).

Method

Each of the Ss was asked to imagine that he was a realtor who was trying to come to some agreement with another realtor regarding the number of acres of land to be sold at a particular time and the cost per acre. The objective in arranging this sale was to accumulate as much profit for the subject as possible, regardless of how much the other made. Thus the Ss had an individualistic rather than a cooperative or a competitive orientation.

Pairs of Ss were escorted, one at a time, into separate booths. They were seated on either side of a large screen that prevented them from seeing each other. Moreover, during the bargaining all communication was conducted by means of standard message slips. Thus the experimental conditions insured the anonymity of the Ss.

Offers. There were two ways in which the Ss could offer terms for agreement. Offer slips could be used to communicate the terms of a particular offer to the other realtor; an offer could also be communicated by sending a notice slip, but, in this case, the offer was made as part of a threat.

Threat. Each of the realtors could reduce the other's profits by a certain percentage. Before he actually reduced the other's profits, however, he was required to warn the other of his intentions. The notice slip constituted a threat that told its receiver that unless he accepted a certain offer, which was indicated thereon, the sender might reduce his profits.

Aggression. If a realtor sent a notice, he was permitted to send a stock sale slip on his following turn. (Each realtor could send no more than one stock sale per trial.) If a realtor received a stock sale slip, his profits for that trial were reduced by a certain percent.

A realtor's threat potential was defined as the percentage by which he could reduce the other realtor's profits. In this experiment, Ss were assigned threat potentials of 90 percent, 50 percent, 20 percent, and 10 percent. Thus the Ss were paired with each other in one of six types of pairs: three equal types, 90–90, 50–50, and 10–10; and three unequal types, 90–10, 50–10, and 20–10.

Each of the Ss had a profit table that indicated to him the amount of profit that he and his opponent would make for any of the twenty possible combinations of number of acres and cost per acre. For any combination of these factors, there was a difference of 500 between the profits of each of the Ss, i.e., in one-half the combinations one of the Ss had the 500 advantage, while in the other half the other one had it. Each was also supplied with a table that indicated the value of profits that remained after he was aggressed against by the other realtor.

For each of the six conditions, there were eight pairs of male undergraduates who served as Ss. Each pair participated in eight bargaining trials. Each trial was terminated at the end of six minutes if no agreement had been reached.

Results

In general, the results indicate that if one or both of the bargainers issue a threat at the start of negotiations or if threat or aggression occurs during the negotiations, the likelihood that an agreement will be reached is reduced (tables 10.2, 10.3, 10.4). These findings are con-

TABLE 10.2. Relation between the Use of Threat
and the Presence of Agreement

	Agreement	No agreement
Notice (threat) is *not* first communication of either realtor	24	9
Notice (threat) is first communication of either realtor	3	12

$X^2 = 11.650$; p<.001

TABLE 10.3. Relation between the Use of Aggression
and the Presence of Agreement

	Agreement	No agreement
Neither of the realtors aggressed during their first trial	26	9
One or both the realtors aggressed during their first trial	1	12

$X^2 = 17.081$; p<.001

TABLE 10.4. Relation between the Threat-Aggression
Sequence and the Presence of Agreement

	Agreement	No agreement
Neither of the realtors threatened or aggressed during their first trial	15	0
One or both the realtors threatened, but neither aggressed during their first trial	11	9
One or both the realtors threatened and aggressed during their first trial	1	12

$X^2 = 24.181$; p<.001

sistent with those reported in the preceding chapter, which indicated that the use of threat involves the bargainers in a threat, counter-threat, and aggression sequence and, consequently, reduces the likelihood of successful bargaining.

The data (see table 10.5) concerning the effects of magnitude of threat in the equal pairs do not show a simple trend. Those pairs with most power to harm one another (the 90–90 pairs) seem to use threat least, aggress least, and agree and profit most, while those pairs with

TABLE 10.5. Mean for Individual Bargainers in Equal and Unequal Pairs

	Equal			*Unequal*		
	90–90	50–50	10–10	90–10	50–10	20–10
1. No. of threats initiated	2.8	4.1	3.9	4.5 3.4	3.9 2.5	3.0 4.5
2. Ratio of no. of counterthreats made to no. of threats received	.33	.64	.55	.59 .46	.69 .51	.65 .66
3. Ratio of no. of aggressions made to no. of threats made	.43	.50	.47	.20 .49	.60 .42	.60 .43
4. Ratio of yielding to being threatened	.22	.21	.16	.30 .24	.19 .22	.07 .11
5. No. of agreements with other's offer	3.5	2.3	2.2	3.0 4.0	2.0 3.0	2.0 1.5
6. Profits before reduction for loss	33	28	31	36 31	33 29	29 20
7. Net profits after reduction for loss	31	26	31	36 26	32 25	19 19

middling power to harm one another (the 50–50 pairs) appear to use threat most, aggress most, and profit least; the pairs with the least power to harm one another (the 10–10 pairs) fall in between the other two types. (These results are statistically significant only for the use of threat, although the trends for the other measures are quite similar.)

Within the unequal pairs, the player with the greater ability to harm the other threatens more frequently than the weaker player, except in those pairs where the difference between the players is small (the

20–10 pairs). In these latter pairs, the weaker bargainer threatens more often; the stronger bargainer aggresses more often, except that the strongest bargainer aggresses least per threat issued. (This diminished aggression is not explainable by the assumption that the subject's threats produce disproportionate yielding from his opposite number.) The more unequal the pairs are in terms of their threat potential, the greater is their rate of agreement and their joint profit. Moreover, the individual profits of both the stronger and weaker bargainers are larger as the inequality of the bargainers within the pair increases.

A comparison of the equal and unequal bargaining pairs shows no significant overall differences between them. A pair-by-pair comparison reveals, however, some interesting results. Comparing the 90–90 pairs with the 90–10 pairs, it is apparent that both the stronger and the weaker bargainers make more threats than the equal bargainers. However, the players in the 50–50 pairs threaten more than do the players in either the stronger or weaker position in the 50–10 pairs.

Discussion

The results support the view that the use of threat and aggression interferes with the development of profitable agreements. In addition, they suggest that the employment of threat and aggression is less likely between bargainers who both have either very much or very little power to harm one another than between bargainers with moderate power to harm. In the one case, the threat potential seems too powerful to risk its employment, and, in the other, it is too insignificant to suppose that it would have much effect. When the bargainers in our experiment had unequal threat potential, the greater the discrepancy between their power, the more likely they were to reach agreements and the greater were their profits. The power discrepancy appeared to facilitate agreement by providing a structure about which the bargainers could coordinate their expectations: the cues regarding who should agree to the other's offer and who should receive what share of the profits were and are relatively clear. Nevertheless, it is evident that many subjects were not willing to accept a lesser profit because of their lesser threat potential. The refusal to accept inferior outcomes was greatest when the other's superiority in ability to inflict harm was small.

Experiment VII: The Effects of the Need to Maintain Face [3]

In our discussion of the effects of threat upon bargaining, we suggested that being threatened tends to evoke resistance and counterthreat if the threatener is perceived by the threatened as not having the right to expect deference. To allow oneself to be unjustly intimidated by someone who is not clearly superior is to suffer a loss of face. Rather than permit such a loss of esteem, people will frequently engage in a costly struggle to prevent the other from obtaining an advantage. The present experiment, which was Bert Brown's dissertation, is concerned with some of the determinants of the need to save and restore face in a bargaining situation.

The main hypotheses of the experiment are: (1) the need to maintain face is increased when the bargaining occurs before an audience of significant others; (2) when the reaction of the audience indicates that face has been lost rather than maintained, the bargainer will seek to restore his face by actions directed against the other bargainer who has made him lose face, even at a cost to himself; and (3) his willingness to suffer costs in order to harm the other will be lessened if his costs are known to the other.

Method

Subjects and design of experiment. Sixty adolescent male volunteers (15–17.5 years of age) from New York City public high schools were randomly assigned to conditions in a 2×3 factorial experiment. The independent variables were audience feedback (three levels) and information given to subjects about the other's knowledge of their own costs for retaliating (two levels).

Experimental situation. All subjects, except for those in control groups, were told that they would be observed and evaluated by an audience (classmates) while participating in a bargaining task. Their classmates were purportedly (but not actually) watching from behind a one-way mirror that opened onto the experimental room. Several procedures were employed to strengthen the credibility of this manipulation. Among these was the playing of a tape recording of muffled

---

3. This experiment was conducted by Bert R. Brown and is more fully reported in Brown (1968).

male voices, periodic laughter, the shuffling of furniture, etc., behind the one-way mirror during the first ten trials. Subjects were not permitted to see or communicate with the other participants during the experiment. The subject and his opponent sat on opposite sides of a 6' × 6' separator panel. Unknown to the subjects, the other participant in each pair was a confederate of the experimenter (a stooge) whose behavior was programmed as highly competitive and exploitative in all conditions of the experiment.

Subjects were systematically exploited in the first ten trials of a twenty-trial experiment. Next, all but the control subjects received feedback from the "audience" about their appearance during those trials. In the second ten trials, subjects were given the option of retaliating or of ignoring their exploitation and thereby increasing their own outcomes. Control subjects were told nothing about being observed and received no feedback.

The bargaining task. The task used was a modification of the Acme-Bolt two-person trucking game. In the present experiment, the function of the gates was modified; they were used as "toll gates," which on any single trial were controlled by only one player. On each trial, the player was required to either charge the other, one of several tolls, or permit him to pass through without charge. The rules stated that if a toll was charged one could either accept the charge or refuse payment. Acceptance insured passage; refusal meant that one was required to back out of the narrow path immediately and take the longer route. Players were informed that decisions for each trial were irreversible and that they would not be penalized for time spent in making decisions about tolls, since the interval between receiving the toll announcer card and sending a notice of payment or a refusal-to-pay card was electronically timed and subtracted from the total time to completion.

Orientation. Subjects were given an individualistic motivational orientation; they were instructed to try to earn as much as possible for themselves and to be unconcerned with the amount earned by the other participants. They were told that they could keep whatever they earned (added to or subtracted from a $4.00 real money stake given them at the outset). Their final payoff was determined by the summed earnings on each trial with appropriate adjustments for tolls paid out, tolls collected, and expenses. A series of practice trials was given in which subjects were thoroughly familiarized with the apparatus, the procedures for charging tolls, and the alternating strategy in which both players gain. A drawing of lots was prearranged to assure that the stooge "won" control of the gate for the first ten trials and the subject took control for the last ten.

Stooge's program–first ten trials. The stooge charged high tolls during these trials, causing subjects to lose a sizable portion of their stake. These tolls were:

Trial number	1	2	3	4	5	6	7	8	9	10
Toll charged by stooge (in cents)	10	30	50	40	30	20	50	40	20	50

The toll charged on each trial was determined by the trial number. If a subject avoided the tollgate by taking the alternate route from the outset, the stooge closed the gate anyway, waited a short while, and then proceeded to his own destination without charging a toll. (The stooge's apparatus permitted him to know the whereabouts of the subject's truck at all times, but the latter enjoyed no such advantage.) Avoiding the tollgate in this fashion resulted in a loss of about fifteen cents. The stooge, on the other hand, gained approximately twenty cents, since his way through the direct route was unobstructed. Refusal to pay a toll after reaching the gate resulted in heavy loss (about eighty cents) because of the increased time needed to back down almost the full length of the direct route. Whenever a subject agreed to pay a toll, the stooge allowed the subject's truck to move through the narrow roadway, ahead of his own.

Following every trial, an announcement of the time taken by each to complete the trip was made (corrected for time spent in negotiating toll payment). Subjects were thus confronted with highly exploitative opponents who caused them heavy losses. This situation was so structured that subjects were free to respond in a number of ways to the stooges' high-handedness—but to no avail.

Stooge's program during the second ten trials. The stooge was programmed to travel the direct route and to pay all tolls he was charged. After paying, he moved directly to his destination. If the subject tried to block, the stooge refused to yield for thirty seconds— or until the subject backed up to let him pass. After the subject yielded, the stooge allowed him to proceed.

Audience-feedback manipulations. After the tenth trial, both the stooges and the subjects were handed several sheets, identified by the experimenter as the audience's evaluations of them. (This procedure was omitted in the control condition.) Blank sheets were given to the stooges, but the subjects received one of the two following sets of handwritten feedback:

"Looked foolish" feedback

1. Acme was weak. Bolt made him pay a lot of high tolls and lose.
2. Bolt was out to beat Acme, and he really made Acme look like a sucker.
3. Bolt played tricky. He ran rings around Acme and made him lose a lot. Acme looked pretty bad.

"Did not look foolish" feedback

1. Bolt made Acme pay a lot of high tolls, but Acme looked good because he tried hard and played fair.
2. Bolt was out to beat Acme and make him look like a sucker, but Acme played fair and looked good.
3. Bolt was rough and tricky but Acme came out okay because he played it straight.

Subject's toll schedule. Subjects were given the following toll schedule for the second ten trials:

| Toll you may charge | 00 | 10 | 15 | 20 | 30 | 40 | 50 |
| Costs to self | 00 | 00 | 00 | 10 | 25 | 40 | 60 |

The toll schedule permitted subjects to either retaliate by charging higher tolls or maximize their gains by charging smaller ones. Retaliation, however, involved a dilemma: the more severe the retaliation chosen, the higher one's own costs. Subjects could charge any toll or permit free passage on each trial. That charging higher tolls would reduce their outcomes accordingly was explained to subjects. Tolls were charged by passing a card, with the amount preprinted on it, through a narrow slot in the separator panel. It was through the same slot that subjects had passed a pay or refuse-to-pay notice to the stooge.

Knowledge-of-costs manipulations. In one condition, the experimenter, in plain view, handed the stooge a paper and told him that it was a copy of the subject's toll schedule. The subject, therefore, knew that the stooge was aware of his costs. In a second condition, subjects were assured that the other players would be kept ignorant of their costs. This manipulation was introduced after subjects received the audience feedback. No information was given about (1) whether the audience was told their costs or (2) the stooge's toll costs.

Performance measures. The main dependent variables were (1) the number of trials in which subjects charged tolls of more than fifteen cents and (2) the amount they spent to charge these tolls. These measures reflected willingness to sacrifice "own" gains for the opportunity to retaliate. In addition, the total payoffs earned by subjects were examined; this measure provides an overall index of bargaining efficiency. The predictions made for this variable parallel those relating to toll-charging behavior.

Results

Comparability of subjects in the first ten trials and effectiveness of the experimental manipulations. Steps were taken, before examinining the data bearing on the hypotheses, to determine the comparability of subjects during the first ten trials and to check on the effectiveness of the manipulations. Analyses disclosed no significant differences in total time to reach destination, number of trials in which subjects refused to pay tolls, or number of trials in which subjects avoided the tollgate—that is, traveled the alternate route. Similarly, there were no significant differences in perceptions of the stooges' behavior, as measured by midexperimental questionnaire items, on such dimensions as peaceful-hostile, cooperative-competitive, generous-selfish, and yielding-unyielding. The overall means indicated that the subjects saw the stooges as competitive, unyielding, and moderately selfish and hostile. Finally, the effectiveness of the audience-feedback manipulations was tested by items embedded in the postexperimental questionnaire. These items showed that the subjects believed that they were under observation by their classmates, and they were strongly influenced by the feedback. As intended, subjects in the "looked foolish" condition reported that the audience saw them as significantly more "foolish looking" than subjects in the "not foolish" condition. Other differences were all in the expected directions.

Toll-charging behavior and payoffs earned by subjects. The main experimental results are shown in table 10.6. Analysis of the *frequency* with which tolls of more than fifteen cents were charged revealed significant effects of the audience feedback, of the other's knowledge of the subject's costs, and of the interaction of these variables. Table 10.6 shows that subjects who received derogatory feedback retaliated more frequently than either those who received the more favorable feedback or control subjects. Retaliation was less frequent when a subject knew that the other player was informed of his costs than when costs were kept unannounced.

TABLE 10.6. Mean Number of Trials on Which Subjects
Charged Tolls Involving Costs to Self

	Audience Condition		
Other's Knowledge of Subject's Costs	*"Looked foolish"*	*"Did not look foolish"*	*Control, no feedback*
Other knew own costs	2.30	0.90	1.70
Other ignorant of own costs	7.00	2.20	4.30

It was predominantly in the other-ignorant-of-own-costs condition that the audience-feedback manipulations produced significant differences in the frequency of retaliation. Each of the three means differed significantly from the other two. In contrast, in the other-knew-costs condition there were no significant differences between either audience-feedback condition and the control condition.

In addition to examining the frequency of retaliation, we also studied the *amount* that subjects spent to retaliate. These results are shown in table 10.7. Analysis revealed that the differences among the "audience" conditions are significant for both "knowledge" conditions but are, as for the frequency variable, significantly more pronounced when the subject thought the other was ignorant of the subject's costs.

TABLE 10.7. Mean Payoffs Expended in Charging Tolls
of More than 15 Cents

	Audience Condition		
Other's Knowledge of Subject's Costs	*"Looked foolish"*	*"Did not look foolish"*	*Control, no feedback*
Other knew own costs	0.23	0.10	0.21
Other ignorant of own costs	1.03	0.25	0.67

We next examine the effects of the experimental manipulations on overall bargaining efficiency (reflected in the payoffs that subjects earned). Overall payoffs were determined by summing trial payoffs (obtained by subtracting the time to destination on each trial from a base of sixty cents) and making appropriate adjustments for tolls paid out, tolls collected, and "own" costs. The results reveal significant differences in payoffs only for the audience-feedback effect. The difference between the two other's-knowledge-of-subject's-costs conditions did not reach significance but was in the expected direction. Subjects receiving the "looked foolish" feedback earned significantly less than the remaining subjects.

There were more prolonged collisions in the "looked foolish" condition than in either of the other two conditions. Thus subjects who received the derogatory feedback sought to reduce the stooge's payoff in two ways: by charging him higher tolls and by trying to delay him in the narrow path. Both strategies reflect a willingness to sacrifice own outcomes in order to inflict heavier losses on the other player.

Why were subjects in the "looked foolish" condition drawn into such self-destructive bargaining strategies? The suggestion has been made that these bargainers attempted to restore face after humiliation by trying to reassert their capability and strength. To test this formulation, subjects were asked how hard they tried to "appear strong" to the other in the second half of the experiment, with responses ranging from "tried very hard" (9) to "didn't try at all" (1). Statistical analysis revealed sharp differences due to audience-feedback but no differences due to the "knowledge" manipulations or to their interaction. Table 10.8 shows that concern with appearing strong was more prevalent in the "looked foolish" condition than in either the "not foolish" or control groups. It was, presumably, this potent motivational factor that caused humiliated subjects to retaliate against the other players.

TABLE 10.8. Mean Extent to Which Subjects Tried to
Appear Strong to the Other Players
During the Second Ten Trials

	Audience Condition		
Other's Knowledge of Subject's Costs	*"Looked foolish"*	*"Did not look foolish"*	*Control, no feedback*
Other knew own costs	6.90	4.60	5.50
Other ignorant of own costs	8.00	5.80	5.30

Discussion

The results of this experiment leave little room for doubt. When bargainers have been made to look foolish and weak before a significant audience by an aggressive opponent, they are more likely to retaliate than if their exploitation by the other has not led to a public loss of face. Moreover, retaliation will be undertaken despite the knowledge that doing so may require the sacrifice of all, or large portions of, one's possible earnings. Such behavior will be most likely, however, when bargainers believe that their costs of retaliating are unknown to their opponents. In our experiment, a significant finding was that humiliated subjects soon discovered a means of retaliation that went beyond charging high tolls. This involved causing head-on collisions and then blocking for prolonged periods. They thus spread the conflict beyond the limits set by the rules of the game.

While the feedback given to subjects in the "looked foolish" condition served to increase their concern with looking strong, the "not foolish" feedback had an opposite effect. It encouraged subjects to focus on increasing their own payoffs rather than on reducing those of the other player. The "not foolish" feedback not only intimated that the Ss were evaluated positively by the audience, but it also suggested that the stooges were *disfavored* for being high-handed and charging expensive tolls. The "not foolish" feedback implicitly placed value on playing fair and thereby communicated to the subjects what they had best *not* do if they wanted the audience's continued good favor. Thus it is likely that subjects in the "looked foolish" condition feared a loss of status and, consequently, of face for not retaliating; in the "not foolish" condition, it was retaliation and subsequent audience disapproval that posed the threat to esteem. Hence, the need to maintain esteem was not only responsible for the retaliation in the "looked foolish" condition, but it may also have been responsible for the restraint shown in the "not foolish" condition.

EXPERIMENT VIII: THREAT, PUNITIVE POWER, AND BARGAINING[4]

This study, which was Peter Gumpert's dissertation, was stimulated in part by methodological criticisms of the initial Deutsch and Krauss

4. This experiment was conducted by Peter Gumpert and is reported more fully in Gumpert (1967).

experiment by Kelley (1965). The major criticisms were that (1) the original experiment did not clearly distinguish between threatening and harmful behavior, since the gate could be used for both; (2) the obtained differences resulted from the fact that the gates force the players to take the alternative route if they are competitive, but if the players in the no-gate situation are competitive, they are forced to confront one another and work out an agreement; and (3) the experiment employed trivial incentives and imaginary money, and it appeared that the readiness to cooperate would be increased if more important incentives were employed. Although I have pointed out elsewhere (Deutsch 1966a, 1969a) my reasons for accepting the first criticism and rejecting the second and third, the experiment was designed by Gumpert so as not to be vulnerable to any of the three. In addition, the experiment was designed to investigate an extension of the theoretical analysis of the effects of threat and punitive power.

If we contrast threat ("If you do A or fail to do B, I will do X or fail to do Y, which will be to your detriment.") and punishment ("I have done X or failed to do Y, to your detriment, because you have done A or failed to do B."), it is evident that threat has a more tentative character than punishment. It refers to a possibility in the future rather than to an actuality in the past or present. A threat is more revokable than a punishment. Threat is also usually less costly to the threatener and the threatened than is punishment. Thus it is usually easier, less costly, and less dangerous to threaten than to punish.

The preceding comparison of threat and punishment suggests that, if a bargainer has the capacity to threaten as well as to punish, he is more likely to start by threatening than by punishing. But if a bargainer threatens another and the other does not comply, the threatener is faced with the problem that, if he does not carry out his threat, his credibility and the future usefulness of his threat may be considerably lessened. Punitive power must be employed if the power to threaten is to be preserved. Threat, then, is *tempting* to use, and once used, it opens the *gateway* to the use of punitive power. Thus one could predict that if one compared situations in which bargainers could aggress or punish, but had no capacity to threaten one another, with situations in which bargainers could threaten and aggress or punish one another, then one would expect more frequent use of punitive power in the latter.

Similar reasoning could be applied to the possession of low as well as high levels of punitive power as compared to the possession of high levels only. Low levels of precisely controllable punitive power may be thought of as having some of the characteristics and consequences of threats. Namely, they are more tempting to employ than higher levels and may serve as a gateway to the use of higher levels of power. This suggests the possibility that the possession of precisely graduated weapons, which vary from low to high punitive power, may be more dangerous to the outcome of bargaining than the availability of weapons that have only high punitive power.

The experiment reported below varies threat availability and graduation of punitive power in a 2 × 2 factorial design. A control condition in which neither threat nor punitive power was available was included primarily to provide evidence for the prediction that the availability of ungraduated punitive power without corresponding threat capability would not interfere with bargaining in the game.

The research was carried out using the Deutsch and Krauss version of the trucking game but incorporating various changes to take into account the alternative interpretations that have been suggested by Kelley (1965) and others.

1. The gates and long alternative paths were removed from the game. In their stead, some bargainers were given the power to impose large financial penalties on one another and send specific threatening messages.
2. Subjects who wished to earn money were recruited for the experiment. They played the trucking game for significant amounts of money.

Two general predictions can now be stated:

1. Since threat is likely to be viewed by bargainers as a potentially useful and effective influence device, and since the bargainers are likely to be less aware than we of the possible deleterious consequences of threat use, bargainers who possess threat capability will have higher aspiration levels before the game begins than will bargainers who do not have threats.
2. Bargaining in the conditions in which threat and/or graduated control of punitive power is available will become more competitive than bargaining in the condition in which no threats and

only imprecise control of punitive power are available. This greater competitiveness will be reflected in an increasing use of punitive power, greater "deadlocking" in the one-lane section of the pathway, reduced outcomes, and more negative ratings by the bargainers of their feelings for one another.

Method

Subjects. Subjects were 180 male undergraduate students, who agreed over the telephone to participate in response to a newspaper advertisement that promised "up to $4.00 for an hour's participation" in small-group research. When subjects made appointments, the scheduler explained to them that the actual amount they earned would depend strictly on what they did and on what happened to them in the two-person "experimental game" in which they would take part.

Procedure. Subjects were assigned to the Acme or Bolt position in the Acme-Bolt trucking game by a lottery procedure in which each thought he had been the first to draw a position card from a cup; actually, the second subject to arrive chose from two identical cards. The subjects in a pair did not see or speak with one another until the experiment was concluded. Pairs were assigned to the various experimental treatments by a random procedure. All subjects were given an individualistic motivational orientation.

The subjects' attention was directed to a road map on their tables that showed the routes and distances for the two trucking companies, and it was pointed out to them that Bolt's route was "somewhat longer" than Acme's. One consequence of this, they were told, was that Bolt's trips took longer than Acme's trips and that therefore Bolt could not earn as much money in the game as Acme could. The tape explained:

Since your earning capabilities are somewhat different, we'll be comparing your performance—that is, your total time for all the trips—with how other people that have operated your truck in the past have done. And if you do better than the average for people in your position, you'll be awarded a fifty-cent bonus at the end of the experiment. Now I can't tell you until the end of the experiment what the average times for other Acmes and other Bolts have been up to now. *However, I do want you to remember that you drew the Acme and Bolt positions in a fair lottery, so you will be expected to avail yourselves of any advantages you feel you might have in the game.*

The above instructions were given in an attempt to accomplish two purposes: first, to focus the attention of the subjects on their own incomes, rather than on those of the other players, via the bonuses; second, to maintain, as much as possible, the subjects' feeling that their statuses were, in fact, equal.

Subjects were then introduced to the problem presented by the one-lane section of road and were told about the consequences of meeting one another on the one-lane road—that it was impossible for the two trucks to pass one another while on the one-lane road, and that, therefore, one had to give way to the other on every trip. Subjects were told that the beginning and the end of each trip would be signaled and that each would know the position of his own truck (but not the position of the other player's truck) at all times. They were also told that they would learn whenever one truck was blocking the other's forward movement on the one-lane section of road by means of a message appearing on their game consoles.

At this point in the instructions, threats and/or penalties were introduced in some conditions as "another strategy available to you in the game." Differences among the conditions are described below:

In the threat graduated penalty condition (TGP), subjects were told that they could, once per trip during any trip, penalize the other player ten, twenty, thirty, forty, or fifty cents. These penalties, they were told, would not be added to their own earnings but would be subtracted from the earnings of the other player. In order to impose a penalty, subjects set the amount of the penalty on a rotary switch on their penalty panels and pressed a "delivery button," which sent information to the other (and to the experimenter) concerning the magnitude of the penalty that had been imposed. Subjects were told that they could, if they wished, also send the other player ". . . a message to tell him that you might penalize him on a trip." This message was sent via the other electric panel mounted on the subject's console. The message was read to the subjects, and appeared written on the message panel.

> I intend to go through first. If I meet you anywhere on the one-lane road, I will let you go through before me, *but I will cause you to lose* ——— *cents.*

The magnitude of the threat message was set by the subject, and the message was delivered, in the same way that the penalties were controlled. Subjects were told that the messages and penalties could be used independently of one another. In order to preserve, as much as possible, the independence of trials, subjects were instructed to return the threat and penalty magnitude switches to their lowest settings at the end of each trip. At the same time, subjects were told, the message lights would be reset by the experimenter from the control room.

In the no threat graduated penalty condition (NTGP), subjects had only one supplementary panel available—the penalty panel. The magnitude of the penalty imposed and its delivery were controlled by the subject exactly as in the TGP condition. No mention of messages was made in the instructions, although the instructions were in other respects the same as in the TGP condition.

In the threat nongraduated penalty condition (TN-GP), subjects had two supplementary panels, one for sending penalties and the other for sending threat messages. The magnitude of the threats and penalties, however, was set by the experimenter at fifty cents and could not be varied by the subjects. Panels in this condition were arranged so that the subjects were not aware of the possibility of lesser threats and penalties for some subjects; no rotating knob for setting threat and penalty levels was visible, and the threat message read, ". . . but I will cause you to lose fifty cents."

In the no threat nongraduated penalty condition (NTN-GP), only the penalty panel, which as in the TN-GP condition was present at fifty cents, was made available to the subjects.

In all the conditions involving threats and/or penalties, it was made very clear to the subjects that they did not have to use these devices unless they wished to do so. The threats and/or penalties available to the subjects in these various conditions were in all cases bilateral; no unilateral conditions were employed in this experiment.

In the no threat-no penalty condition (NTNP), neither the threat nor the penalty panels were visible, and all instructions having to do with them were deleted. Thus this condition served as a control for the availability of these devices.

Following the instructions described above, the subjects were told about the sequence of events they could expect in the experiment. They went through three practice trips and then twelve real trips in the trucking game; they completed brief questionnaires after the practice trips, after the sixth real trip, and after the final trip.

The subjects were told that, although they would be following the experimenter's instructions during the three practice trips, the last two of these would be made for money which would form part of their total earnings for the game. In the first of the three practice exercises, the subjects' trucks met in deadlock in the center of the one-lane road. They were kept in deadlock for approximately ten seconds, after which Acme was instructed to reverse his truck while Bolt continued forward. When Bolt's truck was off the one-lane road, Acme was instructed to move forward to his destination. The subjects' times and payoffs were not announced after the completion of this exercise. In the second practice exercise, Bolt was instructed to stop his truck just short of the one-lane section of the road; he waited there until Acme left the one-lane section and was then instructed to proceed. When both subjects' trucks had completed their trips, times and payoffs were announced; these were kept constant for all pairs in all conditions. Acme earned forty cents, and Bolt earned twelve cents. For the third exercise, this procedure was reversed. This time, Acme waited just short of the one-lane section of road until Bolt left it, and then Acme was instructed to proceed to his destination. Times and payoffs were announced. Acme earned twenty-three cents, and Bolt earned thirty-one cents. Thus the subjects learned that, if they were reasonably efficient in using an alternation strategy to resolve their conflict, they could both earn a considerable amount of money in the game. Actually, with perfect coordination and continuation of the alternation pattern, Acme could earn a maximum of $5.40 and Bolt a maximum of $4.00, exclusive of bonuses.

Subjects who were in the various conditions in which threats and/or penalties were made available to them were instructed to send simulated threats and/or penalties before the first practice exercise began. In the two graduated conditions, they were instructed to send a threat and/or a penalty of thirty cents, after which they returned the rotating knobs on those panels to their lowest positions. Subjects in the nongraduated conditions, of course, sent a fifty-cent threat and/or penalty. Penalties and threats were not mentioned or used at any time during the practice trips.

After each trip in the actual game, the experimenter announced each player's travel time, his before-penalty payoff, and (when applicable) the amounts of any penalties imposed.

Postexperimental interview. After the subjects had completed the final two tasks, they were introduced to one another, and the nature and purposes of the experiment were thoroughly explained to them. When all their questions had been answered, they were paid what they had earned in the game (although all subjects received at least $2.50 simply for their participation in the experiment).

Results

Threat availability and aspiration level. The analysis in the introductory section of this experiment suggests that threat is viewed by bargainers as a potential aid to bargaining. Thus prior to the bargaining, bargainers with threats available should have been more optimistic about their performance than bargainers without threats. The pregame questionnaire, administered after the practice trials but before the game began, asked the subjects to estimate the average number of seconds that it would take them and their partners to complete each of the first six trips. The optimism of the subjects about their future performance can be assessed by comparing the threat conditions with their no threat counterparts. Table 10.9 presents the mean expectations for the bargainers in all conditions. Statistical analysis indicates that the bargainers who possess a threat capability expect to do better than those without such a capability; Acme, who has the shorter path, expects to do better than Bolt.

TABLE 10.9. Mean Pre-Game Performance Expectation, in Seconds [1]

	Experimental Conditions				
Bargainer's Position	*NTN-GP*	*NTGP*	*TN-GP*	*TGP*	*NTNP*
Acme	44.1	43.0	41.8	38.9	42.2
Bolt	50.2	47.9	46.0	47.3	49.7

[1] Lower numbers indicate more optimistic expectations.

Table 10.10 presents what might be seen as a tentative indicator of felt competitiveness before the game. Each subject's pregame estimate of his own probable average performance was subtracted from his estimate of his partner's probable average performance. An inspection of the means indicates that subjects in the threat condition were more optimistic about both their relative and their absolute performances than were subjects in the no threat conditions. Although this result just misses the .05 level of statistical significance, it is close enough to be tantalizing. In any case, it is clear that threats were, at the outset, viewed as potentially useful by bargainers who had them available. The question of whether the threats were, in fact, used and whether their use had the anticipated consequences for bargaining will be answered in the following sections.

TABLE 10.10. Mean Difference between Estimates of
Other's and Own's Anticipated Performance [1]

	Experimental Conditions				
Bargainer's Position	*NTN-GP*	*NTGP*	*TN-GP*	*TGP*	*NTNP*
Acme	+3.7	+3.7	+6.0	+4.7	+4.9
Bolt	−9.3	−10.1	−8.0	−7.1	−9.7

[1] For Acme bargainers, *larger positive* numbers indicate anticipations of better relative performance; for Bolt bargainers, *smaller negative* numbers indicate anticipation of better relative performance.

The use of threats and punitive power. Most of the bargainers who had threats available used them at least once during the game; twenty-four out of thirty Acme bargainers and twenty-seven out of thirty Bolt bargainers did so. That threats were used often in the game by both bargainers can be seen in table 10.11. Overall, bargainers used threats on about 40 percent of their trips. Those bargainers who used threats at least once used them about 57 percent of the time on the average. The data on threats also demonstrate that bargainers tended to use threat messages early in the game. Thirty-seven percent of all the bargainers in the threat conditions used threats during the first trip, and 67 percent of them had delivered a threat by the end of the second trip. By the end of the first half of the game, 82 percent of the bargainers had threatened their bargaining partners.

TABLE 10.11. Mean Number of Trips in Which Threat
Messages and Penalties Were Utilized

	Bargainer's	*Experimental Conditions*			
Data	*Position*	*NTN-GP*	*NTGP*	*TN-GP*	*TGP*
Threat	Acme			4.6	4.5
	Bolt			5.4	4.9
Penalty [1]	Acme	0.7	3.1 [1]	3.3 [1]	3.1 [1]
	Bolt	0.7	3.2 [1]	2.9 [1]	2.7 [1]

[1] Significance level of differences between the NTN-GP condition and the other conditions (by Dunnett's t-test) is $p < .05$.

If the threat messages had been merely useful for coordinating moves in the game, as many bargainers probably expected, bargainers who had threats would not have had to use their penalties at all. The data are inconsistent with such a view of the threats. In the TN-GP condition, ten out of fifteen Acme bargainers and ten out of fifteen Bolt bargainers used their penalties at least once. In the NTGP condition, fourteen out of fifteen Acme and thirteen out of fifteen Bolt bargainers used their penalties at least once. The data for the NTGP condition are comparable to the data in the two threat conditions: eleven out of fifteen Acme bargainers and ten out of fifteen Bolt bargainers used penalties sometime during the game. But in the NTN-GP condition only four out of fifteen bargainers and four out of fifteen Bolt bargainers imposed penalties. A comparison of the frequencies in the NTN-GP condition with those in the other three conditions yields striking differences. Clearly, bargainers who possessed threats, graduated control over their penalties, or both were more likely to impose at least one penalty than were bargainers who had no threats and only nongraduated punitive power.

Our theoretical analysis suggested that bargaining in the conditions in which threat and/or graduated control of punitive power was available would become more competitive than bargaining in the NTN-GP condition—and that this competitiveness would be reflected in an increasing use of punitive power as the bargaining progressed. Table 10.12 divides the game into four blocks of three trips and presents the mean amount of penalty imposed by bargainers in the four penalty conditions. Neither Acme nor Bolt bargainers in the NTN-GP condition imposed penalties during the last block of three trips; the

TABLE 10.12. Mean Amount of Penalty per Trip
Imposed by Bargainers (Cents)

		Trips			
Bargainer	*Condition*	*1–3*	*4–6*	*7–9*	*10–12*
	NTN-GP	5.6	5.6	1.1	0.0
Acme	NTGP	8.9	6.9	8.0	5.6
	TN-GP	12.2	13.3	11.1	18.9
	TGP	6.2	10.9	6.4	14.0
	NTN-GP	4.4	4.4	2.2	0.0
Bolt	NTGP	6.4	8.4	10.7	11.1
	TN-GP	11.1	13.3	7.8	16.7
	TGP	6.4	10.2	9.3	9.8

amount of penalty used decreased from the first to the last block of trials. For the other conditions, taken collectively, there was a tendency for an escalation of penalty use from the first to the last block of trials. However, it should be noted in passing that a considerable reduction of penalty use between the second block and the third block of trips is apparent in three of the four penalty conditions.

This result is probably accounted for by the midgame questionnaire that was administered after the sixth trip and that asked bargainers to reflect on the first half of the game. It seems likely (1) that many bargainers were stimulated by the questionnaire to attempt to do better during the second half of the game and (2) that they might have resolved to try to be more moderate in their use of penalties. The data for the last two blocks of trips indicate that, for the most part, these attempts at moderation were unsuccessful.

Since no record was kept of the sequence of events within a trip, we have no direct evidence of the development of competitive spirals of threat-counterthreat and penalty-counterpenalty within a given trip. But some indication of how the bargainers tended to respond to each other's overall use of penalties may be seen in the correlations between the total amounts of penalty imposed by Acme and Bolt bargainers in the various conditions. The correlations are quite high: .84 in the NTN-GP condition, .95 in the NTGP condition, .69 in the TN-GP condition, and .92 in the TGP condition. All are significant beyond the .01 level, and none is significantly different from any other. If one bargainer imposed penalties, then, the other bargainer was likely to impose them also.

The data on threat and penalty use have clearly demonstrated that threat messages were used by most bargainers to whom they were available, and that the availability of threats and/or graduated control of penalties led to frequent use of the penalties. Though it is less clear, there is also some evidence to support the notion that the use of penalties increased over time in the conditions in which bargainers had threats available or could exercise quantitative control over their penalties; in any case, penalty use tended to remain relatively high in those conditions, whereas it tended to drop off in the condition in which bargainers had no threat messages and only a high level of punitive power available to them. The effects of the use of threats and penalties on other aspects of bargaining are discussed below.

Travel time and deadlocking. The amount of time that the bargainers spent traveling from their starting points to their destinations is a reflection of the amount of difficulty they experienced in bargaining, including coordination difficulties and mutual deadlocking on the one-lane section of their pathway. Bargainers learned in the practice trips that if they achieved near-perfect coordination and alternated first use of the one-lane section, Acme could reach his destination in an average time of about thirty-eight seconds per trip and Bolt in about forty-eight seconds per trip. How they fared in the game is shown in table 10.13.

TABLE 10.13. Travel Time, Reported Feelings, and Payoffs

Measure	Bargainer	Experimental Conditions				
		NTNP	NTN-GP	NTGP	TN-GP	TGP
Mean travel time per trip	Acme	45.4	46.1	60.8	56.0	49.5
	Bolt	54.2	52.1	68.4 [1]	63.4	58.2
Number of trips in which deadlock took place		.3	3.1	5.9 [1]	4.9	5.7 [1]
Reported feelings about other bargainer, midgame questionnaire [2]	Acme	35.2	41.8	38.8	34.6	33.4
	Bolt	36.3	41.9	34.3	27.1 [1]	22.9 [1]
Reported feelings about other bargainer, postgame questionnaire	Acme	37.5	40.9	38.2	32.4	35.8
	Bolt	39.5	40.1	37.2	24.4 [1]	29.1
Mean outcomes per trip (cents)	Acme	+24.6	+21.1	0.0	+1.9	+11.6
	Bolt	+16.2	+14.9	−6.2	−7.3	+2.5
Mean number of trips in which both bargainers made profits	Combined	10.5	10.0	7.1 [1]	7.1 [1]	7.3

[1] A significant level of difference ($p < .05$) is indicated between the NTN-GP condition and the condition with which it is compared by a superior 1.

[2] Lower numbers indicate more negative feelings.

The error variance for the overall travel-time data was very high in this experiment, due to a number of bargaining pairs in the NTGP and TN-GP conditions who engaged in exceedingly long deadlocks during the game. Therefore, although the NTN-GP condition travel-time means for both bargainers are lower than those in the other penalty conditions, only the Bolt bargainers in the NTGP condition have consistently higher means ($p < .02$) than their NTN-GP counterparts. However, the surprisingly low travel time for both bargainers in the TGP condition should be noted. Apparently, competitiveness in the TGP condition was not expressed by long deadlocking.

But shorter-term deadlocking *was* engaged in by TGP bargainers. Table 10.13 presents the mean number of trips in which a deadlock of five seconds or more took place between a pair of bargainers; five seconds, in our judgment, was enough to distinguish between an instance of inadvertent miscoordination and one of deliberate blocking. TGP bargainers were apparently able, for some reason, to confine their competitive behavior to the use of threats and penalties and to brief pro forma deadlocks. Though the evidence is weaker for the TN-GP condition, the data, overall, provide a reasonably good case for the assertion that dysfunctional mutual blocking was engaged in more by bargainers who had threats and/or graduated control over penalties than by bargainers in the NTN-GP condition.

Bargainers' reports of feelings toward one another. Items in the midgame and postgame questionnaires asked bargainers to rate their position on a sixty-one-dot rating scale describing a continuum of feelings toward the other, ranging from "angry and annoyed" to "warm and friendly." These data (table 10.13) do not provide strong support for the prediction; although the means for the NTN-GP condition reveal less negative feelings than those in the other three penalty conditions, the stable differences were limited to Bolt bargainers in the two threat conditions. It may well be that Acme, because of his advantage over Bolt, felt less entitled to express anger or annoyance at his partner than did Bolt.

The bargainers' outcomes. Since the bargainers' payoffs were determined by their travel times and the penalties imposed on them by their fellow bargainers, it seems somewhat redundant to present data on payoffs. However, other investigators have depended heavily on outcome data, and it may therefore be of interest to look at bargainers' outcomes in the present experiment. Table 10.13 presents the mean payoffs per trip for Acme and Bolt bargainers. Because these data are as plagued by high error variance as are the travel-time data, an alternative measure of payoff is also presented: the mean number of trips in which *both* bargainers in the various conditions made some profit. The mean-payoff-per-trip data indicate that, of the three conditions in which competitive bargaining was expected to develop, bargainers in the TGP earned most. But even Acme bargainers in that condition earned only half as much as did Acme bargainers in the NTN-GP condition. The relatively high payoffs in the TGP condition reflect the fact that TGP bargainers were able to avoid the extremely lengthy deadlocks that seemed to take place in the NTGP and TN-GP conditions.

Summary and Conclusion

The pattern of results for the NTN-GP condition closely parallels that for the NTNP condition; so close was the parallel, in fact, that the data for these two conditions might plausibly have been pooled to test some of the major predictions. Clearly, the lack of a threat capability combined with only a high level of punitive power does not have demonstrably deleterious effects on bargaining. Comparing the NTN-GP condition with the others in which penalties were available, the results of the experiment can be summarized as follows:

1. Bargainers who had threats available to them had higher aspiration levels before the game began than did bargainers without threats, probably indicating that the deleterious effects of the threats were not anticipated by the bargainers.

2. The threat messages were heavily used by most of the bargainers who had them.

3. The availability and use of threats resulted in the early and continuing use of punitive power by a large proportion of the bargainers.

4. Bargainers who did not have threats but did have graduated control of their penalties also began using the penalties early in the game and continued using them throughout the game. Bargainers in the NTN-GP condition, on the other hand, used their penalties very seldom in the early stages of the game and not at all later in the game.

5. Somewhat different patterns of competitiveness emerged in the NTGP, TN-GP, and TGP conditions. Penalty use in the two threat conditions tended to escalate with the passage of time as compared with that in the NTN-GP condition. In the NTGP condition, penalty use led also to lengthy mutual blocking on the one-lane pathway. Although TGP bargainers engaged in more blocking than did NTN-GP bargainers, the blocking tended to be of short duration. As was predicted, then, more competitive behavior of various sorts took place in the NTGP, TN-GP, and TGP conditions than took place in the NTN-GP condition.

Considering the subject population and certain features of the experimental procedure, the results of this experiment are particularly striking. The subjects, according to their own reports in the postexperimental interview, were highly motivated to maximize their monetary outcomes, and the experimenter very strongly encouraged this motivation in his instructions to them. The message of the practice trips was certainly unmistakable, and the absence of gates and alternative routes in the present version of the trucking game made coordination difficulties quite trivial; the efficiency of the bargaining in the NTNP and NTN-GP conditions attests admirably to that fact. Furthermore, the experimenter announced travel times and penalties after each trip, and the midgame questionnaire served to focus the bargainers' attention on their satisfaction with their outcomes. Yet, in the face of all that, bargainers in some conditions continued to penalize one another and/or block one another's progress to the point that their outcomes were drastically reduced.

The bearing of the results of the experiment reported here on the controversy in the literature over the effect of threats upon interpersonal bargaining is perfectly clear. The results lend unambiguous support to the notion that threat availability in mixed-motive bargaining tends to lead to the development of competitive rather than cooperative processes and thus to a reduction in the joint outcomes of the bargainers.

We have suggested that threats (and small amounts of punitive power) are more *tempting* to use as a means of influencing a possibly recalcitrant other than are large amounts of punitive power. Doing so seems easier, less costly, and less dangerous. Yet, the availability of threats and small graduated amounts of punitive power *can* open the gateway to the use of larger amounts of punitive power and to the more frequent uses of small amounts of such power. The gateway is apparently opened by two related processes. Threats, to be credible, must be supported by punitive power if they fail initially, and threats, as well as punitive power, tend to elicit resistance and the use of counterthreats and counteraggressions; thus the initial threat or aggression is unlikely to be effective in achieving its objective. Had our subjects been more concerned about relative power and "face," and less concerned about their individual earnings, one might have expected that the mutual harm resulting from the availability of threats and graduated punitive power might have been even greater than was the case.

11. Structural and Attitudinal Factors in Bargaining

Our studies of bargaining have been guided by the assumption that the ease or difficulty of resolving a conflict is influenced by the relative strengths of the cooperative and competitive interests of the bargainers: the stronger their cooperative interests, the easier it is to resolve the conflict; the stronger their competitive interests, the more difficult it is to resolve. The research on the effects of threat has presupposed that the use of threat, given the social context of our experiments, would strengthen the competitive interests of the bargainers in relation to one another and that this, in turn, would make it more difficult for the subjects to come to a cooperative agreement about how to share the main route in the Acme-Bolt bargaining game. In the present chapter, we consider several factors, other than the availability of threat, that we anticipated might influence the bargaining process by affecting the relative balance of the cooperative and competitive interests of the bargainers. Three experiments are reported: (1) The Effects of Size of Conflict; (2) The Effects of "Locking Oneself In" During a Game of Chicken; and (3) Structural and Attitudinal Factors in Bargaining.

EXPERIMENT I: THE EFFECT OF SIZE OF CONFLICT AND SEX OF EXPERIMENTER UPON INTERPERSONAL BARGAINING [1]

Fisher (1964) has pointed out that the issues over which nations go to war are the big issues, which rarely can be adjudicated. In the Cuban missile crisis, neither the United States nor the Soviet Union would

1. This experiment was done by the present author in collaboration with Donnah Canavan and Jeffrey Rubin and is reported more fully in Deutsch, Canavan, and Rubin (1971).

have been willing to negotiate about an issue such as freedom or communism in the Western Hemisphere, although they were able to negotiate about the much smaller issue of the location of seventy-two weapons systems. Fisher's thesis is the familiar one that small conflicts are easier to resolve than large ones. However, he also points out that the participants may have a choice in defining the conflict as a large or a small one.

One enlarges a conflict by dealing with it as a conflict between large rather than small units (a racial conflict rather than a conflict between two individuals of different races), as a conflict over a large, substantive issue rather than over a small one (being treated fairly or being treated unfairly on a particular occasion), as a conflict over a principle rather than over the application of a principle, as a conflict whose solution establishes large rather than small substantive or procedural precedents. Many other determinants of conflict size could be listed. For example, an issue that bears upon self-esteem or a change in power or status is likely to be more important than an issue that does not affect these things. Illegitimate threats or attempts to coerce are likely to increase the size of the conflict and thus increase the likelihood of a competitive process.

Conflict size may be defined as being equal to the expected difference in the value of the outcomes that a person will receive if he wins compared with the value he will receive if the other wins a conflict. A person "wins" a conflict if he obtains outcomes that are satisfying to him; the more satisfying they are to him, the more he wins. This definition implies that conflict size will be small for a person who believes that both parties can win and large if he thinks that one person will lose (have less than satisfactory outcomes) if the other wins. This definition also implies that the size of a given conflict may be larger for one person than for the other. One person may expect that his outcomes will be quite satisfactory even if the other wins, while the second may believe that his outcomes will be adversely affected if the other wins.

I have defined conflict size subjectively, in terms of expected outcomes. In simple and easily grasped situations, there is likely to be a close correspondence between the objective and subjective definitions, so that the expected difference in outcomes will neatly parallel the actual differences that occur when one or the other person wins. Having, in the Acme-Bolt trucking game, a very simple, objective method for varying the size of conflicts, Donnah Canavan, Jeffrey Rubin, and I decided to conduct an experiment on the effects of size using this game. In addition, we studied the effects of the sex of the experimenter because pilot runs suggested that different results might be obtained by a male and a female experimenter.

Method

The two independent variables of this experiment, conflict size and sex of the experimenter, were used in a 3 × 2 factorial design with fifteen pairs of Ss in each cell. Undergraduate male subjects were recruited during the summer from ads in *The Village Voice* and the *Columbia Spectator*. The ads promised that Ss could earn up to $4.00 an hour by participating in an experiment. Pairs of Ss were randomly composed. They came to the laboratory in such a way that they did not meet on arrival. They were seated at separate tables in an experimental room (in such a way that they could not see each other) and were instructed not to speak to each other at any time. Each subject was given $1.00 as his initial "stake" in the game.

After listening to taped instructions that explained the bargaining game and the experimental apparatus, the Ss were led through a series of five practice trials to familiarize them with the various actions that could be taken—including the use of the gates. Next, they were given a brief preexperimental questionnaire to complete. The actual game was then begun, time and pay for each player being announced at the end of each of the twenty trials in the game. Upon completion of the game, the Ss were asked to fill out a postexperimental questionnaire. Finally, they were introduced to each other and paid, and the purpose of the experiment was carefully explained to them.

Subjects were given an individualistic motivational orientation; they were told to attempt to make as much money for themselves as possible, regardless of how well or how poorly the other player did. They could do this by moving their trucks from start to destination in the shortest possible time. The Ss were told that for each trip in the game they would each be given a certain amount of capital and that operating expenses (based on the time taken to go from start to destination) would be deducted from this capital (at the rate of a penny a second), leaving their net earnings for that trial. It was emphasized that the money was real and that each subject would keep whatever he earned. On each trip there was a maximum allowable loss of seventy-five cents per player, such that additional time spent on that trip would not result in further losses. Each trip was allowed to run for a total of 180 seconds, or three minutes.

Conflict size was experimentally manipulated by varying the length of the one-lane section of the main route. In low-conflict conditions, this one-lane section was only four units in length, while in middle- and high-conflict conditions, it was ten and eighteen units long, respectively. The total length of the main route was held constant at twenty units in all conditions; similarly, the length of the alternate route remained constant in all conditions. Thus while in low-conflict conditions only 20 percent of the main route was one-lane wide (conflict size 4), in medium conflict 50 percent was one-lane wide (conflict size 10), and in high-conflict conditions it was one-lane wide for 90 percent of the total distance (conflict size 18). In order to hold constant the maximum amount of money that Ss in different conflict-size conditions could make, the Ss started with different amounts of money in the three conditions. Thus if players chose the optimally cooperative solution to the bargaining problem and coordinated effectively, they could make the same amount of money in *all* conflict-size conditions. Four-unit pairs began each trip with forty-eight cents each—so that on any optimally coordinated trip, the pair member to go through the one-lane section first (P_1) could make a maximum of twenty-three cents, while the player to go through second (P_2) could make a maximum of eighteen cents. Similarly, ten-unit pairs began each trip with fifty-two cents apiece, such that P_1 and P_2 could make a maximum of twenty-seven cents and fourteen cents, respectively. Finally, eighteen-unit pairs began each trip with fifty-seven cents each—with P_1 and P_2 making a maximum of thirty-two cents and nine cents, respectively. Thus in all three conflict conditions the *maximum joint pay* on a trip equalled forty-one cents.

In manipulating the second independent variable, *sex of experimenter,* half the Ss in each of the size conditions were run by a male experimenter (M), the other half being run by a female experimenter (F). All the Ss heard the same taped instructions, the voice being that of a male but clearly not that of M. Both M and F employed identical experimental procedures (including the phraseology used in greeting Ss, in leading them through the practice trials, and in reporting scores after each trial of the actual game). Face-to-face contact between experimenter and Ss was brief, involving the greeting and direction of Ss to the experimental room and the administration of two written questionnaires. The Ss knew that they were being observed by the experimenter from behind a one-way vision screen, and they knew that the other S was also a male.

The dependent measures in this experiment may be grouped as follows:

1. *Bargainers' game behavior.* This information included such variables as mean joint payoff (in cents); number of alternations (an alternation being characterized as a sequence in which a player who was first to go through the one-lane section on one trip is second to go through on the next trip); number of trials in which both pair members have positive outcomes (i.e., number of "cooperative trials"); number of maximum losses (minus seventy-five cents); total time lost in deadlock (in seconds); total amount of gate use; number of trials on which at least one player finishes on the alternate route.

2. *Bargainers' attitudes toward themselves, their bargaining partners, and the bargaining game.* This information was obtained from subjects' ratings on pre and postexperimental questionnaires. The prequestionnaire was administered after the practice trials, while the postquestionnaire was administered after the twenty trials. Both questionnaires asked the S to rate himself *and* the other on a variety of attributes, using sixty-point scales. The attributes were: friendly, yielding, typically male, sharing, excitable, careful, considerate, fair, slow, competitive. Other questions measured the S's aspiration level, his objectives in the game, and his minimal acceptable outcome.

Results

The game data. Table 11.1 and figure 11.1 present a summary of the game data as a function of the experimental variables. It is evident that as conflict size increased, joint payoff decreased. In addition, the Ss who had a female experimenter had worse outcomes than those with a male experimenter. There was also a definite increase in joint payoff over the course of the twenty trials. However, the Ss run by the male increased their joint payoffs over the twenty trials considerably more than did the Ss run by the female. Moreover, the Ss in the smallest conflict had little improvement in their joint payoffs during the twenty trials (starting off at a fairly high level and remaining there), while the Ss in the two larger conflicts had a marked increase in their outcomes from the first block to the last block of trials.

The other measures that are shown in table 11.1 provide related evidence that as size of conflict increased, cooperation became more difficult. There were fewer trials in which both players had positive outcomes; there were more trials in which both players had negative outcomes; there were more trials of maximum deadlock and loss; there were more trials in which one or both players finished on the alternate path; and there were more trials in which both Ss used their gates (this last result is not quite statistically significant). These mea-

TABLE 11.1. Means for Three Conflict Sizes and for
Male and Female Experimenters

	Size 4			Size 10			Size 18		
	M	F	Av	M	F	Av	M	F	Av
Joint payoff per trial in cents	12.68	12.05	12.37	18.35	−.55	8.90	−1.87	−26.68	−14.28
No. of trials in which both Ss in a pair had positive outcomes	15.20	14.73	14.97	14.53	11.20	12.87	10.60	6.13	8.37
No. of trials of maximum losses (−.75)	1.53	.80	1.17	1.27	2.73	2.00	4.67	5.20	4.94
No. of trials in which both Ss in a pair had negative outcomes	2.60	2.73	2.67	1.73	4.60	3.17	4.47	8.27	6.37
No. of trials in which one or both of pair finished on alternate route	1.93	3.26	2.10	1.40	4.07	2.74	5.40	10.60	8.00
No. of trials in which both Ss used gates	1.40	2.20	1.80	1.20	3.00	2.20	2.27	5.80	4.04

sures are also consistent in indicating that our male Ss had more difficulty cooperating with one another (or were more competitive) when
the experimenter was a female rather than a male graduate student.

Although the statistical analysis revealed no significant size by sex
interactions, inspection of the data in table 11.1 showed that the Ss
who were run by the male experimenter tended to be as cooperative in
conflict size 10 as their counterparts in conflict size 4. Figure 11.1,
which plots the mean joint payoff per trial by trial blocks, also indicates that, after the initial block of trials, the Ss run by the male in

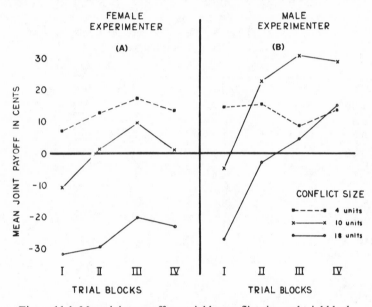

Figure 11.1. Mean joint payoff per trial by conflict size and trial block.

conflict size 10 were the most cooperative pairs in the entire experiment. We must turn to the questionnaire data to see what light can be
shed on this deviant result.

The questionnaire data. Statistical analysis revealed that on the postquestionnaire Ss perceived their partners as less hostile, less greedy,
less reckless, less unfair, less alert, less competitive and less typically
male than they had indicated on the prequestionnaire. On the other
hand, they saw their partners as more yielding, more easygoing and
more considerate than they had expected them to be on the prequestionnaire. The change in the Ss' perception of themselves mirrors the

change in their perception of their partners, except for the fact that there were no significant differences in perceptions of their own maleness, recklessness, and alertness. The obtained differences between the pre and postquestionnaire paralleled the actual increase in cooperative interaction that occurred from the initial to the final trials.

It is interesting to note that the preexperiment questionnaire indicated that the Ss run by the female experimenter anticipated, at the outset of the game, that their game-playing would be more hostile, more unfair, and more competitive than did the Ss run by the male. A similar analysis of the postexperiment questionnaire showed that the difference in unfairness was eliminated. Possibly the Ss discovered that they were no more unfair than the other players and that unfairness is a relative matter. The behavioral data from the game were, thus, consistent with the differences in self-anticipations of the Ss run by the two different experimenters.

The prequestionnaire data also indicated that the Ss in conflict size 10 initially saw their opposing players as likely to be more unfair and more competitive than did the Ss in the other experimental conditions. They also thought that the other players would be considerably more competitive than they themselves: the anticipated difference between self and other in competitiveness was greatest for conflict size 10 (see table 11.2). The Ss run by the male experimenter in conflict size 10 did not anticipate being competitive themselves and, in behavior, they were not. Thus these Ss, expecting their pairmates to be competitive but finding that they were not, experienced a marked disconfirmation of their expectations about the other's behavior. Possibly, this disconfirmation led to a quick and radical shift of their view of the relative competitiveness of themselves and the other.

TABLE 11.2. Perceived Differences between Self and Other in Competitiveness before and after the Game, as a Function of Conflict Size and Sex of the Experimenter

	Size 4		Size 10		Size 18		*Statistical Significance*	
	M	F	M	F	M	F	Size	Sex
Pre-Competitiveness	−19.8 [1]	−6.9	−25.9	−20.7	−9.3	1.9	.05	n.s.
Post-Competitiveness	29.5	43.9	59.8	4.9	32.2	10.2	n.s.	.05
Pre-Post Change	49.3	50.8	85.7	25.6	41.5	29.2		

[1] A minus sign indicates that the other was rated as more competitive than the self; a plus sign indicates that the self was rated as more competitive.

By the end of the game, these Ss viewed the other to be considerably more cooperative but rated themselves as considerably less cooperative than was initially the case. As figure 11.1 indicates, the disconfirmation of these Ss' expectations was followed by an early improvement in the cooperativeness of the pairs in this condition. Although the somewhat deviant results for conflict size 10 run by the M seem explainable in terms of the disconfirmation of the Ss' initial expectations that the other players would be rather more competitive than they, we do not have any basis for explaining their initial expectations.

Discussion

Our results support the idea that decreasing the size of a conflict makes it easier for bargainers to come to an agreement that is mutually rewarding. These results are consonant with research on intrapsychic conflict, which also indicates that such conflict is easier to resolve when the opposing forces are small rather than large in magnitude (see chapter 3). They are also consistent with research on labor-management conflict, which suggests that negotiations are more likely to lead to peaceful outcomes when they focus on specific issues rather than on the ideological frame of reference of the parties in dispute (see chapters 5 and 13). While we believe that our findings and the related results of other research are valid, it does seem reasonable to suppose that, under certain conditions, a large conflict may seem so potentially dangerous that, if it cannot be suppressed or evaded, it leads to strong pressure to come to a quick agreement. It would be worthwhile to do research to identify the conditions under which this hypothesized result might occur.

   If size of conflict is an important determinant of the likelihood of a cooperative process of conflict resolution, it may well be, as Roger Fisher has suggested, that "issue control" is as crucial as arms control to the peace of the world. The escalation of conflict typically involves a broadening of the scope of conflict as well as an intensification of the issues involved. Issue control would, however, be directed toward narrowing and limiting the scope of the conflict, making the issues as specific and focused on the here and now as possible. There is a considerable literature on the escalation of conflict, but very little has been written on the fractionation of conflict. We suspect that most people know how to increase the size of conflict but that they are not so adept at reducing its scope. Thus there seems to be a definite place for imaginative research to help develop a technology for conflict reduction.

Our results have also indicated that the experimenter may have significant effects upon the behavior of the subjects during an experiment. Our attractive female experimenter evoked more competitive behavior from our male undergraduates than our male experimenter. It is, of course, impossible to tell whether it was the gender differences between our experimenters or other personality differences systematically or accidentally associated with the sex differences that led to the significant effects. Nevertheless, reviewing our own previous research on interpersonal bargaining in the light of this finding, it appears that our subjects have been most competitive when they and the experimenter were opposite in sex and most cooperative when they were of the same sex. That is to say, we cannot conclude from the present experiment that it is the increased sense of "maleness" in the face of a female experimenter that produced the enhanced competition; possibly, an increased sense of "femaleness" among female subjects with a male experimenter would have had parallel results. It seems entirely possible that some of the nonreplications of findings in the experimental literature may be due to the fact that the sex of the experimenter, in relation to the sex of the subject, was not considered in the replication.

EXPERIMENT II: THE EFFECTS OF "LOCKING ONESELF IN" DURING A GAME OF "CHICKEN" [2]

Such terms as *brinkmanship, the rationality of irrationality,* and *the doctrine of the last clear chance* have been much in vogue among intellectuals (e.g., Schelling 1960) who are concerned with formulating a rationale to guide strategic choices in a situation of international conflict. The basic notion underlying these different terms is that a bargainer will gain an advantage if he can commit himself irrevocably, so that the last clear chance of avoiding mutual disaster rests with his opponent. A child who works himself up to the point that he will have a temper tantrum if his parents refuse to let him sit where he wants in a restaurant is using this bargaining tactic. So is the driver

2. This experiment was done in collaboration with Roy J. Lewicki and is more fully reported in Deutsch and Lewicki (1970).

who cuts in front of someone on a highway while appearing to be deaf to the insistent blasts of the other's horn. And so is a nation that tells another nation that its national honor and the sacrifices of its soldiers do not permit withdrawal or defeat.

It is evident that this type of bargaining maneuver can sometimes be very effective. Yet, we wondered, would one expect this type of bargaining tactic to be effective when both sides could resort to it? We also wondered whether it is as suitable for a continuing relationship as it might be for a single, unrepeated encounter. To investigate these questions, Roy Lewicki and I employed a modified version of the Acme-Bolt bargaining game.

Two basic modifications were made in the usual Acme-Bolt game. First, the game was altered so as to resemble more closely the adolescent game of "chicken" by instructing the subjects that if their two trucks met at any point along the one-way section of the main path, the encounter would be defined as a collision. If a collision occurred, the trial would be terminated; both subjects would then be penalized one cent for each second used from the start of the trial to the time of the collision. (A collision would thus cost each player at least twenty cents.) The second modification entailed introducing a commitment device as a replacement for the gates. The commitment device ("the lock") enabled the subject to lock his truck into forward gear so that it had to move forward. Once locked, the position of the gear could not be altered during the trial; hence, the truck was committed irreversibly to moving forward. When a subject used the lock, the other player was informed of this action by a clear, unambiguous signal.

The subjects in all the experiments described below were adolescent males attending high schools in New York City. They were recruited by advertisements offering them the opportunity to earn up to $4.00 per hour. Ten pairs of subjects were used in each of the experimental conditions in each of the experiments. Subjects were selected in such a way that the members of a bargaining pair did not know one another. On arrival, they waited together in a common reception room. During the experiment, the subjects were seated at separate tables in such a way that they did not see each other; they were instructed not to speak to each other at any time. Each subject was given $2.00 as his initial stake in the game. On each table was an electronic panel, labeled *Acme Express Company* or *Bolt Express Company*. Money was to be earned by moving the trucks from the start position to the destination in the shortest possible time. For each trip that did not end in a collision, each company would be paid a fee of sixty cents; operating expenses would be deducted from this fee at the rate of one cent per second. It was emphasized that the money was real and that the Ss would be allowed to keep whatever they earned in the task. In this experiment, unlike the procedure in our other experiments, the subjects were always aware of the other's choice of route and his location on that route; they were told that if their two trucks should meet head-on at any point, the encounter would be defined as a collision. If a collision occurred, the trial would immediately end, and each subject would be penalized for the amount of time taken from start to collision at the rate of one cent per second.

Following instructions on the actual operation of the apparatus (selecting a route, moving the trucks, etc.), subjects were led through a series of five practice trials that illustrated the various possible actions in the game, including the use of the locks and collisions. All subjects, unless otherwise noted—as in the third experiment, were given instructions that stressed an individualistic orientation.

Several different versions of this experiment were conducted: an experiment involving a one-trial game; a second one with a twenty-trial game; a third, which compared the effects of "chicken" versus "social problem-solving" orientations; and a fourth, which investigated the effects of the timing of the commitment decision.

The One-Trial Game

The subjects in this version of experiment II played in one of three experimental conditions: *bilateral lock,* both possessed locks; *unilateral lock,* only Acme possessed the lock; and *no lock,* neither player possessed the lock. The subjects were led to believe that they were participating in a one-trial game; however, following completion of the initial trial, they played an additional trial. In the second trial, the no lock pairs became the bilateral lock pairs and the bilateral lock became the no lock pairs; Bolt got the lock from Acme in the second unilateral lock condition.

The results (see table 11.3) indicated no statistically significant differences among the three experimental conditions on the first trial, although there was a tendency for a lower level of joint outcomes as one moved from the no lock to the unilateral lock to the bilateral lock conditions. In the unilateral lock condition, Acme, who possessed the commitment device, had significantly better payoffs than did Bolt, who possessed no such device.

In the second one-trial game, there was significant improvement in the joint outcomes of the pairs in the unilateral lock condition, with a reduction in the relative advantage for the player possessing the commitment device: Bolt did not display as much advantage over Acme as Acme did over Bolt. The pairs who were in the bilateral lock condition during the first one-trial game and in the no lock condition during the second game improved their joint outcomes considerably,

TABLE 11.3. Mean Payoffs in Cents and Mean Number of
Collisions in the One-Trial Games and the
First Trial of the Twenty-Trial Game
(N = 10 pairs of subjects in each condition in each game.)

	No Lock	Unilateral Lock	Bilateral Lock
First One-Trial Game			
Acme payoff	−9.0	−.5	−3.8
Bolt payoff	5.5	−12.1	−12.5
Acme + Bolt	−3.5	−12.6	−16.3
Acme − Bolt	−14.5	11.6	8.7
No. of collisions	3	4	5
Second One-Trial Game			
Acme payoff	−7.0	2.7	−7.5
Bolt payoff	4.6	8.1	−8.8
Acme + Bolt	−2.4	10.8	−16.3
Acme − Bolt	−11.6	−5.4	−1.3
No. of collisions	3	2	6
First Trial of Twenty-Trial Game			
Acme payoff	6.6	4.8	2.0
Bolt payoff	−1.6	−2.9	9.8
Acme + Bolt	5.0	1.9	11.8
Acme − Bolt	8.2	7.7	−7.8
No. of collisions	2	2	1

while the pairs who shifted to the bilateral lock from the no lock condition worsened their joint outcomes; there was no effect due to the sequence of experiencing the lock.

These results indicated that a commitment device provided the player who possessed it with a relative advantage over his partner. However, there was no evidence that he had any advantage over players in the no lock condition, where neither player had such a device. But there was evidence to indicate that when both players were able to publicly commit themselves irreversibly to "going through first" they did worse then when neither could do so.

A Twenty-Trial Game

The above were the results for the single encounter for a one-trial game. What would happen if the players expected the encounters to be repeated? To investigate this question, we conducted another experiment that completely paralleled the one just described except that the pairs played the game for twenty trials. At the outset they knew that there would be more than one trial, but they did not know how many until they finished.

If we compare the results (see table 11.3) for the first trial of the twenty-trial game with those of the first one-trial game, it is evident that the bargaining pairs did better when they were anticipating a longer game; the difference was most marked for the bilateral lock condition. Again, there was no advantage for Acme, who possessed the lock, in the unilateral lock condition as compared to Acme in the no lock condition; however, he did better than Bolt, with whom he was paired in the one-sided condition.

The overall results were not surprising, since the one-trial game is clearly more competitive in structure than the longer game, which permits an equitable solution of alternation. However, we were surprised by the relatively favorable outcomes in the bilateral lock condition.

If we examine the overall results for the twenty trials (see table 11.4), we find much the same findings as for the first trial: no significant differences in mean joint payoffs among the conditions, b\ the bilateral lock condition tended to do best; the possessor of the commitment device did significantly better than the other player with

TABLE 11.4. Mean Payoffs per Trial in Cents and Mean Number
of Collisions in the Twenty-Trial Games
(N = 10 pairs of subjects in each condition.)

	(1) No Lock	(2) Uni- lateral Lock	(3) Bi- lateral Lock	(4) Social Problem- Solving Bilateral Lock	(5) "Chicken" Bilateral Lock	(6) Pre- Trial Bilateral Lock
Acme payoff	5.06	4.50	6.65	5.47	−14.14	9.11
Bolt payoff	3.61	−.42	7.12	8.24	−14.26	6.50
Acme + Bolt	8.67	4.08	13.77	13.71	−28.40	15.61
Acme − Bolt	1.45	4.92	−.47	−2.77	−.12	3.61
No. of collisions	5.6	5.8	5.0	4.8	10.7	4.9

whom he was paired in the one-sided condition but had no reliable advantage over the players in the other conditions; there was some improvement in outcomes from the initial to the final block of trials for all conditions, but it was most marked in the no lock condition (see figure 11.2). A dominance-submission pattern occurred in only

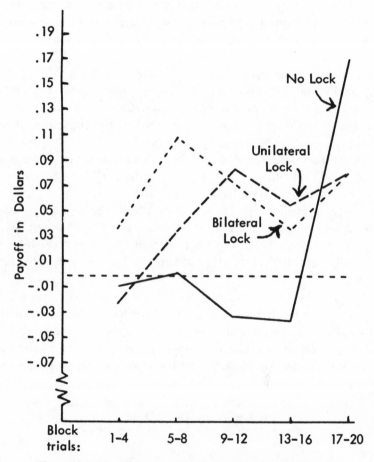

Figure 11.2. Mean joint payoff plotted against four-trial blocks.

four of the ten pairs in the unilateral lock condition (rarely in the other conditions); the other six pairs were characterized by frequent collisions before settling down to an alternation pattern that gave them low but essentially equal outcomes.

The unexpectedly favorable outcomes for the bilateral lock require an explanation. We found clues in a more detailed examination of the way the locks were used in this condition as compared with the way they were used in the unilateral lock condition (see table 11.5). In the unilateral condition, the subject who had the lock employed it predominantly in such a way as to seek to obtain an advantage over his pairmate. In contrast, in the bilateral condition, the subjects mostly used the lock as a coordination device to signal whose turn it was to use the one-way road. In this condition, the subjects commonly alter-

TABLE 11.5. Mean Number of Times Lock Was Used on
Two Adjacent Trials and Mean Number of
Times Lock Was Used per Pair in
the Twenty-Trial Game

Experimental Conditions	(1) No. Times Lock Used on Adjacent Trials [2]	(2) No. Times Lock Used	$\frac{(1)}{(2)}$
Unilateral lock [1]	8.9	11.0	.81
Bilateral lock	5.1	16.2	.31
"Chicken" bilateral lock	7.4	15.3	.48
"Social problem-solving" bilateral lock	3.4	11.4	.30
"Pre-period" bilateral lock	4.9	17.9	.27

[1] Since only one player in each of the 10 pairs had a lock in the unilateral lock condition, the maximum number of lock uses was 200 and the maximum number of times a lock could have been used in two adjacent trials was 190; the corresponding maximum for the bilateral lock conditions was 400 and 380, since both players in each of the 10 pairs per condition could employ their locks.

[2] If a player employed his lock on adjacent trials but only after the other player had passed through the one-lane section of the road, this was not counted here. Some players used their lock this way even though they cooperated in an alternating pattern. The measure in column (1) provides an indication of an attempt to obtain more through the use of the lock than an alternating pattern would offer.

nated, so that one player would go first on one trial and second on the next trial. When it was his turn to go first, a player would signal this by employing his lock. Using the lock as a signaling device in this way apparently lessened the ambiguity and indecision and led to less loss of time (and, hence, better outcomes) as compared with the no lock condition.

Shure, Meeker, and Kelley (unpublished) have described a similar use of a locking mechanism as a coordination device in a study patterned after our earlier Acme-Bolt bargaining experiments. Their results were obtained in an experimental context that I considered to be rather cooperative. Reviewing our own experimental situation in this light, it became evident that we had created an experimental context that was rather more cooperative than that in our previous research. Unlike the subjects in our previous experiments with threat, the subjects in our present experiment saw each other, knew the other was also from a local high school, and waited together in the same room before they took part in the experiment. They could also expect to leave together after the experiment. In our earlier experiment, we had been able to eliminate any prior social contact before the bargaining game. Data from the postexperimental questionnaire support our interpretation of the cooperativeness of the context. These data indicate that the subjects, in describing their motivations during the game, ranked the desire to "cooperate with the other player" and the desire to "maximize own outcome" as equally important and as considerably more important than the desire to "do better than the other person." The experiments described below were designed to provide a further test of our interpretation of our unexpected findings for the bilateral lock condition.

"Chicken" Versus Problem-Solving Instructions

The third version of this experiment involved two additional bilateral lock conditions: a cooperative and a competitive one. Our assumption was that the results for the cooperative condition would parallel our prior results with the bilateral lock (i.e., the use of the lock for coordination purposes) but that this would not be so for the competitive condition. We created the cooperative condition by using social problem-solving instructions and the competitive condition by using "chicken" instructions.

The *"chicken" instructions* were as follows:

> There are two of you who are going to play a game of "Chicken." This experiment has been designed to separate people into two groups: those who give in under pressure, and those who do not. We are interested in observing, when two people are under pressure, who will "chicken out" or back down first. In this game it is possible to win or lose money. It is possible for both of you to profit, or

for both of you to lose, or for one of you to profit and the other to lose; this all depends on how you play the game. I want you to feel that it is important for you to earn as much money as you can or lose as little as possible in this game.

The *social problem-solving instructions* were as follows:

There are two of you who are going to engage in a social problem-solving game. This experiment has been designed to separate people into two groups: those who can arrive at a solution to a problem which will bring maximum benefits to both of the players, and those who cannot work out this solution. We are interested in observing what types of people can arrive at this solution. In this game it is possible to win or lose money. It is possible for both of you to profit, or for both of you to lose, or for one of you to profit and the other to lose; this all depends on how you play the game. I want you to feel that it is important for you to earn as much money as you can or to lose as little as possible in this game.

Table 11.4 presents the major results. From a comparison of columns 3 and 4, it is obvious that the original bilateral lock condition had effects that were rather similar to the cooperative, social problem-solving bilateral lock condition. Our explanation of the findings for the bilateral condition seems reasonably well supported. It is also evident that the competitive motivations induced by the "chicken" instructions lead the subjects in this condition to frequent collisions and substantial losses. As figure 11.3 reveals, under "chicken" instructions, the losses occurred throughout the entire series of trials.

The Timing of the Commitment Decision

In a fourth experiment, we allowed the subjects to have a period of five seconds before each trial in which they could lock their trucks into forward gear without the opponents knowing that this had occurred until the trial had actually started. In addition, as in the other bilateral lock condition, the subjects could employ the lock after a trial had begun. Thus in the pretrial period, one subject would not know what the other had done at the moment when he (the former) had to make his decision about whether or not to use the lock. We speculated that this uncertainty about the other's action during the pretrial period might lead the subjects to be more suspicious of one

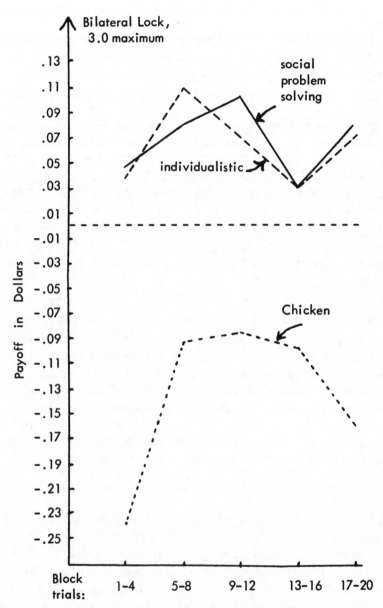

Figure 11.3. Mean joint payoff over four-trial blocks for the three bilateral lock conditions.

another and that their mutual suspicions might increase their readiness to use the lock. If our speculation were correct, then the pairs in this condition would do worse than those in the bilateral lock condition without the pretrial period for decision.

The results do not support our speculation. Columns 6 and 3 of table 11.4 reveal essentially no differences between these two bilateral lock conditions. The locks were employed during an average of 8.1 trials in the bilateral lock condition without the pretrial decision period and during 8.8 trials in the other condition (of which 5.5 were initiated in the pretrial period and 3.3 during the trials). Overall, there was as much cooperativeness in the latter experimental condition as in the former one.

Discussion

Sermat (1962, 1967) has studied the effects of commitment using a mixed-motive matrix game, which, like our "chicken" game, is characterized by the quality that joint defection from mutual cooperation is more costly to both participants than dominating or being dominated by the other. In his study, the subjects were playing against a preprogrammed stooge who chose a dominating strategy on each of the first fifty trials in all conditions. In one condition, the subjects were led to believe that they were playing with another player who was making his choice trial by trial. In a second condition, they were led to believe that the other player was present but had committed himself to a strategy for the entire series of trials—so that all his choices were already fixed. The third condition was similar to the second except that the subjects were told that the other player was no longer present. In the fourth condition, they were informed that they would be playing against a fixed program and that there was no other subject involved. Sermat's results indicated that the subjects were least likely to make a yielding (cooperative) response in the first condition and most likely to make it in the fourth condition; the subjects in the other two conditions showed intermediate reactions, yielding more than the subjects in the first condition but less than those in the fourth.

These results suggest, on the one hand, that a subject is more likely to yield to another's dominating strategy the less the possibility of influencing it by resistance. On the other hand, the less-frequent yielding to the fixed program when the subject perceives the fixed other to be human rather than merely mechanical suggests that subjects are willing to experience lower outcomes, even when doing so has no other utility than to harm and express resistance to another who seeks more than a fair share.

A comparison of our results with Sermat's has many inherent difficulties because of the differences in experimental tasks and conditions. Nevertheless, it is apparent that, on the average, our subjects, playing against other real subjects and each being unprogrammed, played more cooperatively than did his subjects when his subjects thought that they were playing against other humans who were not already committed to a given program of behavior. Sermat's subjects were, of course, playing against a very competitive preprogrammed stooge, while our subjects were playing with other people who, like themselves, were inclined to be cooperative under the general circumstances of our experiment.

Except when they were prompted to be competitive by the "chicken" instructions, the competitive structure of the single-trial game or the one-sided possession of the lock, our subjects, generally, did not seek an advantage over the other player. As a consequence, they usually did not employ their locks as a commitment tactic to influence the other to yield disproportionately. The lock was more customarily used as a coordination device (i.e., it was used by the subject when it was his turn to go first). Evidence for these assertions is presented in table 11.5. It can be seen that except in the "chicken" and unilateral lock conditions, the subjects rarely employed their locks on two or more successive trials (i.e., they did not seek to prevent the other from alternating with them in priority on the one-lane path). The lock was used most frequently for this purpose in the unilateral lock condition.

It is interesting to examine in detail the results for the twenty-trial, unilateral lock condition (see table 11.6). Several different types of interactions occurred. In three of the ten pairs in this condition, the possessor of the lock never employed it; in two of these pairs, the lock possessor allowed the other player to have an advantage. Collisions occurred infrequently, and all the subjects in these pairs had moderately good outcomes. In a fourth pair, the lock possessor attempted to use his lock exploitatively in the first several trials but met resistance from the other player. The pair then settled on an uneasy alternation pattern, which was periodically disrupted by collisions; they had low positive outcomes. In a fifth pair, the lock possessor was somewhat more persistent in his initial attempts to dominate, but he met with prolonged resistance. It was not until the fourteenth trial that this pair worked out a persisting pattern of alternation; the result was that both players suffered a moderately high loss.

In the remaining five pairs, the lock possessor persistently used his lock on a minimum of 85 percent of the trials. The resulting outcomes were very much a function of the amount of resistance displayed by the other player. In one case, the lock user met with no resistance whatsoever—with the result that this subject had the highest individual outcome of any of the subjects participating in the experi-

TABLE 11.6. Statistics for Ten Pairs in the
Unilateral Lock Condition

Pair	No. Trials of Collisions	No. Trials in Which Outcome Was Higher for		No. Trials Lock Used	No. Trials Lock Used on Adjacent Trials	Total Payoff	
		Acme	Bolt			Acme	Bolt
1	0 [1]	6	13	0	0	1.20	1.68
2	2	9	9	1	0	1.77	1.78
3	2	8	10	3	0	1.60	2.08
4	7	8	5	3	2	.77	.15
5	10	5	5	9	8	−1.79	−1.71
6	0	20	0	20	19	4.55	.63
7	4	15	1	19	11	2.34	−.06
8	9	10	1	18	15	.39	−1.56
9	11	9	0	20	19	−.45	−2.23
10	13	5	2	17	15	−1.19	−2.13

[1] In one trial, Acme and Bolt both took the alternate route.

ment. (His outcome pulls up the average outcome of Acme in the unilateral lock condition in such a way as to give a distorted view of Acme's typical outcome in this condition.)

As the resistance of Bolt increased, with a resulting increase in the number of collisions, both Acme's and Bolt's outcomes decreased. However, Acme consistently did better than Bolt when he used his lock persistently, even when both players ended up with negative outcomes. None of the players without a lock was ready to have a collision on every trial in order to force the player with the lock to yield. It is apparent that possession of the lock increased the risk-taking resolve of Acme, and this, in turn, gave him a relative advantage over

Bolt. Yet it also must be evident that the relative advantages over Bolt did not commonly result in a good outcome for Acme. If we look at the six players who used their locks aggressively in this condition, three had positive and three had negative outcomes (see rows 5–10 in table 11.6). The mean outcome for these six players was .64; while this was considerably better than the -1.18 mean outcome of their paired Bolts, it was still a low outcome. It was not half as good as the average outcome of the four unaggressive Acmes in this condition (see Rows 1–4); their mean outcome was 1.34. Not only did the nonaggressive Acmes do better for themselves, but their paired Bolts did much better than the Bolts with aggressive partners. They had a mean outcome of 1.68.

The tendency for aggressive use of the lock by one player to induce resistance in the other player, with lowered outcomes for the pair, was general across conditions. Lumping all the bilateral lock conditions, one finds a significant association in numbers of aggressive usages of the lock between paired players (see table 11.7). Also, if one compares the mean outcomes for pairs with three or more aggressive lock usages with those having two or less, the paired outcomes are significantly higher for the latter (see table 11.8).

TABLE 11.7. Association in the Number of
Aggressive Lock Uses between Acme and
Bolt in Same Pair for All Bilateral
Lock Conditions Combined

		Bolt	
		2 or less	3 or more
Acme	2 or less	22	4
	3 or more	4	10

NOTE: $X^2 = 12.5637$; $p < .001$

TABLE 11.8. Mean Joint Outcomes for Pairs
with Three or More Aggressive Lock Usages
Compared with Those with Two or Less

2 or less (N = 22)	3 or more (N = 18)
1.82	-1.37

NOTE: $t = 3.04$; d.f. $= 38$; $p < .01$

Conclusion

Let us summarize the conclusions gained from our initial work on the effect of commitment on bargaining. First, there are many interesting questions that warrant further research in this area; our study is a first step rather than a concluding or conclusive one. It would, for example, be useful to study the effects of introducing uncertainty about the irrevocability of the commitment. This could be done in any number of ways—e.g., allow the subjects to buy a key to their lock but increase the cost of the key at intervals after the initiation of the trial. Second, adolescent boys may be more sensible than they are given credit for and possibly less collision-prone than American statesmen and some of their social-science advisors. They are sufficiently prudent to resist the temptation to lock themselves into positions from which they cannot reverse if they know they are going to have repeated encounters with someone who has a similar capacity. However, when they are prompted to be competitive by the game of "chicken" by a single encounter, or by their own dispositions, some of their prudence—and some of their money—is lost. Third, having a commitment device gives the player a relative advantage over the person with whom he is bargaining, but it also can lead to a preliminary hassle over the attempt to dominate, with neither player ending up in a superior position. In any case, there is no evidence to suggest that the bargainer with a commitment device does better than the bargainer without such a device when each is facing a player who does not have one. Perhaps all this can be summed up by saying that locking oneself into an irreversible position in order to gain an advantage is rarely more beneficial than cooperating with the other for mutual gain, and it has the prospect of leading to be a mutually destructive contest of willpower.

EXPERIMENT III: STRUCTURAL AND ATTITUDINAL FACTORS IN INTERPERSONAL BARGAINING [3]

Social psychologists typically postulate two classes of determinants to explain the behavior of interacting persons. One class is structural. It consists of certain aspects of the social environment in which the in-

---

3. This study is more fully reported in Krauss (1966).

teraction is set. Included are such factors as communication networks, status systems, systems of goal interdependence, and ecological distributions. In the present experiment, which was the dissertation study of Robert M. Krauss, we are concerned with the system of goal interdependence. The other class is attitudinal. This consists of the perceptual, evaluative, and affective orientations of the interacting individuals toward one another.

It seems usually to be the case that the structural and attitudinal orientations of interacting individuals are mutually consistent. For example, when two individuals are promotively interdependent (that is to say, when goal attainment by one increases the probability of goal attainment by the other), it is typically the case that they like, trust, and respect each other (e.g., Deutsch 1949b; Gottheil 1955; Lott and Lott 1960; Mizuhara and Tamai 1952). Furthermore, attitudinal orientations established before interaction will affect the character of the subsequent interaction: people who are positively oriented will behave more cooperatively than people who are negatively oriented (see Borah 1963; Ex 1959; Rice and White 1964).

These two sets of findings, taken together, suggest the hypothesis that the relationship between attitudinal and structural orientations is not adventitious but rather tends toward a preferred equilibrium or balanced state. A model for such a process is Heider's (1958) theory of cognitive balance. We will assume that a cooperative structure (one in which the participants are interdependent in a mutually facilitative way) is in balance with positive interpersonal attitudes and that a competitive structure (one in which the participants are interdependent in a mutually obstructive way) is in balance with negative interpersonal attitudes. Such an assumption is intuitively plausible and is consistent with the evidence cited above.

One difficulty with applying balance-type theories to specific situations is that it is often difficult to specify in advance which of the available modes of balance restoration will be adopted by the subject. Theoretically, balance is restored by changing the weakest element. However, such an approach poses some problems, since it is difficult to measure in any comparable form the strength of such qualitatively different elements as structures and attitudes. In such cases, the investigator frequently resorts to an experimental manipulation that differentially anchors (i.e., makes differentially resistant to change) one or another of the elements under investigation.

In the present experiment, we were able to create positive or negative attitudes on the part of our subjects toward each other by means of an experimental induction. We assumed that an experimentally induced attitude could be strongly anchored and made resistant to change by linking it to the person's self-esteem system and that without such a linkage the attitude would be weakly anchored.

The theory employed here predicts that, when a participant in a bargaining situation is faced with an imbalance between the structure of his relationship with another individual and his attitude toward that individual, the mode of balance restoration will be determined by the extent to which his attitude is resistant to change. When the attitude is strongly anchored, he will resolve the imbalance by behaving in a manner consistent with the attitude; when it is weakly anchored, he will resolve it by changing his attitude and behaving in a manner consistent with the structure of his relationship.

In previous experiments, subjects who were cooperatively oriented bargained more effectively (i.e., were better able to come to mutually profitable agreements) and used an available means of threat less frequently than did competitively oriented subjects. In the present experiment, it is hypothesized that bargaining effectiveness will be high (1) where the bargaining structure is cooperative and there are no strongly anchored negative attitudes; or (2) where there are strongly anchored positive attitudes. In effect, we are hypothesizing that bargaining effectiveness will be determined by the interaction of anchoring with the structural and attitudinal factors. Similarly, the frequency with which an available means of threat is used will covary with bargaining effectiveness: the more frequently threat is employed, the less effective bargaining will be.

Method

Overview of experiment. Eighty pairs of female subjects were randomly assigned to the cells of a $2 \times 2 \times 2$ factorial experiment that consisted of two levels of bargaining structure—cooperative (COOP) and competitive (COMP); two levels of attitudes—positive (POS) and negative (NEG); two levels of attitudinal anchoring—strong (SA) and weak (WA). Subjects filled out an opinion questionnaire, then listened to taped task instructions. A fictitious questionnaire, ostensibly belonging to each subject's partner in the experiment, was then distributed. In it, the partner's responses were either similar or dissimilar to

his own. On the basis of this information, subjects were asked to rate
each other on an Interpersonal Judgment Scale (Byrne 1961). Next,
they received instructions designed to produce either strong or weak
anchoring of their attitude toward the other player plus the instructions that produced the bargaining structure. The subjects then played
the Acme-Bolt bargaining game for ten trials. The bargaining game
was employed in the same manner as in our initial studies. Finally,
each rated his partner again on the Interpersonal Judgment Scale.

Subjects

One hundred and sixty experimentally naive female clerical employees of the Bell Telephone Laboratories served as subjects. Their ages
ranged from eighteen to thirty-five years, with a mean age of about
twenty-four. All were high school graduates.

Ten pairs were run in each of the eight cells of a $2 \times 2 \times 2$ factorial
matrix. They were assigned randomly to their treatments, with the restriction that the members of a pair had to come from different offices. This was necessary to keep each subject from discovering her
partner's identity. To further prevent identification, their arrival times
were staggered by about five minutes.

Manipulation of Independent Variables

Structure. Because the structure of the task permits only one player to
pass through the one-way section at a time, the experimental task im-
poses a discrepancy between the positive payoffs obtainable by the
subjects on any given trial. The competitiveness of this structure was
modified by manipulating the manner in which goal attainment for
one subject was affected by the other's goal attainment through a system of bonuses. In the Coop conditions, each subject received a bonus
based on 20 percent of the other player's profit. That is, 20 percent of
the other player's profit was added to, or 20 percent of the other's
losses were subtracted from, the subject's own profit. In the Comp
condition, the bonus was negative in sign. That is, each player had 20
percent of the other player's losses added to his own profits.

Attitudes. Positive or negative attitudes were induced by a modification of a technique developed by Byrne (1961). In the present experiment, each subject received a questionnaire containing twenty
statements of opinion and calling for a binary (agree-disagree) response. Shortly thereafter, each subject received a questionnaire that

ostensibly had been filled out by her partner but that actually had been filled out by the experimenter. In the Pos conditions, the responses to seventeen of the twenty statements in the fictitious questionnaire agreed with the subject's own responses. In the NEG conditions, seventeen of the twenty responses disagreed with the subject's own. The subject was asked to use the other person's questionnaire to get a picture of that player and to formulate an idea of what "she's really like." Then she was asked to rate the other player by filling out a modified version of the Interpersonal Judgment Scale. One of Byrne's six items (on personal morality) was omitted. Subjects rated their partner's intelligence, cooperativeness, considerateness, likability, and desirability as a work partner.

Attitudinal anchoring. Differential anchoring was achieved by a verbal induction. In the SA condition, subjects were told that they had received sufficient information to form a very accurate picture of the other player and that "the normal, well-adjusted individual, the sort of person who understands himself and others and who gets along with people reasonably well" was quite accurate at evaluating others on the basis of this sort of information. The WA instructions simply stated that the information provided was insufficient to form the basis for an accurate judgment. The instructions for the SA and WA conditions were given in an informal and offhanded manner, suggesting that they were not a part of the experiment proper.

Results and Discussion

A total of eighty-five pairs of subjects were run. Five pairs were eliminated from the analysis,[4] leaving eighty pairs, ten in each experimental condition.

Effectiveness of the attitudinal induction. The effectiveness of the attitudinal manipulation in creating positive or negative attitudes may be assessed by examining the initial rating on the Interpersonal Judgment Scale. Since the exchange of questionnaires ostensibly took place before the structural or attitudinal anchorage conditions were created, attitudes should have been uncontaminated by the other treatment effects. Subjects judged their partners to be more intelligent, coopera-

4. Two pairs were eliminated because of equipment breakdowns, one because of an error by the experimenter in giving the instructions, one because one of the subjects claimed she was unable to comprehend the instructions, and one because the pair became stalemated for 5 minutes on the first trial.

tive, considerate, likable, and desirable as work partners under the positive attitude treatment than under the negative attitude treatment.

Bargaining effectiveness. The major predictions were concerned with relations between the independent variables and bargaining effectiveness. Bargaining effectiveness is defined as the extent to which the parties jointly maximized the value of their outcomes. It will be remembered that payoffs were simple transformations of time (Payoff = sixty minus time in seconds). However, the actual payoffs were contaminated by the COOP—COMP manipulation. Therefore, time itself was used as an index of bargaining effectiveness.[5]

TABLE 11.9. Cell Means for Bargaining Effectiveness,
Gate Use, and Attitude Change

		Bargaining Effectiveness (T_j') [1]		Gate Use [2]		Attitude Change [3]	
	Structure	*Pos. Att.*	*Neg. Att.*	*Pos. Att.*	*Neg. Att.*	*Pos. Att.*	*Neg. Att.*
Strong att. anchoring	COOP	2.28	3.31	1.9	8.5	+0.60	+1.10
	COMP	2.52	3.01	3.7	5.5	+0.75	−1.20
Weak att. anchoring	COOP	2.36	2.67	3.4	4.4	−0.30	+1.85
	COMP	2.93	3.08	6.6	7.7	−2.10	−0.20

[1] The lower the T_j' score the greater the bargaining effectiveness.
[2] $N = 10$ observations (pairs) per cell.
[3] Second rating minus first rating. $N = 20$ observations per cell.

We hypothesized that bargaining effectiveness would be determined by the interaction of the anchoring variable with attitude and structure. Inspection of table 11.9 reveals this to be the case. Of particular interest is the configuration of the interaction effects. The interaction of anchoring and attitude is graphed in figure 11.4 and anchoring and structure in figure 11.5. As figure 11.4 indicates, when anchoring is strong, positive attitudes result in more effective bargaining (i.e., in bargaining that takes less time), and negative attitudes result in pro-

5. Since the distribution of time scores was positively skewed, a log transformation was performed. T' (the Index of Bargaining Effectiveness) is defined as follows:

$$T' = \log_{10}(t - C)$$

where t is the time (in seconds) to completion of a given trip and C is the minimum possible time minus one. The joint effectiveness score (T_j') of a pair of subjects (a and b) is defined as the sum of their transformed time scores: $T_j' = T_a' + T_b'$.

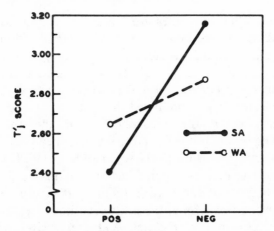

Figure 11.4. Interaction of attitude and anchoring on Index of Bargaining Effectiveness (T_j'). (A low score indicates high effectiveness.)

longed conflict with poor outcomes to the subjects. This difference is statistically significant. When attitudinal anchoring is weak, the difference between the positive and negative attitude treatments is not significantly different from zero. Conversely, as figure 11.5 indicates, where anchoring is weak, a cooperative bargaining structure produces significantly more effective bargaining than a competitive structure. Under SA, no difference is found.

Thus where attitudes are relatively labile (i.e., WA), the attitudinal effect is attenuated, and the reward structure of the task has a deter-

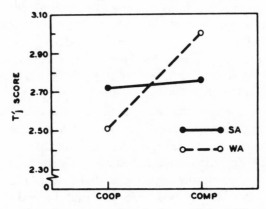

Figure 11.5. Interaction of structure and anchoring on Index of Bargaining Effectiveness (T_j'). (A low score indicates high effectiveness.)

mining effect. Where attitudes are relatively resistant to change (i.e., SA), the initial attitude determines the direction of interaction, and the effect of the reward structure is minimal.

Use of gates. Each pair of subjects was assigned a gate score, based on the number of trials (out of ten) in which one or both players had closed their gates. It was predicted that gate use would be influenced by the bonus structure and the attitudes toward the other, with the attitudes having more powerful effects when they were strongly anchored and less powerful effects when they were weakly anchored. Clearly, this was the case; significant interactions of attitudinal anchoring with attitude and with bargaining structure were observed. When anchoring was strong, the positive attitude treatment produced relatively infrequent use of gates, and the negative attitude treatment produced relatively frequent use. This difference was statistically significant. When anchoring was weak, the difference between the positive and negative attitude treatments was not significantly different from zero. Similarly, when anchoring was weak, the frequency of gate use was significantly higher in the competitive condition than in the cooperative. When anchoring was strong, the difference was not significant. The similarity between the findings for gate use and the measure of bargaining effectiveness was not surprising since the product-moment correlation between these two variables is fairly high ($r = +.73$).

Attitude change. Subjects' ratings of their partners on the pre- and postgame administration of the Interpersonal Judgment Scale were summed across the five items and the difference of the sums was calculated [Diff = (Post − Pre)]. As the cell means indicate, subjects who interacted in a COOP structure tended to view their partners somewhat more favorably subsequent to their interaction than did subjects in the COMP conditions. In addition, attitude and anchoring interacted significantly. The interaction is graphed in figure 11.6. From the figure, it is clear that it is the combination of attitude and anchoring that determines the direction of attitude change. With WA, positive attitudes become less positive, and negative attitudes become less negative; when the attitudinal anchor is strong, the difference in change for positive versus negative attitudes is nonsignificant.

General discussion. It was assumed that individuals attempt to achieve a state of cognitive balance between the structure of their relationships with others and their affective or attitudinal orientations.

In effect, it was postulated that interpersonal conflict creates a potential situation of intrapersonal conflict. When structures and attitudes are in balance, no intrapersonal conflict exists, and the individual is free to behave in an unambivalent manner toward his counterpart. Indeed, his behavior is in a sense "overdetermined"; the influence of structures and attitude is mutually reinforcing. However, when these factors are imbalanced, a state of intrapersonal conflict exists—which the individual can resolve in one of two ways: by orienting his behav-

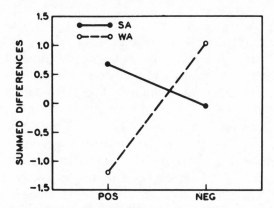

Figure 11.6. Interaction of attitudes and anchoring for summed differences between first and second administration of five-item Interpersonal Judgment scale.

ior to make it consonant with his attitude, or by changing his attitude so that it is consonant with his behavior. In the present experiment, the mode of balance restoration was determined by the degree of anchorage of the interpersonal attitude. When anchorage was strong, the effect of attitude was marked and the effect of structure was minimal; when it was weak, this effect was reversed. Bargaining, then, for our subjects consisted, at least partly, of an attempt to maintain cognitive balance.

12. Strategies of Inducing Cooperation: Experimental Studies

The experiments reported here studied several behavioral strategies to see which is most effective in eliciting cooperation from someone whose behavior is not initially and persistently cooperative. The effectiveness of the strategies was investigated in a two-person laboratory game that permits players to act altruistically, cooperatively, individualistically, defensively, or aggressively toward one another. One of the players in each game was always an accomplice of the experimenter; he followed a predetermined strategy in response to the true subject's behavior in the game. The true subject, of course, did not know that he was playing with an experimenter's accomplice.

The different strategies are described in detail in the next section. They are briefly characterized here to permit a discussion of their rationale. One strategy, termed *turn the other cheek,* had the accomplice respond to attacks or threats by exhibiting altruistic behavior (doing something that rewarded the other) and by showing cooperative behavior otherwise. The *nonpunitive* strategy had the accomplice react self-protectively rather than with counterthreats or counterattacks when the subject threatened or attacked; otherwise, he reciprocated the subject's behaviors. The *deterrent* strategy had the accomplice respond threateningly to any noncooperative acts of the subject and also had him counterattack when attacked; he responded cooperatively to any cooperative behavior from the subject. The remaining strategies are different types of *reformed sinner* strategies. Here, the accomplice played in a very threatening and aggressive manner during the first fifteen trials of the game but then dramatically changed his behavior by disarming on the sixteenth trial. In one form of the reformed sinner strategy, the accomplice followed a turn-the-other-cheek strategy after the sixteenth trial; in another, he followed a nonpunitive strategy; in the third he used a deterrent strategy.

314

The three basic strategies (turn the other cheek, nonpunitive, deterrent) were selected in an attempt to represent, even if only crudely, three widely held positions regarding how to elicit cooperation. The turn-the-other-cheek strategy seeks to elicit cooperation by appealing to the social conscience and goodwill of the subject; such an approach has characterized many religious groups and the advocates of nonviolence. The deterrent strategy attempts to elicit cooperation by use of the carrot and the stick—i.e., by rewarding cooperation and punishing noncooperation; it appeals to the economic motives of the subject by increasing the costs of noncooperative behavior. In so doing, it does not distinguish between the psychological effects of reward and those of punishment. The implication is that rewards and punishments exist on a psychologically unidimensional continuum. Such an approach often characterizes viewpoints that have been described as rationalistic, utilitarian, authoritarian, tough-minded, disciplinarian, and militaristic; these viewpoints are, of course, not necessarily similar in other respects. The nonpunitive strategy places its emphasis on rewarding cooperation and on neutralizing or nonrewarding aggressive behavior; it appeals to the self-interests of the subject through positive rather than negative incentives and thus attempts to avoid the misunderstanding and hostility that may result from the subject's experience of punishment. This type of strategy is often popular among progressive educators, psychotherapists, liberals, the "tender-minded," and the like.

We assumed that if the subjects were individualistically oriented, so that they were out to do as well as they could for themselves, they would tend to exploit the accomplice if he employed the turn-the-other-cheek strategy. Thus it could be anticipated that the subjects' game outcomes in this condition would be relatively high while those of the accomplices would be relatively low, with the discrepancy between their outcomes being quite large. In addition, the subjects, being individualistically oriented, could be expected to have difficulty in understanding why anyone would use such a strategy, and they might think that its use was stupid or bizarre. In contrast, we expected the nonpunitive strategy to elicit cooperation from the subjects and, hence, to result in relatively high outcomes for both the accomplices and the subjects. The deterrent strategy, in comparison with the nonpunitive one, was expected to be relatively ineffective in eliciting cooperation, and it was anticipated that the game outcomes for both the subjects and accomplices would be relatively low. It was expected that the deterrent strategy would produce the most competitive behaviors (defensive and aggressive) of any of the strategies.

The reformed sinner strategies were expected to elicit aggressive and defensive behavior from the subjects during the first fifteen trials when the accomplice was being threatening and aggressive (i.e., being a "sinner"). However, we had no clear expectations as to how the subjects would respond to the accomplice who reformed and then adopted a turn-the-other-cheek strategy. On the one hand, we thought it possible that the subjects would seek revenge and might exploit the accomplice even more than in the condition where the turn-the-other-cheek strategy was not preceded by aggressive behavior. On the other hand, it seemed possible that the reform would be accepted as genuine and its form as appropriate and, further, that the accomplice's earlier display of aggressiveness would serve to deter the subjects' temptation to exploit. The former reaction would produce even more exaggerated differences than we were predicting for the simple turn-the-other-cheek strategy. The latter reaction would make the results for the reformed sinner version of this strategy resemble the results predicted for the nonpunitive strategy—i.e., both subjects and accomplices would do relatively well. We also expected that, after the reform had been clearly established, the reformed sinner-nonpunitive strategy would be effective in eliciting cooperation and would result in relatively high outcomes for both players.

Several different experiments were conducted. The first compared the effectiveness of five different strategies in a relatively noncompetitive situation.[1] The strategies compared were: turn the other cheek, nonpunitive, deterrent, reformed sinner-turn the other cheek, and reformed sinner-nonpunitive. A second experiment studied the effectiveness of these strategies in a more competitive situation and also investigated the reformed sinner-deterrent strategy. A third experiment examined two different versions of the deterrent strategy.[2] The last experiment [3] studied the three basic strategies in a situation where the temptation to take advantage of the other was high. In one condition

1. The first experiment was done in collaboration with Yakov Epstein, Donnah Canavan, and Peter Gumpert. It is more fully reported in Deutsch et al. (1967).
2. The second and third experiments were done with the collaboration of Barbara Bunker and King Collins.
3. The fourth experiment was done with the collaboration of Mary Chase.

in this situation, the different strategies were employed vis-à-vis another who had higher power; in the second condition, both participants had equal power. The methodology and results of the first experiment are reported in detail to provide a baseline for the description of the other studies.

EXPERIMENT I: STRATEGIES OF INDUCING COOPERATION

Experimental Procedure

Subjects. Ss were drawn from a pool used in several experiments running concurrently in our laboratory. They were recruited from summer-session graduate courses at Teachers College, through advertisements placed in the Columbia University newspaper and through notices placed at Actors Equity. The recruitment appeal stressed the opportunity to earn up to $4.00 per hour as well as the opportunity to participate in a scientific experiment. The Ss used in this experiment consisted of a fairly diverse group of thirty-eight men and sixty-seven women who were randomly selected from the subject pool and randomly assigned to the various experimental conditions.

Experimental Situation and Instructions

During the course of the experiment, the Ss were seated in separate cubicles. They did not see or speak to one another before or during the experiment. The experimental situation utilized a two-person game. This game differed from the ones employed in the experiments previously described in this book. It was invented to permit a less ambiguous interpretation of the meaning of different behaviors by the subjects and also to allow a clearer distinction between the nonpunitive and deterrent strategies than the other games permit. Recorded instructions for the game were played to the Ss over a tape recorder. A transcript of the instructions follows:

> There are two of you who are going to play a game in which you can either win money or lose money. I want you to earn as much money as you can regardless of how much the other earns. This money is real and you will keep whatever you earn. I am going to give you each thirty cents to begin with—that is, at this time you each have thirty cents. You can lose this thirty cents or earn more

money, depending on how you play the game. This game consists of a series of trials; you each have a pegboard in front of you. This board is divided into two areas: a resource area and an allocation area. Your task on each of these trials will be to select one peg from the resource area and place it in the allocation area. At the end of each trial, you will be told what the other has chosen for that trial and how much money you have each won or lost on that trial.

Now let me tell you something about these pegs; there are five different kinds of pegs: black, white, blue, red, and green. In addition, there are two specially shaped markers—orange and beige—and they each have pins on the top of them.

Whenever you choose a black peg, it will earn money for you, regardless of what the other player chooses. Whenever you choose a white peg, it will earn money for the other player but not for you. Blue pegs are worth a large amount of money if you both choose them on the same trial, but they are only worth a small amount of money if they are not matched on the same trial. Red pegs can only be used to attack the other and to take away his money. Green pegs can only be used to defend your money from his attacks. Red pegs and green pegs are worth nothing unless they are used in an attack. Orange markers indicate that you wish to attack the other player. Beige markers indicate that you have disarmed—that is, you have destroyed all the red attack pegs that you have accumulated up to that trial.[4]

Now let me tell you specifically how much each peg is worth. On each trial that you choose a black peg, we will give you six cents. That is, you will earn six cents for each black peg that you choose, regardless of what the other player chooses. On each trial that you choose a white peg, we will give the other player seven cents. That

---

4. In designing the game we tried to have the choice of a given peg be a clear indicator of a given type of interpersonal behavior. Thus, the selection of a white peg was considered to be an altruistic or ingratiating behavior; the blue peg was equated with cooperative behavior; the choice of a red peg was thought to be a threatening, competitive behavior; the selection of a green peg was considered to be a defensive move; the use of the orange peg manifested aggressive behavior; and the beige peg expressed a desire to reform and engage in nonthreatening and nonaggressive activity. For the Ss, we did not label the pegs or describe the meanings we attributed to them. However, as our results indicate, the Ss gave the pegs the interpersonal meanings we had intended for them.

is, the other player will be given seven cents for each white peg that you choose. Whenever you and the other player both choose blue pegs on the same trial, we will give each of you nine cents. So, if you and the other match in choosing blue pegs on the same trial, we will give each of you nine cents. . . . However, if you choose a blue peg and he chooses a different colored peg, then your blue peg will only be worth one cent. Similarly, if he chooses a blue peg but you do not, his blue peg will only be worth one cent. That is, blue pegs when matched on the same trial are worth nine cents to each player. But if they are not matched on that trial, they are worth only one cent to the player choosing the blue peg. Red pegs and green pegs are different from the other pegs in that they are worth nothing unless they are used in an attack. If you choose to attack, this means that you will be pitting your red attack pegs against the other's green defense pegs. In an attack, a red peg and a green peg cancel each other. If the attacker has more red pegs than the number of green pegs that the defender has, then each of these extra pegs will take six cents from the defender. That is, if you attack and you have a greater number of red pegs than he has green pegs, then you will win six cents from him for each red that you have over and above the number of greens he has. However, if the defender has more green pegs than the number of reds that the attacker has, then each of the defender's extra green pegs will take six cents away from the attacker. That is, if the defender has more green pegs than the attacker has reds, then the defender will win six cents from the attacker for each green that he has over the number of reds that the attacker has. Remember, you attack only with your reds and defend only with your greens. Thus it is impossible to attack unless you have some red pegs. Pegs that are used in an attack cannot be used again. This means that after each attack, the attacker starts off with no red pegs and the defender starts off with no green pegs. Of course, the green pegs of the attacker and the red pegs of the defender remain; they were not used in the attack. If you want to attack, you should take an orange attack indicator for that trial of play. Play will be stopped until you have both heard the results of that attack. Your orange attack indicator constitutes your choice for that trial.

Now let me describe how the game is actually played. At the beginning of each trial, we will announce the trial number. At that time, you will choose one peg of any color from the resource area and place it in the allocation area. Put the peg in the row number corresponding to the trial number. That is, on trial one, place the peg in row 1. On trial two, row 2, and so on. Make sure to place the peg in the hole which is the same color as the peg. Blue pegs go in blue holes, black pegs in black holes, and so on. After you have made your choices, we will announce the results of that trial to both of you. On the table, there is a paper which can be used to keep a record of the game. This paper is used to record the other's choice, also what you expect the other to choose, and also the amount of money that you have each won or lost on that trial. When we announce the trial number, write down the color peg that you intend to choose for that trial in the column entitled *My Choice*. Next, write down the color peg that you expect the other player to choose in the column entitled *I Expect Other to Choose*. Then make your choice on the board. When you have both made your choices, we will announce the result of that trial to each of you. You will then record your gains or losses in the column entitled *My Gains or Losses,* and you will record the other's gains or losses in the column entitled *Other's Gains or Losses.* There is one other feature of the game I want to tell you about. You may disarm yourself of your red attack pegs, that is, on any trial you may destroy all the red attack pegs that you have accumulated up through that point. If you wish to disarm, you should select a beige disarmament marker as your choice for that trial. Thus after disarming, you begin the next trial with no red attack pegs. We have given you a good deal of information. You have a summary sheet which describes the various pegs and what they are worth. Now take a moment to look over this sheet. All right, are there any questions?

Ss were then run through a series of practice trials. The following instructions were given to them:

1. "Player one, please select a black peg, and player two, please select a black peg. Player one, what would you have won or lost had that been a real trial?" (Experimenter waited for an answer. If it was incorrect, he gave the correct answer and explained it.) "Player two, what would you have won or lost had that been a real trial?" (Experimenter waited a period for the answer.)

2. "Player one, please select a black peg. Player two, please select

a red peg." (Experimenter repeated questioning procedure as in step 1 above.)

3. "Player one, please select a blue peg. Player two, please select a white peg." (Again, questioning procedure was repeated as in step 1 above. In this case, however, player two, the accomplice, appeared to have responded in error and the experimenter said): "Player two, that's not quite correct. If you choose white, the other player receives seven cents and you receive nothing. But, in addition, he also receives one cent for the blue peg he selected that was not matched. So that on this trial you received zero cents and he received a total of eight cents —seven cents for the white you selected and one cent for the unmatched blue."

4–10. The pegs that the subjects were asked to select were varied as follows on practice trials 4 through 10.

Steps	Player One	Player Two
4	white	black
5	blue	blue
6	red	red
7	red	green
8	green	red
9	orange	red
10	green	beige

On step 9 the attack procedure was reviewed as follows: "Stop! Player one has attacked player two. One moment, please. Up to this point, player one has made two reds, while player two has made only one green. Thus in this attack, player one, who has one more red than the number of greens that player two has, has won six cents from player two. Player two has lost six cents in this attack."

On step 10 the disarmament procedure is reviewed. On this step, player two had selected beige and therefore had disarmed. Consequently, he was told that he now had no red pegs in the allocation area. Players were then asked to replace all the pegs into the resource area and were told the game was now about to begin.

The Ss played the game for sixty trials. Typically, the experiment lasted a total of one and a half to two hours.

Experimental Design

Five experimental conditions and one control condition were run. In the control condition, two true Ss played the game with one another.

In the five experimental conditions, Ss were paired with an accomplice of the experimenter who played in accordance with one of the predetermined strategies.

1. *Turn the other cheek.* The accomplice chose blue on the first trial, white on the second trial, and blue on the third trial—no matter what the actual S chose. Thereafter, he chose blue, except that he chose white if the S had chosen red or orange on the preceding trial.

2. *Nonpunitive.* The accomplice chose blue on the first three trials. Thereafter, he matched what the S chose on the preceding trial, with the following exceptions: if the S chose red or orange, the accomplice chose green; if the S chose to disarm (beige), then the accomplice chose blue; if the S chose green, the accomplice chose blue.

3. *Deterrent.* The accomplice chose blue on the first trial and whenever the S chose blue, white, or beige. To a choice of black, green, or red by the S, he responded with red; if S chose orange (attack), he counterattacked with an orange on the next trial.

4. *Reformed sinner–turn the other cheek.* The accomplice attacked by choosing orange on the third, ninth, and twelfth trials; otherwise, he chose red during the first fifteen trials. On the sixteenth trial, he disarmed completely by choosing beige, and, thereafter, he chose blue, white, and blue and followed the turn-the-other-cheek strategy (as described in point 1. above).

5. *Reformed sinner–nonpunitive.* For the first sixteen trials, the accomplice behaved in exactly the same manner as indicated in point 4 above. On the seventeenth, eighteenth, and nineteenth trials, he chose blue and, thereafter, followed the nonpunitive strategy described in point 2.

Although fifteen Ss were run in each of the experimental conditions (with twenty pairs in the control condition), an examination of our data soon revealed that not all the Ss in each condition were exposed to the strategy we had assigned for them. For example, in the first three conditions, Ss who made blue choices both initially and throughout received exactly the same responses from the accomplices, and, hence, they were not exposed to different treatments. For this reason, we decided to eliminate from our analysis of results those Ss who did not get exposed, differentially, to the strategy to which they were assigned.[5] In the turn-the-other-cheek strategy, we eliminated

5. For analytic purposes, we have not separated statistically the male and female Ss because the numbers of male and female Ss, when broken down by experimental

four Ss who did not experience a white choice after the first three trials; in the nonpunitive condition, nine Ss were eliminated because they did not experience a green choice in response to their red or orange choice; in the deterrent treatment, five Ss were lost because they did not experience a red choice at any time. In the reformed sinner–turn-the-other-cheek condition, three Ss were eliminated who did not experience a white choice after the first three trials of reformed behavior by the accomplice. In the reformed sinner—nonpunitive çondition, eight Ss were eliminated because they did not experience a green choice in response to red or orange choices.

By the criteria we used for eliminating Ss from the experimental conditions, any S who chose blue throughout would have been taken out of our sample. These, of course, were the Ss who behaved most cooperatively. To produce a parallel reduction in our control groups of paired true Ss, we eliminated nine of twenty control pairs who chose blue throughout the game. For analytic purposes, one member of each control pair was then randomly assigned to be compared with the true Ss in the various experimental conditions, and the other member was assigned to be compared with the accomplices.

Results

The meaning of the pegs. To obtain measures of the emotional meaning of the various moves available to the Ss in the game, they were asked to rate, in a postexperimental questionnaire, each of the different-colored pegs on three nine-point scales: bad-good, strong-weak, active-passive. Analysis of variance indicates that the pegs differed significantly from one another in the ratings they received; this is so for each of the three scales. It is evident from the data presented in table 12.1 that the selection of a red or orange peg was evaluated unfavorably but was associated with strength and activity.

A blue peg was also associated with strength and activity, but it was favorably evaluated. The black peg was rated as less strong and

---

conditions, were small and disproportionately distributed among the Ss who were actually exposed to the different strategies. A preliminary analysis of various data, comparing the overall results for males and females without regard to experimental conditions, revealed no statistically significant differences. The number of males (M) and females (F) in each condition is listed below: *Turn the Other Cheek*—3M, 8F; *Nonpunitive*—2M, 4F; *Deterrent*—2M, 8F; *Reformed Sinner–Turn the Other Cheek* —2M, 10F; *Reformed Sinner–Nonpunitive*—3M, 4F; *Control*—3 male pairs, 8 female pairs.

less active than the blue, red, or orange pegs but stronger and more active than the green, white, or beige pegs. These latter were thought of as being on the passive and weak side, the white peg being rated the most passive and the weakest. The black, green, white, and beige pegs were rated rather less favorably than the blue pegs but rather more favorably than the red or orange ones. The green, beige, and white pegs received quite similar ratings.

TABLE 12.1. Mean Ratings of the Pegs
(N = 85)

	Bad (1)– Good (9) [1]	Active (1)– Passive (9)	Strong (1)– Weak (9)
Black (Individualistic)	6.54	5.27	4.67
Blue (Cooperative)	7.87	3.17	3.21
White (Altruistic-Ingratiating)	5.47	6.39	6.13
Red (Aggressive)	3.49	2.30	3.40
Green (Defensive)	5.77	5.65	5.29
Orange (Attack)	3.82	2.22	2.98
Beige (Disarm)	5.12	6.16	5.52

NOTE: The data represent the ratings by all Ss who participated in the experiment, including those who were not exposed to the strategies, who completed the postexperimental questionnaire.

[1] The numbers in the parentheses indicate the numerical values associated with each end of the bipolar scales.

The ratings of the pegs seem consistent with our a priori conceptions of their interpersonal meanings. Further support for the appropriateness of our a priori conceptions came from the names that the Ss ascribed to them. On the postexperimental questionnaire, we asked the Ss to select from a list the two names that would "best capture the meaning of moving that particular peg" for the black, blue, white, red, and green pegs. Below is a list of the three most frequently selected names for each peg, with the number of Ss selecting each name being given in parenthesis:

Black peg: cautious (30), independent (29), selfish (18)
Blue peg: cooperative (43), mutual (35), co-working (26)
White peg: benevolent (32), philanthropic (30), foolish (19)
Red peg: aggressive (52), combative (26), hostile (17)
Green peg: protective (45), antiweapon (27), self-preservative (26)

Financial Outcomes

In a game that permits a variety of behavior, one of the best measures of the overall process is the outcome of behavior. Our data provide four measures of outcome, all of which are relevant to a comparison of the effectiveness of the different behavioral strategies. These measures are: the joint outcome of the two players, the outcome of the S, the outcome of the accomplice, and the difference between the outcomes of the S and the accomplice. Figures 12.1–12.4 graph these different outcome data for each of the six conditions by blocks of fifteen trials.

Joint outcomes. It is evident from figure 12.1 that joint outcomes improved with the number of trials in almost all conditions. However, analyses of variance reveal that there were differences among the conditions in the initial and final outcome levels as well as in the amount of change in outcomes between the initial and final trial blocks.[6] The turn-the-other-cheek strategy produced a high initial joint outcome, which did not improve consistently over trials. The nonpunitive strategy also resulted in a relatively high initial joint outcome, but it got higher with each succeeding trial block. In contrast, the deterrent strategy had a relatively low initial joint outcome, and, although it increased with trials, the increase was comparatively small. As might be expected, the joint outcomes in the first fifteen trials were quite low in both reformed sinner conditions. However, after the "reform" took place on the sixteenth trial, there was a substantial and rapid improvement in outcomes. The improvement was more rapid and the joint outcomes reached a higher level in the turn-the-other-cheek rather than in the nonpunitive–reformed sinner strategy. It is of interest to note that the turn-the-other-cheek strategy produced higher outcomes in the last two blocks of trials when preceded by aggressive behavior during the first block of fifteen trials than if employed from the very

6. Here, as with most of our measures, two separate two-way analyses of variance were done: conditions $\times$ trial blocks (using all four trial blocks), and conditions $\times$ trial blocks (using the last three trial blocks only). Each trial block consisted of 15 trials. For the four trial block analysis of *joint outcomes* the effects of conditions ($F = 4.69$, $df = 5/51$, $p < .001$), trial blocks ($F = 67.70$, $dr = 3/153$, $p < .001$), and the interaction ($F = 9.03$, $df = 15/153$, $p < .001$) were all clearly significant. Similarly, for the three trial block analysis of *joint outcomes*: conditions ($F = 5.18$, $df = 5/51$, $p < .001$), trials ($F = 23.09$, $df = 2/102$, $p < .001$), and interaction ($F = 2.90$, $df = 10/102$, $p < .005$) were all significant.

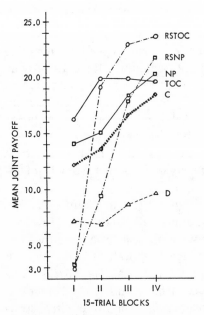
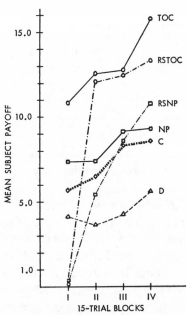

Figure 12.1. Mean joint payoffs (given
in cents, divided by ten) for Ss and
accomplices, by 15-trial blocks. Conditions are indicated as follows:
RSTOC, *reformed sinner—turn the
other cheek* (N = 12); RSNP, *reformed sinner — nonpunitive* (N = 7);
NP, *nonpunitive* (N = 6); TOC, *turn
the other cheek* (N = 11); C, *control*
(N = 11); D, *deterrent* (N = 10).

Figure 12.2. Mean subject payoffs
(in cents, divided by ten), by 15-trial
blocks. Conditions are indicated by
initials as in figure 12.1.

start of the game. The control groups, composed of paired true Ss,
had joint outcomes that were about midway between those obtained
in the deterrent and the nonpunitive strategies.

The subject's outcome. From figure 12.2, it is evident that the Ss
had the best outcomes in the turn-the-other-cheek condition (as could
be expected from the accomplice's behavior in this strategy) and the
worst outcomes when the accomplice was employing the deterrent
strategy. The control groups of naive Ss did not do as well as the Ss
who were exposed to the nonpunitive strategy, but they did better
than those who experienced the deterrent strategy.[7]

The accomplice's outcome. Figure 12.3 gives the answer to the

7. For the four trial block analysis of Ss *outcomes,* the effects of conditions
(F = 14.25, df = 5 / 51, p < .001), trial blocks (F = 63.15, df = 3 / 153, p < .001), and in-

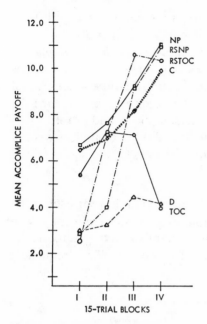

Figure 12.3. Mean payoffs of accomplices (in cents, divided by ten), by 15-trial blocks. Conditions are indicated by initials as in figure 12.1.

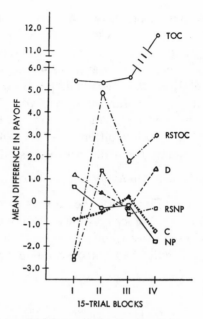

Figure 12.4. Difference between subject and accomplice payoffs (in cents, divided by ten), by 15-trial blocks. Conditions are indicated by initials as in figure 12.1.

question of which strategy benefited the accomplice most. Evidently, the nonpunitive strategy was considerably more rewarding than either the turn-the-other-cheek or the deterrent strategy. Although the outcomes for the accomplice who employed the deterrent strategy were, on the average, worse than those for the turn-the-other-cheek strategist, the outcomes for the former improved over the last several trial blocks but worsened for the latter. The "sinners who reformed" did relatively well after they reformed (but poorly while being aggressive). The turn-the-other-cheek–reformed sinner had a faster improvement rate than did the nonpunitive–reformed sinner. Also, it is of interest to note that the differences between the two turn-the-other-cheek strategies were substantial and increased with succeeding trial blocks,

---

teraction (F = 9.03, df = 15 / 153, p < .001) are all significant. For the three block analysis, conditions (F = 13.99, df = 5 / 51, p < .001) and trial blocks (F = 15.96, df = 2 / 102, p < .001) are significant but not their interaction (F = .78, dr = 10 / 102).

while the opposite was true for the two nonpunitive strategies. Here, the differences were small and they decreased with trials.[8]

Differences in outcomes between the subject and the accomplice. It is evident from figure 12.4 that the Ss did much better, and consistently so, than the accomplices *only* in the turn-the-other-cheek condition. A similar trend was found in the reformed sinner–turn-the-other-cheek condition once the accomplice had "reformed." Otherwise, the differences between the Ss and the accomplices were insubstantial and did not necessarily favor the Ss.[9]

Choices Made by the Subjects

Figure 12.5 charts the choices made in each condition for each of the four trial blocks. Over all the conditions and trials, the blue pegs were chosen most frequently, and then came the black, red, green, orange, and white pegs in descending order of frequency. The frequencies

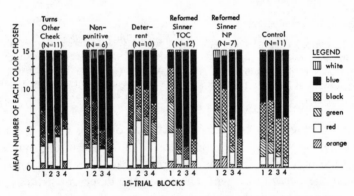

Figure 12.5. Mean numbers of each color chosen by 15-trial blocks.

8. For the four trial block analysis of *the accomplices' outcomes*, there are significant effects of conditions $(-20.15, df=5/51, p<.001)$, trial blocks $(F=20.81, df=3/153, p<.001)$, and interaction $(F=37.91, df=15/153, p<.001)$. For the three trial block analysis, there are significant effects of conditions $(F=14.9, df-5/51, p<.001)$, trial blocks $(F=9.91, df=2/102, p<.001)$, and also of the interaction $(F=3.22, df-10/102, p<.005)$.

9. For the four trial block analysis of *the differences between the outcomes of the Ss and their paired accomplices*, significant differences were obtained for conditions $(F=4.13, df=5/51, p<.01)$, trial blocks $(F=4.00, df=3/153, p<.01)$, and the interaction $(F=2.05, df=15/153, p<.01)$. For the three trial block analysis, significant differences were found only for the conditions $(F=3.34, df=3.34, df=5/51, p<.025)$.

with which the different pegs were chosen varied, of course, as an interacting function of both the strategy to which the Ss were exposed and the trial block in which the choices were made. Thus the turn-the-other-cheek strategy induced the Ss to make relatively more aggressive moves (red and orange choices) and to decrease the relative frequency of their defensive (green) and individualistic (black) actions as the trials proceeded. On the other hand, the nonpunitive strategy led the subjects to increase the proportion of their cooperative (blue) moves as they decreased their individualistic (black) and aggressive (orange and red) choices. The deterrent strategy elicited from the Ss a gradual decrease in individualistic choices, an increase in and then a subsidence of aggressive activity, and finally an increase in cooperative choices. In the "sinner" stage of the reformed sinner strategies, the subjects reacted with a relatively high level of aggressive, defensive, and individualistic behavior and a low frequency of cooperative choice. After the reform by the accomplice, the turn-the-other-cheek—reformed sinner elicited a rapid increase in cooperative behavior, which was paralleled by a decrease in individualistic, aggressive, and defensive actions. The increase in the frequency of cooperative choices and the accompanying decrease in the noncooperative behaviors did not occur so rapidly after the reform in the nonpunitive—reformed sinner strategy. The control groups of paired true Ss showed a gradual increase in cooperative activity with a gradual decrease in defensive and aggressive behaviors. Their level of individualistic activity did not alter much over the trials.

Analyses of variance were made on the frequency data for each type of choice by condition and trial block. Separate analyses were done excluding and including the first block of trials (i.e., the trials before the accomplice reformed in the reformed sinner conditions). A brief description of the results of these analyses for each type of choice follows.[10]

White pegs. Relatively few of the Ss made this type of move in any of the conditons, and no significant differences were obtained among the conditions. There was a significant decrease in the use of these pegs during the last three trial blocks.

10. To conserve space, we shall not present the details of the analyses of variance performed on the usage of each of the colored pegs but rather only the significant differences. We note that the "beige" pegs were not employed at all by the subjects. As table 12.1 indicates, this peg was not viewed with much favor by our subjects, and they could signal their good intentions through the use of the blue peg.

Blue pegs. There was a significant overall increase in cooperative choices per trial block the more times the game had been played. There was also a significant interaction between conditions and trial blocks for the last three trial blocks as well as for all trial blocks. Apart from the responses to the reformed sinners before they reformed, the fewest cooperative choices were elicited by the deterrent strategy. The most frequent cooperative responses were made to reformed sinner–turn the other cheek. All strategists except the deterrent strategy ended up eliciting more cooperative behavior than the control condition of paired true Ss.

Black Pegs. There was a significant overall decrease in the number of individualistic choices made over the course of the four trial blocks. No decrease occurred in response to the nonpunitive and the turn-the-other-cheek strategists.

Green pegs. There was a significant overall decrease in the number of defensive weapons used by the Ss over the last three trial blocks as well as over all four blocks. The decrease over the four blocks is most marked in the reformed sinner conditions and not evidenced in the deterrent and nonpunitive conditions. During the last three trial blocks, significantly more defensive weapons were chosen by the Ss in response to the deterrent strategy than to any other condition.

Red pegs. There was a significant overall decrease in the choice of aggressive weapons over the block of four trials and for the last three trials. However, in the turn-the-other-cheek condition, the frequency of red choices increased from trial block to trial block. Aggressive weapons were chosen most frequently by the Ss who were exposed to the deterrent and the turn-the-other-cheek strategies and least frequently by the Ss in the control condition.

Orange pegs. In general, few attacks were made by the Ss; attacks decreased significantly over all four trial blocks and also over the last three blocks. However, there was a slight increase in attacks over the four trial blocks in response to the deterrent and turn-the-other-cheek strategies; the largest decrease between the initial and final blocks occurred in the Ss exposed to the reformed sinner strategies.

Other Findings

Table 12.2 presents some data obtained from the postexperimental questionnaires about the impressions that the Ss formed of the accomplices in the various experimental conditions. The Ss perceived the accomplices in the nonpunitive condition as the most cooperative, most stable, and most fair; they were also perceived as being relatively kind, generous, and peaceful. The accomplices using the turn-the-other-cheek strategy were also perceived relatively favorably on the just-mentioned characteristics; they were viewed as the most kind, generous, and peaceful. The deterrent strategists were rated as the most uncooperative, least kind, and most selfish of the accomplices; they were also considered to be relatively unstable and almost as aggressive as the reformed sinners. Not surprisingly, the highest instability was attributed to the accomplices employing the reformed sinner–turn-the-other-cheek strategy. Finally, it is of interest to note that the Ss who were exposed to the deterrent strategy expressed the least desire to play the game again.

TABLE 12.2. Means of Ss' Ratings from the
Postexperimental Questionnaire

	T.O.C.	Non-P	Det.	R.S.–T.O.C.	R.S.–Non-P	Control	Sig.[1] level
Ratings of Other as:							
Aggressive (1)–Peaceful (9)	7.73	6.60	4.90	4.42	4.29	6.00	p<.10
Fair (1)–Unfair (9)	3.09	1.60	3.77	3.75	4.42	3.75	not sig.
Kind (1)–Cruel (9)	2.30	2.80	4.60	4.33	3.86	4.00	p<.10
Stable (1)–Unstable (9)	2.30	1.20	4.60	5.33	4.44	3.88	p<.005
Selfish (1)–Generous (9)	7.70	5.60	4.90	4.92	5.14	5.13	p<.05
Cooperative (1)–Uncooperative (9)	2.90	1.00	6.20	4.50	3.29	4.38	p<.001
Own desire to play again (1)	1.81	1.60	5.33	2.00	2.00	2.20	p<.005

[1] Based on one-way analyses of variance with d.f. for F usually being 5/47. Not all Ss filled out the questionnaire.

Discussion of Results

The results of the present experiment are consistent with, and extend, the findings of other investigators. Solomon (see chapter 8) studied the effects of three strategies upon the development of interpersonal trust in a two-person Prisoner's Dilemma game: an *unconditionally benevolent* strategy (the accomplice always chose to cooperate no matter what the S chose), a *conditionally benevolent* strategy (the accomplice chose cooperatively on the first trial and, thereafter, matched the choice made by the S on the preceding trial), and an *unconditionally malevolent* strategy (the accomplice always chose noncooperatively,

no matter what the S chose). The turn-the-other cheek and unconditionally benevolent strategies resemble one another in that they are
both unconditionally cooperative and they both appeal to conscience.
The nonpunitive and conditionally benevolent strategies both stress
reciprocation—with the exception that the former strategy defends itself against threat and aggression but does not reciprocate them. (In
the Prisoner's Dilemma game, it is impossible to tell whether a noncooperative action is defensive or aggressive in intent.) The unconditionally malevolent strategy was not matched by any of our strategies,
except during the first fifteen trials of both the reformed sinner strategies.

Solomon found that his Ss exploited the accomplices who were
unconditionally benevolent and were puzzled by their behavior; the Ss
responded competitively to the unconditionally malevolent strategy
and liked these accomplices least; and they responded most cooperatively to the conditionally benevolent accomplices and liked them
most. Our results parallel Solomon's: our Ss behaved most competitively during the fifteen trials when the accomplices in the reformed
sinner conditions were being threatening and aggressive; they tended
to exploit the turn-the-other-cheek accomplices; and they behaved
most cooperatively in the nonpunitive treatment.[11]

Bixenstine and Wilson (1963), in a study also employing the Prisoner's Dilemma game, have reported a finding similar to the result
that we obtained with our turn-the-other-cheek and reformed sinner–
turn-the-other-cheek strategies. They compared two strategies that
used the same overall percentage of cooperative choices (50 percent)
during 200 trials but that differed in their sequencing of choices. In
one strategy, the accomplices chose cooperatively in 95 percent of
the first 40 trials, while in the other they chose cooperatively in only
5 percent of these trials; in both strategies, they chose cooperatively
in 50 percent of the next 20 trials, i.e., trials 41–60. Although
their Ss responded slightly more cooperatively during the first 40
trials, to the accomplices who were programmed to choose coop-

---

11. Lave (1965), also using the Prisoner's Dilemma game, studied three stategies:
Unconditionally Benevolent (called "Gandhi" by Lave), *Unconditionally Malevolent*
(called "Stalin"), and a seductive strategy (called "Khrushchev") which was malevo-
lent but occasionally chose cooperatively to seduce the S into cooperation. The
"Ghandhi" strategy elicited most cooperation, the "Khrushchev" next most, and the
"Stalin" least.

eratively in 95 percent of the initial trials they responded considerably more favorably in the next 20 trials to the accomplices who had initially chosen a low rather than a high level of cooperation. These results paralleled our findings that the reformed sinner–turn-the-other-cheek strategist elicited more cooperation after the reform than did the accomplice who employed the turn-the-other-cheek strategy initially and through-out the game.

Shure, Meeker, and Hansford (1965) studied the effectiveness of a "pacifist" strategy in a bargaining game modeled after our Acme-Bolt trucking game (see chapter 9). In their experiment, they induced the real Ss to adopt a dominating rather than a cooperative strategy by having each S play the game as a respresentative of a team, i.e., as one who would share the game's outcome equally. The two teammates of the S were, in fact, confederates of the experimenters and they, by majority vote, pressured the S to adopt a dominating strategy before the start of the game; during the initial trials, they sent messages to the S to get him to maintain a dominating strategy. The S was exposed to an accomplice who always acted cooperatively and who required the S to use force (which the S thought would cause a painful electric shock to the accomplice) if the S wished to exploit him. In one experimental condition, the pacifist accomplice communicated his conciliatory intent, presented a statement of fair demands, and emphasized his refusal to use the shock and his intention to force the other to shock him if the other was going to remain unfair. In another condition, no direct communication was allowed among the players.

The results of this effort indicate that only a small proportion of the Ss did not exploit the pacifist accomplice; the proportion of Ss who switched from a dominating, exploitative strategy to a cooperative one increased significantly under the communication condition, but it was not a large increase. Further findings showed that it made little difference whether the pacifist accomplices explicitly disarmed or not, and it made little difference whether or not the Ss received information about the accomplices that indicated that the accomplices were Quakers who were morally committed to a position of nonviolence.

Our results with the turn-the-other-cheek strategy were consistent with the findings obtained by Shure et al. in their study of the pacifist strategy, although their results were considerably more extreme than ours. (In our experiment, the accomplices using the turn-the-other-cheek strategy elicited as much cooperation as the control Ss and had outcomes that were about as good as these Ss.)˙The extremity of their results was undoubtedly due to their having "fixed" their Ss into a dominating strategy by the group pressures under which they were placed. This was not the case for our Ss. Shure et al viewed their results as supporting the "harsh and unflattering" judgment that the pacifist's tactics invited exploitation and aggression even among those who did not begin with such intentions. Their interpretation is too unqualified. Not only does it ignore the group pressures upon the subjects to be exploitative, but it also ignores the social reality of the experiment. From the experimenter's instructions, the Ss could assume that both players had the experimenter's approval and encouragement to seek "selfish" outcomes and, also, that the experimenter's provision of means to attempt to dominate the other invited and legitimized their usage. In a sense, the pacifist was violating the implicit norms of the experimental situation as established by the experimenter and was appealing to exterior social values whose relevance had been deliberately minimized by the arrangements and paraphernalia of the experiment. (Ss were isolated in separate cubicles; they had no personal contact; they didn't know each other's names; if they communicated at all, it was through a computer; etc.) In such a context, the pacifist strategy might have been experienced as puzzling or even incredible, and as saintly but inappropriate. And, in fact, the turn-the-other-cheek strategy was often puzzling to *our* Ss; moreover, it was the only one in which some felt that they were not playing with a real person.

It is interesting to note that the reformed sinner–turn-the-other-cheek strategy was considerably more effective in eliciting cooperation than the simple turn-the-other-cheek strategy. The data of table 12.2 suggest that, in the former condition, the initially aggressive behavior of the accomplice served to create an image of a relatively unstable and potentially aggressive person whom it was wise not to provoke lest he be temped to revert to his aggressive ways. It seems likely, however, that, if we had run this condition for a longer series of trials, the cooperation by the Ss would have started to decrease.

The deterrent strategy was ineffective apparently because the Ss tended to perceive the threats made by the accomplice as aggressive rather than as deterrent in intent. Table 12.2 indicates that the accomplice using this strategy was rated relatively high in aggressiveness, selfishness, cruelty, and uncooperativeness. On the other hand, the nonpunitive strategy, which used defensive rather than threatening tactics to handle noncooperation by the Ss, was quite effective in eliciting cooperation and favorable evaluations from the Ss. It is of interest to note that the reformed sinner–nonpunitive strategy also elicited considerable cooperation, despite the relatively unfavorable ratings that the accomplices received. Unlike our expectation for the other reformed sinner strategy, we would not expect cooperation to deteriorate in a longer series of trials.

EXPERIMENT II: THE EFFECTS OF STRONGER INCENTIVES TO COMPETE UPON THE DIFFERENT STRATEGIES

The second experiment replicated the first one—with several modifications. The modifications include: the addition of a reformed sinner-deterrent condition; a change in the values of the pegs so that the incentive for competitive behavior was increased; minor alterations in the strategies; more careful procedures to insure that all the subjects fully understood the game; and the use of an equal number of male and female subjects in each of the conditions. There were few differences in the results for the males and females; consequently, the findings are not presented separately for the two sexes.

The values for the pegs in experiments I and II are indicated in table 12.3. Clearly, the incentives for cooperation decreased, while the incentives for competitive behavior increased in the second as compared to the first experiment.

The strategies followed by the accomplice of the experimenter were essentially the same as those in the first experiment.

1. *Turn the other cheek.* The accomplice chooses blue on trial one.

TABLE 12.3. The Monetary Values of the
Pegs in Experiments I and II

Type of Peg	Experiment I	Experiment II
Black	6¢	5¢
Blue	9¢ or 1¢	7¢ or 0
White	7¢ to other	6¢ to other
Red	6¢	17¢
Green	6¢	17¢
Orange	attack	attack
Beige	disarm	disarm

From then on, if the subject chooses either white, blue, or beige on a particular trial, the accomplice chooses blue on the following trial. If the subject chooses either black, red, green, or orange, the accomplice chooses white on the next trial.

2. *Nonpunitive.* The accomplice chooses blue on trial one. From then on, if the subject chooses white, the accomplices does likewise; similarly, if the subject chooses black, the accomplice does also. If the subject chooses blue, green, or beige, the accomplice chooses blue; if the subject chooses red or orange, the accomplice selects green.

3. *Deterrent.* The accomplice chooses blue on trial one. From then on, if the subject chooses white, blue, or beige, the accomplice picks blue. If the subject selects red, green, or black, the accomplice chooses red; if the subject selects orange, so does the accomplice.

4, 5, 6. *Reformed sinner.* In the reformed sinner conditions, the accomplice selects orange on the third, ninth, and twelfth trials; otherwise he chooses red through trial fourteen. On the fifteenth trial, he disarms by picking beige, and on the sixteenth trial he selects blue. From then on, the accomplice follows either the turn-the-other-cheek, the nonpunitive, or the deterrent strategy.

7. *Control.* Two real subjects of the same sex are run with each other.

Results of the Second Experiment Compared
with Results of the First.

The results of the second experiment were very similar to those of the first. We shall consider here only the differences between the two.

The meaning of the pegs. Although the meaning of the pegs remained essentially the same, there were some clear shifts. Whereas in the first experiment red and orange were evaluated least favorably, white and beige were considered in the least favorable light in the second experiment. Unlike the situation in the first experiment, blue was rated no more favorably than black. Green was rated as more active and stronger in the second experiment, more so than blue or black. This shift represented an increase for green and a decrease for blue.

The changes indicate that the pegs involved in competitive interaction (red, orange, and green) increased in favorableness in the second experiment, while the pegs that were involved in cooperative or altruistic action (blue, white, and beige) decreased; the individualistic peg (black) remained the same. It is relevant to note that, in the second experiment, the aggressive pegs (orange and red) were more favorably regarded in the conditions where they were used most (TOC, RS-TOC, D, RS-D) and least favorably where they were used least (NP, RS-NP, C). Increased use may well have led to increased positive evaluation.

Financial outcomes. A direct comparison between the outcomes in the two experiments would be meaningless because of the differences in values of the pegs in the two. Nevertheless, it is possible to compare how the various strategies did vis-à-vis one another in the two experiments. Table 12.4 presents the average outcomes per block of three trials for the subject and the accomplice and the sum or joint outcome of the subject and the accomplice. This is done separately for the first fifteen trials and the last forty-five trials.

TABLE 12.4. Mean Payoffs per Block of Three Trials for the Various Experimental Conditions for Trials 1–15, 16–60

	Joint		Subject		Accomplice	
Condition	1–15	16–60	1–15	16–60	1–15	16–60
Turn Other Cheek	21.0	24.3	25.7	40.4	−4.8	−16.1
Nonpunitive	19.8	35.9	10.0	17.8	9.8	18.1
Deterrent	5.6	10.9	1.9	1.5	3.7	9.4
R.S.–Turn Other Cheek	1.6	32.3	−.8	46.1	2.4	−13.8
R.S.–Nonpunitive	2.2	20.8	−2.9	10.9	5.1	9.9
R.S.–Deterrent	2.9	9.3	.4	7.5	2.4	1.7
Control	10.3	21.0	6.3	9.9	4.0	11.2

If we examine the data for the initial fifteen trials, we find results that parallel those of the earlier experiment. The reformed-sinner strategies had the worst joint outcomes as well as the poorest individual outcomes for the subject and the accomplice, with the accomplice doing somewhat better than the subject. The deterrent strategy was next worst, having even worse outcomes than the control group. The nonpunitive strategy produced relatively high joint payoffs, with both the subject and the accomplice doing equally well. In contrast, the subject did considerably better than the accomplice in the turn-the-other-cheek strategy; their joint outcome was high even though the average accomplice lost money in their condition.

The results for the last forty-five trials do exhibit some contrasts with those of the initial experiment, even though they mostly duplicate the earlier findings. The major difference is in the reformed sinner–turn-the-other-cheek condition. In the second experiment, unlike the first one, the accomplice employing this strategy did rather poorly, worse than all but the consistent turn-the-other-cheek accomplice. The accomplices in both the turn-the-other-cheek strategies in the second experiment were heavily exploited by the subjects who, as a result, ended up with by far the highest outcomes. In the first experiment, the initially aggressive play of the accomplice in the reformed sinner–turn-the-other-cheek condition appeared to inhibit the exploitative behavior of the subject. This was obviously not the case under the more competitive conditions of the second experiment.

The results again confirmed the superiority of the nonpunitive strategy. It resulted in relatively high earnings for both the accomplice and the subject, with higher joint returns and higher payoffs for the accomplice than in any of the other conditions. However, the reformed sinner–nonpunitive strategy was considerably less effective than the consistent nonpunitive strategy; much less so than in the initial experiment. Although the Reformed sinner–nonpunitive strategy was generally superior to the deterrent and the reformed sinner–deterrent strategies, and although it is definitely superior to the turn-the-other-cheek strategy in terms of the accomplice's payoff, the control condition did just as well on all outcome measures.

The deterrent strategies had the lowest joint outcomes and also the poorest subject outcomes of all the conditions. This paralleled the results of the first experiment. The reformed sinner–deterrent condition did worse than the consistent deterrent condition. Thus all three reformed sinner strategies did relatively poorly in the second experiment, more so than in the first one.

Color choices. The alterations in values of the pegs from the first to the second experiment produced the expected changes. There were significant decreases in the number of blue and black choices and significant increases in the number of red, green, and orange choices. Clearly, the values of the pegs in the second experiment predisposed the subjects to behave more aggressively and less cooperatively.

Figures 12.6a and b chart the percentage of blue choices for the different blocks of trials; figures 12.7a and b present a comparable picture for the red choice. It is evident that the nonpunitive strategy was the only one to elicit frequent and early cooperative choices from the subjects. This strategy was as effective in this regard in the second

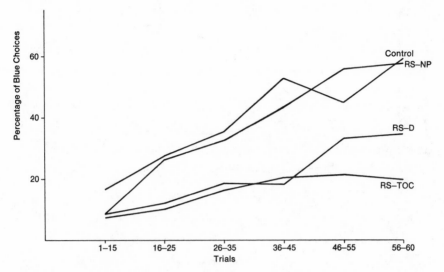

Figure 12.6a. Percentage of blue choices by trial blocks for Ss in *Control, RS-NP, RS-D,* and *RS-TOC* conditions.

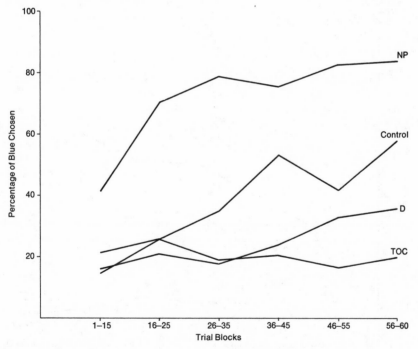

Figure 12.6b. Percentage of blue choices by trial blocks for Ss in *NP, Control, D,* and *TOC* conditions.

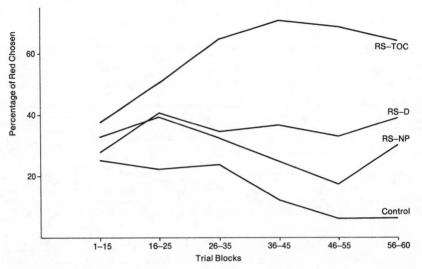

Figure 12.7a. Percentage of red choices by trial blocks for Ss in *RS-TOC, RS-D, RS-NP,* and *Control* conditions.

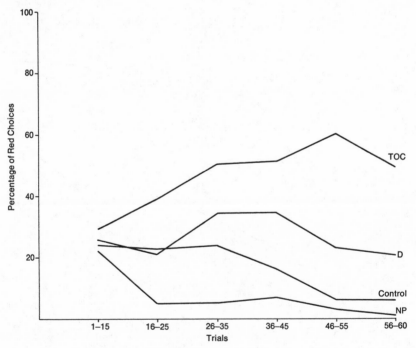

Figure 12.7b. Percentage of red choices by trial blocks for Ss in *TOC, D, Control,* and *NP* conditions.

experiment as in the first. All the other strategies were less effective in eliciting cooperation under the more competitive conditions of the second experiment. The decrease in effectiveness was most marked for the turn-the-other-cheek strategies, particularly for the reformed sinner version of this strategy. The results for the red choices complemented those for the blue choices. The fewest such choices occurred in situations where the subjects were exposed to the nonpunitive strategy, while the most frequent red choices were made by subjects who faced an accomplice who was employing a turn-the-other-cheek strategy.

Discussion of Results

The value of the pegs in the second experiment as compared to the first favored competitive choices, and, as a result, the choices of the subjects were more competitive. This was true in all the conditions except when the subjects were exposed to a consistently nonpunitive strategy. This strategy was highly effective in eliciting cooperative behavior under the competitive incentives of the second experiment as well as in the less competitive situation. In contrast, the turn-the-other-cheek strategies decreased markedly in their effectiveness. Under the more competitive incentives of the second experiment, the reformed sinner–turn-the-other-cheek accomplice was exploited much more than in the initial experiment. Unlike the situation in the first experiment, the accomplice's aggressive play in the early trials did not inhibit the subject from yielding to the temptation to take advantage of him.

Apart from the differences cited above, the results of the experiments were similar. The nonpunitive strategies were more effective in eliciting cooperation from the subjects and in producing better outcomes for the accomplices than the deterrent strategies, which were, in turn, more effective than the turn-the-other-cheek strategies.

EXPERIMENT III: A COMPARISON OF TWO VERSIONS OF THE DETERRENT STRATEGY

The third experiment contrasted the relatively threatening deterrent strategy of the second experiment with a milder variant of the same strategy. In the milder variant, the accomplice chose black rather than red in response to a subject's choice of black. Rather than threaten the subject when he chose individualistically, and therefore noncooperatively, the accomplice made a matching choice. The earlier variant of the deterrent strategy, in effect, sought to deter all forms of noncooperative behavior; the later variant tried to deter only the production of weapons, aggressive (red) or defensive (green).

Results

The subjects in the initial, harsher deterrent condition rated the red and orange pegs as being significantly stronger than did the subjects in the milder treatment. The accomplices employing the later deterrent strategy were rated as being less aggressive and nicer than the ones in the earlier condition. However, despite these differences in the postexperimental ratings (and they were the only significant differences between the two conditions in the various ratings), the subjects exposed to the two variants of the deterrent strategy exhibited few differences in their actual behavior. There were no reliable differences in their choices of blue (cooperative), black (individualistic), or white (altruistic) pegs. The subjects exposed to the harsher deterrent treatment, however, did choose defensively (the green pegs) significantly more often, while the subjects exposed to the milder variant chose aggressively (the red pegs) more often. Although the number of attacks (the orange pegs) did not differ for the two treatments over the sixty trials, the subjects in the milder variant attacked the accomplices more frequently in the early trials and less frequently in the later trials than did the subjects in the harsher variant.

In terms of outcomes, there were no reliable differences between the accomplices in the two conditions; nor were there overall differences in the joint payoffs. However, the subjects did slightly, but significantly, better when they had to contend with the milder rather than harsher deterrent.

Discussion

The milder as well as the harsher deterrent strategies were both relatively ineffective in eliciting cooperative behavior from the subjects when compared with the nonpunitive strategy. Both the deterrent strategies elicited a good deal of weapons choices from the subjects: in the milder variant, there was a favoring of aggressive over defensive weapons, while in the harsher one, the two types of weapons were equally favored. These results are in striking contrast with the nonpunitive treatment; in the latter, few weapons of either type were chosen by the subjects.

EXPERIMENT IV: THE EFFECTIVENESS OF THE DIFFERENT
STRATEGIES AS A FUNCTION OF POWER
AND COMPETITIVENESS

In this experiment, the three basic strategies—turn the other cheek, nonpunitive, and deterrent (in its milder version)—were compared with one another under two conditions: one in which the accomplice's and the subject's weapons had *equal power,* and one in which the accomplice's weapons were of *weaker power,* having only half the strength of the subject's weapons. In addition, the values of the various color choices were altered so as to increase the temptation to engage in aggressive action and the risk of choosing cooperatively. All subjects in this experiment were male college students.

Table 12.5 presents the values for the different color choices; table 12.6 presents the strategies.

Results

The data, not surprisingly, indicate that the accomplices in all strategy conditions did better when their weapon power was equal rather than weaker than the subjects'; the subjects did better when their power was stronger rather than equal to the accomplices'. The total or joint outcomes were, however, somewhat better under the equal rather than unequal power conditions—except in the control group.

From table 12.7, it is evident that the accomplice did worst with the turn-the-other-cheek strategy, the control groups did next worst, and the deterrent and nonpunitive strategies were equally effective (or ineffective). The level of mutual cooperation was low even in the two most effective strategies—the joint payoffs were less than half of what would have been obtained from optimal cooperation.

The color choices also revealed the high level of noncooperation. Table 12.8 indicates the percentage of choices that involved attacks and/or weapons (i.e., choices of orange, red, or green). It is evident that a fairly high level of aggressive and defensive behavior occurred among the subjects in all conditions—but especially in the turn-the-other-cheek and control conditions. The fewest such choices occurred in response to the nonpunitive strategy in the equal power condition.

TABLE 12.5. The Monetary Values of the Different Color Choices in Experiment IV

Type of Color	Stronger and Equal Power	Weaker [1] Power
Black	6	6
Blue	0 if chosen by one person, 8 if chosen by both	0 if chosen by one person, 8 if chosen by both
White	0 to person selecting it, 5 to other person	0 to person selecting it, 5 to other person
Orange	20 each when other chooses blue on same trial, otherwise 10	10 each when the other chooses blue on same trial, otherwise 5
Red	0 until activated by orange, then worth 10 each	0 until activated by orange, then worth 5 each
Green	0 until activated by other's orange, then worth 10 each	0 until activated by other's orange, then worth 5 each
Beige	cancels own unused reds	cancels own unused reds

[1] In the *weaker power* condition, the subject had the stronger power while the accomplice had the weaker power.

TABLE 12.6. The Strategies Followed by the Accomplice

	Accomplice's Choice on the Next Trial [1]		
Ss Choice	Turn Other Cheek	Nonpunitive	Deterrent
Black	Black	Black	Black
White	Blue	Blue	Blue
Blue	Blue	Blue	Blue
Beige	Blue	Blue	Blue
Green	Blue	Blue	Red
Orange	White [2]	Green	Orange
Red	White [2]	Green	Red

[1] All three strategies chose blue on the first trial.

[2] If the subjects chose orange or red in an unbroken string, the accomplice chose blue one-third of the time in a predetermined asymmetrical pattern to make his behavior more credible to the S.

TABLE 12.7. Mean Payoff by Three Trial Blocks

Condition	Joint Payoff	Subject's [1] Payoff	Accomplice's Payoff
Turn the Other Cheek			
Equal power	18	34	−15
Unequal power	14	39	−24
Nonpunitive			
Equal power	23	13	9
Unequal power	16	16	0
Deterrent			
Equal power	20	9	10
Unequal power	17	16	0
Control			
Equal power	7	2	4 [2]
Unequal power	13	20	−7 [2]

[1] 12 subjects were in each of the 8 conditions.
[2] 2 real subjects were employed in the control condition.

TABLE 12.8. Percentage of Trials in Which the Subject's Choice Was Orange, Red, or Green

Choice	*Turn Other Cheek*		*Nonpunitive*		*Deterrent*		*Control*	
	Equal	*Unequal*	*Equal*	*Unequal*	*Equal*	*Unequal*	*Equal*	*Unequal*
Orange	39.7	55.9	17.2	24.1	23.5	22.6	33.8	38.1
Red	20.7	20.5	13.8	25.0	13.8	20.8	25.3	26.9
Green	2.8	1.4	2.9	3.6	15.5	10.8	15.1	7.4
TOTAL	63.2	77.7	33.5	52.6	52.8	54.2	74.2	72.4

The subject who had stronger power than the accomplice was more likely to make an aggressive choice.

Discussion of Results

Under conditions of strong temptation to engage in aggressive action and of high risk for cooperative behavior, it is not surprising that there were a sizable number of aggressive and defensive choices by the subjects. Only in response to the nonpunitive accomplices, who had equal power with them, did the subjects engage in such behavior significantly less than half the time. When the subjects had stronger power than the accomplices, even in response to the nonpunitive strategy, the temptation to be aggressive was hard to resist—even more so than when the subjects and the accomplices had equal power. The subjects in the control groups and those exposed to the turn-the-other-cheek strategies were most apt to be aggressive, while those confronting the nonpunitive or deterrent conditions were least likely to be so. Such aggressive behavior paid off for the subjects only when the accomplices employed a turn-the-other-cheek strategy and the subjects had greater power than the accomplices. In a complementary way, the accomplices did poorly under all conditions when they had lower power then the subjects—especially in the turn-the-other-cheek and control conditions. The nonpunitive and deterrent accomplices coped more successfully with their pairmates than did their counterparts in the turn-the-other-cheek and control conditions under both equal and unequal power conditions. However, even in these latter conditions the outcomes for the accomplices (and also the subjects) were low. It seems likely that these results reflect the rather strong incentives for competition and the weak incentives for cooperation that were built into the situation by the values assigned to the different color choices.

CONCLUSION

We have studied several basic types of strategies for inducing cooperation. It is well to stress that each type has many different variants and that it would be mistaken to conclude that the results obtained in our experiments for a given type would hold for all its variants. For example, the less threatening variant of the deterrent strategy used in the third and fourth experiments elicited considerably less negative attitudes, although rather similar behavior, than the harsher variant used in the first two experiments. Also, it is well to recognize that the impact of a given strategy may be great or small, depending on the social context and circumstances in which it is employed. Thus it seems likely that the effectiveness of the turn-the-other-cheek strategy is very much influenced by the competitiveness of the situation; the more competitive the incentives of the other, the more likely it is that such a strategy will be massively exploited. However, it should be noted that this strategy was consistently exploited in all our experiments except when it had been preceded by a show of strength (the reformed sinner variant) in the first experiment. On the other hand, if we consider the deterrent strategy—in comparison with the control situation—it seems plausible to speculate that such a strategy may become relatively more effective as the conditions become more competitive. Under relatively cooperative conditions, it induces the other to see the accomplice as being hostile and aggressive, and provocatively so. On the other hand, when the circumstances strongly elicit competitive behavior, then the deterrent strategist is less aggressive than the control subject, who is operating on unsystematic impulse rather than on deliberate plan and tends to be vindicative.

The effectiveness of the nonpunitive strategy varied least from situation to situation. In none of the experiments were any of the other strategies more effective than the nonpunitive one in eliciting cooperation and reducing aggression. Only under the extremely competitive conditions of the fourth experiment was this strategy no more effective than the deterrent strategy, and, even then, when the accomplice had equal power with the subject, he elicited less competitive behavior when he employed a nonpunitive rather than a deterrent strategy.

It is the task of future investigations to specify more precisely and in greater detail the conditions under which the various strategies of inducing cooperation are most effective and to identify strategies that are effective over a wide range of conditions. It is often man's lot to need to obtain another's cooperation under conditions that are unclear and in situations when little is known about the other.

PART THREE: CONCLUDING ESSAY

13. Factors Influencing the Resolution of Conflict

INTRODUCTION

The purpose of this chapter is to summarize the typical features of destructive and constructive conflicts. The emphasis will be on the contrast between competitive and cooperative processes of conflict resolution. In this connection, we shall also discuss the processes of perception and commitment that tend to reinforce and augment whichever mode of conflict resolution has been initiated. Next, we shall consider the factors that determine which mode of conflict resolution will be dominant. Underlying this discussion is the assumption that conflict between parties with cooperative rather than competitive relations is likely to be less destructive. Yet, it is obvious that the relations between conflicting parties may be incorrigibly competitive. Under such circumstances, the regulation of conflict to limit its destructiveness becomes an objective. In this context, we shall discuss the circumstances affecting the likelihood of effective conflict regulation. Finally, we shall consider some of the special issues relating to conflicts between the weak and the strong.

THE COURSE OF DESTRUCTIVE CONFLICT

Destructive conflict is characterized by a tendency to expand and escalate. As a result, such conflict often becomes independent of its initiating causes and is likely to continue after these have become irrelevant or have been forgotten. Expansion occurs along the various dimensions of conflict: the size and number of the immediate issues involved; the number of motives and participants implicated on each side of the issue; the size and number of the principles and precedents that are perceived to be at stake; the costs that the participants are

351

willing to bear in relation to the conflict; the number of norms of moral conduct from which behavior toward the other side is exempted; and the intensity of negative attitudes toward the other side.

The processes involved in the intensification of conflict may be said, as Coleman (1957, p. 14) has expressed it, "to create a 'Gresham's Law of Conflict: the harmful and dangerous elements drive out those which would keep the conflict within bounds." Paralleling the expansion of the scope of conflict, there is an increasing reliance upon a strategy of power and upon the tactics of threat, coercion, and deception. Correspondingly, there is a shift away from a strategy of persuasion and from the tactics of conciliation, minimization of differences, and enhancement of mutual understanding and goodwill. Within each of the conflicting parties, there is increasing pressure for uniformity of opinion and a tendency for leadership and control to be taken over by those elements that are militantly organized for waging conflict through combat and taken away from those that are more conciliatory.

The tendency to escalate conflict results from the conjunction of three interrelated processes: (1) competitive processes involved in the attempt to win the conflict; (2) processes of misperception and biased perception; and (3) processes of commitment arising out of pressures for cognitive and social consistency. These processes give rise to a mutually reinforcing cycle of relations that generate actions and reactions that intensify conflict.

Other factors, of course, may serve to limit and encapsulate conflict so that a spiraling intensification does not develop. Here, we refer to such factors as: the number and strength of the existing cooperative bonds, cross-cutting identifications, common allegiances and memberships among the conflicting parties; the existence of values, institutions, procedures, and groups that are organized to help limit and regulate conflict; and the salience and significance of the costs of intensifying conflict. If these conflict-limiting factors are weak, it may be difficult to prevent a competitive conflict from expanding in scope. Even if they are strong, misjudgment and the pressures arising out of tendencies to be rigidly self-consistent may make it difficult to keep a competitive conflict encapsulated.

Competitive effects. In chapter 2, I characterized the essential distinctions between a cooperative and competitive process and described their social psychological features in some detail. Here, I shall only highlight some of the main features of the competitive process, those that tend to perpetuate and escalate conflict. Typically, a competitive process tends to produce the following effects:

1. Communication between the conflicting parties is unreliable and impoverished. The available communication channels and opportunities are not utilized, or they are used in an attempt to mislead or intimidate the other. Little confidence is placed in information that is obtained directly from the other; espionage and other circuitous means of obtaining information are relied upon. The poor communication enhances the possibility of error and misinformation of the sort that is likely to reinforce the preexisting orientations and expectations toward the other. Thus the ability to notice and respond to the other's shifts away from a win-lose orientation becomes impaired.

2. It stimulates the view that the solution of the conflict can only be imposed by one side or the other by means of superior force, deception, or cleverness. The enhancement of one's own power and the complementary minimization of the other's power become objectives. The attempt by each of the conflicting parties to create or maintain a power difference favorable to his own side tends to expand the scope of the conflict from a focus on the immediate issue in dispute to a conflict over the power to impose one's preference upon the other.

3. It leads to a suspicious, hostile attitude that increases the sensitivity to differences and threats while minimizing the awareness of similarities. This, in turn, makes the usually accepted norms of conduct and morality that govern one's behavior toward others who are similar to oneself less applicable. Hence, it permits behavior toward the other that would be considered outrageous if directed toward someone like oneself. Since neither side is likely to grant moral superiority to the other, the conflict is likely to escalate as one side or the other engages in behavior that is morally outrageous to the other.

Misjudgment and misperception. In our preceding discussion of the effects of competition, it was evident that impoverished communication, hostile attitudes, and oversensitivity to differences could lead to distorted views of the other that could intensify and perpetuate conflict. In addition to the distortions that are natural to the competitive process, there are other distortions that commonly occur in the course of interaction. Elsewhere (Deutsch 1962, 1965), I have described some of the common sources of misperception in interactional situations. Many of these misperceptions function to transform a conflict into a competitive struggle—even if the conflict did not emerge from a competitive relationship.

Let me illustrate with the implications of a simple psychological principle: the perception of any act is determined both by our perception of the act itself and by our perception of the context within which the act occurs. The contexts of social acts are often not immediately given through perception, and often they are not obvious. When the context is not obvious, we tend to assume a familiar context—one that seems likely in terms of our own past experience. Since both the present situations and the past experiences of the actor and perceiver may be rather different, it is not surprising that the two individuals will interpret the same act quite differently. Misunderstandings of this sort are very likely, of course, when the actor and the perceiver come from different cultural backgrounds and are not fully informed about these differences. A period of rapid social change also makes such misunderstandings widespread as the gap between the past and the present widens.

Given the fact that the ability to place oneself in the other's shoes is notoriously underemployed and underdeveloped in most people, and also given that this ability is impaired by stress and inadequate information, it is to be expected that certain typical biases will emerge in the perceptions of actions during conflict. Thus since most people are strongly motivated to maintain a favorable view of themselves but are less strongly motivated to hold such a view of others, it is not surprising that there is a bias toward perceiving one's own behavior toward the other as being more benevolent and more legitimate than the other's behavior toward oneself. This is a simple restatement of a well-demonstrated psychological truth: namely, that the evaluation of an act is affected by the evaluation of its source—and the source is part of the context of behavior. For example, research has shown that American students are likely to rate more favorably an action of the United States directed toward the Soviet Union than the same action directed by the Soviet Union toward the United States. We are likely to view American espionage activities in the Soviet Union as more benevolent than similar activities by Soviet agents in the United States.

If each side in a conflict tends to perceive its own motives and behavior as more benevolent and legitimate than those of the other side, it is evident that the conflict will spiral upward in intensity. If Acme perceives its actions as a benevolent and legitimate way of interfering with actions that Bolt has no right to engage in, Acme will be surprised by the intensity of Bolt's hostile response and will have to escalate its counteraction to negate Bolt's response. But how else is Bolt likely to act if he perceives his own actions as well-motivated? And how unlikely is he not to respond to Acme's escalation with counter-escalation if he is capable of doing so? To the extent that there is a biased perception of benevolence and legitimacy, one could also expect that there will be a parallel bias in what is considered to be an equitable agreement for resolving conflict: should not differential legitimacy be differentially rewarded? The biased perception of what is a fair compromise makes agreement more difficult and thus extends conflict. Another consequence of the biased perception of benevolence and legitimacy is reflected in the asymmetries between trust and suspicion and between cooperation and competition. Trust, when violated, is more likely to turn into suspicion than negated suspicion is to turn into trust. Similarly, it is easier to move from cooperation to competition than in the other direction.

There are, of course, other types of processes leading to misperceptions and misjudgments. In addition to the distortions arising from the pressures for self-consistency and social conformity (which are discussed below), the intensification of conflict may induce stress and tension beyond a moderate optimal level and this overactivation, in turn, may lead to an impairment of perceptual and cognitive processes in several ways. It may reduce the range of perceived alternatives; it may reduce the time perspective in such a way as to cause a focus on the immediate rather than the overall consequences of the perceived alternatives; it may polarize thought so that percepts will tend to take on a simplistic cast of being black or white, for or against, good or evil; it may lead to stereotyped responses; it may increase the susceptibility to fear- or hope-inciting rumors; it may increase defensiveness; it may increase the pressures for social conformity. In effect, excessive tension reduces the intellectual resources available for discovering new ways of coping with a problem or new ideas for resolving a conflict. Intensification of conflict is the likely result as simplistic thinking and the polarization of thought push the participants to view their alternatives as being limited to victory or defeat.

Paradoxically, it should also be noted that the availability of intellectual and other resources that can be used for waging conflict may make it difficult, at the onset of conflict, to forecast the outcome of an attempt to impose one's preference upon the other. Less inventive species than man can pretty well predict the outcome of a contest by force through aggressive gesturing and other displays of combat potential; thus they rarely have to engage in combat to settle "who shall get what, when." However, the versatility of man's techniques for achieving domination over other men makes it likely that combat will arise because the combatants have discordant judgments of the potential outcomes. Unlike his hairy ancestors, the "naked ape" cannot agree in advance who will win. Misjudgment of the other side's willingness and capability with respect to fighting has sometimes turned controversy into combat as increased tension has narrowed the perceived outcomes of conflict to victory or defeat.

Process of commitment. It has long been recognized that people tend to act in accord with their beliefs; more recently, Festinger has emphasized in his theory of cognitive dissonance that the converse is also often true: people tend to make their beliefs and attitudes accord with their actions (see chapter 3 for a further discussion). This pressure for self-consistency may lead to an unwitting involvement in and intensification of conflict because one's actions have to be justified to oneself and to others. The tragic course of American involvement in the civil war in Vietnam provides an illustration.

In an unpublished paper presented a number of years ago (Deutsch 1966b), I wrote:

> How did we get involved in this ridiculous and tragic situation: a situation in which American lives and resources are being expended in defense of a people who are being more grievously injured and who are becoming more bitterly antagonistic to us the more deeply we become involved in their internal conflict? How is it that we have become so obsessed with the war in South Vietnam that we are willing to jettison our plans for achieving a Great Society at home, neglect the more important problems in South America and India, and risk destroying our leadership abroad?
>
> The most direct statement of the reason for our continued involvement is the fact that we are involved: our continued involvement justifies our past involvement. Once involved it is exceedingly difficult to disengage and to admit, thereby, how purposeless and unwitting our past involvement has been. I am stating, in other

words, that we are not involved because of any large strategic or moral purpose and that any such purposes we now impute to our involvement are ex post facto rationalizations.

As a nation, we stumbled into the conflict in South Vietnam. At every step of increasing involvement, we were led to believe that with some small additional help (economic aid, then military advisers, then the use of American heliocopters, then the combat use of American soldiers, then massive air intervention by American planes, then bombing of the North, then massive intervention of American troops, and so on) we would not risk a major conflict but yet would help to build an independent, stable country that could stand on its own feet. We have over and over again acted on the tempting assumption that with just a little more investment we would prevent the whole thing from going down the drain.

This type of assumption is one with which we are familiar in connection with the psychology of gambling. We all know of the losing gambler getting deeper and deeper into a hole, who keeps on betting with the hope that by so doing he will recover his initial losses. Not all losing gamblers submit to the gambler's temptation, of course. But those whose sense of omnipotence is at stake, those who are too proud to recognize that they cannot overcome the odds against them are vulnerable to this type of disastrous temptation.

In addition to the gambler's temptation, I shall describe briefly three other processes of gradual and unwitting commitment. One is the previously discussed process of *dissonance-reduction*. As Festinger (1961) has pointed out: "Rats and people come to love the things for which they have suffered." Presumably they do so in order to reduce the dissonance induced by the suffering, and their method of dissonance-reduction is to enhance the attractiveness of the choice which led to their suffering: only if what one chose was really worthwhile would all of the associated suffering be tolerable. Did we not increase what we perceived to be at stake in the Vietnam conflict as it has become more and more costly for us? Were we not told that our national honor, our influence as a world leader, and our national security were in the balance in the conflict over this tragic little land?

Silvan Tomkins (Tomkins and Izard 1965) has described a process of *circular, incremental magnification* which also helps to explain the widening of involvement and the monopolization of thought. He suggests that it occurs if there is a sequence of events of this type: threat, successful defense, breakdown of defense and re-emergence of threat; second successful defense, second breakdown of defense and re-emergence of threat, and so on until an expectation is generated that no matter how successful a defense against a dreaded contingency may seem, it will prove unavailing and require yet another defense. This process is circular and incremental since each new threat requires a more desperate defense, and the successful breakdown of each newly improved defense generates a magnification of the nature of the threat and the concurrent effect which it evokes. The increasing and obsessive preoccupation of American officials with Vietnam may, in part, reflect just such a process: time and time again, they assumed that a new and more powerful defense or assault against the Vietcong would do the trick only to find that a new and more powerful military commitment was required.

Let me, finally, turn to an everyday process of unwitting involvement: *situational entrapment*. The characteristic of this process is that behavior is typically initiated under the assumption that the environment is compliant rather than reactive—that it responds as a tool for one's purposes rather than as a self-maintaining system. Well-intentioned actions sometimes produce effects opposite to those intended because the actions do not take into account the characteristics of the setting in which they take place. By now, we are all aware that an unintended consequence of some public health measures in Latin America was the population explosion. Only now are we beginning to recognize that some consequences of the types of aid we have given to underdeveloped countries are to hinder their economic development and to foster a need for ever-increasing aid. Similarly, one may propose that the nature of the American intervention in Vietnam served to weaken the opposition to the Vietcong, demoralize those in Vietnam who were able and willing to rely on the Vietnamese to solve their problems without foreign control, increase the strength and resolution of the Vietcong, and otherwise produce the responses which required an increasing involvement and commitment of American resources and men just to prevent an immediate overturn of the situation.

A destructive conflict such as the one in Vietnam can be brought to a conclusion because the costs of continuing the conflict become so large in relation to any values that might be obtained through its continuance to one or both sides that its senselessness becomes compellingly apparent. The senselessness is likely to be most apparent to those who have not been the decision makers, and thus have little need to justify the conflict, and to those who bear the costs most strongly. Destructive conflict can also be aborted before running its full course if there is a strong enough community or strong third parties who can compel the conflicting parties to end their violence. We in the United States are in the unfortunate position that, relative to our prestige and power, there is neither a disinterested third party nor an international community that is powerful enough to motivate us to accept a compromise when we think our own interests may be enhanced by the outcome of a competitive struggle. Peace in Vietnam might have occurred much earlier if the United Nations, or even our friends, could have influenced us.

THE COURSE OF PRODUCTIVE CONFLICT

The question I wish to consider now is whether there are any distinguishing features in the process of resolving conflict that lead to constructive outcomes. Do lively, productive controversies have common patterns that are distinctive from those characterizing deadly quarrels?

I had expected to find in the social science literature more help in answering these questions than I have found so far. For example, the writings on personality development unfortunately have little to say about productive conflict; the focus is on pathological conflict. Yet, each of us knows from his own personal experiences as well as from the biographies of such men as Freud, Darwin, and St. Augustine that intense inner conflict is often (but not necessarily) the prelude to major emotional and intellectual growth. Similarly, the voluminous literature on social conflict neglects productive conflict between groups. It is true that the long standing negative view of social conflict has yielded to an outlook that stresses the social functions of conflict. Nevertheless, apart from the writings of people connected with the nonviolence movement, little attempt has been made to distinguish between conflicts that achieve social change through a process that is mutually rewarding to the parties involved in the conflict and one that is not. Yet, change can take place either through a process of confrontation, which is costly to the conflicting groups, or it can take place through a process of problem solving, which is mutually rewarding to the conflicting groups. My own predilections have led me to the hunch that the major features of productive conflict resolution would be similar, at the social level, to the processes involved in creative thinking. Let me first turn to the processes involved in creative thinking. For an incisive, critical survey of the existing literature, see Stein (1968).

Creative Thinking. The creative process has been described as consisting of several overlapping phases. Although various authors differ slightly in characterizing the phases they all suggest some sequence such as (1) an initial period that leads to the experiencing and recognition of a problem that is sufficiently arousing to motivate efforts to solve it; (2) a period of concentrated effort to solve the problem through routine, readily available, or habitual actions; (3) an experience of frustration, tension, and discomfort that follows the failure of customary processes to solve the problem and leads to a temporary withdrawal from the problem; (4) the perception of the problem from a different perspective and its reformulation in a way that permits new orientations to a solution to emerge; (5) the appearance of a tentative solution in a moment of insight, often accompanied by a sense of exhilaration; (6) the elaboration of the solution and the testing of it against reality; and finally, (7) the communication of the solution to relevant audiences.

There are three key psychological elements in this process: (1) the arousal of an appropriate level of motivation to solve the problem; (2) the development of the conditions that permit the reformulation of the problem once an impasse has been reached; and (3) the concurrent availability of diverse ideas that can be flexibly combined into novel and varied patterns. Each of these key elements is subject to influence from social conditions and the personalities of the problem solvers.

Thus consider the arousal of an optimal level of motivation, a level sufficient to sustain problem-solving efforts despite frustrations and impasses and yet not so intense that it overwhelms or prevents distancing from the problem. Neither undue smugness, satisfaction with things as they are, a sense of helplessness, terror, nor rage is likely to lead to an optimal motivation to recognize and face a problem or conflict. Nor will a passive readiness to acquiesce to the demands of the environment, nor even the willingness to fit oneself into the environment no matter how poorly it fits oneself. Optimal motivation presupposes an alert readiness to be dissatisfied with things as they are and a freedom to confront one's environment without excessive fear combined with a confidence in one's capacities to persist in the face of obstacles. The intensity of motivation that is optimal will vary with the effectiveness with which it can be controlled: the more effective the controls, the more intense the motivation can be without having disruptive consequences.

Thus one of the creative functions of conflict resides in its ability to arouse motivation to solve a problem that might otherwise go unattended. A scholar who exposes his theories and research to the scrutiny of his peers may be stimulated to a deeper analysis when he is confronted with conflicting data and theoretical analysis by a colleague. Similarly, individuals and groups who have authority and power and who are satisfied with the status quo may be aroused to recognize problems and be motivated to work on them as opposition from the dissatisfied makes the customary relations and arrangements unworkable and unrewarding and/or as they are helped to perceive the possibilities of more satisfying relations and arrangements. Acceptance of the necessity for a change in the status quo, rather than a rigid, defensive adherence to previously existing positions, is most likely, however, when the circumstances arousing new motivations suggest courses of action that contain minimal threat to the social or self-esteem of those who must change.

Thus although acute dissatisfaction with things as they are and the motivation to recognize and work at problems are necessary for creative solutions, these things are not sufficient. The circumstances conducive to the creative breaking-through of impasses are varied, but they have in common that "they provide the individual with an environment in which he does not feel threatened and in which he does not feel under pressure. He is relaxed but alert" (Stein 1968). Threat induces defensiveness and reduces both the tolerance of ambiguity and the openness to the new and unfamiliar; excessive tension leads to a primitivization and a stereotyping of thought processes. As Rokeach has pointed out, threat and excessive tension lead to the closed rather than open mind. To entertain novel ideas that may at first seem wild and implausible, to question initial assumptions of the framework within which the problem or conflict occurs, the individual needs the freedom or courage to express himself without fear of censure. In addition, he needs to become sufficiently detached from his original viewpoints to be able to see the conflict from new perspectives.

Although an unpressured and unthreatening environment facilitates the restructuring of a problem or conflict and, by so doing, makes it more amenable to solution, the ability to reformulate a problem and develop solutions is, in turn, dependent upon the availability of cognitive resources. Ideas *are* important to the creative resolution of conflict, and any factors that broaden the range of ideas and alternatives cognitively available to the participants in a conflict will be useful. Intelligence, the exposure to diverse experiences, an interest in ideas, a preference for the novel and complex, a receptivity to metaphors and analogies, the capacity to make remote associations, an independence of judgment, and the ability to play with ideas are some of the personal factors that characterize creative problem solvers. The availability of ideas is also dependent upon such social conditions as the opportunity to communicate with and be exposed to other people who may have relevant and unfamiliar ideas (i.e., experts, impartial outsiders, people facing similar or analogous situations), a social atmosphere that values innovation and originality and encourages the exchange of ideas, a social tradition that fosters the optimistic view that, with effort and time, constructive solutions can be discovered or invented to problems that initially seem intractable.

The application of full cognitive resources to the discovery and invention of constructive solutions to conflict is relatively rare. Many more resources are available for the waging of conflict. The research and development expenditures on techniques of conflict waging or conflict suppression, as well as the actual expenditures on conflict waging, dwarf the expenditures for peace building. This is obviously true at the national level, where military expenditures dominate our national budget. I would contend that this is also true at the interpersonal and intergroup levels. At the interpersonal level, most of us receive considerable training in waging or suppressing conflict, and we have elaborate institutions for dealing with adversary relations and for custodial care of the psychological casualties of interpersonal conflict. In contrast, there is little formal training in the techniques of constructive conflict resolution, and the institutional resources for helping people to resolve conflicts are meager indeed.

Cooperative problem solving. In a cooperative context, a conflict can be viewed as a common problem in which the conflicting parties have the joint interest of reaching a mutually satisfactory solution. As I have stressed throughout this work, there is nothing inherent in most conflicts that makes it impossible for the resolution of conflict to take place through a cooperative process. It is, of course, true that the occurrence of cooperative conflict resolution is less likely in certain circumstances and in certain types of conflict than in others. We shall consider some of the predisposing circumstances in a later section.

As our discussion of cooperation in chapter 2 indicated, there was a number of reasons why a cooperative process is likely to lead to productive conflict resolution:

1. It aids open and honest communication of relevant information between the participants. The freedom to share information enables the parties to go beneath the manifest to the underlying issues involved in the conflict and, thereby, to facilitate the meaningful and accurate definition of the problems they are confronting together. It also enables each party to benefit from the knowledge possessed by the other and thus to face the joint problem with greater intellectual resources. In addition, open and honest communication reduces the likelihood of the development of misunderstandings that can lead to confusion and mistrust.

2. It encourages the recognition of the legitimacy of the other's interests and of the necessity to search for a solution that is responsive to the needs of each side. It tends to limit rather than expand the scope of conflicting interests and thus minimizes the need for defensiveness. It enables the participants to approach the mutually acknowledged problem in a way that utilizes their special talents and enables them to substitute for one another in their joint work so that duplication of effort is reduced. Attempts at influence tend to be limited to processes of persuasion. The enhancement of mutual resources and mutual power becomes the objective.

3. It leads to a trusting, friendly attitude, which increases sensitivity to similarities and common interests, while minimizing the salience of differences. It stimulates a convergence of beliefs and values.

It can be seen that a cooperative process produces many of the characteristics that are conducive to creative problem solving—openness, lack of defensiveness, and full utilization of available resources. However, in itself, cooperation does not insure that problem-solving efforts will be successful. Such other factors as the imaginativeness, experience, and flexibility of the parties involved are also determinative. Nevertheless, if the cooperative relationship is one to which both parties are strongly committed, it can withstand failure and temporarily deactivate or postpone an apparently irreconcilable conflict. Or, if the conflict cannot be delayed, cooperative relations will help to contain it so that the contest for supremacy can occur under agreed upon rules.

Benevolent misperception. Just as competitive processes tend to produce characteristic forms of misperception and misjudgment, so, too, with cooperative processes. Cooperation tends to minimize differences and enhance the perception of the other's benevolence. These typical distortions often have the effect of dampening conflict and making escalation unlikely. The consequence of benevolent misperceptions is to limit the frequency and intensity of experienced opposition. It is thus not surprising that research has shown that more happily married as compared with less happily married couples are more often characterized by benevolent misperceptions of their mates rather than by an accurate view of the doubts and hostilities entertained by their spouses. It is also not surprising that other research (Keiffer 1968) has suggested that people with mutually cooperative expectations and orientations may engage in "premature cooperation." They may not explore their differences sufficiently or confront the issues between them with enough depth to enable them to come to a well-grounded, stable agreement. "Premature cooperation" may lead to a superficial, unsatisfying, and unstable agreement before the underlying issues in the conflict have been worked through.

Cooperative commitment. Earlier, I discussed several processes of unwitting involvement and commitment to a course of competitive action: dissonance reduction, the gambler's fallacy, circular, incremental magnification, and situational entrapment. These processes, similarly, can seduce one into being more deeply involved in a cooperative relationship even when the relationship is having little fruitful consequence. Past investments, already established facilities, procedures, and institutions, obligations to third parties, and situational pressures may operate to bind one to a cooperative relationship. This is so even when the emotional attachments to the other and the perceived utility of the relationship do not by themselves warrant its continuation. The bonds of a cooperative relationship may be cemented in loyalty, obligation, conformity, guilt, or convenience as well as in personal attachment and personal gain. The existence of bonds other than those based on utility and personal attitude provides a basis for continuity and stability in the face of fluctuations in personal attitude and personal gains.

FACTORS AFFECTING THE COURSE OF CONFLICT

In the preceding sections, I have described the typical features of constructive and destructive conflicts. Now I turn to a consideration of the factors that influence the course that a conflict takes. There are, inevitably, endless specific matters that may affect whether or not a conflict takes a constructive or a destructive direction. It is useful to have some simplifying idea that emphasizes central determinants and permits a proliferation of specific detail as this becomes necessary.

In reviewing the work presented thus far in this volume—my earlier theoretical analysis of the effects of cooperation and competition upon group process and my subsequent work on factors influencing whether a cooperative or a competitive relationship would develop (which has been described under such labels as "trust and suspicion," "bargaining," and "conflict resolution")—a major simplifying idea has occurred to me which I shall label *Deutsch's crude law of social relations.* It is that the *characteristic processes and effects elicited by a given type of social relationship (cooperative or competitive) tend also to elicit that type of social relationship.* Thus the strategy of power and the tactics of coercion, threat, and deception result from, and also result in, a competitive relationship. Similarly, the strategy of mutual problem solving and the tactics of persuasion, openness, and mutual enhancement elicit, and also are elicited by, a cooperative orientation.

Table 13.1 presents in condensed, outline form some of the basic ideas involved in my analysis of the effect of cooperation and competition that was presented in chapter 2. In review, the theory states that the effects of one person's actions upon another will be a function of the nature of their interdependence and the nature of the action that takes place. Skillfully executed actions of an antagonist will elicit rather different responses than skillful actions from an ally, but a bumbling collaborator may evoke as much negative reaction as an adroit opponent. The theory links type of interdependence and type of action with three basic social-psychological processes—which I have labeled *substitutability, cathexis,* and *inducibility*—and it then proliferates a variety of social-psychological consequences from these processes as they are affected by the variables with which the theory is concerned. Here, I wish to focus attention on the consequences.

The point is that if you take a situation in which there is a mixture of cooperative and competitive elements (most bargaining and conflict

TABLE 13.1. Basic Concepts in the Analysis of the
Effects of Cooperation and Competition

Type of Perceived Interdependence between P and O	*Type of Action by O*	*Effects of O's Actions on P*	*Some Theoretically Expected Consequences of an Exchange of Effective Actions between P and O in Cooperative and Competitive Relationships*
Promotive: P's and O's goals are linked in such a way that their probabilities of goal attainment are positively correlated; as one's chances increase or decrease so does the other's chances.	Effective: (O's action increases O's chances of goal attainment and, thus, also P's.)	Positive substitutability: P will not need to act to accomplish what O has accomplished. Positive cathexis: P will value O's actions and will be attracted to O in similar, future situations (i.e., as a fellow cooperator). Positive inducibility: P will facilitate O's actions and be open to positive influence from O.	Task orientation: highlighting of mutual interests; coordinated effort with division of labor and specialization of function; substitutability of effort rather than duplication; the enhancement of mutual power becomes an objective. Attitudes: trusting, friendly attitudes with a positive interest in the other's welfare and a readiness to respond helpfully to the other's needs and requests.
	Ineffective: (O's action decreases O's chances of goal attainment and, thus, also P's.)	Negative substitutability: P will need to act to accomplish what O has failed to accomplish. Negative cathexis: P will reject O's actions and will reject O in similar, future situations (i.e., as a fellow cooperator). Negative inducibility: P will hinder O's actions and be negatively influenced by O.	Perception: increased sensitivity to common interests while minimizing the salience of opposed interests; a sense of convergence of beliefs and values. Communication: open, honest communication of relevant information; each is interested in accurately informing as well as being informed; communication is persuasive rather than coercive in intent.

TABLE 13.1—*Continued*

Type of Perceived Interdependence between P and O	Type of Action by O	Effects of O's Actions on P	Some Theoretically Expected Consequences of an Exchange of Effective Actions between P and O in Cooperative and Competitive Relationships
Contrient: P's and O's goals are linked in such a way that their probabilities of goal attainment are negatively correlated; as one's chances increase, the other's decreases.	Effective: (O's action increases O's chances of goal attainment and, thus, decreases P's chances.)	Negative substitutability: P will need to act to accomplish what O has accomplished. Negative cathexis: P will dislike the occurrence of O's successes and will reject O as a future competitor. Negative inducibility: P will hinder or block O's actions and react negatively to O's influence attempts.	Task orientation: emphasis on antagonistic interests; the minimization of the other's power becomes an objective. Attitudes: suspicious, hostile attitudes with a readiness to exploit the other's needs and weakness and a negative responsiveness to the other's requests. Perception: increases sensitivity to opposed interests, to threats, and to power differences while minimizing the awareness of similarities.
	Ineffective: (O's action decreases O's chances of goal attainment and, thus, increases P's chances.)	Positive substitutability: P will not need to repeat O's mistakes. Positive cathexis: P will value the occurrence of O's failures and will prefer O as a future competitor. Positive inducibility: P will facilitate O's blunders and be ready to help O make mistakes.	Communication: little communication or misleading communication; espionage or other techniques to obtain information the other is unwilling to give; each seeks to obtain accurate information about the other but to mislead, discourage, or intimidate the other; coercive tactics are employed.

situations are of this nature), you can move it in one direction or the other by creating as initial states the typical consequences of effective cooperation and competition. All this may be summarized by saying that "cooperation breeds cooperation, while competition breeds competition." However, such a summary is much too condensed; there are other factors determining the course of conflict resolution in addition to the type of social process involved. Below is an outline of factors affecting conflict resolution that highlights crucial determinants.

Process

In table 13.1, the last column presents, in summary form, some of the key consequences of effective actions in a cooperative and a competitive relationship. Above, we have indicated that these characteristic effects tend, as initiating conditions, to elicit the same processes that have given rise to them. Thus a conflict orientation that highlights mutual interests, seeks the enhancement of mutual power, and defines the conflict as a mutual problem is more likely to take a constructive course than an orientation that emphasizes antagonistic interests, seeks to maximize power differences, and defines the conflict in win-lose terms. Similarly, a trusting, friendly orientation to the other, with a positive interest in the other's welfare and a readiness to respond helpfully to the other's needs and requests, is less likely to lead to a destructive conflict then a suspicious, hostile attitude, with a readiness to exploit the other's needs and weaknesses and a negative responsiveness to the other's requests. A perceived similarity in beliefs and values, a sense of common bonds and interests between oneself and the other, is more likely to produce a constructive conflict than a sense of opposed beliefs and values. Full, open, honest communication free of malevolent distortion, which is persuasive rather than coercive in form and intent, is less likely to lead to destructive conflict than blocked, misleading, or autistic communication.

Prior Relationship

The stronger and more salient the existing cooperative as compared with the competitive bonds linking the conflicting parties, the more likely it is that a conflict will be resolved cooperatively. The total strength of the cooperative bonds is a function of their importance as well as their number. There are obviously many different types of bonds: superordinate goals, mutually facilitating interests, common allegiances and values, linkages to a common community, and the like. These bonds are important to the extent that they serve significant needs successfully. Thus experiences of successful prior cooperative relationships between two individuals or groups enhance the likelihood of present cooperation; experiences of failure and disillusionment in attempts to cooperate make such cooperation unlikely. On the other hand, the past experience of costly competitive conflict does not necessarily enhance the probability of cooperation, although this is a possible result.

The Nature of the Conflict

There are several fundamental dimensions of conflict that I would like to spotlight here: the size of the conflict, the centrality of the issues involved, the rigidity of the issues, the number of issues involved and their interconnectedness, the consensus on issue importance, and the degree to which the conflict is acknowledged.

Conflict size. We have seen earlier that one of the characteristics of destructive conflicts is that they tend to grow in size. In a corresponding way, the research reported in chapter 11 and the theoretical discussion of intrapsychic and intergroup conflict strongly indicate that larger conflicts are more likely to take a destructive course than smaller ones. I have suggested in chapter 11 that *conflict size* might be defined as being equal to the expected difference in the value of the outcomes that a person would receive if he wins, compared with the values that he would receive if the other wins the conflict. An implication of this definition is that the more concordant the views and interests of the conflicting parties are, the smaller will be the size of their conflict. A conflict may be big because the participants perceive themselves to have important interests that are in opposition to one another, or it may be large, despite the congruence of their interests, because they have opposing views of how to pursue their important mutual interests—each thinking that his own proposed course would be favorable and the other's would be disastrous to their common interests. Thus to reduce the size of conflict, one may focus on diminishing the perceived opposition in values and interests of the conflicting parties or on decreasing the perceived opposition in their beliefs and policies about achieving their common values and interests as well as on shrinking the perceived importance of what is at stake in the conflict.

There are various techniques that can be employed to diminish perceived opposition in interests or beliefs; these include controlled communication (Burton 1969), role reversal (Cohen 1950; Rapoport 1960), and encounter group exercises (Schutz 1967). These techniques essentially assume that perceived opposition can be reduced if the conflicting parties can be led to see how much they have in common, if their differences can be seen in the context of their similarities and agreements. They also commonly assume that if misunderstandings are eliminated through improved, open, full, direct communication between the parties, their perceived differences will decrease. While this is often the case, removal of misunderstanding sometimes sharpens the awareness of conflicting interests or beliefs, an awareness that had been beclouded by benevolent misunderstandings (Johnson 1967).

It is somewhat surprising that, in the literature dealing with the therapeutic management of conflict, there has been relatively little focus on what Fisher (1964) has labeled *issue control*. Controlling the importance of what is perceived to be at stake in a conflict may be one of the most effective ways of preventing the conflict from taking a destructive course. Many conflicts may be defined in a way that either magnifies or minimizes the size of the disputed issues. In general, "here-now-this" conflicts, which are localized in terms of a given time and place and specified in terms of particular, delimited actions and their consequences, are much easier to resolve constructively than conflicts that are defined in terms of principles, precedents, rights, etc., so that the issues transcend time and space and are generalized beyond the specific action to personalities, groups, races, or other large social units or categories. Thus when a quarrel starts to center on personalities or group membership rather than specific actions, it usually takes a nonproductive turn. Similarly, when a discussion focuses on rights or principles rather than on what is specifically taking place at a given time and locale, it is not likely to be fruitful.

There is, however, an asymmetry about conflict size that should be noted. Insofar as a conflict involves a change in the status quo, keeping the conflict small may favor lack of change. This is particularly likely to be the case when there is a social inertia or bias in favor of the status quo. In such an instance, those who wish to bring about change may have to enlarge the conflict sufficiently to motivate those who see no reason to be interested in altering things as they are. Thus those endeavoring to preserve the status quo may seek to minimize conflict so that it seems not worth bothering about, while those attempting to bring about a change may try to enhance it so that it can become a focus of concerned attention.

Issue rigidity. The perceived lack of satisfactory alternatives or substitutes for the methods of achieving the outcomes or for the actual outcomes initially at stake in the conflict makes for *issue rigidity*. If an academician wants a salary increase and will not accept a promotion as a substitute, he and his financially pressed university may find themselves embroiled in an irreconcilable conflict, a conflict that would be readily resolved if a promotion were an acceptable alternative. Sometimes, motivational and intellectual limitations may lead the parties to perceive issues more rigidly than reality dictates—as when an insecure child stubbornly insists that he cannot make "duty" except in his own potty. However, it is also evident that a harsh reality may very much limit the possibility of finding acceptable substitutes and narrowly restrict the possibilities open to the conflicting parties. If there is insufficient food, shelter, clothing, medicine, or anything else required for physical and psychological survival, conflict over such necessities will often take on a desperate quality.

Issue rigidity is not only determined by the psychological and environmental resources available to the conflicting parties but also by the nature of the issue. Certain issues are less conducive to conflict resolution than others. "Greater power over the other," "victory over the other," "having more status than the other" are rigid definitions of conflict, since it is impossible on any given issue for each party in conflict to have outcomes that are superior to the other's.

Centrality of the issues. Any issue that infringes upon something considered to be vital to a person's physical well-being, socio-economic position, self-esteem, or defense against anxiety is *central*. The more central an issue is considered to be, the more likely it is to be viewed as an important or large issue and the more apt it is to be defined as a rigid one. Thus conflicts over issues that are considered to be central by both sides are often the most irreconcilable ones. The centrality of an issue is determined not only by the substantive significance of the issue, or by what values are perceived to be at stake, but also by the perceived vulnerability of the person. The more vulnerable a person considers himself to be in a given area, the more likely it is that he will view an issue bearing upon that area as a central one. There are, of course, immense differences among people in how wide a margin of security they require in order not to feel vulnerable. Those who require a large margin will generally seek to avoid conflict over central issues and, if cornered into such a conflict, will often experience it as a life-and-death struggle with no holds barred. Thus to avoid provoking the other to engage in a desperate struggle, one should avoid challenging him in his vulnerable, central regions.

The number and interdependence of the issues. A conflict in which the winner takes all and the loser gets nothing is likely to be more bitterly contested than one in which there are victories for both sides. If victories are possible for both, there is no longer one winner and one loser; rather there is a winner for each issue in the conflict. Thus it seems evident that, if a "single" conflict can be broken down into a number of separate issues so that it is no longer an all-or-nothing matter, the conflict is less likely to take a destructive course. It would, of course, do little good if all the separate issues were so interconnected that a loss on one inevitably implied a loss on all the others.

Consensus on the importance of different issues. Just as breaking down a large bundle of issues into its separate components may favor the sense of multiple victors, so may a lack of consensus on the significance of the issues. If one side considers issue A to be important and B to be insignificant while the other thinks that A is of little import and B is crucial, it is apparent that their disagreement in valuing the issues will facilitate the resolution of a conflict between them over the two issues.

Consciousness of the issues. In chapter 3, we pointed out that unacknowledged or unconscious conflict is considered harder to resolve than conflict that is recognized by the parties involved. Similarly, conflict between parties who do not recognize the existence and legitimacy of one another is more likely to be destructive than if they do. There are two major forms of unacknowledged conflict: displaced conflict and latent or repressed conflict. In displaced conflict, the conflict is shifted from the issue of primary concern to another associated issue. (See chapter 1 for a further discussion of the types of conflict.) Thus a man and wife who have an unacknowledged conflict about affection may displace their conflict into the sexual arena. They may anticipate that it would be less painful to argue about the frequency and timing of sexual relations than to discuss their needs for affectionate regard from one another.

The fashionable assumption in social science writing, except among behavior therapists, is that it is unproductive to deal with the manifest conflict unless the underlying conflict is also surfaced and faced. However, there are enough recorded instances of successful experiences in dealing with manifest conflict and thus paving the way to a productive confrontation of unacknowledged conflicts to question whether this assumption is universally valid. Successful management of the manifest conflict may give the conflicting parties the courage to face the more fundamental conflict, which was previously too anxiety-arousing to recognize. Nevertheless, it seems reasonable to expect that, unless the underlying conflict is ultimately faced, it will remain a breeding ground for various new manifest conflicts.

Repressed, latent conflict occurs when one of the conflicting parties is sufficiently dominant to make the weaker party forego any overt, conflicting behavior in pursuit of its objectives. The common result of such repression is the build-up of a malaise in the subordinate party, which takes such various forms as depression, listlessness, passive aggressiveness, and psychosomatic ailments—all accompanied by an underlying pent-up rage. Repressed conflict has malconsequences not only for the suppressed party but also for the dominant one. In addition to the passive resistance and the continuous threat of a violent outbreak of the pent-up rage from the repressed, it creates attitudes of superiority in the dominant that interfere with a cooperative confrontation of the issues in dispute once the conflict has surfaced.

The Characteristics of the Parties in Conflict

The ideologies, personalities, social positions, and personal resources of the conflicting parties all play a role in determining whether a given conflict will take a cooperative or a competitive course. They do so in two primary ways. First, they may lead directly to a more favorable evaluation of one process or the other. Thus the strategy and tactics associated with competitive struggle may seem more manly or intriguing than those associated with cooperation. Consider the contrasting popular images of the soldier and the diplomat. Or, one's image of self as tough, invincible, and unbeatable may lead one to expect that there is more to gain from competition than from cooperation. Second, they may evoke an interaction process that may result in misunderstanding and negative feelings and may, in turn, stimulate a competitive orientation to the conflict. Alternately, the characteristics of the parties may create a social process that will engender a sense of mutual understanding and compatibility which, in turn, may give rise to a cooperative orientation. That is, certain types of people will rub one another the wrong way and as a result be negative in their orientation, while other pairings of people will find one another very congenial, and, as a consequence, they will be cooperatively oriented.

There has, as yet, been only a small amount of systematic research on the personal determinants of conflict behavior. Terhune (1970 a, b) has provided an excellent recent survey of this research. My discussion, which follows below, is indebted to Terhune's summary but is not confined to it.

First of all, it is important to note that the magnitude of the effect of personality variables is very much influenced by the situation. The more competitive or threatening the situation (as determined by such factors as the available outcomes and the behavior of the other side), the smaller is the difference in behavior among different personality types. In such situations, people of various personality types all tend to be pushed toward competitive behavior. On the other hand, a cooperative situation permits the various personality types to display different behavior (see Kelley and Stahelski 1970, for related research).

Second, the personal characteristics of one side cannot fruitfully be considered apart from those of the other side. Thus, if *both* sides have high aspirations, so that each wants the major share of the available outcome, then a cooperative process is less likely than if their aspirations permit both to be satisfied. The latter would be the case if both had low aspirations or if one had low and the other had high aspirations. It is evident that some personality characteristics lead to compatibility when each member of an interacting pair displays the characteristic; with other characteristics, compatibility is fostered by dissimilarity.

Similarities in beliefs, attitudes, and values—i.e., in basic perspectives—are usually conducive to compatibility and, hence, to cooperative resolutions of conflict. Exceptions to this generalization occur in relation to competitive (dog-eat-dog) conceptions of the world and also in relation to ideologies and doctrines, which, although similar in conception, claim priority or preeminence for their adherents. Dissimilarity in outlook often leads to antagonistic relations because it is experienced as a fundamental threat to one's conception of reality and thus to one's security. On the other hand, similarity between members of a dyad in the need to dominate, to lead, to have high status, or to possess a given person or object exclusively may foster competition, whereas dissimilarity may evoke cooperation.

Clinical research on married couples (Dicks 1967) suggests that married couples are likely to deal with conflicts most productively when they have similar beliefs, attitudes, and values but a complementary dissimilarity in overt and covert needs, so that, for example, the husband's overt independence and covert dependence are complemented by the wife's overt dependence and covert independence. Presumably, each spouse obtains vicarious release of his own covert strivings from the other's overt behavior; he also obtains direct satisfaction in their reciprocal overt and covert roles.

It is reasonable to hypothesize that certain personality traits are compatible with a wide range of personalities, while other traits will be congenial to only a few. Thus Terhune (1970) reports that such personality characteristics as aggressiveness, authoritarianism, need for dominance, suspiciousness, dogmatism, tendency to derogate others, exploitativeness, and Machiavellianism tend to produce costly conflict and that cooperation is more likely to result from personalities that are egalitarian, trusting, open-minded, tolerant of ambiguity, high in need for achievement, favorable in their view of human nature. In other words, a bossy person or a suspicious person is likely to rub more people the wrong way and apt to have a narrower range of cooperative relations than a person who is egalitarian or trusting. The former types are, as a consequence of their experiences, less likely to expect others to be cooperative and are thus more apt to have pessimistic views about the possibilities of initiating a successful cooperative process.

Internal conflict and dissension within the respective parties to conflict is another characteristic that may affect the course of conflict between them. Internal conflict may result in increased external belligerence as a tactic to increase internal cohesiveness, or it may lead to external weakness and possibly tempt the other side to obtain a competitive advantage. Internal instability also interferes with cooperative conflict resolution by making it difficult to work out a durable, dependable agreement.

Estimations of Success

Many conflicts have an unplanned, expressive character in which the course of action taken is an expression of both the quality of the relationship between the participants and the characteristics of the individual participants. Other conflicts are guided by an instrumental orientation in which courses of action are consciously evaluated and chosen in terms of how likely they are to lead to satisfying outcomes. Many factors influencing the estimations of success of the different processes of conflict resolution could be listed. Those who perceive themselves to have a clear superiority in power are likely to favor an unregulated competitive process; those who perceive themselves as having a legal superiority in "rights" are likely to favor adversary relations that are regulated by legal institutions; those who are concerned with the long-range relationships, with the ability to work together in the future, are more likely to favor a cooperative process. Similarly, those who have been excluded from the cooperative process and expect the regulations to be stacked against them may think of the competitive process as the only one offering any potential of satisfaction.

Third Parties

The attitudes, strength, and resources of interested third parties are often crucial determinants of the course of conflict. Conflict between the conflicting principals may be instigated or aggravated by a third party wittingly or unwittingly—as, for example, when a child struggling with his own oedipal feelings attempts to provoke a quarrel between his parents. As the phrase *tertium gaudens* suggests, third parties can often obtain power by playing two potential rivals off against each other. The conditions under which this can be done successfully are not well understood. Research by Geis (1964) suggests, however, that those who are high rather than low in Machiavellianism are apt to be more successful in doing it.

The intervention of third parties is often constructive (see chapter 8, experiment IV). The mere intervention of an outsider in the conflict may serve to unify the conflicting parties against the outsider: both the conflicting parties may agree that it is their private conflict and both may fear or resent the intrusion of an outsider into their private affairs. It is not unusual for a violently quarreling couple to turn aggressively against someone who tries to intervene in their slugfest. Here, the third party inadvertently, by his intervention, activates and makes more salient the cohesive bonds between the conflicting parties. Third parties who are prestigeful, powerful and skillful may deliberately facilitate a constructive resolution of a conflict by using their prestige and power to encourage such a resolution and by helping provide the problem-solving resources (institutions, facilities, personnel, social norms, and procedures) to expedite discovery of a mutually satisfactory solution. The next section considers in greater detail the role of third parties in the regulation of conflict.

THE REGULATION OF CONFLICT

It is evident that conflict can be limited and controlled by institutional forms (e.g., collective bargaining, the judicial system), social roles (mediators, conciliators, referees, judges, policemen), social norms (fairness, justice, equality, nonviolence, integrity of communication, etc.), rules for conducting negotiations (when to initiate and terminate negotiations, how to set an agenda, how to present demands, etc.), and specific procedures (hinting versus explicit communication, public versus private sessions, etc.). These societal forms may be aimed at regulating how force may be employed, as in the code of a duel of honor or in certain rules of warfare; or it may be an attempt to ascertain the basic power relations of the disputants without resort to a power struggle, as is often the case in the negotiations of collective bargaining and international relations; or it may be oriented toward removing power as the basis for determining the outcome of conflict, as is often the case in judicial processes.

With regard to regulated conflict, it is pertinent to ask three central questions: (1) What are the conditions necessary for the institutionalization and regulation of conflict? (2) What are the conditions that make it likely that the regulations will be adhered to by the parties in conflict? and (3) What are the conditions under which the institutions and procedures will be used to wage conflict competitively or to resolve it cooperatively? Why would adversaries engage in a duel of honor rather than attempt to kill one another without regard to any rules? In a duel, when would a duelist prefer to die rather than to cheat? Under what conditions will the duelists use the rules to attempt to kill one another, and under what conditions will they use the same rules to restore mutual honor and esteem?

The Development of Conflict Regulation

For conflict regulation to develop, several preconditions seem required. First of all, the conflicting parties must themselves be organized. As Dahrendorf (1959, p. 226) has pointed out: "So long as conflicting forces are diffuse, incoherent aggregates, regulation is virtually impossible." *Unless each party is sufficiently internally coherent and stable to act as an organized unit so that the actions of its components are controlled and unified in relation to the conflict, it is evident that regulation cannot be effectively developed or maintained.* Thus one is not likely to engage in a duel of honor with an opponent who is so unstable and impulsive that his actions are uncontrollable—and it cannot be predicted with confidence that he will follow the rules.

Second, *each party to a conflict must be willing to recognize the legitimacy of the other party and be committed to accepting the outcome of the regulated conflict, even if it is considered to be unfavorable to his interest.* For example, an employer who is confronted with demands from a number of his workers may feel that those demands do not represent the wants of the majority of his employees and may refuse to recognize them. Under such conditions, it is unlikely that the conflict between the employer and his workers will be limited and regulated by rules and procedures that are acceptable to both sides. Also, if either an employer or a union makes clear its intention to refuse to accept the outcome of a regulated conflict if it believes the outcome is undesirable, there is little incentive for the other side to submit to being regulated. Similarly, it is hard to have a duel of honor if your opponent is not willing to accept your right to challenge him. Nor are you likely to participate in such a duel if you know that your opponent will attempt to have you injured in some underhanded way if he is defeated fairly by you.

Third, it should be noted that *the conflicts that are regulated are not likely to be the unprecedented ones.* A conflict that is recurrent provides a base of experience for developing the procedures, institutions, facilities, and social roles for limiting its destructiveness. It would be reassuring to be able to report some evidence that demonstrates that repeated experience with a given type of conflict leads to its more productive management. Unfortunately, I could find no significant research bearing upon this issue.

Finally, and perhaps most importantly, *the regulation of conflict is most likely to develop when both sides to a conflict are part of a common community.* This is so for several reasons. The community may be adversely affected by an unrestrained conflict and may, hence, exert pressures on the conflicting parties to regulate and limit their conflict and to follow the rules once they have been agreed upon. In addition, as members of a common community having similar values, traditions, and language, it may be easier for the conflicting parties to agree on rules and procedures for regulating the conflict than if they do not have this correspondence of background. Also, a common community is likely to help provide the knowledge, resources, and facilities that can expedite the development of methods of regulating a conflict. Prior experience with similar conflicts may have led the community to develop institutions and procedures for dealing with the type of conflict in which the parties are engaged. A duel of honor presupposes that the duelists have a common code of honor, a code to which all members of a given community will adhere if they want to be esteemed within that community. It also presupposes a set of social roles and procedures that have been carefully articulated within the community and that help to limit and specify the actions that may be taken by the adversaries.

Adherence to the Rules

A full examination of the conditions that influence whether rules (norms, agreements, contracts, laws, and the like) are adhered to or violated would lead to a discussion of the different forms of rule violation and social deviance, their genesis and control. Such an undertaking is beyond the scope of this work. However, it seems reasonable to assert that adherence to the rules is more likely when:

1. *The rules are known.* How accessible is the information about the rules? How much publicity have they been given and through what media of communication? How motivated and able is the individual to acquire and absorb knowledge of the rules?

2. *The rules are clear, unambiguous, and consistent.* How easy is it to understand the rules, and how clear are their implications? If one conforms to one rule, does this lead to a violation of other rules because the rules are not internally consistent?

3. *The rules are not perceived to be biased against one's own interests.* How fair are the rules? Do they give the adversary an advantage he would not otherwise have?

4. *The other adheres to the rules.* With how much confidence can one predict that the other side will also follow the rules if one abides by them? If the other violates the rules, will it be out of ignorance or mischief?

5. *Violations are quickly known by significant others.* If violations of the rules occur, how quickly will they be identified? How much advantage will the violator gain before the violation is detected? Who will know of the violations, and how influential are they?

6. *There is significant social approval for adherence and significant*

social disapproval for violations. How strong are the internalized values of conscience in the conflicting parties? Do important people and groups in the community care about whether the rules are supported or violated? Are esteem and other social benefits granted for adherence to the rules, and are there significant negative sanctions for those who violate them?

7. *Adherence to the rules has been rewarding in the past.* Have the prior experiences with the rules been rewarding or frustrating? Is there a legacy of trust or suspicion with regard to the rules and the way they have been administered in the past?

8. *One would like to be able to employ the rules in the future.* Do the adversaries envision a future that will be better because they have worked toward the preservation of the current system of rules, or is the outcome of the specific conflict more important to them than the preservation of the system? Is the system of conflict regulation held in such disrepute that the conflict participant is more concerned with destroying the system than with resolving the specific conflict?

Effective Conflict Regulation

Although adherence to the rules may be a necessary condition for conflict to be regulated productively, is it obviously not sufficient. Limited warfare as well as cooperative exchanges may be guided by rules. It is relevant to ask, for example, under what conditions the institutions and procedures of collective bargaining between union and management result in industrial peace rather than in industrial warfare.

One of the most extensive studies that attempts to answer this question was carried out under the aegis of a committee, the National Planning Association, that included many of the leading scholars and practitioners of industrial relations in the United States. The results of this investigation were published in fourteen monographs, which included case studies of harmonious union-management relations in many different industries and in many different contexts. In the conclusions to their final report (National Planning Association 1953), they list the following basic causes of industrial peace:

1. There is full acceptance by management of the collective bargaining process and of unionism as an institution. The company considers a strong union an asset to management.

2. The union fully accepts private ownership and operation of the industry; it recognizes that the welfare of its members depends upon the successful operation of the business.

3. The union is strong, responsible, and democratic.

4. The company stays out of the union's internal affairs; it does not seek to alienate the workers' allegiance to their union.

5. Mutual trust and confidence exist between the parties. There have been no serious ideological incompatibilities.

6. Neither party to bargaining has adopted a legalistic approach to the solution of problems in the relationship.

7. Negotiations are "problem-centered"—more time is spent on day-to-day problems than on defining abstract principles.

8. There is widespread union-management consultation and highly developed information-sharing.

9. Grievances are settled promptly, in the local plant whenever possible. There is flexibility and informality within the procedure.

In brief, negotiations involving conflicts of interest are more likely to have acceptable outcomes for the parties involved to the extent that they take place in a context of cooperative relations. Harmonious relations are less likely to occur if either or both sides (1) feel that their existence or their rights are under threat from the other side; (2) think that their survival is endangered by external competition from other firms or from other rival unions; (3) are torn by internal factionalism that gets displaced onto the union-management relationship; (4) have little local autonomy so that agreements cannot be responsive to local conditions; (5) are constantly subjected to changing conditions due to such factors as changes in technology, alterations in the market, seasonal variations, and turnover in management or union personnel.

So far in this section, we have discussed the regulation of conflict in some detail and tried to outline the answers to three central questions: (1) What are the conditions necessary to the institutionalization and regulation of conflict? (2) What are the conditions that make it likely that the regulations will be adhered to by the conflicting parties? and (3) What are the conditions under which the institutions and procedure will be used to wage conflict competitively or resolve it cooperatively? Now, we shall discuss the role of third parties in regulating, aborting, or undoing a malignant process of conflict resolution. The question is: How can a third party intervene therapeutically if negotiations are deadlocked or unproductive because of misunderstandings, faulty communications, the development of hostile attitudes, or the inability to discover a mutually satisfying solution?

If one examines such roles as those of the mediator in industrial negotiations (Douglas 1962; Stevens 1963; Kressel 1972), the intervenor in community disputes (Cormick 1971), the psychotherapist doing marital therapy (Bach and Wyden 1969), the human relations consultant working with intergroup conflicts of various sorts (Chalmers and Cormick 1971; Walton 1969), or the international conciliator (Iklé 1964; Jackson 1952; Bailey 1971; Edmead 1971; and Pechota 1971), a number of common functions can be identified.[1] These are considered below.

Helping the conflicting parties identify and confront the issues in conflict. Conflicts are often suppressed, avoided, or evaded and sometimes, as a consequence, displaced. A married couple may be irritated with one another over trivia because they have not faced directly their conflicting views about their respective household responsibilities. One of the major tasks of a third party is to help the conflicting parties identify and confront the issues about which they disagree. There are many ways in which this can be done. First of all, the mere presence of a supportive, skilled, neutral, discreet third party may sufficiently relieve the anxieties of the conflicting parties about the possibilities of an uncontrolled, catastrophic blowup that they will be able to deal with issues that they might otherwise think would be too hot to handle. In addition, his presence may serve as a continuing reminder and prod to come to grips with the issues, to get down to the real business. Second, a third party may try to alter the asymmetries in motivation, power, or legitimacy between the conflicting parties. Such asymmetries often lead to conflict evasion or suppression. Conflict is more likely to be faced openly if both (rather than one) of the conflicting parties are motivated to deal with the issues, if the balance of power is such that neither side can impose its decision on the other, and if both sides recognize the other's legitimacy. Thus in a dispute between the First Spanish Methodist Church in East Harlem and a community protest organization called the Young Lords Organization (YLO), the

---

1. In addition to drawing upon relevant literature, I have drawn upon my own experience as a psychotherapist working with individuals, couples, and families and also upon some experience as a consultant working on problems of intergroup relations.

Board of Mediation for Community Disputes helped legitimize the YLO and give it a degree of stature by recognizing it as representative of a given constituency (Cormick 1971). In addition, by vouching for the YLO's "reasonableness" and willingness to heed an agreement, the prestigious board placed considerable pressure upon the church to enter negotiations with a group it previously had refused to acknowledge. Third parties can not only aid the conflicting parties to confront one another, but they may also help identify the real issues in conflict. The rhetoric of the conflicting parties, or the proliferation of issues during a protracted dispute, may obscure the underlying issues. A skillful third party who can interview each party separately, as well as view them in interaction, may develop a clear picture of what they agree and disagree about, and he may be able to use this picture to help *them* identify the substance of their conflict.

Helping provide favorable circumstances and conditions for confronting the issues. A third party can help create an atmosphere within which meaningful discussions may occur by providing a meeting place on neutral ground where the conflicting parties can be divorced from the immediate pressures and disruptions due to everyday irritations. In addition, by his intervention he can frequently regulate the degree of tension between the parties by suggesting that they move to more or less "hot" issues; by creating restraints to inhibit certain kinds of destructive behavior; or by using encouragement to foster constructive actions. Thus he can often stimulate sufficient tension to keep a serious dialogue going or remove the excess tension that might disrupt a productive encounter. Also, he can help arrange and time confrontations so that the conflicting parties are both ready to engage in the discussion and so that neither of the conflicting parties feels that the readiness to engage in a dialogue is an admission of weakness.

Helping remove the blocks and distortions in the communication process so that mutual understanding may develop. Doing this entails such diverse activities as: stimulating sufficient communication from both parties so that the less articulate as well as the more articulate can both express their views fully; translating so that the communications are understood the same way by both sides; and training the conflicting parties in how to communicate more effectively and how to check whether they are being understood by one another. In marital conflicts, for example, it is not uncommon for one spouse to be more articulate and more dominant than the other. The marital therapist must see to it that both sides to the conflict get expressed. It is also not unusual for husbands and wives to misunderstand one another; wives more often use the particularistic language of a personal-emotional relationship, in which statements are verifiable in terms of subjective feelings, while husbands more commonly employ the universalistic language of impersonal social relations, in which statements are objectively verifiable. Thus a wife will say, "I'll be ready in a minute," and mean, "I'll be ready in what I feel will be a short time." But her husband may interpret the statement in clock time. Wives frequently are hurt because their husbands do not say "I love you" often enough. Husbands, typically, assume that having said that they love their wives implies that they will continue to love them unless the husbands say otherwise. Therefore, reiteration seems unnecessary to the men. A skilled third party will understand the sociocultural differences that lead one side to misunderstand the other and will not only serve as a translator but will also help the two sides understand the contexts and frameworks that give the other's communications their meaning. In addition, he will train them to use feedback to check how well they are understanding the other by verifying, from time to time, that the other has said what one thinks he has said and, similarly, that the other has understood what one has intended to communicate.

4. *Helping establish such norms for rational interaction as mutual respect, open communication, the use of persuasion rather than coercion, and the desirability of reaching a mutually satisfying agreement.* In other words, the conflicting parties are helped to fight fairly, that is, to fight under rules that prevent them from hitting one another below the belt or from yelling foul when a fair but intense exchange is taking place (Bach and Wyden 1969). This is perhaps one of the most important functions of the third party when he is dealing with inexperienced disputants. The inexperienced are likely to engage in such tactics as: hitting at the other side's sensitive spots; generalizing rather than being specific, so that the issues in conflict become broad and diffuse rather than limited and clearly focused; defining issues in absolutistic terms that leave no room for give and take or in moralistic terms that imply that if the other yields, he is confessing guilt; issuing ultimatums and threats that imply that the other has no alternative but to yield; and bluffing indiscriminately so that is is impossible to know when one should be taken seriously.

Fair rules of procedure are valuable in any kind of discussion but are vital in conflicts. The essence of fair rules is that they are unbiased. Adherence to such rules implies that each of the conflicting parties is willing to let the other do unto him that which he does unto the other. Such rules give both sides equal opportunity to state positions and respond to the other. In addition, they limit or define the kinds of injury that each side can inflict upon the other. They also make each side responsible for the positions it takes and the behavior it engages in, so that neither side can disregard reality, lie at will, nor attribute its actions to others and, by so doing, disown them. Further, such rules often require each party, when criticizing the other, to offer the other an alternative in the form of a "yessable proposition" (Fisher 1969). Such a proposition states specifically what kind of decision or action is wanted from the other and is not merely a statement of dissatisfaction with what the other is doing or offering. Even if the other is willing to surrender, he must know what he is to do so that his surrender will be recognized and will lead to a cessation of hostilities.

Fair rules for regulating conflict provide a basis for resolving a conflict when no other basis for agreement can be found: first choice goes to the winner of the contest. However, the winner in a fair contest is not necessarily the sole survivor as may be the case in an uncontrolled test of power. The value and procedures regulating the conflict may select the winner on some other criterion than the relative physical might of the contestants. A conflict between husband and wife or between the United States and one of its citizens may be settled by a judicial process whose rules permit the contestant with the stronger legal claim to win even though his physical prowess may be weaker. Or the rules may make the contest one of intellectual rather than physical power. Thus, through the rules that are employed in regulating conflict, a society may encourage the survival of certain values and the extinction of others because the rules tend to favor those who possess the resources of one rather than the other—e.g., those who possess moral right rather than physical might.

Although norms that encourage fair rules for fighting are useful in limiting the destructiveness of a struggle, they are often not sufficient to encourage cooperative negotiations. The latter are facilitated by norms that emphasize recognition of the other's legitimacy, mutual respect, the desirability of a mutually satisfying agreement, and open communication. The third party, by recognizing the legitimacy of

both sides, by treating each side with respect, by encouraging direct-
ness of communication, and by emphasizing that stable agreements
are based on mutual satisfaction, can do much to promote a social
framework that is conducive to cooperative negotiations rather than
merely fair combat.

5. *Helping determine what kinds of solutions are possible and
making suggestions about possible solutions.* By careful listening and
probing, the third party can often discover the aspirations and expectations of each side and learn how rigidly fixed they are. Sometimes a
solution requires that the aspirations of one or both of the conflicting
parties be altered and made more realistic. If each conflicting party is
expecting the other side to do what is impossible for it to do, each has
to redefine his aspirations before a solution is possible. A discontented
wife cannot reasonably expect her introverted husband to become a
social lion, and a union cannot realistically hope that an employer
will pay wages that will be substantially higher than those paid by his
competitors and that will, as a consequence, drive him out of business. The third party can use his expert knowledge and authority to
try to curb unrealistic aspirations. He can often go beyond this to
make suggestions for potential agreements that could be acceptable to
both sides. In doing so, he may find it necessary to help the conflicting
parties redefine their problem so that previously unconceived alternatives may be considered. Thus, for example, a third party may suggest
that the solution to a money dispute about who gets what share of the
financial pie may lie in pooling efforts to enlarge the pie that is to be
shared. Of course, a third party who offers a specific suggestion
should do it in a way that will enable the conflicting parties to feel
that they may accept or reject the suggestion, that it is a solution that
they "own" and for which they are responsible if they agree to it.

6. *Helping make a workable agreement acceptable to the parties
in conflict.* Although a feasible compromise or a productive solution
to the conflict may be known to the conflicting parties, they may be
resistant because each may feel that such an agreement will seem like
a retreat and result in a loss of face. Various tactics are available to a
third party in overcoming this kind of resistance. He may emphasize
the futility and costs of false pride—no better agreement is likely to
be reached and the costs of continued strife may be unbearable. Alter-
natively, he may try to present the agreement so that each side can
think it has won a victory. This may happen if each side is led to be-

lieve that he has obtained what he wanted on a crucial issue. Or, the third party may apply pressure to achieve agreement through such tactics as threatening to withdraw if an agreement is not reached within a specified time, confining the conflicting parties to a locked room until they agree, and enlisting the public or other significant parties in support of the agreement. Although forced agreements are generally not desirable because the parties may not feel committed to them, it is sometimes true that disputants have to be forced to accept an agreement that they normally would be happy to accept in order to create the impression among their constituents that they did the only thing they could under the circumstances.

7. *Helping make the negotiators and the agreement that is arrived at seem prestigeful and attractive to interested audiences, especially the groups represented by the negotiators.* The negotiators of an agreement may be the principals to the conflict, or they may be agents or representatives of the conflicting parties. In the latter case, the agreement must be acceptable to the principals as well as to the negotiators. However, even when the principals do the negotiating, their subsequent attitudes toward any agreement at which they arrive will be, in part, determined by the reactions of significant others to it. Thus it is useful for the third party to help the negotiators sell the agreement, that is, make it appear meritorious and warranting approval and support.

I have outlined above the functions that a third party can perform in helping conflicting parties come to a constructive resolution of their conflict. But how does this third-party role get established and accepted? Elmore Jackson's (1952) historical survey of mediation in his book *Meeting of Minds* suggests that such social institutions as mediation are most apt to develop when there are powerful third parties, as in a cohesive community, with an interest in preventing destructive strife because of the damage it does to the community or because of the harm it does to the parties in conflict. It seems reasonable to speculate that such institutions initially arise in response to the occurrence of destructive conflict as an attempt to limit the destructiveness. It also seems probable that if the third-party role develops a reputation for being successful in preventing or limiting destructive conflict, and if such third parties are easily accessible to act as mediators, conciliators, or counselors, parties in conflict who have reached an impasse will tend to seek help before rather than after engaging in a destructive struggle. If the foregoing speculations are correct, then, it would be socially valuable to encourage the development of highly visible neighborhood conciliation centers that could be used by people or groups who are involved in unproductive conflict. There is, I suggest, a general lack of readily accessible, prestigeful, skilled, impartial, discreet, third parties to help those entangled in bitter conflict. Family controversies, neighborhood disputes, intergroup conflicts, and the like would often be resolved more productively if such help were easily available.

I have indicated above that third parties can help in resolving disputes constructively to the extent that they are *known, readily accessible, prestigeful, skilled, impartial,* and *discreet.* Each of these qualities is necessary if conflicting parties are to seek out help and receive it successfully from third parties. Perhaps the most ambiguous of these terms is *skilled.* What are the skills of a "skilled" mediator, therapist, or conciliator, and how are they acquired? At this time, there are no good answers to these questions. This is partly due to a lack of clear criteria for success; it is partly due to the discreet, nonpublic nature of many of the third party's activities, which makes them difficult to observe and study; it is partly the mystique of traditional views that emphasize the elusive, idiosyncratic, personal nature of all third-party interventions; and it is partly the lack of a systematic theory of intervention into conflicts. It seems abundantly clear that answers to these questions will require systematic inquiry into the assumptions underlying the interventions in conflict of mediators, conciliators, and the like and systematic study of different kinds of interventions and their effects.

CHANGING THE COURSE OF CONFLICT

By now, it should be evident that I believe that a *mutually cooperative* orientation is likely to be the most productive one for resolving conflict. Yet it must be recognized that the orientations of the conflicting parties may not be mutual. One side may experience the conflict and be motivated to resolve it; the other side may be content with things as they are and not even be aware of the other's dissatisfaction. Or, both may recognize the conflict, but one may be oriented to a win-lose solution while the other may be seeking a cooperative resolution. We have suggested earlier that the usual tendency for such asymmetries in orientation is to produce a change toward mutual competition rather than mutual cooperation. It is, after all, possible to attack, overcome, or destroy another without his consent, but to co-operate with another, one must be willing or, at least, compliant.

How can Acme induce Bolt to cooperate in resolving a conflict if Bolt is not so inclined or if Bolt perceives his interests as antagonistic to Acme's? There is, obviously, no single answer to this question. What answer is appropriate depends upon such factors as: the nature and motivation of Bolt's noncooperation, the particular resources and vulnerabilities of each party, and their relationships to third parties. However, it is evident that the search for an answer must be guided by the realization that there are dangers in certain types of influence procedures. Namely, they may boomerang and increase open resistance and alienation, or they may merely elicit sham or inauthentic cooperation with underlying alienation.

Let me summarize, from my discussion of social influence in chapter 6, some hypotheses about the types of influence procedures that are likely to elicit resistance and alienation:

1. *Illegitimate techniques,* which violate the values and norms governing interaction and influence that are held by the other, are alienating (the greater the violation, i.e., the more important and the more numerous the values being violated, the greater the resistance). It is, of course, true that sometimes an adaptation-level effect occurs so that a norm loses its illegitimacy if it is violated frequently; at other times, the accumulation of violations tends to produce an increasingly negative reaction.

2. *Negative sanctions* such as punishments and threats tend to elicit more resistance than do positive sanctions such as promises and rewards. What is considered to be rewarding or punishing may also be influenced by one's adaptation level; the reduction of the level of the rewards that are customarily received will usually be viewed as negative.

3. Sanctions that are *inappropriate* in kind are also likely to elicit resistance. Thus the reward of money rather than appreciation may decrease the willingness to cooperate of someone whose cooperation is engendered by affiliative rather than utilitarian motives. Similarly, a threat or punishment is more likely to be effective if it fits the crime than if its connection with the crime is artifi-

cial. A child who breaks another child's toy is punished more appropriately if he has to give the child a toy of his own as a substitute than if he is denied permission to watch TV.

4. Influence that is *excessive* in magnitude tends to be resisted; excessive promise or reward leads to the sense of being bribed, and excessive threat or punishment leads to the feeling of being coerced.

I have, so far, outlined what one should *not* do if one wants to elicit authentic cooperative conflict resolution. Let me turn now to the question of what courses of action can be taken to induce cooperation. I wish to focus on a particularly important kind of conflict: conflict between those groups that have considerable authority to make decisions and relatively high control over the conventional means of social and political influence and those groups that have little decision-making authority and relatively little control over the conventional means of influence. Although there have always been conflicts between the ruler and the ruled, between parents and children, and between employers and employees, I suggest that this is the characteristic conflict of our time. It arises from the increasing demand for more power and prosperity from those who have been largely excluded from the processes of decision making, usually to their economic, social, psychological, and physical disadvantage. The racial crisis in the United States, the student upheavals throughout the world, the revolutionary struggles in the underdeveloped areas, the controversies within and between nations in eastern Europe, and the civil war in South Vietnam: all these conflicts partly express the growing recognition at all levels of social life that social change is possible, that things do not have to remain as they are, that one can participate in the shaping of one's environment, and that one can improve one's lot.

It is apparent that those who are content with their superior roles in the decision-making process may develop a vested interest in preserving the status quo and appropriate rationales for this purpose. These rationales generally take the form of attributing superior competence (more ability, knowledge, skill) and/or superior moral value (greater initiative, drive, sense of responsibility, self-control) to oneself compared to those of lower status. The rationales are usually accompanied by sentiments that lead their possessors to react with disapproval and resistance to attempts to change the power relations and with apprehension and defensiveness to the possibility that these attempts will succeed. The apprehension is often a response to the expectation that the change will leave one in a powerless position under the control of those seeking revenge for past injustices.

What can a less powerful group (Acme) do to reduce or overcome the defensiveness of a more powerful group (Bolt) and to increase the latter's readiness to share power? Suppose, in effect, that as social scientists we were consultants to the poor and weak rather than to the rich and strong. What would we suggest? Let me note that this would be an unusual and new position for most of us. If we have given any advice at all, it has been to those in high power. The unwitting consequence of this one-sided consultant role has been that we have too often assumed that the social pathology has been in the ghetto rather than in those who have built the walls to surround it, that the disadvantaged are the ones who need to be changed rather than the people and the institutions who have kept the disadvantaged in a submerged position.

But given the resistance and defensiveness of those in high power, what can we recommend to those in low power as a strategy of persuasion? The process of persuasion starts with the communicator's having a message that he wants to get across to the other. He must have an objective if he is to be able to articulate a clear and compelling message. Further, in formulating and communicating his message, it is important to recognize that it will be heard not only by the other but also by one's own group and by other interested audiences. The desirable effects of a message on its intended audience may be negated by its unanticipated effects on those for whom it was not intended.

I suggest that Acme's message to Bolt, to be effective, should include the following basic elements:

1. *A clear statement of the specific actions and changes being requested of Bolt.* Bolt should know what is expected of him so that he can fulfill Acme's expectations if he so desires. Presumably, Bolt is more apt to do what Acme wishes if Bolt believes that it is possible for him to do so. He is more likely to believe that this is the case if Acme's wants are perceived to be specific and limited rather than if they are viewed as vague and unbounded.

2. *An appreciation of the difficulties, problems, and costs that Bolt*

anticipates if he complies with Acme's wishes. Such an appreciation should be combined with an expressed willingness to cooperate with Bolt to overcome the difficulties and reduce the costs. This willingness entails a readiness on Acme's part to consider Bolt's proposals and counterproposals and to modify his own initial proposals so that a mutually responsive agreement can be reached.

3. *A depiction of the values and benefits that Bolt will realize by cooperating with Acme.* In effect, if Bolt can be persuaded that he has more to gain than to lose by doing what Acme wants, obviously, he is more likely to do it. The important gains reside in the possibility that Bolt, by sharing power with Acme, may enhance Acme's general cooperativeness and thus markedly increase Bolt's fulfillment of his own objectives. Thus there are many instances in labor-management, student-faculty, and warden-prisoner relations that indicate that the more powerful party has gained enormously through enhancing the power (and thus the sense of responsibility) of the weaker party. In addition, other dissatisfactions that Bolt has experienced in his relationship with Acme may be reduced by Acme's enhanced cooperativeness. Other sources of potential gain for Bolt reside in the enhanced reputation and goodwill that he will obtain from influential third parties and in the greater fulfillment he will experience when Acme is content rather than dissatisfied with their relationship.

4. *A statement of the negative, harmful consequences that are inevitable for Bolt's values and objectives if Acme's wishes are not responded to positively.* In effect, Bolt has to be led to understand the costs of nonagreement—so that he can realize that the costs of agreement are not the only ones to be taken into account. Potential costs for Bolt of a failure to come to an agreement include: the losses resulting from a decrease in Acme's future cooperativeness, including the possibility of Acme's total noncooperation; losses in esteem and goodwill, and also possibly the loss of cooperation, of significant third parties; losses due to active attempts to embarrass, harass, obstruct, or destroy the interests of Bolt by Acme or his sympathizers.

5. *An expression of the power and resolve of Acme to act effectively and unwaveringly to induce Bolt to come to an acceptable agreement.* Acme's unshakable commitment to induce a change may affect Bolt by convincing him that Acme's needs are serious rather than whimsical and thus deserve fulfillment. It may also persuade Bolt that the pressure from Acme will not diminish until an acceptable

agreement has been reached. However, if Bolt has no concern whatsoever for Acme's needs and no belief that Acme's pressure will be sufficiently strong to be disturbing, Acme must attempt to develop, mobilize, and publicize its power sufficiently to convince Bolt that negotiation would be a prudent course of action.

A message that contains the above elements strongly commits Acme to his objective yet suggests that the means of attaining it are flexible and potentially responsive to Bolt's views. Because the objective is articulated so as to be specific and limited, it is more likely to be considered by Bolt as feasible for him to accept than is one stated in more generalized and grandiose terms. The message provides Bolt with the positive prospect that change will result in enhanced social and self-esteem and will yield the benefits to be derived from increased cooperation from Acme. It also indicates the negative results to be expected from lack of change. Although Acme's firm intent to alter the status quo is made evident, his stance throughout is cooperative. The possibility of a true mutual exchange is kept open with explicit recognition that the dissatisfactions and the problems are not one-sided.

Rage or fear in the low-power group often makes it impossible for the members of that group to communicate a message of the sort described above. Rage leads to an emphasis on destructive, coercive techniques and precludes offers of authentic cooperation. Fear, on the other hand, weakens the commitment to the steps necessary to induce a change and lessens the credibility regarding the idea that compliance will be withdrawn if change does not occur. Rage is potentially a more useful emotion than fear since it leads to actions that are less damaging to the development of a sense of power and, hence, of self-esteem. Harnessed rage or outrage can be a powerful energizer for determined action, and if this action is directed toward building one's own power rather than destroying the other's power, the outrage may have a socially constructive outcome.

In any case, it is evident that when intense rage or fear is the dominant emotion, the cooperative message outlined here is largely irrelevant. Both rage and fear are rooted in a sense of helplessness and powerlessness; they are emotions associated with a state of dependency. Those in low power can overcome these debilitating emotions by their own successful social action on matters of significance to them. In the current slang, they have to "do their own thing"; it cannot be given to them or done for them. This is why my emphasis has been on the sharing of power, and thus increasing one's power to affect one's fate, rather than on the sharing of affluence. While the sharing of affluence is desirable, it is not sufficient. In its most debilitating sense, poverty is a lack of power and not merely a lack of money. Money is, of course, a base for power, but it is not the only one. If one chooses to be poor, as some members of religious or pioneering groups do, the psychological syndrome usually associated with imposed poverty—a mixture of dependency, apathy, small time-perspective, suspicion, fear and rage—is not present.

Thus the ability to offer and engage in authentic cooperation presupposes an awareness that one is neither helpless nor powerless, even though one is at a relative disadvantage. Not only independent action but also cooperative action requires a recognition and confirmation of one's capacity to "go it alone" if necessary. Unless one has the freedom to choose *not* to cooperate, there can be no free choice *to* cooperate. Black power is thus a necessity for black cooperation, black cooperation with blacks as well as with whites. Powerlessness and the associated lack of self- and group esteem are not conducive to either internal group cohesiveness or external cooperation. Black power does not, however, necessarily lead to cooperation. This is partly because, in its origin and rhetoric, black power may be oriented against white power and thus is likely to intensify the defensiveness of those with high power.

However, even if power is "for" rather than "against," and even if it provides a basis for authentic cooperation, cooperation may not occur because it is of little import to the high-power group. This group may be unaffected by the positive or negative incentives that the low-power group controls; it does not need their compliance. Universities can obtain new students; the affluent nations no longer are so dependent upon the raw materials produced in the underdeveloped nations; the white industrial society does not need many unskilled Negro workers.

Apart from resigning into apathy, what can a low-power group do in such situations? Basically, there is only the possibility of increasing its relative power sufficiently to compel the other to negotiate. Relative power is increased by either of two means: increasing one's own power or decreasing the other's power. Attempts to change power can be directed at altering the resources that underlie power (such as wealth, physical strength, organization, knowledge, skill, trust, respect, and affection), or it can be directed toward modifying the effectiveness with which the resources of power are employed. Potential power may not be converted into effective power because those who possess such power may not be aware of their power, or they may not be motivated to use it, or they may use their power inefficiently and unskillfully so that much potential power is wasted. Thus, as we have seen in chapter 5, effective power depends upon the following key elements: (1) the control or possession of resources to generate power; (2) the awareness of the resources one possesses or controls; (3) the motivation to employ these resources to influence others; (4) skill in converting the resources into usable power; and (5) good judgment in employing this power so that its use is appropriate in type and magnitude to the situation in which it is used.

By operating on one or more of the key elements listed above, a low-power group can work to increase its own power or to decrease the power of the high-power group opposing it. There are, of course, endless ways in which each of the key elements can be affected; which of the ways are suitable to employ at any given time will be determined by the particular circumstances. Nevertheless, it is safe to assume that low-power groups generally lack control over the resources, such as money, guns, and official position, that are immediately related to economic, military, and political power. Their primary resources are discontented people and having "justice" on their side.

The utility of people as a resource of power is a function of their *number,* their *personal qualities* (such as their knowledge, skill, dedication, and discipline) their *social cohesion* (as reflected in mutual trust, mutual liking, mutual values, and mutual goals), and their *social organization* (as expressed in effective coordination and communication, division of labor and specialization of function, planning, and evaluation). Numbers of people are obviously important but undoubtedly not as important as their personal qualities, social cohesion, and social organization. A large, inchoate mass of undisciplined, ineffectual people are at the mercy of a small, dedicated, disciplined, well-organized, cohesive group. Most large groups are controlled by less than 10 percent of their membership by virtue of organized activity in the face of a passive mass membership.

If one examines such low-power minority groups as the Jews, the Chinese, and the Japanese, which have done disproportionately well in the United States and in other countries to which they have migrated, it is apparent that these groups have been characterized by high social cohesion and effective social organization combined with an emphasis upon the development of such personal qualities as skill, dedication, and discipline. Similarly, the effectiveness of such guerrilla forces as the Vietcong has been, in part, due to their social cohesion, social organization, and personal dedication. Clearly, the development of these characteristics is of prime importance as a means of increasing the power of one's group.

In chapter 4 we considered some of the determinants of cohesion. Here I would add that groups become cohesive by formulating and working together on issues that are specific, immediate, and realizable. They become effectively organized as they plan how to use their resources to achieve their purposes and as they evaluate their past effectiveness in the light of their experiences. It is apparent that the pursuit of vague, far-in-the-future, grandiose objectives will not long sustain a group's cohesiveness. Nor will the exclusive pursuit of a single issue be likely to sustain a long-enduring group unless that issue proliferates into many subissues. Those intent upon developing social cohesion and social organization should initially seek out issues that permit significant victories quickly; they should set out on a protracted, indeterminate struggle only after strongly cohesive and effective social organizations have been created.

So far, I have stressed personal qualities, social cohesion, and social organization as resources that can be developed by low-power groups to enhance their power. Typically, such resources are vastly underdeveloped in low-power groups; however, they are necessary to the effective utilization of almost every other type of resource, including money, votes, tools, force, and the like. Low-power groups often have two other key assets that can be used to amplify their other resources: discontent and the sense of injustice. If intense enough, these may provide the activating motivation and the continuing determination to change the status quo. They are the energizers for individual and social action to bring about change. Moreover, to the extent that the basis for discontent and the nature of the injustice can be communicated to others so that they experience it, if only vicariously, then supporters and allies will be attracted to the side of the low-power group. And increasing the number of one's supporters and allies is another important way of increasing one's power.

As we have seen in earlier chapters, discontent and the sense of injustice may be latent rather than manifest in a subordinated group. Neither the consciousness of oneself as disadvantaged nor the consciousness of being a member of a class of disadvantaged people may exist psychologically. If this is the case, "consciousness-raising" tactics are necessary precursors to the development of group cohesion and social organization. The diversity of consciousness-raising tactics has been illustrated by the variety of techniques employed in recent years by women's liberation groups and black power groups. They range from quasi-therapeutic group-discussion meetings, through mass meetings and demonstrations, to dramatic confrontations of those in the high-power groups. It is likely that a positive consciousness of one's disadvantaged identity is most aroused when one sees someone, who is considered to be similar to oneself, explicitly attacked (or disadvantaged) because of his disadvantaged identity but also sees the attack resisted successfully. The attack and resistance reveal both the wound and its cure.

By raising to consciousness the discontent and sense of injustice, a powerful and persisting energy for change is activated. If this energy can be harnessed through skilled and disciplined action by dedicated individuals in effectively organized, cohesive groups, then a very powerful instrument for social change has been forged, and the situation of the low-power group has been radically altered. It is now in a position to offer significant positive or negative incentives to those in high power. The positive incentives are those deriving from enhanced cooperation, while the negative incentives are those of noncooperation, harassment, obstruction, or destruction.

Negative incentives are the losses that the high-power group, or "haves," expects to experience as a consequence of a power struggle with the low-power group, or "have-nots." As Alinsky (1971, p. 152) has pointed out: "The basic tactic in warfare against the Haves is a mass political jujitsu: the Have-Nots do not rigidly oppose the Haves, but yield in such planned and skilled ways that the superior strength of the Haves becomes their own undoing." As in physical jujitsu, the inertia, momentum, and imbalance of the adversary are used as weapons against him.

Thus, as Alinsky further suggests, ". . . since the Haves publicly pose as the custodians of responsibility, morality, law and justice (which are frequently strangers to each other), they can be constantly pushed to live up to their own book of morality and regulations. No organization, including organized religion, can live up to the letter of its own book."

Alinsky (1971) cites many examples of tactics in which bureaucratic systems were ensnarled in their own red tape by pressure to live up to their own formally stated rules and procedures. Tactics of this sort may center upon demanding or using a service that one is entitled to, a service that is not ordinarily used so massively and for which the institution is not prepared to provide in large volume without excessive cost to itself. For example, banks may be disrupted by a massive opening and closing of accounts, department stores by massive returns of purchases, airports by a massive use of their toilets and urinals by visitors, and so forth. Or, the tactics may center upon disobedience to a rule or law that cannot be enforced in the face of massive noncompliance. Thus landlords cannot afford to throw out all tenants who refuse to pay rents in a cohesive rent strike or schools to dismiss all students who disobey an obnoxious regulation—if the students are united in their opposition.

Related to the tactic of clubbing the haves with their own book of rules and regulations is the tactic of goading them into errors such as violating their own rules or regulations. If they can be provoked into an obvious disruption of their own stated principles, then segments of the high-power group may become disaffected with the resultant weakening of the haves. In addition, previously neutral third parties may, in response to the violations by those in power, swing their sympathies and support to the have-nots.

In general, it is a mistake to think that a high-power group is completely unified. Most groups have internal divisions and conflict among their most active members; further, only a small proportion of their members are likely to be active supporters of current policy. The conflicts among those who are active in the high-power groups and the distinction between active and passive members provide important points of leverage for the have-nots. The internal conflict can be exacerbated by fostering mutual suspicion and by playing one side against the other. The passive compliance of the inactive majority of the haves may disappear as their leaders are provoked into intemperate errors and as they are subject to ridicule and embarrassment by their inability to cope effectively with the persisting harassments and nuisances caused by the have-nots.

The power of the haves, as is true of any group, depends upon such tangibles as control over the instruments of force, an effective communication system, and an effective transportation system and upon such intangibles as prestige and the aura of invincibility. While a low-power group may not be able to interfere seriously with the tangible bases of power of the haves without engaging in illegal, destructive actions of sabotage, it has many legal means of tarnishing and weakening their intangible sources of power. Ridicule and techniques of embarrassment are most effective weapons for this purpose. Here, as elsewhere, inventiveness and imagination play an important role in devising effective tactics. Alinsky, a master at inventing such tactics, illustrates with the following hypothetical example (1971, p. 141):

> Imagine the scene in the U.S. Courtroom in Chicago's recent conspiracy trial of the seven if the defendants and counsel had anally trumpeted their contempt for Judge Hoffman and the system. What could Judge Hoffman, the bailiffs or anyone else, do? Would the judge have found them in contempt for farting? Here was a tactic for which there was no legal precedent. The press reaction would have stunk up the judge for the rest of time.

Other tactics of embarrassment and ridicule include the picketing of such people as slum landlords, key stockholders, and management personnel of recalcitrant firms and other such wielders of power in situations that are embarrassing to them—e.g., at their homes, at their churches or synagogues, at their social clubs. The advantage of such tactics as ridicule and embarrassment is that they are often very enjoyable for those in low power and very difficult for those in high power to cope with without further loss of face.

Over the preceding several pages, I have discussed some of the strategies and tactics available to low-power groups in their attempt to compel a resistant high-power group to agree to a change in their relations. My discussion was meant to be suggestive rather than comprehensive. It was also intended to indicate that apathetic resignation or destructiveness are not the only responses available in the face of a contrary authority. It is possible to increase the power of the have-nots by developing their personal resources, social cohesion, and social organization so that they have more influence. And in jujitsu fashion, it is possible for the have-nots to employ some of the characteristics of the haves to throw the haves off balance and reduce their effective opposition.

CONCLUSION

As I review this last section, where I have functioned as a self-appointed consultant to those in low power, I am struck by how little of what I have said is well grounded in systematic research or theory. Social scientists have rarely directed their attention to the defensiveness and resistance of the strong and powerful in the face of the need for social change. They have not considered what strategies and tactics are available to low-power groups and which of these are likely to lead to a productive rather than a destructive process of conflict resolution. They have focused too much on the turmoil and handicaps of those in low power and not enough on the defensiveness and resistance of the powerful; the former will be overcome as the latter is overcome.

Is it not obvious that, with the great disparities in power and affluence within nations and between nations, there will be continuing pressures for social change? And is it not also obvious that the processes of social change will be disorderly and destructive unless those in power are able, or enabled, to lower their defensiveness and resistance to a change in their relative status? Let us refocus our efforts so that we will have something useful to say to those who are seeking radical but peaceful social change. Too often in the past, significant social change in the distribution of power has been achieved at the cost of peace; this is a luxury that the world is no longer able to afford.

Bibliography

Adams, S. 1953. Status congruency as a variable in small group performance. *Social Forces* 32:16–22.

Adorno, T. W.; Frenkel-Brunswick, E.; Levinson, D. J.; & Sanford, R.. N. 1950. *The authoritarian personality*. New York: Harper and Brothers.

Alinsky, S. D. 1971. *Rules for radicals: A practical primer for realistic radicals*. New York: Random House.

Aronson, E., & Carlsmith, J. M. 1963. Effect of the severity of threat on the devaluation of forbidden behavior. *Journal of Abnormal and Social Psychology* 66:584–88.

Asch, S. E. 1956. Studies of independence and conformity: I. A minority of one against a unanimous majority. *Psychological Monographs* 70, whole no. 416.

Atkinson, J. W. 1964. *An introduction to motivation*. New York: American Book Company.

Bach, G. R., & Wyden, P. 1969. *The intimate enemy: How to fight fair in love and marriage*. New York: Morrow.

Back, K. W. 1951. Influence through social communication. *Journal of Abnormal and Social Psychology* 46:9–23.

Bailey, S. D. 1971. *Peaceful settlement of disputes: Ideas and proposals for research*. Unitar PS no. 1. New York: United Nations Institute for Training and Research.

Banton, M. *Race relations*. 1967. New York: Basic Books.

Barker, R. G. 1942. An experimental study of the resolution of conflict by children. In Q. McNemar and K. Merrill, eds., *Studies in personality*. New York: McGraw-Hill.

Barnard, C. I. 1946. Functions and pathology of status systems in formal organizations. In W. F. Whyte, *Industry and society*. New York: McGraw-Hill.

Beattie, J. H. M. 1969. Awareness of group and self in small-scale societies. Paper presented at UNESCO Conference on inter-group relations at Cannes, September 1969.

Benoît-Smullyan, E. 1944. Status, status types and status interrelations. *American Sociological Review* 9:151–61.

Berger, J.; Zelditch, M., Jr.; & Anderson, B. 1966. *Sociological theories in progress*. Vol. 1. Boston: Houghton Mifflin.

401

Berkowitz, L. 1957. Effects of perceived dependency relationships upon conformity to group expectations. *Journal of Abnormal and Social Psychology* 55:350–54.

Bixenstine, V. E., & Wilson, K. V. 1963. Effects of level of cooperative choice by the other players in a prisoner's dilemma game: Part II. *Journal of Abnormal and Social Psychology* 67:139–47.

Blake, R. R., & Mouton, J. S. 1961a. Comprehension of own and outgroup positions under intergroup competition. *Journal of Conflict Resolution* 5:304–10.

Blake, R. R., & Mouton, J. S. 1961b. Loyalty of representatives to ingroup positions during intergroup competition. *Sociometry* 24:177–83.

Blake, R. R., & Mouton, J. S. 1962a. Overevaluation of own group's product in intergroup competition. *Journal of Abnormal and Social Psychology* 64:237–38.

Blake, R. R., & Mouton, J. S. 1962b. Comprehension of points of communality in competing solutions. *Sociometry* 25:56–63.

Borah, L. A., Jr. 1963. The effects of threat in bargaining: Critical and experimental analysis. *Journal of Abnormal and Social Psychology* 66:37–44.

Boulding, K. E. 1962. *Conflict and defense: A general theory.* New York: Harper & Row.

Brock, T. C., & Buss, A. M. 1962. Dissonance, aggression, and evaluation of pain. *Journal of Abnormal and Social Psychology* 65:197–202.

Brock, T. C., & Buss, A. H. 1964. Effects of justification for aggression and communication with the victim on postaggression dissonance. *Journal of Abnormal and Social Psychology* 68:403–12.

Brown, B. R. 1968. The effects of need to maintain face on the outcomes of interpersonal bargaining. *Journal of Experimental Social Psychology* 4:107–121.

Brown, J. S. 1957. Principles of intrapersonal conflict. *Journal of Conflict Resolution* 1:135–54.

Burnstein, E., & Zajonc, R. B. 1965a. Individual task performance in a changing social structure. *Sociometry* 28:16–29.

Burnstein, E., & Zajonc, R. B. 1965b. The effect of group success on the reduction of status incongruence in task-oriented groups. *Sociometry* 28:349–62.

Burton, J. 1969. *Conflict and communication.* New York: Macmillan.

Byrne, D. 1961. Interpersonal attractiveness and attitude similarity. *Journal of Abnormal and Social Psychology* 62:713–15.

Byrne, D. 1969. Attitudes and attraction. In Leonard Berkowitz, ed., *Advances in experimental social psychology.* Vol. 4. New York: Academic Press.

Campbell, A. 1971. *White attitudes toward black people.* Ann Arbor, Michigan: Institute for Social Research.

Campbell, D. T. 1965. Ethnocentric and other altruistic motives. In D. Levine, ed., *Nebraska symposium on motivation.* Lincoln: University of Nebraska Press.

Cantril, H. 1965. *The pattern of human concerns.* New Brunswick, N.J.: Rutgers University Press.

Cartwright, D., ed. 1959. *Studies in social power.* Ann Arbor, Michigan: Institute for Social Research.

Cartwright, D., & Zander, A. F., eds. 1968. *Group dynamics: Research and theory,* 3rd ed. New York: Harper and Row.

Cervin, V. B., & Henderson, G. P. 1961. Statistical theory of persuasion. *Psychological Review* 68:157–66.

Chalmers, W. E., and Cormick, G. W., eds. 1971. *Racial conflict and negotiations: Perspectives and first case studies.* Institute of Labor and Industrial Relations, The University of Michigan–Wayne State University, Ann Arbor, Michigan.

Chase, M. 1971. Categorization and affective arousal. Ph.D. dissertation, Teachers College, Columbia University.

Cheney, J.; Harford, T.; & Solomon, L. 1971. The effects of communicating threats and promises upon the bargaining process. Unpublished manuscript, Boston University.

Christie, R., & Cook, P. 1958. A guide to published literature relating to the authoritarian personality through 1956. *Journal of Psychology* 45:171–99.

Clark, K. B. 1967. Address at the U.S. Commission on Civil Rights Conference, Washington, D.C., November 17.

Cohen, J. 1950. Technique of role-reversal: The study of international conferences. *World Federation for Mental Health* (Paris meeting), August–September.

Coleman, J. S. 1957. *Community conflict.* Glencoe, Ill.: Free Press.

Coleman, J. S. 1969. Race relations and social change. In Irwin Katz & Patricia Gurin, eds., *Race and the social sciences.* New York: Basic Books.

Collins, B. E., & Guetzkow, H. 1964. *A social psychology of group processes for decision-making.* New York: Wiley.

Cormick, G. W. 1971. Year end report to the Ford Foundation. Board of Mediation for Community Disputes, January 1, 1970, to December 31, 1970.

Coser, L. 1956. *The Function of social conflict.* Glencoe, Ill.: Free Press.

Dahl, R. A. 1968. Power. In D. L. Sills, ed., *International Encyclopedia of the Social Sciences,* Vol. 12. New York: Macmillan.

Dahrendorf, R. 1959. *Class and class conflict in industrial society.* Stanford: Stanford University Press.

Darwin, C. R. (1859). *On the origin of species by means of natural selection; Or, the preservation of favored races in the struggle for life.* New York: The Modern Library, 1936.

Davidson, B. 1961. *The African slave trade: Precolonial history, 1450–1850.* (Orig. pub. as *Black Mother.*) Boston/Toronto: Atlantic Monthly; Little Brown.

Davies, J. C. 1962. Toward a theory of revolution. *American Sociological Review* 27:5–19.

Davis, K. E., & Jones, E. E. 1960. Changes in interpersonal perception as a means of reducing cognitive dissonance. *Journal of Abnormal and Social Psychology* 61:402–10.

Deutsch, M. 1949a. A theory of cooperation and competition. *Human Relations* 2:129–51.

Deutsch, M. 1949b. An experimental study of the effects of cooperation and competition upon group process. *Human Relations* 2:199–231.

Deutsch, M. 1958. Trust and suspicion. *Journal of Conflict Resolution* 2:265–79.

Deutsch, M. 1960a. The effect of motivational orientation upon trust and suspicion. *Human Relations* 13:123–39.

Deutsch, M. 1960b. Trust, trustworthiness, and the F-scale. *Journal of Abnormal and Social Psychology* 61:138–40.

Deutsch, M. 1960c. The pathetic fallacy. *Journal of Personality* 28:317–32.

Deutsch, M. 1961. The interpretation of praise and criticism as a function of their social context. *Journal of Abnormal and Social Psychology* 62:391–400.

Deutsch, M. 1962a. Cooperation and trust: Some theoretical notes. In M. Jones, ed., *Nebraska symposium on motivation*. Lincoln: University of Nebraska Press.

Deutsch, M. 1962b. A psychological basis for peace. In Q. Wright, W. M. Evan, & M. Deutsch, eds., *Preventing World War III: Some proposals*. New York: Simon and Schuster.

Deutsch, M. 1965. A psychological approach to international conflict. In G. Sperrazzo, ed., *Psychology and international relations*. Washington, D.C.: Georgetown University Press.

Deutsch, M. 1966a. Comments on Kelley's comments. In K. Archibald, ed., *Strategic interaction and conflict*. Berkeley: University of California Press.

Deutsch, M. 1966b. Vietnam and the start of World War III: Some psychological parallels. Presidential address before the New York State Psychological Association, May 6.

Deutsch, M. 1969a. Socially relevant science: Reflections on some studies of interpersonal conflict. *American Psychologist* 24:1076–92.

Deutsch, M. 1969b. Conflicts: Productive and destructive. *Journal of Social Issues* 25:7–41.

Deutsch, M. 1972. Awakening the sense of injustice. Paper presented at Conference on Problems of Injustice in American Society, University of Waterloo, May 26–28.

Deutsch, M.; Canavan, D.; & Rubin, J. 1971. The effects of size of conflict and set of experimenter upon interpersonal bargaining. *Journal of Experimental Social Psychology* 7:258–67.

Deutsch, M., & Collins, M. E. 1951. Interracial housing: A psychological evaluation of a social experiment. Minneapolis: University of Minnesota Press.

Deutsch, M.; Epstein, Y.; Canavan, D.; & Gumpert, P. 1967. Strategies of inducing cooperation: An experimental study. *Journal of Conflict Resolution* 11:345–60.

Deutsch, M., & Krauss, R. M. 1960. The effect of threat on interpersonal bargaining. *Journal of Abnormal and Social Psychology* 61:181–89.

Deutsch, M., & Krauss, R. M. 1962. Studies of interpersonal bargaining. *Journal of Conflict Resolution* 6:52–76.

Deutsch, M., & Lewicki, R. 1970. "Locking-in" effects during a game of chicken. *Journal of Conflict Resolution* 14:367–78.

Deutsch, M., & Solomon, L. 1959. Reactions to evaluations by others as influenced by self-evaluation. *Sociometry* 22:93–112.

Deutsch, M.; Thomas, J. R. H.; & Garner, K. A. 1971. Social discrimination on the basis of category membership. Unpublished manuscript, Teachers College, Columbia University.

Dicks, H. V. 1967. *Marital tensions; Clinical studies towards a psychological theory of interaction.* New York: Basic Books.

Dollard, J.; Miller, N. E.; Doob, L. W.; Mowrer, O. H.; & Sears, R. H. 1939. *Frustration and aggression.* New Haven: Yale University Press.

Dollard, J., & Miller, N. E. 1950. *Personality and psychotherapy.* New York: McGraw-Hill.

Douglas, A. 1962. *Industrial peacemaking.* New York: Columbia University Press.

Edmead, F. 1971. *Analysis and prediction in international mediation.* Unitar PS no. 2. New York: United Nations Institute for Training and Research.

Edwards, W. 1954. The theory of decison-making. *Psychological Bulletin* 51:380–417.

Erikson, E. H. 1964. *Insight and responsibility.* New York: Norton.

Etzioni, A. 1968. *The active society: A theory of societal and political processes.* New York: Free Press.

Ex. J. 1959. The nature of contact between co-operating partners and their expectation concerning the level of their common achievement. *Acta Psychologica* 16:99–107.

Exline, R. V., & Ziller, R. C. 1959. Status congruency and interpersonal conflict in decision-making groups. *Human Relations* 12:147–62.

Feierabend, I. K., & Feierabend, R. L. 1966. Aggressive behaviors within politics, 1948–1962: A cross-national study. *Journal of Conflict Resolution* 10:249–71.

Fenichel, O. 1945. *The psychoanalytic theory of neuroses.* New York: Norton.

Festinger, L. 1954. A theory of social comparison processes. *Human Relations* 7:117–40.

Festinger, L. 1961. The psychological effects of insufficient reward. *American Psychologist* 16:1–11.

Festinger, L.; Schachter, S.; & Back, K. 1950. *Social pressures in informal groups: A study of human factors in housing.* California: Stanford University Press.

Fiedler, F. E. 1964. A contingency model of leadership effectiveness. Vol. 1. In L. Berkowitz, ed., *Advances in experimental social psychology.* New York: Academic Press.

Fiedler, F. E. 1967. The effect of inter-group competition on group member adjustment. *Personnel Psychology* 20:33–44.

Fisher, R. 1964. Fractionating conflict. In R. Fisher, ed., *International conflict and behavioral science: The Craigville papers.* New York: Basic Books.

Fisher, R. 1969. *International conflict for beginners.* New York: Harper and Row.

Form, W. H. 1951. Stratification in low and middle income housing areas. *Journal of Social Issues* 7:109–31.

French, J. R. P., & Raven, B. 1959. The bases of social power. In D. Cartwright, ed., *Studies in social power.* Ann Arbor: University of Michigan.

Freud, S. (1930). *Civilization and its discontents.* In J. Strachey, ed., *The standard edition of the complete psychological works of Sigmund Freud.* Vol. 21. London: Hogarth Press, 1961.

Gallo, P. S., Jr. 1966. Effects of increased incentives upon the use of threat in bargaining. *Journal of Personality and Social Psychology* 4:14–21.

Gallo, P. S., & McClintock, C. G. 1965. Cooperative and competitive behavior in mixed-motive games. *Journal of Conflict Resolution* 9:68–78.

Galtung, J. 1964. Foreign policy opinion as a function of social position. *Journal of Peace Research* 1:206–31.

Garner, K. A., & Deutsch, M. 1973. The effects of dissimilar goal orientations and differing expectations about the partner on cooperative behavior in a prisoner's dilemma game. Unpublished manuscript, Teachers College, Columbia University.

Geis, F. L. 1964. Machiavellianism and success in a three-person game. Ph.D. dissertation, Columbia University.

Genovese, E. D. 1965. *The political economy of slavery: Studies in the economy and society of the slave South.* New York: Pantheon.

Gerard, H. B. 1953. The effect of different dimensions of disagreement on the communication process in small groups. *Human Relations* 7:313–25.

Glass, D. C. 1964. Changes in liking as a means of reducing cognitive discrepancies between self-esteem and aggression. *Journal of Personality* 32:531–50.

Goffman, E. 1955. On face-work: An analysis of ritual elements in social interaction. *Psychiatry* 18:213–31.

Goldhamer, H. 1968. Social mobility. In D. L. Sills, ed., *International Encyclopedia of the Social Sciences.* Vol. 14. New York: Macmillan.

Gottheil, E. 1955. Changes in social perception contingent upon competing or cooperating. *Sociometry* 18:132–37.

Grant, D. A. 1956. Analysis-of-variance tests in the analysis and comparison of curves. *Psychological Bulletin* 63:141–54.

Grossack, M. 1954. Some effects of cooperation and competition on small group behavior. *Journal of Abnormal and Social Psychology* 49:341–48.

Gumpert, P. 1967. Some antecedents and consequences of the use of punitive power by bargainers. Ph.D. dissertation, Teachers College, Columbia University.

Gumpert, P.; Deutsch, M.; & Epstein, Y. 1969. The effect of incentive magnitude on cooperation in the prisoner's dilemma game. *Journal of Personality and Social Psychology* 11:66–69.

Hammond, K. R. 1965. New directions in research in conflict resolution. *Journal of Social Issues* 21:44–66.

Hare, A. P. 1962. *Handbook of small group research*. New York: Free Press.

Harris, M. 1968. Race. In D. L. Sills, ed., *International Encyclopedia of the Social Sciences*. Vol. 13. New York: Macmillan.

Hartmann, N. 1932. *Ethics*. Vol. 2 of *Moral values*. New York: Macmillan.

Heider, F. 1958. *The psychology of interpersonal relations*. New York: Wiley.

Heilman, M. 1972. Attitudes, expectations, and behavior in response to threats and promises as a function of the influencer's reputation. Ph.D. dissertation, Teachers College, Columbia University.

Herman, S. N. 1970. *Israelis and Jews: The continuity of an identity*. New York: Random House.

Hernes, G. 1969. On rank disequilibrium and military coups d'etat. *Journal of Peace Research* 1:65–72.

Himmelstrand, U. 1969. Tribalism, nationalism, rank-equilibration, and social structure. *Journal of Peace Research* 2:81–104.

Hollingshead, A. B. 1949. *Elmstown's youth*. New York: Wiley.

Homans, G. C. 1961. *Social behavior: Its elementary forms*. New York: Harcourt, Brace and World.

Hornstein, H. 1965. The effects of different magnitudes of threat upon interpersonal bargaining. *Journal of Experimental Social Psychology* 1:282–93.

Hover, J.; Garner, K.; Kaplan, S. P.; & Deutsch, M. 1972. The effects of threats which vary in their rationale, demand and consequence components. Unpublished manuscript, Teachers College, Columbia University.

Hyman, H. H. 1969. Social psychology and race relations. In Irwin Katz & Patricia Gurin, eds., *Race and the social sciences*. New York: Basic Books.

Iklé, F. C. 1964. *How nations negotiate*. New York: Harper & Row.

Jackson, E. 1952. *Meeting of minds*. New York: McGraw-Hill.

Jahoda, M. 1958. *Current concepts of positive mental health*. New York: Basic Books.

Janowitz, M. 1969. Patterns of collective racial violence. In H. D. Graham & T. R. Gurr, eds., *The history of violence in America*. New York: Praeger.

Johnson, D. W. 1967. Use of role reversal in intergroup competition. *Journal of Personality and Social Psychology* 7:135–41.

Johnson, S. 1772. *The rambler*. Publisher unknown.

Journal of Conflict Resolution. 1957. 1:1–104.

Keiffer, M. G. 1968. The effect of availability and precision of threat on bargaining behavior. Ph.D. dissertation, Teachers College, Columbia University.

Kelley, H. H. 1965. Experimental studies of threats in interpersonal negotiations. *Journal of Conflict Resolution* 9:79–105.

Kelley, H. H., & Stahelski, A. J. 1970. Social interaction basis of cooperators' and competitors' beliefs about others. *Journal of Personality and Social Psychology* 16:66–91.

Kerner, O. 1968. *Report of the United States National Advisory Commission on Civil Disorders*. New York: Bantam Books.

Korten, D. C. 1962. Situational determinants of leadership structure. *Journal of Conflict Resolution* 6:222–35.

Krauss, R. M. 1966. Structural and attitudinal factors in interpersonal bargaining. *Journal of Experimental Social Psychology* 2:42–55.

Krauss, R. M., & Deutsch, M. 1966. Communication in interpersonal bargaining. *Journal of Personality and Social Psychology* 4:572–77.

Kressel, K. 1972. *Labor mediation: An exploratory study*. New York: Association of Labor Mediation Agencies.

Laqueur, W. 1968. Revolution. In D. L. Sills, ed., *International Encyclopedia of the Social Sciences*. Vol. 13. New York: Macmillan.

Lasswell, H. D., & Kaplan, A. 1950. *Power and society*. New Haven: Yale University Press.

Lave, L. B. 1965. Factors affecting cooperation in the prisoner's dilemma. *Behavioral Science* 10:26–38.

LeVine, R. A., & Campbell, D. T. 1972. Ethnocentricism: Theories of Conflict, ethnic attitudes, and group behavior. New York: Wiley.

Levy, S. 1953. Experimental study of group norms: The effects of group cohesiveness upon social conformity. Ph.D. dissertation, New York Univeristy.

Lewicki, R. J., & Rubin, J. Z. 1971. A model of promise and threat use in interpersonal bargaining. Unpublished manuscript, Yale University and Tufts University.

Lewin, K. 1931. Environmental forces in child behavior and development. In C. Murchison, ed., *A handbook of child psychology*. Worcester, Mass.: Clark University Press.

Lewin, K.; Dembo, T.; Festinger, L.; & Sears, P. S. 1944. Level of aspiration. In J. McV. Hunt, ed., *Personality and the behavior disorders*. New York: Ronald Press.

Lewin, K.; Lippitt, R.; & White, R. K. 1939. Patterns of aggressive behavior in experimentally created "social climates." *Journal of Social Psychology* 10:271–99.

Likert, R. 1961. *New patterns of management*. New York: McGraw-Hill.

Loomis, J. L. 1957. Communication and the development of trust. Ph.D. dissertation, New York University.

Loomis, J. L. 1959. Communication and the development of trust. *Human Relations* 12:305–15.

Lott, B. E., & Lott, A. J. 1960. The formation of positive attitudes toward group members. *Journal of Abnormal and Social Psychology* 61:297–300.

Luce, R. D., & Raiffa, H. 1957. *Games and decisions: Introduction and critical survey*. New York: Wiley.

Lundberg, G. A., & Beasley, V. 1948. Consciousness of kind in a college population. *Sociometry* 2:59–74.

Mack, R. W., & Snyder, R. C. 1957. The analysis of social conflict—toward an overview and synthesis. *Journal of Conflict Resolution* 1:212–48.

Margolin, J. B. 1954. The effect of perceived cooperation or competition on the transfer of hostility. Ph.D. dissertation, New York University.

Mazrui, A. A. 1969. Scotland and Biafra: Problems of post-imperial fragmentation. Paper presented at UNESCO Conference on inter-group relations at Cannes, September.

McCall, G. J., ed. 1970. *Social relationships*. Chicago: Aldine.

McClintock, C. G., & McNeel, S. P. 1966a. Reward and score feedback as determiners of cooperative and competitive game behavior. *Journal of Personality and Social Psychology* 4:606–13.

McClintock, C. G., & McNeel, S. P. 1966b. Reward level and game playing behavior. *Journal of Conflict Resolution* 10:98–102.

McGrath, J. E., & Altman, I. 1966. *Small group research: A synthesis and critique.* New York: Holt.

Mead, G. H. 1934. *Mind, self and society.* Chicago: University of Chicago Press.

Mead, M. 1937. *Cooperation and competition among primitive peoples.* New York: McGraw-Hill.

Merton, R. K. 1957. *Social theory and social structure.* rev. ed. Glencoe, Ill.: Free Press.

Michels, R. (1911). *Political parties: A sociological study of the oligarchical tendencies of modern democracy.* New York: Dover, 1959.

Miller, N. E. 1944. Experimental studies of conflict. In J. McV. Hunt, ed., *Personality and the behavior disorders.* Vol. 1. New York: Ronald Press.

Miller, N. E. 1948. Theory and experiment relating psychoanalytic displacement to stimulus response generalization. *Journal of Abnormal and Social Psychology* 43:155–78.

Mintz, A. 1951. Non-adaptive group behavior. *Journal of Abnormal and Social Psychology* 46:150–59.

Mizuhara, T., & Tamai, S. 1952. Experimental studies of cooperation and competition. *Japanese Journal of Psychology* 22:124–27.

Myrdal, G. 1944. *An American dilemma: The Negro problem and modern democracy.* New York: Harper & Brothers.

Naess, A. 1958. A systematization of Gandhian ethics of conflict resolution. *Journal of Conflict Resolution* 2:140–55.

National Planning Association. 1953. *Causes of industrial peace.* Washington, D.C.: National Planning Association.

Newcomb, T. M. 1948. Attitude development as a function of reference groups: The Bennington study. In M. Sherif, ed., *An outline of social psychology.* New York: Harper & Brothers.

Parsons, T., & Bales, R. F. 1955. *Family, socialization and interaction process.* Glencoe, Ill.: Free Press.

Pechota, V. 1971. *Complementary structures of third-party settlement of international disputes.* Unitar PS no. 3. New York: United Nations Institute for Training and Research.

Porter, L. W., & Lawler, E. E. 1965. Properties of organization structure in relation to job attitudes and job behavior. *Psychological Bulletin* 64:23–51.

Rabbie, J. M., & Horwitz, M. 1969. The arousal of ingroup-outgroup bias by a chance win or loss. *Journal of Personality and Social Psychology* 13:269–77.

Rabbie, J. M., & Soutendijk, S. 1967. Beloning, discriminatie en intergroepsattitude. Unpublished report, Institute of Social Psychology, University of Utrecht.

Rapoport, A. 1960. *Fights, games and debates.* Ann Arbor: University of Michigan Press.

Raven, B. H., & Eachus, H. T. 1963. Cooperation and competition in means-interdependent triads. *Journal of Abnormal and Social Psychology* 67:307–16.

Rice, G. E., & White, K. R. 1964. The effect of education on prejudice as revealed by a game situation. *Psychological Record* 14:341–48.

Roberts, B. C. 1969. On the origins and resolution of English working-class protest. In H. D. Graham & T. R. Gurr, eds., *The history of violence in America*. New York: Praeger.

Rokeach, M. 1960. *The open and closed mind*. New York: Basic Books.

Rosenblatt, P. C. 1964. Origins and effects of group ethnocentrism and nationalism. *Journal of Conflict Resolution* 8:131–46.

Rummel, R. J. 1969. Dimensions of foreign and domestic conflict behavior: A review of empirical findings. In Dean G. Pruitt and Richard C. Snyder, eds., *Theory and research on the causes of war*.

Sartre, J. P. 1956. *Being and nothingness: An essay on phenomenological ontology*. New York: Philosophical Library.

Schelling, T. C. 1957. Bargaining, communication, and limited war. *Journal of Conflict Resolution* 1:19–36.

Schelling, T. C. 1958. Strategy of conflict: Prospectus for the reorientation of game theory. *Journal of Conflict Resolution* 2:203–64.

Schelling, T. C. 1960. *The strategy of conflict*. Cambridge, Mass.: Harvard University Press.

Schutz, W. C. 1967. *Joy: Expanding Human Awareness*. New York: Grove Press.

Sermat, V. 1962. Behavior in a mixed-motive game as related to the possibility of influencing the other's behavior. Paper read at the meetings of the American Psychological Association, St. Louis. Mimeographed.

Sermat, V. 1967. Sex differences and cooperativeness as a function of the other player's game strategy. Working Paper no. 224. Center for Research in Management Science. University of California at Berkeley, July.

Sherif, M. 1966. *In common predicament: Social psychology of intergroup conflict and cooperation*. Boston: Houghton Mifflin.

Sherif, M.; Harvey, O. J.; White, B. J.; Hood, W. R.; & Sherif, C. W. 1961. *Intergroup conflict and cooperation: The robbers cave experiment*. Norman, Oklahoma: University Book Exchange.

Shure, G. H.; Meeker, R. J.; & Hansford, E. A. 1965. The effectiveness of pacifist strategies in bargaining games. *Journal of Conflict Resolution* 9:106–17.

Siegel, S., & Fouraker, L. E. 1960. *Bargaining and group decision making*. New York: McGraw-Hill.

Simmel, G. 1955. *Conflict*. New York: Free Press.

Simon, B., & Weiner, H. 1966. Models of mind and mental illness in ancient Greece: I. The Homeric model of mind. *Journal of the History of the Behavioral Sciences* 2:303–14.

Skolnick, J. H. 1969. *The politics of protest*. New York: Ballantine Books.

Snowden, F. M. 1970. *Blacks in antiquity: Ethiopians in the Greco-Roman experience*. Cambridge, Mass.: Harvard University Press.

Solomon, L. 1960. The influence of some types of power relationships and game strategies upon the development of interpersonal trust. *Journal of Abnormal and Social Psychology* 61:223–30.

Stein, M. I. 1968. The creative individual. In manuscript.

Stembridge, B. J., & Deutsch, M. 1972. The effects of similarity and sharing on behavior in a PD game. Unpublished manuscript, Teachers College, Columbia University.

Stevens, C. M. 1963. *Strategy and collective bargaining negotiation.* New York: McGraw-Hill.

Stinchcombe, A. L. 1968. The structure of stratification systems. In D. L. Sills, ed., *International Encyclopedia of the Social Sciences.* Vol. 15. New York: Macmillan.

Stone, J. J. 1958. An experiment in bargaining games. *Econometrica* 26:286–96.

Sumner, W. G. 1906. *Folkways.* New York: Ginn.

Suppes, P., & Carlsmith, J. M. 1962. Experimental analysis of a duopoly situation from the standpoint of mathematical learning theory. *International Economics Review* 3:60–78.

Survey Research Center, University of Michigan, November 1971. In *Group life in America: A task force report.* New York: The American Jewish Committee, 1972.

Swingle, P. G., ed. 1970. *The sturcture of conflict.* New York: Academic Press.

Taft, P., & Ross, P. 1969. American labor violence: Its causes, character, and outcome. In H. D. Graham & T. R. Gurr, eds., *The history of violence in America.* New York: Praeger.

Tajfel, H. 1970. Experiments in intergroup discrimination. *Scientific American* 223:96–102.

Terhune, K. W. 1970a. The effects of personality in cooperation and conflict. In P. Swingle, ed., *The structure of conflict.* New York: Academic Press.

Terhune, K. W. 1970b. From a national character to national behavior: A reformulation. *Journal of Conflict Resolution* 14:203–63.

Thibaut, J. W., & Kelley, H. H. 1959. *The social psychology of groups.* New York: Wiley.

Thoden van Velsen, H. V. E., & van Wettering, W. 1960. Residence, power groups, and intrasocietal aggression. *International Archives of Ethnography* 49:169–200.

Thomas, E. J. 1957. Effects of facilitative role interdependence on group functioning. *Human Relations* 10:347–66.

Tomkins, S. S., & Izard, C. C., eds. 1965. *Affect, cognition, and personality.* New York: Springer.

U.S. Department of Commerce, Bureau of the Census. 1971. *The social and economic status of Negroes in the United States, 1970.* B. L. S. Report no. 394, July.

Van den Berghe, P. L. 1967. *Race and racism.* New York: Wiley.

Wagley, C., & Harris, M. 1958. *Minorities in the New World: Six case studies.* New York: Columbia University Press.

Walton, R. E. 1969. *Interpersonal peacemaking: Confrontations and third party consultation.* Reading, Mass.: Addison-Wesley.

Walton, R. E., & McKersie, R. B. 1965. *A behavioral theory of labor negotiations.* New York: McGraw-Hill.

Wilkenfeld, J. 1969. Some further findings regarding the domestic and foreign conflict behavior of nations. *Journal of Peace Research* 2:147–56.

Williams, R. M., Jr. 1947. The reduction of intergroup tensions: A survey of research on problems of ethnic, racial, and religious group relations. *Social Science Research Council Bulletin* 57:1–153.

Wills, G. 1968. *The second civil war.* New York: Signet Books.

Workie, A. 1967. The effect of cooperation and competition on productivity. Ph.D. dissertation, Teachers College, Columbia University.

Wrightsman, L. S., Jr.; O'Connor, J.; and Baker, Norma J., eds. 1972. *Cooperation and competition: Readings on mixed-motive games.* Belmont, California: Brooks/Cole.

Young, D. 1932. *American minority peoples.* New York: Harper & Brothers.

Zeuthen, F. 1930. *Problems of monopoly and economic warfare.* London: Routledge.

Zipf, G. K. 1949. *Human behavior and the principle of least effort.* Cambridge, Mass.: Addison-Wesley.

Index

413